CAPTAIN BULLEN'S WAR

★ **THE VIETNAM WAR DIARY** ★
OF CAPTAIN JOHN BULLEN

Edited by PAUL HAM

HarperCollinsPublishers

HarperCollins*Publishers*

First published in Australia in 2009
by HarperCollins*Publishers* Australia Pty Limited
ABN 36 009 913 517
www.harpercollins.com.au

HarperCollins*Publishers*
25 Ryde Road, Pymble, Sydney, NSW 2073, Australia
31 View Road, Glenfield, Auckland 0627, New Zealand
1–A, Hamilton House, Connaught Place, New Delhi – 110 001, India
77–85 Fulham Palace Road, London, W6 8JB, United Kingdom
2 Bloor Street East, 20th floor, Toronto, Ontario M4W 1A8, Canada
10 East 53rd Street, New York NY 10022, USA

National Library of Australia Cataloguing-in-Publication data:

Bullen, John, 1936–
    Captain Bullen's war : the Vietnam War diary of Captain John Bullen / John Bullen ; editor: Paul Ham.
    ISBN: 978 0 7322 8843 3 (pbk.)
    Includes index.
    Bullen, John, 1936–
    Australia. Army. Australian Task Force (Vietnam), 1st.
    Australia. Army. Royal Australian Survey Corps.
    Vietnam War, 1961–1975—Veterans—Australia—Biography.
    Vietnam War, 1961–1975—Personal narratives, Australian.
    Vietnam War, 1961–1975—Participation, Australian.
    Vietnam War, 1961–1975—Campaigns—Vietnam—Nui Dat.
    Australia—Armed Forces—History.
    Other Authors/Contributors: Ham, Paul.
959.7043092

Cover and internal design by Matt Stanton
Typeset in 10.5/16.5pt Sabon by Alicia Freile
Printed and bound in Australia by Griffin Press
70gsm Bulky Book Ivory used by HarperCollins*Publishers* is a natural, recyclable product made from
wood grown in sustainable forests. The manufacturing processes conform to the environmental
regulations in the country of origin, New Zealand.

6 5 4 3 2 1   09 10 11 12 13

★ FOREWORD ★

By Paul Ham

Sifting through the letters and diaries that chart the tragicomic passage of the human race, historians occasionally alight upon what I call a 'Eureka' find.

I had such a Eureka find in late 2005, while researching my book *Vietnam: The Australian War*. I was sitting in the Australian War Memorial in Canberra. On the desk sat a dusty old pile of Vietnam War documents, mostly about the Australian reaction to the Tet Offensive of 1968.

Wedged between the dry After Action Reports and 'Body Count' manifests was a photocopied extract from a soldier's diary. Written in a fine running hand of beautifully rounded letters, the very words exerted a tranquil allure among the grim old Olivetti-typed military files. They acted as a kind of mental massage. But it was the suppleness of the prose and the wry, detached voice of the narrator that instantly held my attention.

In the extract, the unnamed diarist recorded that a helicopter pilot had requested permission to 'shoot six cattle north of Nui Thi Vai'.

'Did you say cattle, i.e. cows?' the soldier-diarist wrote.

'That is affirmative,' replied the pilot.

'Why do you want to shoot them?'

'Because they're Viet Cong cattle, that's why.'

'How can you divine the political beliefs of a cow when you're in an aircraft and the cow's on the ground?' the diarist inquired.

I traced this flashpoint to Captain (now Lieutenant Colonel, retired) John Bullen, who served 13 months in Vietnam during 1968 — the worst year of fighting — as officer commanding the Topographical Survey Troop, the Australian map-producing unit.

To my amazement, I found that he now lived in Canberra. A cheerful voice answered the phone when I called in late 2005. I explained my project and John agreed to meet. Thus began the long journey that led to this book.

An officer and a gentleman, John Bullen is one of those rarities in modern Australia: he's not afraid to speak his mind or, in the vernacular, 'take the piss'. Richly irreverent, gimlet-eyed, with a knowing caress for the right detail, John Bullen's diaries are the perfect antidote to the hypocrisy, bombast and sheer callousness of many in politics, the armed forces and the peace movement during that benighted era, the Swinging Sixties. John Bullen, however, takes aim at his targets with a constant eye for the ordinary soldiers and the awful situation in which they found themselves during the Vietnam War: sent by most Australians to 'do their duty' . . . the troops were then condemned for doing it.

Bullen's is the voice of an older, wiser, less deferential Australia; a refreshing reminder that there was once a time when our country wasn't tyrannised by false sentimentality; when we weren't prey to a dangerously humourless strain of political correctness; when we seemed a quieter, funnier, more confident people. Back then, we grieved in private; laughed in public. John Bullen takes us back to a time when we'd rip in regardless, and understatement needed no bloody explanation.

John Bullen is a lot more, to boot: a polymath, who commands several languages; a professional cartographer; and an expert of many disciplines, including military history and Swiss railways.

But above all, Bullen is a natural writer with a finely tuned ear for the comic side in the most desperate situations. Looking back, his contribution clearly made life more bearable for the men around him.

He wrote his experiences down for his family. On his return from Vietnam, these diaries sat in storage for years — until one day in 1985, John showed them to Kit Denton, father of the TV interviewer, Andrew. Kit spent an entire night reading them, and the next day was determined to find a publisher. None emerged: the memory of Vietnam was too raw. So John set the diaries aside and that, it seemed, was that.

Great writing, however — and this is an excellent example of a most difficult genre — always seems to find its deserving readers. So it has proved with John's diaries. When I first set eyes on them, like Kit Denton, I was transfixed. I, too, resolved to find a publisher and HarperCollins, to its great credit, agreed instantly.

For me, simply being involved in seeing Captain Bullen's diaries through to publication, 40 years after they were written, has been a great privilege. I commend these diaries to our country as an acutely observed, wonderfully droll, classic contribution to understanding who we were in Vietnam, what we did there, and why.

PAUL HAM

Author, *Vietnam: The Australian War* and *Kokoda*

★ INTRODUCTION ★

It was my habit to keep a diary whenever engaged for a period of time on a particularly interesting and unusual activity. My surveying and mapping work in remote regions of Western Australia in the early 1960s definitely came into this category. So, too, did my family's move to Europe by sea shortly afterwards.

So when my tour of duty in Vietnam came up, it was perfectly natural for me to keep a diary. But there were additional reasons. I felt that a diary would be a good way to assist my successor as Officer Commanding the Survey Troop in Vietnam to arrive well briefed. My successor had already been appointed — a good friend, Captain Ken Lyons. As events turned out, Ken's posting was delayed to enable Major Peter Constantine to go to Vietnam ahead of him. Ken succeeded Peter a year later, however; so my briefing was definitely not wasted.

Supplementing my letters home, my diary would also serve to keep my family informed of the life I was leading. Accordingly, I set up an arrangement with Ken before I left Australia whereby I would send each completed volume of the diary back through the Army system to him, and he would pass it on to my family.

At that time Ken was studying part-time for a higher degree in surveying at the University of New South Wales. Since my sister Anne was doing advanced studies in a different field and was on staff at the same university, it was simple for Ken to hand my diaries on to her. Anne then forwarded each volume on to our mother in Sydney and she in turn posted them down to my wife, Yvonne, in our Army married quarter at Wodonga in rural Victoria. Thus, for different purposes, my diary kept several people informed, in addition to being my own record of events.

I wasn't keen to go to Vietnam in the first place. I was not long back from Europe where I had been studying hard for over two years for a master's degree, and I was eager to put my knowledge into practice in Australian mapping. Going to Vietnam at this stage seemed to be wasting my newly acquired qualifications, but I naturally accepted my posting to Vietnam as my Army duty.

Once I was in the country, apart from the painfully obvious disadvantage of domestic separation, I was glad I was there. Now outside the narrow technical world I had been in for the last nine years, I was part of the *real* Army and I enjoyed that. I renewed old friendships, met new friends, learnt a lot and gained what I felt was really worthwhile experience.

In Vietnam, life was always busy, often desperately demanding, and frequently I was badly short of sleep. In this situation I could never have written such a comprehensive journal without several chances happily working in my favour.

Many evenings were taken over by work but other evenings were comparatively free, allowing limited time for personal activities or social life. For an officer in a unit close to the Task Force Headquarters, the only social life in the evenings was in the Task Force Headquarters Officers' Mess, where it was customary to screen films every evening. The projector and screen were set up in the lounge and bar building — the only other Mess building being the dining room and kitchen.

Cinema has always been an interest of mine, ever since I first saw Stan Laurel and Oliver Hardy in *Great Guns* and Walt Disney's *Reluctant Dragon* early in 1942. But by 1968 my interest had become more discerning and the American films regularly screened in the Mess had no appeal for me.

For those in the Mess who didn't watch the films, the only alternative was to line the dimly lit bar at the back of the lounge area, where one could have a drink and a chat. But I didn't drink alcohol, orange fizz didn't appeal, so that left only chatting. And chatting interfered with the film soundtrack and was not encouraged by the cinema audience. An enthusiastic member of that audience was the Task Force Commander himself, Brigadier Ron Hughes, commissioned in 1939 and a serious-minded veteran of World War II and Korea, so those inclined to chat at the bar were reluctant to push their luck.

Evenings in the Officers' Mess had little to offer, so I mostly returned to the Survey Troop lines straight after dinner and either caught up on work, or went to my tent and wrote letters or in my diary. Thus, I made plenty of time for entries. I was away for thirteen and a half months and the diary filled nine volumes. All volumes were foolscap-sized (216 x 343 mm) Army notebooks, written on both sides of the paper. The final pile of nine volumes was 10 centimetres high. I recorded everything I found interesting, especially those matters which I thought were most unlikely to be recorded anywhere else. And there was a great deal happening in Vietnam that I found interesting.

My diary is, of course, an on-the-spot record of what I saw or heard at the time, and it lacks the benefit of later analysis. I was always very conscious that, in recording events from my own viewpoint, I often lacked the full story. But there was a war on and I did not have the time or resources of a historian to conduct research, to crosscheck or to analyse. I had to move on, as did the war. Readers should bear this in mind and, with the benefit of their later knowledge, not be too critical of those instances where I was not in possession of the full facts at the time I made an entry. I only wish I had known more and I often tried to find out, but as mentioned, I had to move on.

War is a terrible thing. It is an often shocking mixture of the ghastly, the ridiculous, the heroic, the pathetic, the frivolous, the tragic, the serious and the hilarious. All of these aspects I recorded. We all have our own personal techniques for coping with unpleasantness and difficulty. I guess my method was to make light of the situation whenever I could. Readers should therefore try not to be offended by my cynicism or by my overly cheerful treatment of serious situations. Beneath my cheer, I remained only too conscious of what my infantry colleagues of all ranks were facing daily in Vietnam. They were the reason I was there.

This book is dedicated to the soldiers of the Australian Army who were given a difficult and dangerous job in the Vietnam War, did it cheerfully and very well, but received little thanks.

John Bullen
Canberra, 2008

★ GLOSSARY ★

1ALSG — 1st Australian Logistic Support Group

AFV — Australian Forces Vietnam (including Navy, Army and Air Force)

APC — armoured personnel carrier

ARU — Australian Reinforcement Unit

ARVN — Army of the Republic of Vietnam

ATF — Australian Task Force

Ba Ria (official name Phuoc Le, but often known as Baria) was the capital
of Phuoc Tuy province in which the Australian Task Force concentrated
its operations. Although nominally the capital and certainly the largest
population centre in the province, Ba Ria was no more than a large
village. Phuoc Tuy province is now Ba Ria-Vung Tau

boob — Army slang for military prison or cell; see also 'slot'.

CGS — Chief of the General Staff (nowadays Chief of Army)

CICV — Combined Intelligence Center Vietnam

dai-uy — captain

defensive fire task (DF) — potential target for artillery or mortars,
previously selected and noted, enabling fire to be called down quickly if
attack on the target is needed

fire support base (FSPB or FSB) — a defended and isolated small base
containing fire support, usually artillery, for forward operations
full astern — full speed in reverse (nautical)

GSO2 — General Staff Officer, Grade 2 (a major)

GSO3 — General Staff Officer, Grade 3 (a captain)

HQ AFV — headquarters of Australian Forces Vietnam

LAD — Light Aid Detachment of the RAEME; does light repairs light fire
team — a team of two or three armed helicopters (gunships)

Long Binh — the largest US Army base in Vietnam, home to about 50,000
men, including 66 Engineer Company (Topographic)

MACV — Military Assistance Command Vietnam

MC — Military Cross (or Master of Ceremonies)

10 MID — 10 Military Intelligence Detachment, ARVN

MP — military police

NCO — non-commissioned officer

NGS — South Vietnamese National Geographic Service

Nui Dat — largest Australian camp in Vietnam, where 1st Australian Task Force was based

PF — Popular Force (South Vietnamese)

picquet — guard

PRO — South Vietnamese Province Reconnaissance Unit

PX — post exchange, a retail store for troops at a base

R&C — rest and convalescence leave of five days per year within Vietnam

R&R — rest and recuperation leave of five days per year outside Vietnam

RAA — Royal Australian Artillery

RAEME — Corps of Royal Australian Electrical and Mechanical Engineers, which maintains Army equipment

RAF — Royal Air Force (UK)

RAN — Royal Australian Navy

RAR — Royal Australian Regiment (1RAR = 1st Battalion etc)

RF — Regional Force (South Vietnamese)

RNZA — Royal New Zealand Artillery

ROK — Republic of Korea

RPG — rocket propelled grenade

RTAVF — Royal Thai Army Volunteer Forces

SAS — (Australian) Special Air Service

slot — army slang for military prison or cell; see also 'boob'

Tan Son Nhut — main airport near Saigon

thieu-ta — major

uc dai loi — Australian soldier

USARV — US Army, Republic of Vietnam

USNS — United States Navy ship (not a warship)

USS — United States ship (warship)

VC — Viet Cong, army of the National Liberation Front operating in South Vietnam

Vung Tau— Vietnamese seaside resort, used by Americans and Australians for recreation, and where 1st Australian Logistic Support Group and US installations were located; not then part of a province, Vung Tau was a 'Special Zone' by itself

WO1/WO2 — warrant officer first class/second class

NOTE ON STYLE AND USAGE

Some small liberties in style have been taken in publishing these diaries. John Bullen followed the spelling of Vietnamese words he saw written in 1968; he always wrote 'Viet Nam', for example, which has been changed to 'Vietnam'. Such references have been changed by the publisher to avoid confusion to modern-day readers. Similarly, some military short-hand has been spelt out in full or rephrased to suit non-military readers.

The original diaries included occasional footnotes where John added information he learnt later. These have generally been retained; elsewhere, if appropriate, they have been integrated into a diary entry. Some subsequent clarifications have been inserted as footnotes into this published version by Paul Ham and occasionally John Bullen.

In the period 1968–69 Australia was still using the imperial system of measurement; however, those trained in technical fields, such as survey, frequently used metric measurements. Thus, both were used interchangeably by John Bullen throughout his diaries and no attempt has been made to standardise these. When flying, John was often able to see the aircraft instrument panel, which showed speed in knots and height in feet above sea level. When he couldn't see the instrument panel he made estimates in miles or kilometres per hour and metres or feet above the ground below. Thus two systems of measurement relating to flying are used in the text.

All money values are in Australian dollars, except where specified otherwise. In 1968–69, A$1 was approximately equivalent to US$1.1.

Approximate metric equivalents to imperial measures are as follows:
1 inch = 2.5 cm
1 foot = 30 cm
1 yard = 0.9 m
1 mile = 1.6 km
1 ounce = 28 g
1 pound = 0.45 kg
1 stone = 6.35 kg
1 ton = 1.02 t
1 gallon = 3.8 L
100°F = 38°C

JANUARY

AUSTRALIAN MILITARY FORCES

AAB — 71A
Reprinted Dec, 1964

RECORD BOOK

CONTAINING 96 PAGES

RULED FEINT

On the morning of 17 January 1968, Captain John Bullen boarded HMAS *Sydney* at Garden Island wharf, Sydney, bound for South Vietnam. After seven months living at the Officers' Mess at Randwick, John was leaving to take up the position of Officer Commanding 1 Topographical Survey Troop at Nui Dat. Amid the throng of relatives waving off loved ones were his wife, Yvonne, sons David (aged six) and Peter (aged one), as well as his mother and mother-in-law, none of whom he would see for another 13 months.

On board John was the most senior of only a few officers accompanying 350 troops — a mixed bunch of reinforcements representative of all Army units found in Vietnam. Travelling also was a small Signals detachment on its way to Thailand.

Their warm reception by the Navy was a huge and most welcome anticlimax. As the senior Army officer, John had been worried that the troops might offend their Navy hosts, known to have many traditions unfamiliar to 'pongos' (the Navy nickname for soldiers). Worse still, the ship had a brand-new captain, which could mean a strict new broom sweeping clean. So John gathered all the Army people together the day before they sailed and tried to teach them whatever Navy traditions and jargon (port, starboard, quarterdeck, heads, bulwark, goffa etc) he knew.

He needn't have bothered. A soldier asking politely where he could find the 'heads' (toilet) was cheerfully told 'up towards the sharp end and turn left, mate!' The Navy was completely used to hosting soldiers and made the voyage as pleasant as it could.

PAUL HAM

★

One sailor called to a native trader,
'How much for your wife?'
Native grinned from ear to ear and shouted back,
'Twenty dollars.' Not sure whether he was
merely entering into the spirit of things
or whether he was fair dinkum.
To be certain one would have to see the wife.

★

Wednesday 17 January 1968

Early morning at 05.00 at Personnel Depot at South Head. Breakfast, roll call, and onto the buses by 07.00, and then to Garden Island. Passed through Kings Cross on the way. Someone pulled the buzzer cord in the bus and said, 'Anywhere along here will be fine, thanks, driver!'

Aboard HMAS *Sydney* by 08.30. Sharing a two-man cabin with Captain Neville Bretzke (Catering Corps and bound for Saigon). Total Army complement aboard is about 350, including ten officers. Seem to have all the corps represented except Psychology, Education and Legal. Three men for 1 Topographical Survey Troop are aboard, viz me, Sergeant Eric Clutterbuck, Sergeant Ted Morris.

No frills aboard *Sydney*, especially as far as NCOs and other ranks are concerned. RAN company pleasant, and food is a big improvement after Randwick. Friends and relatives allowed on wharf from 13.30 to 15.00. David showed great interest in cranes, ships and some Bofors guns being repaired. Departure scene fairly restrained — only one obvious case of a last-minute seduction.

HMAS Sydney *bound for Vung Tau.*

Ship sailed 15.30. Light rain. Buzzed in harbour by attractive yawl, with (to the delight of troops and crew) even more attractive girls on board, and also by the Manly hydrofoil ferry *Fairlight*. *Fairlight* was most spectacular as she circled *Sydney* and blew horn several times — a most powerful, clear and sweet note, obviously from a group of finely tuned air klaxons that could only have been made in Italy.[1]

Escorted off the premises and through the Heads by police launch *Nemesis*. Settled baggage and self in and attended briefings on what we'll be doing on board. *Sydney* heading for Manus Island, then Thailand (Sattahip) and then Vietnam (Vung Tau).

Film on in wardroom during evening — *A Certain Smile*. Image on screen poor, sound worse, and the film itself worse still. Stuck out one reel and then quit.

Thursday 18 January 1968

Ship life is getting organised now — activities and training for troops being planned. Activities include lectures, volleyball, shooting, physical training. An ominous warning given — we are heading straight for Cyclone Brenda off the Queensland coast, or maybe Brenda is heading for us — it doesn't matter much. Wind rose to about 60 knots during afternoon and waves rose considerably. Ship rolled heavily in the waves. While on quarterdeck, I happened to look up just in time to see all space beside the ship full of a rearing mass of light-green water, as a huge

[1] Discovered later that the whole vessel, horn and all, comes from Italy.
Horn has three trumpets. — JB

wave burst in. I jumped up on the nearest high object as the water rushed beneath. Two naval officers and two ratings all leapt for the doorway, reached it together and jammed in before rank won. Sea most impressive. We are assured that we're barely at the edge of Brenda and should strike the centre, some 300 miles away, some time during the next day. We can then expect waves to break over the flight deck where vehicles are lashed. What, with this cheerful prospect plus heaving of ship, my stomach feels unsteady, so I missed dinner and went to bed and then tackled the problem of staying in a tipping upper bunk.

Friday 19 January 1968

Stayed in bed during the night — more than a fellow officer managed to do. Fortunately, he was tossed from a bottom bunk. Stomach now fine. Sea and wind quieter — Brenda has obligingly headed off towards Fiji. Played sport in the afternoon — a form of basketball using a quoit. Very hectic and most enjoyable. 'Aren't there any rules?' asked one soldier.

'Oh yes,' said a passing sailor. 'I did hear a whistle once on the last voyage — I think someone had pulled a knife.'

Received the ship's newspaper, a daily publication. Excerpts from it follow:

1. 'The Captain [the redoubtable D.A.H. "Nobby" Clarke], when approached for his service history for this publication, is reported to have replied: "I have no bloody time to write history, I am too busy making it".'

2. Report of an 11-year-old boy shooting his seven-year-old brother dead in their home in Wodonga, their father is in the Army in Vietnam. The address given was about 50 yards from our home in Wodonga.

3. Cricket report: '. . . but this does not detract from the performance of the charging Northants bowler whose balls came off the pitch so fast that the batsmen were hustled into errors.'

4.(i) 'Dear Dorothy Dix, What does my daughter mean when she says that the youth of today is not immoral but merely partaking of a new morality?'
'Dear Reader, Probably that she is pregnant.'

4. (ii) 'Dear Dorothy Dix, I am 17 years old, attractive, and would like to be going out with boys but they don't seem to notice me. Have you any suggestions?'
'Dear Reader, Not until you tell me whether you are male or female.'

4. (iii) 'Dear Dorothy Dix, For the past 50 years I have been too busy making a living to be interested in girls, now that I . . .'
'Dear Reader, Forget it mate.'

5. Full details of Australian Army court martial in Vietnam of a gunner alleged to have murdered an officer.[2]

6. Full details of US Army court martial of several men cutting ears off dead Viet Cong. From statements of all concerned, it seems that no one is telling the truth.

7. Horses for Saturday's races at Moonee Valley and Rosehill.

8. The Geographical Ages of a Woman:
From 15 to 25 — like South America — part virgin and part explored.
From 25 to 35 — like Africa — hot, torrid and mysterious.
From 35 to 45 — like North America — streamlined, efficient and co-operative.
From 45 to 55 — like Europe — devastated but still good.
From 55 onwards — like Australia — everyone knows it's down under but nobody goes there.

[2] See entry for 6 February 1969. — PH

9. Australia's mail strike has gone from bad to worse. Those on board who are still seasick are wishing the Army would be called in and the *Sydney* called back.

Saturday 20 January 1968

Weather now very good and humid, especially those cabins (including mine) which have the sun-scorched flight deck for a ceiling. Cabin temperature about 100°F and humidity probably 100%. Good acclimatisation for Vietnam, I imagine, and I don't find it distressing. Was amused to read predictions for 1977 and 1987 in a magazine in the wardroom and to see that a future event recorded was the death by drowning, of General de Gaulle, following his unsuccessful attempt to Walk On Water. Typically, this came from an English magazine — *Punch*!

Films on in evening. Saw *Guns at Batasi*, a film set in the new independent Africa, perhaps Kenya, but the actors looked more like West Africans. Most amusing film, thanks to Richard Attenborough's caricature of the British regimental sergeant major. Cabin still at 100°F during night. I slept OK, but most of the other officers sleeping nearby took stretchers out onto the quarterdeck for the night.

Sunday 21 January 1968

Another hot day with no training activity. Ship about level with Torres Strait. Captain changed course to chase a rain storm to cool the ship down. Practised man-overboard drill. A float (the man overboard) is tossed over the rail. The diver on duty, wearing overalls, bare feet, cap with lamp, life jacket, knife strapped to leg, tosses a life buoy over and then dives in off the quarterdeck. A

Gemini rubber raft, powered by a Johnson 20 outboard motor and manned with a crew, is now lowered into the water, the ship still doing about 20 knots and with its engines now full astern. Ship stops in about 1 mile. Meanwhile, diver has got to the life buoy, swum with it to the float, been picked up by the raft, which now chases after the ship, and is hauled aboard. Total time: seven minutes.

Played volleyball with Navy officers during afternoon. Standard good and much fun and exercise was had by all. The Captain played and ensured there was never a dull moment. He spent most of the time accusing the opposition of being Bloody Cheats. I got quite a fright when leaping high at the net to block a smash by the Captain. For one horrible moment I thought I was going to end up wearing ball, net, and about 17 stone of captain. Fortunately, he missed both ball and me and muttered, 'There I go — half an hour or two women behind my intentions — same distance in each case!' The Captain has only been with *Sydney* for about five days and seems a very friendly man.

While passing through Trobriand Islands in the Louisiade Archipelago I visited the bridge to have a look at the charts and the ship's navigation equipment. Many rocks and reefs in this area. Captain is there, with towel around middle and bare feet up on the dashboard. He gets up, goes to edge of bridge, looks into water (which looks blue and wet, just as it has done since leaving Sydney Harbour), says, 'We'd better move over a bit,' orders an alteration in the ship's course, and heads the ship off on a new bearing. Meanwhile, navigator and staff seize rubber and fresh pencils and leap at plot to keep track of ship which Captain is driving like a jeep across country.

Captain knows these waters like proverbial back of proverbial hand. His methods are justified by the fact that we haven't hit a thing yet. He keeps up a running commentary all the time, keeping all present in fits of laughter. We passed a huge and beautiful motor cruiser (about the same size as a small Manly ferry and obviously in the millionaire-ownership class) anchored at Kiriwina Island. Captain's speculation as to the activities of such a ship's female complement was hilarious to listen to. Officer of the Watch mentioned later that they've never struck a captain like this one before and that he is excellent, despite his extraordinary manner and appearance — 17 stone, voluble and utterly uninhibited. I was amazed at the temerity of a sub-lieutenant who dared go to the Captain's private cabin and wake him up for a game of volleyball with the junior officers. I was even more amazed when the Captain responded with 'Would I? Bloody hell, let's go!' They knew their man better than I did. Apparently this captain is a legend throughout the Navy and is well known for his competence and eccentricity.

Evening again hot despite strong rain storm. Saw film *Enemy Below*, featuring Robert Mitchum and Curt Jurgens. Unusual to find a war film from USA without romantic interest. Instead it had deep philosophy which was extremely unconvincing.

Monday 22 January 1968

Interesting and very slow passage along the northern New Guinea coast. Captain purposely brought ship to within a mile or so of the coast so that the Army people aboard could see the sites of many fierce struggles in World War II — Buna, Gona, Sanananda, Finschhafen, and the Markham and Ramu Rivers. Finally headed off north towards the Admiralty Islands, passing just to the east of Long Island. Many volcanic islands about, with their attractive symmetrical cone shapes.

More volleyball, this time with Army. The Army is choosing the team to play Navy. I am in Army's second team so standard is low. Washed socks and underclothes — only took about 15 to 20 minutes, but in the steamy atmosphere of the washroom, perspiration was extreme. When undressing afterwards for a shower, underpants were dripping wet. Wrung them out by hand over basin with plug in and got half a cup of sweat out without any difficulty. When one perspires this quantity of moisture, fluid loss is obviously very high indeed. All cabin furniture very hot to the touch — probably about 105°F.

Navy did helicopter flights today. One helicopter took off and immediately crashed from a height of a foot or so. Tail rotor had failed due to incorrect assembly after maintenance. Helicopters are Westland Wessex and are collapsible for stowage in hangars below flight deck. Main rotor blades all fold back along the boom and the boom itself folds sideways to reduce the length of the aircraft. We play volleyball right beside the stowed helicopters — no worry at all to the Navy. Pilots didn't bat an eyelid when a heavy smash landed right on the exposed tail-rotor drive shaft where the boom folds, causing the shaft to oscillate freely.

Night very hot. Everyone from officers' cabins now sleeping on quarterdeck except me. From casual discussion with the Army doctor aboard it seems that my body is becoming acclimatised very rapidly, no doubt assisted by my willingness to remain in the hot, humid environment.

Tuesday 23 January 1968

Arrived at Manus Island early in the morning. Tied up with stern towards the shore and refuelled over six hours or so. Natives came alongside in dugout canoes with outriggers and attempted to sell coconuts, carved wooden objects, shells, beads etc. Quality was low and prices high. I understand from a Navy officer that the carvings are done with workshop equipment at the naval base. Beads were the standard Woolworths plastic type. Several native canoes came close enough to shout to the ship. One sailor called to a native trader, 'How much for your wife?'

Native grinned from ear to ear and shouted back, 'Twenty dollars.' Not sure whether he was merely entering into the spirit of things or whether he was fair dinkum. To be certain one would have to see the wife.

Buffet lunch on board the ship on quarterdeck for the officers and visitors — i.e. officers and wives from the naval base on shore. Met several of the wives and spoke with them. All are there for two years and all of them love the life. Schooling seems to be no problem. New South Wales Education Department has a primary school there, and secondary schooling is done by correspondence or else the child boards in Australia. Wives get one trip back to Australia at Navy expense during their stay, or else a child boarding in Australia may use this to visit parents instead. Recreational facilities are adequate, but shopping is necessarily limited. Nevertheless, almost all the wives were wearing brief mini-dresses and seemed able to keep up with current fashions.

With no wind due to stationary ship, flight deck became extremely hot, and temperature below deck was at its fiercest yet. Cabin temperature would have been about 120°F. Cabin ceiling (which is the flight deck) was too hot to touch, all furniture was very hot indeed, water from the cold tap was so hot that I could not have put my hands in it had it been any hotter.

Ship was delayed about four hours by an accident. When a landing craft was being hauled aboard, the hoisting gear failed and it fell down to the water from a height of about 25 feet. No damage to boat, but four officers in it were injured. All were confronted with the choice of clinging to the vertical safety ropes and being hit by several tons of metal beam coming down above the boat, or slipping down the ropes ahead of the beam. All chose the latter course and suffered severe rope burns to hands and fingers, and one of them suffered arm and head injury also. Accident should not have happened — these landing craft and their hoists were only fitted to the ship two months ago. Only a minute or two prior to the accident, a native canoe had been right underneath the landing craft, but fortunately had got clear before the boat fell.

Attempts to repair hoisting gear failed, so this one landing craft was left at Manus Island — together with two sailors who hadn't turned up after shore leave.

Wednesday 24 January 1968

Intermittent rain all day — some of it so hard that visibility was down to about 100 yards (about half the ship's length). Helicopter exercises, rifle shooting, volleyball, all cancelled. Everyone lying around playing cards or reading girlie magazines. Many spectacular tattoos on the lounging bodies, especially the Navy men. It seems most are done not overseas but in Sydney or Melbourne during any city leave from recruit training. Tattoos can be found almost anywhere — arms, legs, back, chest and reputedly buttocks[3] and penis also! Eagles, ships, flowers, dancing girls, daggers, skulls etc seem to be very popular. Noticed the chaplain at lunch being served his meal by an arm bearing a tattoo of a nude dancing girl, breasts and genital region being fully displayed and drawn in great detail. It didn't put the chaplain off his meal. 'Mother' inscriptions are also very popular, usually linked with a heart, flowers, female head or the ubiquitous dancing girl.

Today chaplains and doctor both had discussions with the troops. The doctor, who has delivered a similar talk at the Jungle

[3] I later saw a huge eye on each buttock of one man. — JB

Training Centre at Canungra each week for the last few years, presented his usual vivid advice, which had many men swearing off hamburgers and doughnuts (as the doctor described badly diseased female organs) and Vietnamese women for life — although the medical statistics of the Australian forces in Vietnam show that these good intentions soon go by the board. The doctor's talk was well summarised by his concluding words: 'Flies spread disease — keep yours buttoned!'

Weather cool outside, but cabin still very hot, though cooler than yesterday.

Thursday 25 January 1968

Cloudy but no rain. Morning spent shooting off the stern at balloon targets dropped into the water. General standard low. Eight men, each with ten rounds of ammunition, were usually only able to hit four out of every eight balloons before they were out of range astern. Apparently the infantry battalions usually hit about seven out of every eight. The Navy did some shooting (the rifles were theirs) but could only hit one or two out of every eight, often missing by several hundred yards.

Much to our horror the ship had a man-overboard practice while shooting was on, and the first we knew of it was when the diver (his coloured cap looking like a balloon) was seen about 200 yards astern of the ship and only about 300 yards from the last lot of balloons in the water. He could easily have been hit by a stray shot, since the Navy men were shooting at the time. Apparently, the diver could hear the shots from the flight deck as the order came for him to dive in from the quarterdeck, and he was distinctly apprehensive about the whole business. It had been arranged that the bridge would warn the firing point of any man-overboard exercise, but this time the warning arrived at the same instant as we noticed the diver in the target area.

After lunch the ship did some gunnery practice with its four Bofors guns at smoke targets laid by helicopters a mile or two away from the ship on either side. Starboard shooting seemed accurate. Port shooting was initially dreadful but settled down later and the shells began to land near the target.

King Neptune ceremony today as we crossed the equator. Victims — all those crossing the line for the first time (which did not include myself) — were heavily daubed with a white mess (probably flour and water) from a large paintbrush and were tipped into a canvas water tank. Unexpectedly, diversion came when a joker set up a fire hose and blasted audience, victims, King Neptune, court and all, then escaped amidst the ensuing confusion.

King Neptune's court, 25 January 1968.

Sky still dull, so outside temperature stayed about 80°F, but cabin was usually 95°F or so.

Friday 26 January 1968

Warm, calm sea, thin cloud. Ship now heading westward in Celebes Sea. Quiet day — volleyball and letter writing. Evening hot as usual. Helicopters practised instrument flying today. Orange screens are placed over windows and pilot wears goggles fitted with blue glass. Pilot can see nothing outside and can just see his illuminated instrument panel.

Saturday 27 January 1968

Hot and sunny, sea still calm. In afternoon the ship passed through Basilan Strait, thereby passing from Celebes Sea to the Sulu Sea (and later to the South China Sea). Travelling westward, we passed north of Basilan Island (well to the north of Sulawesi) and immediately to the south of Mindanao in the Philippines. Passed within a mile or so of the port of Zamboanga, possibly the second largest town or city on Mindanao. Looked quite large — big city buildings, oil tanks, several ships up to 15,000 tons, ferries etc. Several native canoes came close enough to shout to the ship. Some of the soldiers called down to them in most convincing, impromptu native-type talk — '*Lumukalubauwahulamuki!*' etc. The natives called back similarly, both natives and soldiers waving, smiling and shouting. Obviously the synthetic language from the ship didn't stumble accidentally onto anything that the natives found offensive.

Doughnuts for lunch today. A stack of them were left over and served up again for afternoon tea. I suspect that the doctor's horrific venereal disease talk may have had something to do with the doughnuts' unpopularity. The film *The Blue Max* was shown this evening and drew a large crowd — mainly to see Ursula Andress, judging by the applause during the credits. Even the navigator, who lives on the bridge 24 hours a day, came down to see the film. As he appeared, one naval officer got up abruptly and said, 'Mind my seat while I go and get my life jacket, will you?' Audience was disgusted at points in the film where savage cutting by the censor had occurred and annoyance was volubly expressed.

Sunday 28 January 1968

HMAS *Stuart*, a 3000-ton anti-submarine frigate, arrived this morning and came alongside for refuelling by hose from *Sydney*. Various packages and one chaplain were also slung across by rope. Quite interesting to watch. Took some photos. *Stuart* then steamed off ahead for the rest of the day for manoeuvres with *Sydney*. Volleyball matches for ship's championship were held during afternoon. All Army teams defeated in first round. Stayed to watch the final between two Navy teams. Seamen first team beat Petty Officers first team 3–2 in a match that was magnificent to watch — the best game I've ever seen outside Olympic volleyball.

Monday 29 January 1968

Stuart and helicopters from *Sydney* are constantly on anti-submarine patrol, now that we're in operational waters in the South China Sea. On board *Sydney* frequent emergency practices are held; for example, fire, damage control after bombing attack etc. During afternoon *Sydney* practised anti-aircraft firing against parachute flare targets. Shooting very accurate this time.

Read 22 December '67 issue of *Time*, with Bob Hope on the cover. Inside was an article on Rest & Recuperation leave for soldiers from Vietnam, illustrated with four pages of photos of American troops on leave: at the beach at Vung Tau with local girl (sensationally briefly clad); necking in boat in Bangkok with attractive local girl; dancing in Hong Kong dive with most attractive 'hostesses' in spectacular mini-dresses (or are they just long blouses?); and relaxing in a luxurious bath in Taipei beside two nude and shapely girls (presumably masseuses?). I imagine this article must have caused a bit of an uproar back home in

Rest and recuperation, American style, 1967.

USA.[4] Most people realise that this is normal for at least 50% of the troops in Vietnam, but prefer not to be confronted with such spectacular evidence.

In late afternoon, *Stuart* made contact with a submarine. *Sydney* immediately put on full speed and changed course abruptly several times, taking evasive action. *Stuart* hunted the submarine using sonar, and came close enough to fire signal grenades, ordering the submarine to surface and identify itself. The submarine then escaped. It could have been American, Russian or Chinese. Contact again occurred at 22.30 but was again lost.

Stayed up until well after midnight (being Army duty officer) and checked the Army picquets guarding the vehicles on the flight deck and in the hangar. No picquets to be found. Finally rounded up most of them. I doubt that they'll sleep again tonight after what was said.

[4] It did. — JB

Tuesday 30 January 1968

Submarine contact again this morning. *Sydney* dodging while *Stuart* everywhere. Helicopters aloft from *Sydney*. Suddenly, with no warning sound to herald it, an Orion from the US Navy flashed by from behind at an altitude of just above *Sydney*'s flight deck — very low for such a large aircraft. The Orion is an anti-submarine aircraft with interception equipment and rockets visible under its wings. It did a few wide sweeps around *Sydney* and *Stuart* and then disappeared. Submarine still not identified but consensus seems to be Chinese.

Wednesday 31 January 1968

Arrived at Sattahip, Thailand, first thing in the morning to unload troops, vehicles and equipment in SEATO exercise Ramasoon. Troops lined flight deck of *Sydney* as she moved into the wharf. Thai Navy band struck up the most ghastly noise — shrill, raucous, out of tune, out of rhythm — it really was awful. We were then released from the flight deck so I gladly went below to write more letters. Temperature very hot inside ship, hotter still than at Manus Island. Ship sailed at 16.00, after all vehicles and stores had been quickly swung off by crane. One soldier, while lining the flight deck for the ship's departure, was heard to say, 'For Chrissake, let's get this bloody hooker out of here!' This expressed the thoughts of just about everyone aboard, moored as we were in the fierce heat.

FEBRUARY

AUSTRALIAN MILITARY FORCES

AAB — 71A

Reprinted Dec, 1964

RECORD BOOK

CONTAINING 96 PAGES

RULED FEINT

HMAS *Sydney* moored at Vung Tau, South Vietnam, on 3 February 1968. It was the start of Tet, the Buddhist New Year's holiday, and the bloodiest enemy offensive of the Vietnam War was just getting under way — the uprising known as the Tet Offensive, in which tens of thousands of Viet Cong troops threw themselves on South Vietnamese cities.

Vung Tau was a Vietnamese seaside holiday resort, used alike by American, Australian and Vietnam Republic forces, and also by the Viet Cong, for recreation. It had an anchorage where unloading by air was possible, and American and Australian forces both had logistic support bases there. The 1st Australian Logistic Support Group at Vung Tau was Australia's second largest camp in Vietnam, containing supply, transport, stores depots, maintenance, repair, medical and other major support units. The RAAF also had a transport squadron based at the US airfield at Vung Tau.

John's destination, however, was the largest Australian camp in Vietnam, located in a rubber plantation at Nui Dat, some 30 kilometres north of Vung Tau. This was the camp of the 1st Australian Task Force, a fighting formation of about 5000 men whose principal fighting components were three infantry battalions, each of about 900 soldiers. Also at Nui Dat were SAS, artillery, armoured personnel carriers, tanks, engineers, and a collection of support units, including the Topographical Survey Troop, soon to be commanded by John Bullen.

PAUL HAM

★

Meanwhile, above it all, circled a Cessna fitted with a public address system, announcing in Vietnamese: 'Have no fear. We are merely spraying a harmless insecticide. It cannot hurt people. It only hurts mosquitoes.' They made this announcement while the bombs were still dropping and milk jugs were bouncing around on our shaking breakfast table. Must be big mosquitoes here.

★

Thursday 1 February 1968

Preparations for disembarkation at Vung Tau on 3 February. Troops will go off first from forward end of *Sydney*, travelling in American Chinook helicopters, which carry 20 to 30 men. Vehicles and equipment will go off by Skycrane heavy-lift helicopters which can lift 5-ton trucks, and by ship's crane. It is expected that ship will be unloaded completely and reloaded with returning troops and vehicles within five hours.

Have noticed bold white lettering painted on the body of every Army vehicle: 'DELIVERED BY PORT JACKSON–VUNG TAU FERRY SERVICE'; and this inscription on an RAAF bus: 'FLY NAVY THE SAFE WAY AND GET THERE!'[1] Obviously some quick repainting will need to be done on disembarkation. Volleyball this morning — always useful exercise.

[1] Saw this same bus in Vung Tau a month later, still advertising the Navy! — JB

Friday 2 February 1968

Day spent briefing and preparing for departure from ship early morning tomorrow. There is a real risk to ships at Vung Tau, so emergency practices are occurring all over the ship throughout the day.

Saturday 3 February 1968

Aerial unloading by skycrane.

Up at 05.00. Waited in hangar below flight deck. Everyone ready to go at 06.45. First group went up to flight deck. Sounds of huge helicopter landing and taking off were heard. Second group went up. Then came startling news. No more Chinook flights. All troops still remaining (about 300) are to go off by the ship's landing craft.

Apparently heavy fighting, the heaviest of the whole war so far, has broken out throughout South Vietnam. Even Nui Dat and Saigon have been attacked. Most of Saigon is now in Viet Cong hands.

We boarded the landing craft and headed to shore. View just great — steel walls seven feet high all round. After about three miles, we hit the shingle of what I found out later to be Cat Lo. Scrunch! The landing ramp at the bow then dropped. Clang! Splash! 'End of the line! All change here!' shouted the coxswain gleefully. We were now on a shingle beach without a clue as to where

A later landing party admiring the scenery while going ashore.

we were or what to do. 'If our luck's out, we're in Vietnam,' said someone helpfully. All we knew was that the whole country had erupted in flames overnight. As senior man and with no briefing before leaving the ship, I decided we should wait where we were for the time being. Between the lot of us we had one rifle (carried by

L to R: Major General A.L. MacDonald, Vice-Admiral Sir Alan McNicoll and Captain D.A.H. 'Nobby' Clarke contemplating HMAS Sydney's lift well, 3 February 1968.

a cook whose corps didn't know that we aren't supposed to bring weapons because we'll be issued with them in Vietnam) and no ammunition at all. At least our trusty cook had a bayonet and several of us had our clasp knives somewhere in our baggage.

Then a US military police jeep arrived in a smoking hurry. Out jumped a US MP sergeant shouting, 'There's VC coming this way! Take cover and prepare to defend yourselves!' The largest boulder on the shingle beach was about fist size so there wasn't a lot of cover available. And defence? Well, at least a resourceful Australian sergeant was up to the task, scornfully replying to the MP, 'What fuckin' with? Web fuckin' belts?' The MPs disappeared smartly. We did our best to look as inconspicuous as a couple of hundred men on a large flat surface with all their travelling clobber could look.

After about half an hour some Australian trucks appeared, collected us all and drove us through the outskirts of the large logistic support area at Vung Tau. Everywhere American installations stood adjacent to the main airfield. Went past the poor and untidy looking local township and on to the 1st Australian Logistic Support Group (1ALSG) camp. The first Chinook that had left the *Sydney* bound for Nui Dat also arrived — the helicopter had got part of the way to Nui Dat, almost there in fact, and then was forced to return, apparently due to fighting around Nui Dat.

The road to Nui Dat is cut. More news — Ba Ria township near Nui Dat has been shot up heavily.

Waiting on a sand hill within the 1ALSG area for a few hours, we watched unloading of *Sydney* by Skycrane helicopter. Skycrane was huge and made the trucks it carried look tiny. It carried vehicles ashore and brought back damaged vehicles to go back to Australia. One vehicle for return to Australia was a Michigan fork-lift weighing about 5 tons. It fell 500 feet from the Skycrane when the harness gave way, landed in sand and is now totally smashed. Eventually our patient vigil on the sand hill came to an end and the officers were taken to the HQ 1ALSG Officers' Mess for late lunch — big comedown after Navy food.

In mid-afternoon those of us bound for Nui Dat were taken to the American airfield. There were aircraft coming and going all the time — busier than Sydney Airport. Waited at Vung Tau for several hours. While at the airfield, some of us visited the canteen called Uncle Harvey's Saloon. No windows. No doors visible. A dull red light in one corner. When accustomed to the darkness one could make out a bar in another corner, a jukebox in the opposite corner, tables and chairs in between, and nude photographs around the walls. Tremendous noise from jukebox so I soon quit.

At 17.00 we boarded a RAAF Caribou transport aircraft and flew to Nui Dat, the trip only taking about 15 minutes. Plane dived and banked spectacularly to drop height for landing. Have never before seen such a large aircraft thrown about so freely. Probably necessary to lose height rapidly over the only area secure from Viet Cong attack. The Survey Troop vehicle picked up Sergeants Clutterbuck and Morris and me, and drove us to a location about half a mile away.

Reached the Survey Troop in time for the farewell party for Sergeants Rix and Kramer, leaving the next morning now that their replacements have arrived with me. Plenty to talk about, so late to bed.

Sunday 4 – Saturday 10 February 1968

Very busy week. Stocktake of all stores done, files studied, whole Task Force area looked at etc etc — all the normal work of settling in. First impression is all brown with a bit of green. Brown dust everywhere. Task Force area consists of tents and rubber trees — everything dust-covered except the rubber-tree leaves. No rain for two months — dry season now. Wet season due in about two months.

Only two topics of conversation everywhere — replacements and sex: 'When's your replacement due?', 'How long have you been here?', 'My bloody replacement still hasn't arrived!' As for sex, it is obvious that it is considered abnormal not to have sexual relations with local women (or any women, for that matter) while away from Australia. This is recognised as meeting a need analogous to hunger or thirst.

Meanwhile, the war continues. Since 2 February, all forces in Vietnam have been engaged in the heaviest fighting of the whole war. During this week about 24,000 Viet Cong have been killed. Australians have killed about 180 and have lost about ten men. Saigon was partly overrun by three Viet Cong divisions, which are (we hope) being pushed out. Minor attacks have occurred on the Australian Task Force area at Nui Dat. Many towns nearby have nearly been destroyed in the fighting. Nui Dat is cut off by road from Vung Tau but the route should be open soon. Our own guns and mortars are firing sporadically day and night.

One night I watched an American C-47 (equivalent to a DC-3) circling above a nearby village (Hoa Long), directing intermittent streams of machine-gun fire onto targets lit and indicated by a low-flying Cessna. The sight of this slowly circling aircraft, nicknamed Spooky, and its thrusts of red hail towards the ground was both spectacular and chilling. It was also horrible to hear. Its density of fire is extremely high (6000 rounds per minute — a five-second burst will cover a football field with a hail of bullets), and it carries

7 tons of ammunition. The next morning, 31 bodies were found.

Two battalions of Australian infantry, 2nd and 7th, have been out on a big operation against the Viet Cong (Operation Coburg). Third Battalion has remained with the Task Force HQ, and there have been minor contacts on the perimeter each night, usually involving some machine-gun fire, a flare or two, and perhaps mortar fire. This heavy Viet Cong attack throughout Vietnam has been the consequence of the Lunar New Year (Tet or Tet Nguyen Danh), when it is politically expedient to make as good an impression as possible with the local people.

The ARVN (Army of the Republic of Vietnam) has not done much against the VC (Viet Cong — the army of the National Liberation Front). Local examples:

1. VC attack one village, so into it go Australian and American troops from another village, leaving ARVN in charge there. ARVN promptly embarks on two days' looting.

2. Ten VC enter a village 'guarded' by 100 ARVN. VC hold mock trial of top three men in village and then execute them. ARVN, although outnumbering the VC ten to one, hear a disturbance (the ten VC) to the south, so they move further north to avoid trouble.

3. An ARVN force of 150 men attacks a VC stronghold held by about 20 VC. Two ARVN men are wounded. Remainder flee, leaving their commander and an American officer adviser to the mercy of VC. Australian platoon then has to go in and rescue the ARVN commander and the US adviser. Mission successful, but three Australians, including the platoon commander (a lieutenant), were killed. Apparently some ARVN forces are good but most are weak. General consensus of opinion seems to be that ten ARVN = one VC, and that ten VC = one Australian. This sounds boastful but I don't argue against it because the evidence available does appear to support this contention.

What with the various tasks of a handover from one Officer

Commanding (Alex Laing) to another (me), and the continuous row going on all around, this has been a busy week.

Sunday 11 February 1968

Relaxed morning for some lucky people, including myself. Small concert staged at Nui Dat with visiting entertainers flown in from Sydney. Troupe includes male singer — Eden Kane (pleasant manner and the only member of the troupe who could sing); a hypnotist (who weighed about 20 stone); three go-go dancers (who couldn't sing but this didn't matter — they were Maggie Jodrell and sisters Pat and Wendy Sullivan); and an instrumental group of three men. Concert went for about 90 minutes: singing, dancing, hypnotism; that was about the lot. In itself not a marvellous show but the audience made it so and I believe it was the liveliest concert here yet.

The audience consisted mainly of infantrymen from 7th Battalion, who have been in combat against the Viet Cong for the last week or two on Operation Coburg and who were relieved yesterday by 3rd Battalion. These 7th Battalion boys didn't care what they said or whether anyone else cared. Examples:

1. To start off the show, Eden Kane comes to the microphone and says: 'G'day boys. It's a great place here!'

   Immediate reply from up the back: 'Ya can fuckin' 'ave it, mate!'

2. During the opening number of the show, entire troupe is singing on stage, including one girl in a sensational mini-skirt. US Army press photographers move in front of audience taking photos of performers from range of 3 to 5 feet. No one can see. Torrents of abuse. No effect. Then high in the sky the sun glints on a drink can spinning through the air. Good shot? A beauty! Fair on the back of neck of the biggest photographer and bounces high again. He got the message.

3. Girl singer says during the song 'Hava Nageela': 'You fellows aren't doing any work. This is no good.' (She wants them to clap the rhythm.)

   Deep voice from audience: 'Come down here and we'll go all day with you!'

   Girl (amidst much mirth): 'Not on your life.'

4. Girl says: 'Excuse me while I bring on my sister for a duet.' Last half of sentence drowned in a roar from audience at the ambiguity.

5. After the duet one girl says to the other: 'What is it they like about us? Is it our hair?'

   Voice from audience: 'Yeah, pubic!'

   'Or is it our legs? Or is it the mini-skirts?'

   Another voice from audience: 'Step down here and you'll find out soon enough!'

6. During hypnotism session two men are told they are wearing spectacles which see through clothes. One man looks at audience, says: 'Ugh!' and whips off imaginary spectacles and throws them away. Other man keeps spectacles on and heads for the room where the girls are.

The Sullivan Sisters, Wendy & Pat

7. One hypnotised man on stage is told that there is a monkey on a chair and to get it off. No problem. Man lashes out with mighty kick, catches chair right on the centre of gravity and sends it hurtling — imaginary monkey and all — high and hard out into the audience. Obviously a man who doesn't muck about.

8. Hypnotised men on stage are told first that their boots are full of fleas and secondly that there are cats out forward that have to be silenced. This results in a hail of boots flung with immense power into the audience. One really hammered as it streaked over my head. A microphone was knocked flying and someone nearly fell through the bass drum.

9. On arousing a subject, the hypnotist says: '. . . and you'll feel better than you've ever felt before. OK now, one, two, three, wake up! Now mate, how do you feel?'
Answer: 'Fuckin' shit hot, mate!'

As already mentioned, the girls couldn't sing but this didn't matter. They looked good and that was the main thing. One girl was really attractive, and in addition she ensured that her skirt flew waist-high on occasions. The audience responded magnificently! The performers responded very well to the ribaldry from the audience and obviously enjoyed them, resulting in everybody having a most entertaining time.

Had to wait for a vehicle after the show. Got photo of Rocky Camps (Survey Troop driver) cuddling two of the girls. Was amazed at Rocky's speed in getting into position, but as he said: 'Ya don't get anything if ya don't ask!'

Afternoon spent on miscellaneous tasks around camp and preparing for helicopter trip to Long Binh tomorrow to visit 66 Engineer Company (US Army), who are mapping colleagues of the Australian forces. Would have done this trip last week but the war made it impossible. Lines had been cut by VC so we couldn't even ring up. Things look a bit easier now.

POP STAR "SCARED"

POP singer Eden Kane told today how he sat petrified in a Saigon hotel while bombs exploded outside.

"It was real scarey," Kane told reporters Sydney Airport.

Kane was in Vietnam for 14 days with an entertainment troupe.

"It's grand to have my feet planted firmly on Australian soil," he said.

"I liked Saigon and had a wonderful time performing and meeting the Diggers."

● "Professor" a victim

With Kane were other members of the troupe — The Sullivan Sisters, Maggie Jodrell, and hypnotist "Professor" Osma.

"Professor" Le m a said he had survived the perils of Saigon.

He then went and broke an ankle in Singapore.

"The Vietcong didn't get me — I fell off a table trying to adjust a faulty air conditioner," he said.

Eden Kane and his girlfriend Christine Rudas at Sydney Airport.

A special wiggle for the soldiers.

Monday 12 February 1968

Away early — no breakfast — by helicopter to Long Binh with Alex Laing. Travelled in US Army Iroquois helicopter armed with

M60 machine guns on each side at altitude of about 2200 feet above ground. Dense vegetation beneath — not much habitation. Trip took 30 minutes. Flew over American forces camp Bearcat, a huge installation. All trees had been taken down, so the vast expanse of this military camp could be seen at a glance. Went on to Long Binh, the next camp, and we could see Bien Hoa, another huge base, in the distance. Very hard to get used to these huge camps. Long Binh itself is bigger than the entire Australian Army. Arrived at Long Binh, hitched a lift with a passing jeep and went to the Topographic Company to meet the Commander, Captain Joel Cain, and his officers, Lieutenant Skip Skoglund and Warrant Officers Jim Schofield and Bill Brogan. Altogether a most pleasant and helpful lot. Looked over their establishment, about 180 men, impressive map reproduction equipment, and a map depot containing about three million maps.

Buildings, especially the Engineer Group commander's hut, well ventilated with 0.5-inch bullet holes, it being only five days since this small company area was attacked by two Viet Cong battalions, with a savage seven-hour battle following. Despite the overwhelmingly unfavourable odds at this particular spot, US casualties were one killed, while the Viet Cong lost hundreds (there were so many bodies that they bulldozed them into the ground while clearing it to avoid a further surprise attack), and the VC failed to gain a yard of ground. This failure was due to: (i) strength of American position; (ii) many Viet Cong rockets failing to explode; and (iii) deadliness of US helicopter attacks with rockets and machine guns. Atmosphere has not yet calmed down at Long Binh and everyone wears steel helmets everywhere.

Tremendous variety of weapons carried — all types of carbines, rifles, pistols. Our Belgian 9mm pistols were much admired, but we managed to hang onto them. Visited other units in the area and gained much useful information. Between 21.00 and 22.00 I went with Joel Cain on a tour of the defences of his Topographic Company to check that all was as it should be. Flares were being fired everywhere and artillery audible, but no action at all on the front at Long Binh. After checking all bunkers we returned to Joel's room, which had a spare bed, for the night. Listened to Radio North Korea for an hour and heard alleged confession of skipper of USS *Pueblo*, captured by North Korea. Skipper confessed his 'crimes' most abjectly. To bed at 23.00.

Tuesday 13 February 1968

Awakened at 03.30 by news of a Viet Cong ground attack on Bien Hoa camp about 3 miles away. Checked alertness of bunkers around us and informed them of news. Could hear shells exploding in the distance. Back to bed then up at 06.00 for early start to catch plane back to Nui Dat. No space on plane so Alex Laing, Skip Skoglund and I went by US Army jeep to Saigon to catch plane for Nui Dat from there. Fighting still going on in Saigon so best to play safe. Donned flak jackets and American steel helmets, borrowed an arsenal of automatic weapons and set off.

Interesting trip. Country and city similar to Djakarta[2] and environs in many ways — neither rich nor clean. Djakarta preferable — people friendlier there, but of course the Vietnamese are amidst a war and this must make a big difference. Our jeep had frequent fuel blockages and stopped many times.

Jeep finally stopped at • on this sketched map and wouldn't start. At this stage Skip Skoglund said to leave the jeep,

[2] Jakarta. — PH

so we did and got aboard another some 200 yards away. Got to Tan Son Nhut airport, near Saigon, about one minute too late to catch the RAAF Caribou to Nui Dat. Booked on the 15.30 plane instead, and then went to visit Military Assistance Command Vietnam (MACV) and other US forces' HQs, including Intelligence. We even attended a conference on charting, mapping and geodesy.

Went back to airfield with Alex to catch plane and troubles began. Heard our RAAF plane was still at Nui Dat with magneto trouble. We wished to climb instead on the plane about to leave with the vegetable supply for Nui Dat. No, said RAAF, you'll get there, just relax while we get another plane. One hour later — one plane but no petrol. Two hours later — petrol (took one hour to organise a tanker and the Yanks pinched it, so had to wait another hour). Plane finally refuelled by 18.30. Meanwhile, at about 16.00, machine-gun fire had broken out at one end of the airstrip, about a mile or two away. Aircraft dived in and pounded the place with rockets — rather spectacular. Then came mortar and artillery fire and quite a lot of noise. Saigon obviously far from quiet. Read Sydney newspaper brought up by air today. Much fighting in Saigon yesterday. Don't think it's as bad as reported or else we would not have been able to travel through Saigon unmolested today.

Plane took off at 18.30 for Nui Dat. Landed 25 minutes later at Vung Tau, pilot having changed his mind on the way. We realised this shortly after leaving Saigon, because plane was still over swamps and heading almost south. By then dark and no more flights to Nui Dat so we were stuck at Vung Tau and no one at Nui Dat knew where we were. Time was 19.00. RAAF assured us transport, accommodation, food, all organised. After two hours, a Land Rover arrived to take us on the five-minute trip to 1ASLG. Vung Tau black and quiet — curfew is on. Arrived at 1ALSG. Where's dinner (our first meal since yesterday)? 'Oh, we thought you weren't coming so we ate it, but there's half a sandwich left.' Wolfed it down and went to bed. Am beginning to believe impossible yarns I've heard about RAAF inefficiency.

Wednesday 14 February 1968

Flew to Nui Dat at 07.30. Quiet day (for a change). Guns pounding (as usual) at night. Hard to get back to normal routine after two days of American hospitality. All American establishments had coffee available everywhere at all times. Even while patrolling the bunkers (checking defences with Joel Cain) along the outer edge of Long Binh and peering out into the unknown darkness and nearly shooting a Viet Cong (which turned out to be a dog), coffee was available only a couple of yards away. Quite apart from their coffee (they can fight a war without chicken and ice-cream, but not without coffee), the Americans really were most helpful to us.

Thursday 15 February 1968

Drove to Vung Tau during morning on orientation visit. Road not yet completely safe. Everyone in convoy armed and wearing flak jackets. Dry, dusty road south through dry paddy fields for first half of the trip. Then came the town of Ba Ria, badly shot up a week or so ago. Most buildings were either untouched or smashed to bits — there were very few with moderate damage. Road then continued southward along a causeway through mangrove swamp — rather like the road to Port Hedland in Western Australia's nor'-west. Road crossed two bridges which have been smashed and rebuilt many, many times and which look very unsafe.

Arrived at Vung Tau after three-quarters of an hour. Had lunch at the Peter Badcoe Soldiers' Club. Paid only $0.35 for a better meal than I've ever had in the 1ALSG Officers' Mess. Visited the US PX (post exchange or canteen/shop) and did some shopping. Interesting to see liquor prices: 26-ounce de Kuyper crème de menthe for US$1.10 (=A$0.99), 26-ounce Cherry Heering for $3.00 and 26 ounce Bénédictine for $3.00 etc. Electrical and optical goods are also cheap, but minor products such as clothing, toilet articles, stationery etc cost as much as in Australia. Bought 33 postcards for $0.80 — I suspect the Vietnamese cashier made a mistake in my favour but she could speak neither French nor English.

Donned flak jacket again, gun at the ready (I had borrowed a machine carbine for this trip and had five full magazines of ammunition with it), and we set off back to Nui Dat, this time with two infantry Land Rovers in convoy. The infantry were in a hurry and we did the trip in 30 minutes, hanging on grimly as the Land Rover bounced along the road. Lone travel is dangerous and forbidden, so we were forced to keep up when the infantry went through towns at 50 to 55 miles per hour, despite signs saying 'POPULOUS AGGLOMERATION. PLEASE SLOW DOWN TO 10 MPH.' Infantry driver probably gave up in despair after the first two words.

Got back safely to Nui Dat just the same. Quiet evening. Since my arrival in Vietnam I have been surprised at the Australian troops' low regard for the Vietnamese people (although they do hide this attitude from the Vietnamese). I am now beginning to understand it. The apathy of the Vietnamese one sees everywhere hardly inspires sympathy or friendship, and in addition the Australian just does not know who is his friend or his enemy; therefore he must assume them all to be his enemies until friendship is proved beyond any doubt at all.

Friday 16 February 1968

A day working on miscellaneous administrative tasks. Operations against Viet Cong now recording fewer kills. The heavy fighting of the last few weeks is apparently dying down. Mail finally arrived today, the first for the Task Force this week.

Saturday 17 February 1968

Busy day — normal work plus the extra effort of ensuring that no loose ends are left when Alex Laing departs (and I take over) on Monday. Got most things tidied up by 17.00 when the farewell parties for Alex started. The Officers' Mess farewell was brief and Alex and another five to ten officers returned to the Survey Troop for a barbecue. Evening became very noisy: 22 dozen cans of beer were consumed in four hours by about 20 men. Singing of bawdy ballads drowned out the usual pounding of guns and mortars. Not very sensible in a war zone where one could be called upon to defend oneself without warning; however, when so many officers from the Task Force HQ itself are involved, there is little that can be done. Survey Troop soldiers squeezed out of their own facilities not impressed at all.

Despite 22.00 curfew, the party went on until 02.00. The Task Force HQ Sergeants' Mess across the road was also involved in a wild session, which fortunately distracted attention from the disturbance in the Survey Troop area. The Survey show received three smoke grenades, thrown as fireworks, during the evening — one green at 21.00 and two yellow at 23.00 — but the singing continued. Went to bed myself at 23.00.

Sunday 18 February 1968

Today promises to be a hectic day for Alex, with three or four more farewells in various other Officers' Messes he has patronised well. Meanwhile, I took a party of eight of our men down to the beach at Vung Tau for a swimming trip. Swimming parties must be accompanied by an officer, so with two officers in the Survey Troop, this means a fortnightly visit (on Sundays) for each. Interesting trip down — the road busy with the usual Lambro vehicles, a sort of mini-bus with a Lambretta motor scooter chassis and handlebars at the front, containing about eight people when tightly packed. These chug along usually right in the middle of the road.

Spent a leisurely day at Vung Tau. Had a hamburger lunch at the Peter Badcoe Club again. Walked across the road to the beach. Beach very quiet — a few surfers, a few sunbakers and a lot of barbed wire at the back. Went along to the American beach about 500 metres away and quite a different story. Men everywhere, girls everywhere, children everywhere and popular music over a public-address system — just like a normal beach in Sydney. The girls were wearing very brief bikinis — nipples visible over the top of several, and the bottom half of one bikini could not be seen from behind even though

American beach, Vung Tau.

Australian beach, Vung Tau. The soldier at left is Korean.

the wearer was sitting and leaning forward. Saw many busts of most impressive size on many girls, thus disproving the widely held opinion that all Oriental women are flat-chested.

Many girls and men were locked in passionate embraces on the beach. In one instance, a girl pulled a rug over her companion and herself, then they quite clearly removed all of their clothing that would obstruct sexual intercourse and proceeded. Then followed readjustment of clothing and a swim. Many children were selling minor trinkets and pornographic photographs (at exorbitant cost).

Left the beach and went to the American soldiers' club, the Beachcomber. Gift shop, many bars, girls, music — the lot. Had a quick look, then returned to the beach for a swim at the Australian end.

Back at Nui Dat by mid-afternoon. Alex in good health. Due to ill health of many others after last night's session, only one party eventuated today.

Saw James Bond film *You Only Live Twice* in Officers' Mess tonight. The Mess shook with tremendous explosion just as the film atmosphere was explosive: heavy artillery was suddenly being brought to bear on 80 Viet Cong a little distance away. This continued throughout the night — the noisiest yet.

This morning at 01.30 a concerted Viet Cong attack all over the country broke out. The Australian Task Force lost seven killed and 22 wounded. Amidst all tonight's firing I was told at 23.00 to visit the Command Post before breakfast tomorrow. Obviously something serious is happening.

Monday 19 February 1968

Expecting to face an early-morning crisis in the Command Post, I was relieved to find that all that was required of me was urgent supply of maps for a search operation in the village of Long Dien. Easily fixed.

Survey Troop officers' tent.

Alex Laing left this morning. Captain Noel Sproles, second-in-command, arrived today. Most welcome. Our officers' tent will now be a lot tidier. Noel busy settling in and preparing to visit Long Binh tomorrow with WO1 Percy Long for two days with Americans.

Tuesday 20 February 1968

Noel and Perce left early to catch the plane for Long Binh. Visit is for a survey job for Australian Signals (siting a rhombic aerial) and to have a look at 66 Engineer Company there, which I visited a week ago.

Several conferences and two briefings today. Attended 7th Battalion orders group. We are sending four surveyors with 7th Battalion to bring the local map up to date when the battalion infantry have searched Long Dien village for Viet Cong. Operation being mounted swiftly and goes in this afternoon. Two battalions

(2nd and 7th) are being used to sweep and search the Long Dien area — population about 10,000 to 12,000 people, about half of them children. Party set out at 15.00 with 7th Battalion — Sergeant Grant Small, Sergeant Ted Morris, Corporal Graeme ('Willie-the-Keyhole-Peeper') Williams and Sapper Ray Lawson. That intriguing nickname seems to have fallen into disuse, now that Graeme's former days at the School of Survey as the sapper who knew everything that was going on are slipping further into the past.

Attended Amenities conference. Gloomy news — amenities equipment off-loaded from ship at Sydney to make room for tanks. Attended Commander's (Brigadier Ron Hughes's) conference for all unit commanders. Matters mentioned include:

1. Accidents — too many accidental deaths. As Brigadier Hughes said: 'I just don't understand it. How the hell can a bloke enjoy a decent crap when he's being shot at by both sides!'

2. Protection — not enough protective measures for own safety being taken against Viet Cong attack.

3. Noise — too much noise after 22.00. I imagine the farewell party in the Survey Troop lines last Saturday may have had a lot to do with this.

4. Customs — too many breaches of regulations have occurred, mainly with weapons smuggled into Australia.

Wednesday 21 February 1968

Day got off to flying start. After Brigadier Hughes's talk yesterday on accidents, a soldier of 104 Signals Squadron accidentally fired his rifle at 08.00. The bullet missed a sergeant by about a foot, a warrant officer by about a yard, and then passed straight over the Command Post of the Task Force HQ, the Commander's hut, and

THE SURVEY TROOP AND ITS WORK

The 22-man Survey Troop contained two officers, seven field surveyors, five draughtsmen, one photographer, two printers and five other personnel to look after stores, the office, driving and cooking.

The Troop was organised into four groups — the Headquarters (officers and all administrative personnel), the Survey Section (the field surveyors), the Cartographic Section (the draughtsmen), and the Reproduction Section (the photographer and the printers).

Thanks to the US Army, good basic maps of Vietnam already existed, so the Survey Troop did not have to make them. The Troop was not equipped to do so anyway. Its duties were to provide the survey and mapping support that the Task Force needed. The nature of this support changed greatly during the Troop's tour of duty in Vietnam from 1966 to 1971.

Corporal Mario Apfelbaum at his screen press.

Initially, there was much need for field survey (mostly for artillery purposes), and the surveyors were kept very busy. But once done, it was there for good and the surveyors had less to do — as long as the Task Force remained at Nui Dat. Emphasis thus steadily changed to rapid-response mapping, not of standard topographic maps, but of sketch maps for operations, overprints onto standard maps, overlays on tracing paper to go over standard maps, annotated photographic maps, and a wide variety of draughting tasks. We improvised in much of what we did, and we all took pride in being able to meet these challenges, sometimes against apparently impossible deadlines. Occasionally when it really was a case of all hands on deck, I took a pen myself and assisted in a draughting task, especially if we needed free-hand lettering done in a big hurry.

The Troop was equipped lightly as a mobile unit. Its main printing equipment was a specially made lightweight screen press, which could be

dismantled for transport. Screen printing was not greatly suitable for mapping, especially in tropical conditions, but the key factor here was that this press was far more mobile than a heavy lithographic press.

The Troop had progressively added equipment of its own to improve the service it offered. A bombed hospital elsewhere in Phuoc Tuy province yielded stainless-steel sheeting from which photographic developing tanks were hand-made by the Troop's soldiers. A process camera was built from an epidiascope lens and a collection of mechanical parts, star pickets and tar paper by Corporal Bill Snelson, an innovative national serviceman. Eventually, even a lithographic press was obtained from the Troop's US Army counterparts.

Corporal Paul Alderson (front) and Sapper Trevor Marsh (behind) in the draughting hut.

Sapper Mick Sokil in the map store.

After the first two years of accumulating this extra equipment, the Task Force became accustomed to the enhanced service on offer from the Survey Troop — far beyond what had been envisaged when the detachment had embarked from Australia in 1966. We were still officially mobile, but in reality we had become a static installation. A move would have caused an immediate reduction in capabilities and loss of popularity with our customers. Indeed, a move was my worst nightmare as Officer Commanding. Fortunately, the prospect was never realised and we continued to keep our customers happy with the quality and speed of our work.

Map of Nui Dat and environs, overprinted by the Survey Troop to show ground bulldozed clear of vegetation.

then the Officers' Mess. Much excitement. Officers everywhere, from the Brigadier down.

Even more excitement an hour later when 104 Signals Squadron did exactly the same thing again. War is hell.

Another day preparing and printing maps for an operation being undertaken at very short notice. Field party returned from Long Dien. Operation successful but no mapping done. Our party not allowed to start until village completely cleared and by then it was almost time to return. Day spent helping to construct shelters for refugees and carrying water and doing other odd jobs for them. Interesting but tiring day for our party.

Thursday 22 – Friday 23 February 1968

Rocky Camps, our driver, is marvellous at 'obtaining' things we need. On Friday we discussed the need for a firmer path connecting our tents. 'Leave it to me,' said Rocky. Half an hour later he'd produced a 3-ton truck. An hour later, he had emptied two truckloads of coarse gravel right where we needed it. Something like this happens every day but this is his best yet.

Heard today of a dastardly deed done by one of our former members. The Survey Troop needed a transformer to convert 240-volt power to 110-volt power for our American TV set. None was available but HQ Company had a transformer for its TV set. Apparently there was little love between HQ Company and the Survey Troop in those days — different types of people, different interests etc. The Survey people were supposed to use HQ Company facilities, canteen etc but rarely did so due to the enthusiasm of HQ Company for punching the heads of 'intellectuals'. So our man quietly changed some wiring in the HQ Company TV set so that when they next switched it on it blew up in a most spectacular fashion. This meant that their transformer was no longer needed, so we now have it. Fortunately (a) everyone is very reticent on the subject (or we'd get more than our heads punched); and (b) Rocky obtains our requirements by more honourable means.

Mail came in today after a week's non-supply for unknown reasons. Heard of Viet Cong reports of the last few weeks of fighting. Our casualties have been immense. We've lost more armoured personnel carriers than we possess. The people probably believe some of this, despite its absurdity to us.

Saturday 24 February 1968

Noel Sproles and Percy Long returned from their four days at Long Binh with the US Army. Life there is now more exciting than when Alex Laing and I were there a week or so earlier. Long Binh is in constant expectation of attack, and on a couple of occasions rockets were fired into the main position and everyone had to leap underground. Noel and Percy surveyed an aerial in position for the Australian Signals people, and had to organise a patrol to clear the Viet Cong out from the undergrowth before they could start.

Enemy forces appear to be building up for a strike on Saigon. Two Viet Cong divisions are known to be moving into position and they may attack tomorrow morning. Meanwhile the earth and air are pounding with heavy explosions. American B-52 bombers are out on missions and some of their bombs are landing only 2 or 3 miles from here. Flashes can be seen and the concussion is heavy. Our guns and mortars are firing steadily. The heavy 8-inch guns make a tremendous noise and the blast can be felt strongly, although the gun site is a mile from us.

Heard tonight of an accident which befell the Viet Cong a few days ago. During the night a VC battalion was moving silently into position to attack an Australian position. Everything went perfectly until one man made a simple mistake and accidentally discharged his RPG launcher. This caused several casualties in the immediate vicinity. It also happened that, purely by chance, a gunship (helicopter with searchlight and those fearful mini-guns) was cruising above, looking for any force gathering for an attack. One moment the VC battalion was quietly moving into position for the attack, and the next came this accidental explosion. Then the lights went on and the air was full of screaming lead. Casualties were colossal. The VC battalion was carved up and the Australian position was not attacked, thanks to one man's mistake.

Sunday 25 February 1968

Swimming-party day to Vung Tau. I stayed at Nui Dat. Did normal work and managed to find time to lie in the sun for a while and get some letters written.

Monday 26 February 1968

Noisy night last night, mainly from the 7-inch guns of the 1/83 US Artillery Battalion. Many minor jobs to do during day and many minor annoyances for everyone: Amenities never seem able to supply sporting equipment; the PX never seems to have film, radios, etc in stock; and no mail etc. Big pity these things happen. Good morale depends on a lot of these supplies, and I gather that troubles are frequent. Still one can only hope for improvement. Some cloud seen in the air today for a short time. Climate seems very stable at this time of year.

Tuesday 27 February 1968

Awakened at 03.30. Much noise from machine guns, bombs, artillery and aircraft. Puff the Magic Dragon, alias Spooky, was on the prowl again breathing long rasps of fire down to the ground. Many bursts were 10 seconds or longer. Ground target obviously only a mile or two away, because Spooky was directly above us as he circled. Between 07.00 and 08.00 things got rougher, and a series of bomb strikes from a B-52 went in. The concussion from these explosions was very heavy indeed and shook our flimsy buildings and their contents. Strafing by aircraft cannon was also heard.

This coincided, most incongruously, with an American C-123 transport plane spraying insecticide over the Task Force area and surrounding villages, including Hoa Long, now being strafed and bombed. The C-123 roared back and forth at barely above tree-top level. Meanwhile, above it all, circled a Cessna fitted with a public-address system, announcing in Vietnamese: 'Have no fear. We are merely spraying a harmless insecticide. It cannot hurt people. It only hurts mosquitoes.' They made this announcement while the bombs were still dropping and milk jugs were bouncing around on our shaking breakfast table. Must be big mosquitoes here.

Discovered later that at least ten villages within 10 miles of Nui Dat had been hit by Viet Cong last night. Hoa Long, the closest to us (1 to 2 miles away) was the hardest hit, so the retaliation was heaviest on the Viet Cong withdrawal routes from Hoa Long. Meanwhile, tanks just unloaded at Vung Tau and fresh from Australia are now on their way to Nui Dat — a whole squadron of them plus reserve tanks. To impress the locals and the Viet Cong, the tanks will pass through Ba Ria and Hoa Long and test-fire their machine guns on the way.

At 10.00, Noel Sproles and I went on a reconnaissance flight by helicopter (Sioux) for an hour or so. Most interesting flight: altitude between 200 and 1500 feet above ground; terrain flat except for isolated hills; most vegetation a scrubby type of forest. Several rubber plantations seen (the Australian Task Force is in one at Nui Dat which is owned by the Michelin Tyre Company of France). Many paddies, banana fields and other plantations seen. Flew over many villages, viz Ap Suoi Nghe, Xa Binh Gia, Long Tan, Dat Do, Lang Phuoc Hai, Long Hai, Ba Ria, Van Kiep, Long Dien, Long Phuoc, Hoa Long, and back to Nui Dat.

Ap Suoi Nghe is an artificial village built by the Australians to house villagers transplanted from elsewhere. Xa Binh Gia has no less than five churches. Dat Do is surrounded by minefields, but Viet Cong tracks through the minefields could be seen. Lang Phuoc Hai is a densely built up fishing village on the coast and looked most picturesque (from our distance, anyway).

Further down the coast we saw many lovely villas now in ruins. These face the sea at the foot of the Long Hai hills, 1000 feet high. They were built by the French within the last 30 years or so and must have been really beautiful. Large and elegantly styled and surrounded by intricate and ornate garden patterns still visible in the new and haphazard vegetation, these homes are now only crumbling shells. Only walls and roofs remain, and these are in poor condition. This is now a prohibited area for Vietnamese and no one is to be seen except for children and lovers.

Ba Ria, the capital of Phuoc Tuy province, was busy, especially at the marketplace. One very large ruined church there — must visit it by road when safe to do so. Damage to Ba Ria from the Tet Offensive visible from air, with many small blocks of buildings completely levelled. Saw many road blocks along the main road in Long Dien and they looked very substantial — logs etc.

Between the two biggest and most central road blocks (about 200 yards apart) a great Viet Cong flag flew high from a flag pole, its red, gold and blue resplendent in the sun. The Viet Cong do this a lot — fly flags in minefields, at road blocks in towns, outside ARVN posts etc — it helps show their power and daring to the local people. Circled over that flag at about 400 feet altitude but dared go no closer. Very tempting to steal the flag, but I'm told that the last helicopter that tried this was blown out of the sky and totally destroyed by a claymore mine, directed upwards with cord attached. A Viet Cong pulled the cord at the right instant, and when the explosion settled there was no more helicopter recognisable as such. So we left this flag well alone. Disappointed that I didn't have camera — the scene was most attractive.

Had a most pleasant lunch at 161 Recce Flight Mess before returning to our own area. More trouble in Hoa Long — an American truck full of troops returning to Nui Dat from Vung Tau sighted log road block ahead, dodged it, expected to hit mines but didn't, got back on road and continued. Around the next corner was another road block, this time bigger than the truck. Truck did a screaming U-turn and raced back out again. No mines and no shooting but much uneasiness all round.

Surprised in evening by the completely unexpected arrival of an officer stationed in Singapore, who has come to us for a one-month visit. Oh help. The last thing I could have wished for. Purpose of visit: he doesn't know. Neither do I. He's arranged this as some sort of 'orientation and training' visit, but has no aim beyond this. I note that this visit is for the minimum duration to qualify for the Vietnam Medal and war service benefits[3] — or am I being unduly cynical? All that there is to be seen in Vietnam on the survey and mapping side can be seen in a week, so I may as well arrange this for a start. Thus ends a rather eventful day.

[3] Known as a 'swan'. — PH

Wednesday 28 February
– Saturday 2 March 1968

Desperately busy four days. Monthly report to be written and this takes at least a couple of days' full-time work by itself. On top of this have had to play host and guide by day, and work by night. Too busy to write diary. Was working until 02.00 for each of the last three nights.

Tonight not so bad. Our guest has gone off to 3rd Battalion for the afternoon and evening with friends there, and I've managed to catch up with the work at last. His presence has cost me a third to half of the working time of each day so far, but the situation is improving now that I have got many visits organised for him. He is here for exactly 30 days, of which the first nine are to be spent here with us. For the remaining three weeks he will visit Long Binh, Saigon and perhaps Da Lat and Nha Trang. One week would be more than ample for the lot. Don't know how he'll kill the time.

I have been given the job of organising his nine days at Nui Dat. Have let him potter around the Survey Troop for a while and arranged a flight with 161 Recce Flight, a visit to 131 Divisional Locating Battery, a trip to the Australian-built village of Ap Suoi Nghe with the Civil Affairs Unit, a period in the Task Force Command Post as observer and understudy, an orientation tour of the Task Force area, a visit to the Air Intelligence centre at Task Force HQ, and attendance at various conferences and briefings. Being a new boy myself, I was not able to organise all this in a flash, and there is more yet to do. It's been a challenge at a most awkward time but I'm getting there.

Meanwhile, we have other problems. Our photographer, Corporal Bill Snelson, and screen printer, Corporal Lindsay Rotherham, are both due home in Australia by 19 March for discharge. Both are national servicemen and have willingly done a marvellous job. Their replacements, Corporals John Rolfe and Mario Apfelbaum, have been waiting, ready to come, for a couple of months. Army has finally told them to get moving and they will be here in early April. But the rule is that no one can leave Vietnam until his replacement has arrived, so what happens to Bill and Lindsay? After their excellent work here they deserve better thanks than this. Also, Lindsay was hoping to attend a wedding (his own) immediately on return. So I decide to tell Lindsay to go on 18 March since his job can be done by Sapper Bo Hucker for the two to three weeks before Mario arrives. But what about Bill? No problem, says Bill, I know a man who can do my job. I listen and then go over to 4 Field Regiment (Royal Australian Artillery) and head for their HQ Battery. I ask for a loan of Gunner Sprice for a month and for a look at his personal papers. Sure enough, there it is — camera operator, five-year apprenticeship in civilian life before national service got him. HQ Battery only too happy to lend him. He's been on cleaning duties around the camp because they found it difficult to employ him. They're delighted that constructive work can be found for him. He's delighted. And Bill Snelson is grinning like a dead fox.

We now have two and a half weeks to ensure that Gunner Sprice can do the job. However, after one day there seems little doubt about this. He's OK. So Lindsay and Bill can both go home for a well-earned rest, and we should be able to manage OK till Mario and John come.

Back at the war there's been quite a lot of action during the past few days. Viet Cong tunnels have been discovered right on the edge of the Australian position at Nui Dat. Several Australians have been killed and wounded in recent clashes nearby. Amongst Viet Cong weapons captured are several of Swedish, Russian, German and Czech origin. The Divisional Intelligence Unit has been 'rabbiting' in Hoa Long (2 miles away) with A Company of 7th Battalion, under command of Captain Geoff Boscoe (Intelligence) and Major Jake O'Donnell (A Company, 7th Battalion) respectively. They searched Hoa Long a few weeks ago with little success. This time members of 10 MID (Military Intelligence Detachment) of the ARVN accompanied them. The infantry company lined up along a frontage of about 150 metres and moved forward, covering about 40 metres in five minutes. Stop, said the ARVN, you've missed everything. So back they all went, started again, and the ARVN went ahead. This time they took four hours to advance 100 metres and took the whole day to advance 300 metres. Many hides and tunnels were found and almost all contained Viet Cong, both male and female. It was a most successful haul. The pace increased as they got more prisoners, because all prisoners gave accurate information most willingly after 'persuasion' by ARVN, and this information proved most useful. The whole operation was a big success, thanks mainly to 10 MID — nice to record something on the ARVN credit side for a change.

On 29 February a woman was rushed in by helicopter to the Aid Post next to the Survey Troop. She had been in a tunnel and had received in succession: one high-explosive fragmentation grenade, one smoke grenade, and 10 pounds of TNT. At the end of this she was still alive — just. Two days later, still clinging to life — just.

The Viet Cong mined the school at Dat Do today and blew up six children, two of them killed. As I write, rifle and machine-gun fire can be heard quite close — this being in addition to the normal artillery pounding which has been heavier than usual for the past week. To cap things off, our Psychological Operations aircraft did a leaflet drop today — thousands of pieces of paper bearing anti-Viet Cong propaganda. Unfortunately they misjudged the wind and most of the leaflets landed on the Task Force HQ Sergeants' Mess. They all surrendered immediately, hoping for monetary reward.

MARCH

AUSTRALIAN MILITARY FORCES

AAB — 71A
Reprinted Dec, 1964

RECORD BOOK

CONTAINING 96 PAGES

RULED FEINT

Courts martial in Vietnam, as elsewhere, were conducted by an appointed court martial board. The board consisted of a few (usually three or five) officers, one of whom was the chairman. These officers (usually in rank from captain to lieutenant colonel) were regimental officers and advised on legal matters by the judge advocate, a Legal Corps officer (usually a major or captain) appointed for the court martial. The accused was prosecuted and defended by other regimental officers also appointed for the occasion. In more serious cases, the defending and prosecuting officers were both Legal Corps officers.

The accused could nominate a particular officer as defending officer, hoping that he would be available. After John had an early success as defending officer, the word spread and he was soon in demand, mostly by military crims who knew that only a smart legal trick could get them off. Once he started to be used in this way, he declined his services, being uncomfortable with the legal approach to military justice.

PAUL HAM

★

Morning shattered early by the appalling roar of two US Air Force F-100 fighters streaking over the Task Force HQ (and the Survey Troop) at about 600 miles per hour and at an altitude of about 60 to 100 feet above ground. The tree tops swayed as they screeched overhead. All in good fun but the first one (which woke me) gave me a tremendous fright.

★

Sunday 3 March 1968

Up early to take swimming party to Vung Tau for the day. It is only safe to go to Vung Tau in parties of at least two vehicles. On this occasion we went with the Civil Affairs Unit and they wanted an early start in order to get first use of the surf boat.

Uneventful trip down. Visited the Army Education Centre at the camp at Vung Tau with a couple of the chaps who are hoping to pass Leaving English this year. Played table tennis in the Badcoe Club, had an early lunch and went to the beach. Joined a game of softball and failed to hit a ball. Only my fielding saved me from utter disgrace. At least I can still catch. The Australian section of beach quiet — surfboards, barbed wire and about six soldiers swimming or sunbaking. Went along to the American section. As usual much life there: girls, soldiers, beggars, children. One beggar carried a notice saying: 'I am blind. Please give me some money.' Sergeant Eric Clutterbuck held out a $10 note. The blind man opened his eyes wide and clutched eagerly at the note. Eric is now famous for his faith healing.

Walked about 2 miles down the beach to Cap St Jacques itself and photographed a Greek freighter wrecked about two months ago on the rocks right at the southern tip — most surprising since this did not occur in stormy weather and there is a big lighthouse on Cap St Jacques. Walked back past somewhat weather-beaten bars, hotels etc along the beach and back to the American section. Visited The Beachcomber — lots of noise, drinking and girls — and returned to the Australian section for a swim. Entertainment on at the Badcoe Club — popular music played by a Vietnamese group, three youths and a girl. Not much good. Collected party and drove to American PX for shopping. Little on offer — place pretty well cleaned out.

As the only man who had consumed no grog during the day, I drove the Survey Troop Land Rover back. We joined a convoy of one Land Rover and two trucks full of men. Trucks challenged us to a race so we let them pass us. Men were drinking in trucks and dropping beer cans along the road. They stopped just north of Ba Ria for relief of bladders.

Joined another convoy of Land Rovers and went back to Nui Dat. Passed through Hoa Long village on the way. Many sullen faces in Hoa Long, scene of the 'rabbiting' last week. The predominant colour in Hoa Long is brown. Brown soil, brown wooden lean-tos, brown roofs. A pleasant village with no buildings of any importance or attraction at all, but one dares not linger there. Back in Nui Dat we heard of a road accident involving the two trucks we'd been with. One stopped in a cloud of dust; the other drove into the dust at high speed. Two men badly hurt and had to be cut out of wreckage, many bruised and with minor injuries. Second bad road accident in two days — in the other, an Australian armoured personnel carrier hit a stationary Vietnamese truck. This evening a soldier accidentally shot himself in the chest but did not wound himself seriously. Much artillery firing tonight and also some machine-gunning.

Monday 4 March 1968

A couple of rushed mapping jobs today. The Task Force Commander has cut beer quota down to two cans per man per day as a result of all the recent accidents involving liquor. However, this will not stop drinking at Vung Tau.

Many heavy bombing raids some 10 to 20 miles away tonight. Many more holes, tunnels etc have been found on the edge of the Australian position, and Viet Cong have occasionally been sighted. Tanks practised machine-gun fire tonight, their tracer ammunition being most spectacular, especially whenever a ricochet flew high in the sky.

Was sitting with a Vietnamese major at dinner tonight. I've noticed that he never speaks to anyone, nor anyone to him. I spoke to him and smiled, but he did not reply. I then said, 'Préférez-vous parler en français?' His eyes lit up and he beamed with delight and began to talk freely. He's from Hué and has a wife and five children there. He sees them about twice a year and hasn't heard from them since the recent heavy fighting began a month ago. He is with the Intelligence branch of the ARVN. Much to my pleasure, I could understand his French easily — my last French interaction with an Asian was in Holland, with a Vietnamese and a Cambodian, and I found communication very difficult due to their heavy accents. No such trouble this time.

I have also been enjoying an occasional correspondence which began regarding washing with Madame Minh Ha, the laundry proprietor in Ba Ria, who handles the Survey Troop's laundry. She is obviously, from her letters, a well-educated and intelligent woman. I believe she has a

Madame Minh Ha with a 3rd Battalion soldier, 1968.

daughter who is a pharmacist from Saigon University and who is going to Paris shortly. Madame Minh Ha herself has lived a long time in France. I hope to meet her as soon as I can find the time to go on one of the laundry runs. She has very kindly lent me several *Paris-Match* and *Cinémonde* magazines.

Tuesday 5 March 1968

Mail finally came today after several days without. We are informed that mail hold-ups are due to: (i) Australian mail strike in January; (ii) American forces build-up in Vietnam reducing space for mail on Pan Am flights.

Big operation building up in Long Hai hills against Viet Cong. Planned for today are, in sequence: (i) two B-52 bombing strikes; (ii) one drop of 500 gallons of fuel oil; (iii) one drop of napalm without fuses; (iv) one drop of napalm with fuses to cause the whole lot to blow up. Any surviving enemy will then be treated with CS gas.[1] Then the ground attack will go in. Quiet night tonight. Much less shooting than usual.

Wednesday 6 March 1968

Everything happened today. Jobs large and small hit from all directions. Worked 15 hours and it wasn't enough. Viet Cong thought to be building up for new major offensive after Tet.

---

[1] Chlorobenzylidene malononitrile — a kind of tear gas — which temporarily disables its victims. — PH

Thursday 7 – Saturday 9 March 1968

We really are flat chat at the moment. Draughting, photographic and printing jobs coming in all the time, and all of them are high priority. Have been doing draughting work at night myself in addition to my normal administration.

Our guest from Singapore left on Friday to visit the American survey people at Long Binh but he returns in a few days. For the weekend we have two American sergeants visiting from Long Binh. Their presence is most welcome and they are in no way a hindrance.

Action in the Long Hais continues. Two items of interest from the last few days:

1. 161 Battery, Royal NZ Artillery, fired on a Viet Cong stretcher party bearing wounded Viet Cong and caused many casualties (fire being directed by an Australian helicopter). I then discovered that a similar incident had occurred a few days previously. I had thought that this was the sort of thing that one 'didn't do'. Apparently not so.

2. The newly arrived Australian tanks have opened their account. A tank dozer (a normal Centurion tank fitted with bulldozer blade) was clearing scrub. Two Viet Cong were seen. The tank fired two rounds of canister at them from close range. When the dust settled, the Viet Cong and all the vegetation in the vicinity had disappeared. No survivors to tell the tale.

Sunday 10 March 1968

Small amount of cumulus cloud around today — first change in the weather since our arrival. All days cloudless (80–90°F) and nights about 70°F. Very pleasant climate really, but due to the dry season everything is very dusty. (No rain since October.) Dust gets everywhere and penetrates any covering.

Cricket match this morning against the Artillery. Could only muster eight men so we borrowed a few from HQ Company and set out. Played on the new oval at 4 Field Regiment. Concrete pitch, a bulldozed and graded field. Very slow outfield due to loose, dusty soil. Expected to get thrashed so we batted first rather than blunt morale early by having to face a big score. To my surprise, bowling was easy and we scored 129 for the loss of only six wickets when our 70 minutes' batting time ran out. I top-scored with 37 in 40 minutes, which was pretty fast-going — a ball to the boundary was only worth two runs. The highlight of the innings was Sapper Trevor Marsh, who made pathetic attempts to put a bat behind the first three balls bowled to him, missed all three and appeared certain to be bowled by the first straight ball received. Then he suddenly lashed six successive balls to the boundary and several more over it. Then he slipped out of the groove and forgot how to do it. He poked feebly at several more and was soon out for 26 scored in about five minutes.

Our bowling was very steady, and after 55 minutes, with only 15 minutes to go, the Artillery had scored only 40 runs for the loss of three wickets and obviously had no chance of winning, so everyone in our team except me had a bowl and runs came and wickets fell at a furious rate. We gave them an extra 15 minutes' batting time to make a closer finish, but they were all out for only 105, so we won comfortably. Good fun all round, but pretty tiring after charging full tilt around the field in boots for a couple of hours or so.

Two soldiers have returned to Nui Dat to rest and recuperate after five days' R&R in Bangkok. One slept with six different women in five nights. Total expenditure on girls, grog, gifts (including a 120-piece Siamese cutlery set), hotel etc about $500 (or $100 per day). Souvenirs include: (i) a lot of useful literature on Bangkok; (ii) the cutlery set; (iii) a most amusing illustrated prospectus for prostitutes supplied by a hotel organisation; (iv) the VD-free certificate of a prostitute; (v) a possible dose of VD. Quite a holiday. Bit rough to pinch the girl's certificate, though, especially after she saved his life by preventing him from diving at 03.00 from his fourth-floor hotel room into the swimming pool. The certificate was a small booklet, including photo of girl, personal information (e.g. age — 19), name and address of doctor, all on the front page, and thereafter a list of dates with the doctor's stamped signature beside each one. She seemed to have made about two visits a week. The brothel prospectus showed photos of girls, some very beautiful, with captions such as 'Mary, No. 42, you will dream of her all night'.

Swimming party returned from Vung Tau after spending the day there. There were more incidents involving drunken Australians, all from the same unit. Dressed in their best, they overcrowded a truck with drunks and fought with the military police. These incidents still occur because the basic cause of the problem is not being touched. No successful attempt has been made to curb drinking at Vung Tau. The Viet Cong know full well that they can destroy a truck and its load of Australian soldiers any time they like. Trucks of drunks going from Vung Tau to Nui Dat are incapable of defending themselves and often travel as one lone vehicle, despite instructions to the contrary. This happens every Sunday between 16.00 and 18.30.

Humidity in weather has increased a lot during the past week.

Monday 11 – Thursday 14 March 1968

Urgent mapping tasks for the big operation in progress in the Long Hai hills, plus an evening (eight hours) as assistant duty officer at the Task Force Command Post, plus a morning of draughting because no one else in the Survey Troop

can print like this in a big hurry.

As I write, I am listening to the inspiring 'Thoughts of Chairman Mao'. Radio Peking sounds very similar to Peter Sellers's unforgettable rendition on the record *Fool Britannia*. Many stirring stories told. For example: pilot on People's Democratic bombing mission has engine trouble and radios his base. Base recites the appropriate Thought of Chairman Mao applicable to such adversity. Thus inspired, pilot gets engine started. Many similar stories. Then the world news: it is really interesting to hear of the thrashing we're taking in Vietnam. Our casualties are colossal and we are crushed by our losses. Then some singing of suitable anthems, themes being 'Long Live Chairman Mao', 'Oh, Happy Members of the Printers' Union Are We', etc.

Meanwhile, the war continues. Frequent B-52 bombing raids have shaken up the Long Hais. Each bomb weighs about a ton and blows a colossal crater. Have heard many rude remarks about B-52 bombing accuracy. Now I know why. A stick of bombs got stuck in bomb bays of one plane and then fell out later. Result: one friendly village accidentally bombed without warning five miles away from target! Bombs fell within 100 metres of Australian tanks and 50 metres of an Australian infantry position. Unbelievably, casualties both civil and military added up to only one garden and one pond, both of which disappeared (though the pond will now reappear bigger when the wet comes).

We had a survey party out in the Long Hais on Wednesday and Thursday and they got an excellent view of the aerial attacks, which included mini-gun attacks by gunships and strafing by fighters. One F-100 fighter (US Air Force) crashed while on a low-level strafing run. One moment it flew low and fast, the next a colossal explosion. Impossible to determine cause.

USAF F-100 *Super Sabre.*

While on the job, Sergeant Grant Small fell on the rocks on the mountain top, losing his F1 carbine. It bounced on a rock, releasing the safety catch. The carbine then landed on its butt, hard enough to break the butt and shake the bolt back past the magazine. The bolt flew forward, collected a round from the magazine and fired it. The bullet went over Grant's right shoulder. This occurred in the middle of the 2nd Battalion position. One man immediately cocked his M60 machine gun, but apart from that there was no further excitement. Lucky escape for Grant. No one's fault, just a complete accident.

Every night this week I've been working until midnight or thereabouts. Most interesting was the evening (16.00–24.00) as assistant duty officer at the Command Post for the Task Force (13 March). My main task is to keep track of all the patrols, incidents and so on, as they occur, take the appropriate action and record all incidents. This is, in effect, analogous to being at the helm of a huge ship, except that if anything really serious happens, someone of more seniority and experience is immediately brought to the Command Post.

Several incidents did occur. Five Viet Cong were killed in various clashes with Australian patrols. Australian casualties were one man shot in the arm and quite prepared to wait until morning for evacuation. One Australian Cessna yelled for help because he was on fire (cause unknown) but he got safely back to Luscombe airfield at Nui Dat. Artillery showered shells all over the countryside at the slightest provocation. For example, a patrol would report a light seen. Within a minute or two — blam, blam, blam. Patrol would then report light out. The South Vietnamese are not allowed in the fields at night, so any activity detected at night is deemed to be enemy, hence blam, blam, blam, and the patrol counts the bits next morning. Typical action report from a patrol: 'Movement heard. Maybe animals.' Five minutes later: 'Movement heard, definitely not animals. Allowed them to approach us as close as we dared and then we opened up with everything we had.' Five minutes later: 'One Viet Cong killed in action. Kill confirmed.' Five minutes later: 'Three Viet Cong killed in action, one Viet Cong wounded and captured. Three AK-47 (Chinese) light machine guns and two rocket launchers with rockets captured. Also bags of rice and minor equipment. More details after search at dawn. It's a bit dark here.'

Back in the Command Post we learn of a ministerial investigation in Australia to be held into the alleged ill-treatment of a Viet Cong prisoner two years ago. Later discussing this with other officers, it seems highly unlikely that this incident could ever have occurred as described,[2] and it seems that the story is sheer journalistic sensationalism. Shooting up stretcher parties, yes, but ill-treating prisoners, no. The ARVN do this so efficiently that there is no need for Australians to do it. However, the Army, with a brand-new minister (Phillip Lynch, aged 34 and with no military experience whatever), is due for a political panic. RAAF has just had the VIP Flight trouble, and Navy, thanks to HMAS *Voyager*,[3] has remained in the spotlight for four years off and on, so I guess it's the Army's turn now.

Friday 15 – Saturday 16 March 1968

Two busy days, mainly due to the return of our guest from Singapore which naturally took up a fair bit of time that would

[2] It did occur but not as reported. A Viet Cong prisoner under interrogation was forced to swallow half a cup of water before the interrogation was stopped. The event took place in 1966 but did not see the full light of day until 1968. At the time the case prompted a disciplinary hearing and the removal of the officer responsible. — PH

[3] HMAS *Voyager* ran into the path of HMAS *Melbourne* on 10 February 1964 and was cut in half, with the loss of 82 lives. Great controversy surrounded the subsequent investigation and two royal commissions. Nearly 50 years later the issue is still sensitive. — PH

normally have been spent on other work. Farewell party on Friday night for Bill Snelson and Lindsay Rotherham, and Staff Sergeant Peter Rossiter, who are going home after rendering excellent service for the last year. Sergeant Pat Cox arrived on Friday to replace Peter, just in time for the party, but the replacements for Bill and Lindsay won't be here for a while yet.

Much intelligence discovered recently indicates that the Long Hai hills contain about 2000 Viet Cong, heavily armed and living safely in huge natural limestone caves. It is believed that the forthcoming Australian assault on these hills is causing a lot of concern to the Viet Cong and that the Viet Cong are about to attack in various places to distract Australian attention from their vital mountain base. Primary targets are the towns of Ba Ria, Long Dien, Dat Do, the Australian Task Force HQ at Nui Dat, and the big airfields, since it is our air attacks that are greatly feared. So there is an atmosphere of caution and preparedness in the Task Force at the moment.

No attack came on Friday night, but Saturday has brought more intelligence: there are supposed to be about 1000 Viet Cong in the Nui Thi Vai hills, west of Nui Dat and in full view of us. Also, tracks have been discovered of at least four heavy-wheeled tractors which have been towing heavy objects (guns?) a few miles to the north of us. Heavy stores and troops were also landed by sea last night on the coast south-east of Nui Dat. All this adds up to a lot of movement and a lot of people. Meanwhile, our patrolling and reconnaissance have been extended, as the Task Force prepares for its big attack on the Long Hai hills stronghold.

Sunday 17 March 1968

Took swimming party to Vung Tau. Walked along the beach as usual, had pleasant swim, took a few photos. Discovered corpses of several snakes with yellow and black transverse bands. Met Owen Evans whom I knew at Randwick. While on the beach an Australian nurse who knows Owen invited us to a party at 161 Recce Flight at Nui Dat next weekend!!! So the Task Force does live it up, but this isn't much publicised.

Got good exercise on beach from a game of soccer — no rules, every man for himself. Aim: to hog the ball for as long as possible. Had usual hamburger lunch at Peter Badcoe Club. Visited American PX and craft shop. Bought six *Playboy* magazines (the Survey Troop supply) and two slot cars for myself. Cost of two cars (1:24 scale) plus motors was less than $7. They are a Ford GT Spyder and a Ford Galaxie. Would have preferred Porsche, Ferrari or Alfa Romeo, but only American models were available.

Show in progress at the Badcoe Club. Same as last time, but the lead guitarist was very good. Singing was pretty awful. Spent evening preparing for visit to Long Binh tomorrow to seek assistance from 66 Engineer Company for a map-printing job.

Monday 18 — Wednesday 20 March 1968

Took off first thing on Monday for Long Binh with Sapper Paul Alderson in a US Army Bell Iroquois helicopter. No doors and I sat right on the edge. View was absolutely marvellous. Helicopter flew at about 50 to 100 feet for the last few miles to Bearcat. Followed Route 15 nearly all the way. Refuelled at Bearcat and flew on at low level to Long Binh. Saw an Iroquois gunship on the helipad and photographed its fearsome mini-guns. Each gun has six barrels. The gunner wore a flak jacket of the usual drab khaki appearance, but when he turned around, one could see 'KILL' in huge scarlet letters across the back of his jacket. Shortly afterwards the gunship took off and on its underside could be seen 'KILL' in gigantic letters. Hardly an understatement.

Saw many types of helicopters, including the tiny but very fast Cayuse, alias the Flying Tadpole — it looks like a tadpole (just as the Sioux looks like a dragonfly) and is well armed. Also saw a Huey Cobra gunship armed with rockets, cannons and mini-guns — the lot.

Spent the day at 66 Engineer Company. Joel Cain was on leave with wife in Hawaii, since he's now been in Vietnam for three months, after which US forces fly the man from Vietnam to Hawaii (or his preferred R&R destination) and back all free. Many Australians wish a similar system was available to them. The 66 Company most obliging with our printing task, despite heavy commitments of their own.

Up early Tuesday morning to catch dawn helicopter back to Nui Dat. Peaceful night. Things have settled down in the Long Binh area — lights are on and steel helmets are off — for the time being, anyway. Helicopter, piloted by a tall, slim Negro, took off and headed not south but east. Went over a very big American installation (probably Bien Hoa) and then over dense forest, rubber plantations and odd small towns. Was not sure where pilot was heading, but from the way he occasionally glanced at the map he obviously knew what he was doing. Saw a great cloud-shrouded peak ahead and suddenly recognised it as Nui Chua Chan, about 30 miles north-north-east of Nui Dat. We then swung abruptly south and came to Nui Dat after a total flight of about 40 minutes. Flew over the American camp of Blackhorse and also the towns of Xa Binh Gia, Ap Suoi Nghe and various small ARVN camps. The trips both ways were most interesting. Brought about a 100-pound load of photographic equipment and chemicals with me, all given to me by the Americans because it had proved unobtainable through Australian channels.

Back at Nui Dat there has been some excitement. Last night (at 16.30) a Civil Affairs Unit Land Rover received six bursts from an automatic weapon in Hoa Long. The range was 10 to 15 yards but only one bullet hit the vehicle. Occupants escaped. They didn't fire back because of all the women and children around the gunner.

Later the same night an SAS patrol ambushed a Viet Cong party of many men with a tractor, a trailer-load of explosives and a 75mm rocket launcher. Using a trap of four shaped charges (beehive charges) and several claymore mines, the two- or three-man SAS patrol blew up the Viet Cong party. On Wednesday I saw an Intelligence photo of the result. The explosion must have been tremendous. The ground had been wiped clear of vegetation and all character for an area about 100 feet across. Most of the trailer had disappeared. Two large wrecked objects about 60 feet apart appeared to be the major parts of the tractor. Fifteen men had been killed, and 11 of them were in the photo. All corpses were badly damaged. Some had lost limbs and all were thrown at odd angles and looked utterly smashed. Quite a spectacular photo. This happened about 20 miles north-west of Nui Dat.

Difficult day on Wednesday. Intelligence people at Task Force HQ wanted a job done. So did Operations. Said to Ops: 'We're doing this job for Int. Is the same map good enough for you, too?' Answer: 'Yes, go ahead.' Many hours later, job half done, Ops say they want something different. This is the third time in a row that this has happened. Too many chiefs and not enough Indians.

Went for half-hour helicopter reconnaissance on Wednesday afternoon over the Long Hai hills, scheduled for heavy attack in a couple of days, and over the town of Long Hai itself, which is scheduled for a cordon-and-search operation soon. The helicopter was an Iroquois. That's three trips in three days, and the edge seat every time. Wheee! Like travelling in a train with no side walls — seat runs right to the edge of aircraft. Cruising altitude was 2000 feet, low enough to see and high enough to reduce risk of being hit by ground shooting. Only yesterday a helicopter (an Australian

Army Bell Sioux) was shot up by machine gun from the ground: 13 bullets hit the helicopter and one hit the pilot in the upper thigh. Despite his own injury (which landed him in hospital) and the damage to the aircraft, he flew 8 miles back to Nui Dat and landed safely. The helicopter was smoking and was spraying fuel and oil everywhere, the motor was spluttering, but nothing blew up and he got back. The landing was very rough — right in the path of a Caribou about to take off — but no one minded. Pilot was a fairly new second lieutenant.

Thursday 21 March 1968

Some humour in the day's operational reports — bright spots amidst the depressing carnage. Examples:

1. Air strike on a Viet Cong base camp. Results: one bunker destroyed, three bunkers damaged, one military structure destroyed, 20 metres of trench destroyed, 30 metres of trench uncovered, one picnic table destroyed.
2. Artillery fire mission fired 60 shells of 105mm ammunition. Result: one 5-foot baboon killed in action.

The report of the destroyed VC picnic table has gone into the official situation report from the Australian Task Force.

I shall never forget the extraordinary voice of the incredible Texan bomber pilot (American actor Slim Pickens) in the film *Dr Strangelove, Or: How I Learned to Stop Worrying and Love the Bomb*. Apparently he survived his ride on the nuclear bomb and has been posted to Vietnam! While in the Command Post today I heard this unmistakable voice on a radio message — 'Howdy niner. This is Tarzan Raisin thur-ree. Am over objective but Ah cain't see nobahdy here. Does you-all have any other idea? Over.' It was hard to resist the temptation to take the microphone and suggest that he check the contents of his survival kit (nylon stockings, contraceptives, Russian roubles), but I managed to keep a straight face until I got out of the Command Post.

Friday 22 March 1968

Heard a lot of unusual noises and saw a lot of flares in the sky late last night. Discovered this morning that about 15 or so 81mm mortar bombs landed about 500 metres west of the Task Force HQ Command Post and about 600 metres away from the Survey Troop. I had thought it was our own artillery firing.

Our Locating Battery had fixed the position of the mortar base plate immediately, and our artillery was all ready to blast it out of existence but did not do so because an infantry patrol was close to the enemy and was out of radio contact. So enemy got away unscathed. The Task Force Commander has ordered an immediate investigation into the reasons for the loss of radio contact by the patrol.

Had lunch at the 161 Recce Flight Officers' Mess, and met an old friend — Major Tony Hammett, now commander of D Company, 1st Battalion. Tony came back with me to have a look at the Survey Troop. The word spread ahead of him that Major Hammett was here and this caused much alarm and despondency, there being a most unpopular Major Hammett in the Survey Corps in Sydney and everyone presuming (after our current guest's unexpected visit) that this was he. Much delight all round when it was realised that this was the former Captain Hammett who had been such a popular helicopter pilot on field survey jobs in Australia.

Spent late afternoon and evening as assistant duty officer in the Command Post. No mortar attacks tonight. Quiet night instead.

Saturday 23 March 1968

Busy day today: preparation for court martial defence, plus plenty of normal work. Next Tuesday I am to defend at Vung Tau a soldier who skipped off for two months from R&R leave while in Hong Kong. Sounds very serious. However, facts indicate extenuating circumstances. Soldier came from Germany aged eight with parents, returning to Germany aged 14 with parents, but wanted to stay in Australia. Aged 15, he joined German merchant navy. Aged 17, he signed off merchant navy in Australia and joined Army (1963). Perfect record for four and a half years. Went to Malaya. After one and a half years in Malaya and Borneo, he had six weeks in Australia and then went straight to Vietnam with 2nd Battalion. He did not volunteer for any of this overseas service. After well over two years' operational service, his parents (who never wanted him to leave Germany) had become very distressed, so he went to Hong Kong on R&R leave, bought a plane ticket to Frankfurt-am-Main and off he went. After a fortnight at home in Wilhelmshaven, he went to Rotterdam and joined a merchant ship, and worked his passage back to Hong Kong, where he signed off and immediately handed himself into the Army authorities.

Private Wilhelm Harbers is a very quiet but impressive man. Must do all I can for him. Pity trial by combat isn't allowed — he's a body-builder and his torso broadens from waist to shoulders like so \/.

Sunday 24 March 1968

Morning shattered early by the appalling roar of two US Air Force F-100 fighters streaking over the Task Force HQ (and the Survey Troop) at about 600 miles per hour and at an altitude of about 60 to 100 feet above ground. The tree tops swayed as they screeched overhead. All in good fun but the first one (which woke me) gave me a tremendous fright.

First change in the weather since my arrival seven weeks ago. Some grey clouds visible during the morning but disappeared during the afternoon. Morning very busy — many jobs cropped up; unfortunately some of them were presented by people lacking common sense, so time was wasted while these were sorted out. In the course of this, I had an argument with a battalion intelligence officer on a question of map interpretation. I won but it wasted precious time — he finished up admitting that he couldn't read a map.

Work pressure eased during afternoon but night work was necessary, just the same. Much operational activity still going on. Bad aircraft accident today: two US Air Force (USAF) planes (both Bird Dogs, a light reconnaissance plane) collided in mid-air over the Long Hai hills. One was a local-based aircraft from Vung Tau. The other was from Bien Hoa and carried a general and a colonel (the pilot) on a swan, just to look at the country. The latter arrived without warning of its presence and no one knew it was in the area until the two planes collided. The Vung Tau plane lost a wing, crashed, and the crew of two officers was killed. The Bien Hoa plane lost its undercarriage but got safely back to Bien Hoa.

Amazing really that more accidents of this type don't occur. Have made five trips in helicopters here so far, and three trips in Caribous, and the risk of mid-air collision has always impressed me as a major one. I know just how quickly planes can appear from nowhere. There is no radio control in busy areas (except Tan Son Nhut), and control is visual. So far I've only once been in a plane which has actually had to dodge sharply to avoid another, but the risk has always been obvious.

Much shooting late at night: heard a machine gun fire off a full 100-round belt of ammunition in one burst but things settled down after 01.00.

Defending officer's cross-examination notes.

Suitable Question	Facts to be brought out.
• Where were you born?	Germany.
• When did you come to Australia?	1954, aged 8.
• When did you return to Germany?	

②

• Why did you return? • What did you do during those 6 weeks?	3 weeks leave in Adelaide with sis. 3 weeks duty at Enoggera.
• Did you want to return? • Could you have taken more than 3 weeks leave had you wished to?	No.
• Why not?	
• What did you do on return to Germ. Did you then go direct to Vietnam?	Yes.
• Did you volunteer?	
• When did you join Army? When did you come to Vietnam?	No choice. June 67.
• Where did you s. Why did you go absent without leave?	Parents very worried. Both parents lost a brother during WW2. Soldier had been on operational service since Oct 65. Christmas approaching
• How long did you serve in Malaysia in Infantry? • When did you last spend Christmas at home?	7 years ago.
• How long did you spend in Aust. Were your parents happy about you leaving Germany?	Definitely not.
• Why did you go AWOL from Hong Kong?	It seemed to be the best opportunity to see my parents who were very worried.

Monday 25 March 1968

Spent today preparing court martial defence. Travelled by plane to Vung Tau in afternoon.

Tuesday 26 March 1968

Day off to a bad start. Got bawled out by a New Zealand major: 'Captain! Don't you normally salute officers of field rank?'

Somewhat astonished, I told the truth: 'Yes, when I recognise them but I thought you were a second lieutenant until too late to salute.' He got a bit excited at that and then headed off before I could point out that due to the narrow passageway my arm would have hit him in the face had I saluted, but I did come to attention anyway (to which he had not responded). Later heard that this major doesn't seem to be highly regarded.

Court martial went reasonably well. Private Harbers got 40 days' detention. It seemed a lot at first, but I later discovered that the maximum sentence for this offence — absence without leave for two months while on war service — is two years' detention. It also was the lightest sentence awarded at a court martial for many months. The question of guilt did not arise. The only other factor was the mitigating circumstances and I exploited this to the maximum. I achieved my aim, which was to appeal to emotion as well as to reason, and to put a load onto the conscience of the board. Subsequent discussion with the judge advocate indicated that I had done well. The board did not detect several irrelevancies I deliberately introduced to create the desired effect.

Had a brief swim at the beach in the late afternoon. Watched a New Zealand Red Cross nurse (officer status) blatantly ogling about ten soldiers. She also tossed an obvious invitation to me, a complete stranger. Of course she has a monopoly — attractive non-Vietnamese girls are practically non-existent here — but I think she'd manage quite well even in the face of stiff competition. Most interesting to watch her in action. Very full figure, breasts almost spilling out of bra of bikini, attempting to cover up with hand but deliberately missing, frequently bending forwards over the men, occasionally adjusting a pendant tiki almost lost between her breasts, always keeping her bottom swinging even when lying down. Add to all this an attractive face and figure plus a brief bikini and the resultant combination is a bait that few obviously could resist. It was a polished and impressive act, and she made the absolute most of her considerable natural talent. For the last few months, I'm told, she has been sleeping regularly with a married New Zealand officer and irregularly with several others. Now that the New Zealand officer has gone home, she is apparently extending her field further.

Got into trouble today for having a loaded magazine on my pistol. Here at 1ALSG in Vung Tau they insist on weapons being carried at all times, but apparently don't allow them to be loaded. All visitors from Saigon and Nui Dat get caught this way. In the HQ Officers' Mess in the evening everyone (except me in jungle greens) was spick and span in polyester shirt and trousers, complete with all medal ribbons. I did meet a few friends there, but generally did not find the atmosphere hospitable. Could hear in the background the odd unpleasant remark about the Task Force at Nui Dat. There does seem to be some lack of friendliness. Don't know why. Perhaps comparative security at Vung Tau tends to breed discontent? However, I haven't been here long enough to determine the cause.

Am definitely not impressed with the security here. Vietnamese work everywhere in the camp — cleaning, typing, filing, other office work, mess duties. They are everywhere. Some are pretty and flirt with the men. Others just flit silently about. It is reasonable to assume that the layout of this whole camp is known to the Viet Cong. Not only that, but the perimeter defence of the camp is extremely weak. The Chief of the General Staff (CGS — Lieutenant General Daly) is due here in two days. I consider it possible for a one-man Viet Cong party to penetrate this camp in the early hours of the morning, blow the CGS sky high, and be 80 to 90% certain of escaping. In contrast, no Vietnamese (except for the occasional ARVN Intelligence interpreter) are ever allowed into the Task Force base area at Nui Dat, and I feel most uneasy when I see Vietnamese men and girls around the 1ALSG camp and also in every American camp.[4] Won't be sorry to get back to Nui Dat tomorrow afternoon.

Wednesday 27 March 1968

Morning wasted waiting for a court martial today that I am observing to start. Delay caused by late arrival of judge advocate from Saigon. No sooner had the court martial started than it was time for me to leave. This was a soldier charged with shooting himself with intent to avoid military service. Both prosecuting and defending officers were Legal Corps officers. Would have been most interesting and instructive to watch; however, the time couldn't be afforded, so back to Nui Dat.

On landing at Nui Dat I saw an American Huey Cobra helicopter gunship armed with 36 rockets and three mini-guns (i.e. 18 machine-gun barrels). The armament looked deadly. The aircraft itself was long and high, but only 1 metre or less in width, with pilot and co-pilot one behind the other. The plane looks like a striking snake — hence the name. Its emblem was a *Playboy* rabbit.

Played volleyball against A Squadron 3 Cavalry Regiment, and lost 0–3. Next time we'll play on our court which is correct size and to our rules, which do not permit net infringements!

Thursday 28 March 1968

Distraction from normal routine work today was seeing an Intelligence vehicle carrying two captured Viet Cong with their eyes

[4] Heard four days later that a security check of the RAAF base at Vung Tau revealed that five Viet Cong were employed there. — JB

blindfolded. Both were male and looked about 13 or 14 years old, but may have been older. To bed early tonight, being duty officer at Command Post tomorrow morning.

Friday 29 March 1968

Up at midnight to take the shift from midnight to 08.00. Unusually large amount of action. 7th Battalion clashed with Viet Cong near Hoa Long. One Viet Cong killed and an Australian wounded — shot in shoulder and bleeding profusely. Immediate evacuation necessary, so brought RAAF Iroquois helicopter up from Vung Tau and casualty was aboard and heading for hospital about an hour after the first report. Some delay was caused by the enemy still in the vicinity and it was necessary to move another 7th Battalion patrol up to strengthen the first one in order to render the helicopter pick-up safe. All this happened between 01.30 and 02.30. Condition of soldier in hospital reported satisfactory some hours later.

Americans requested clearance to fire on a target near Long Hai village and our artillery assistance. Clearance granted and our artillery, on the other side of the Long Hais, began to fire. First shot went 300 metres too far, so gun was dropped. Second shot hit the intervening mountain, so guns changed to high-angle fire and were immediately on target (VC signalling lights). At about 04.00 lights were seen just west of the Task Force position so the artillery had a go at this too.

Never had a free moment from midnight to 08.00 — most unusual indeed for the night shift. Pretty tired at the end of it — my first go as duty officer alone and with full responsibility. Did routine tasks till 11.00 then to bed till 16.00 and up for more routine work. Early night. Saw the Viet Cong killed early this morning — half his head had been shot away.

Saturday 30 March 1968

Again overcast in the morning. At dawn some rain fell — about eight spots to the square foot. This afternoon flew by RAAF Caribou to Vung Tau to stay overnight at 1ALSG for general court martial of an officer tomorrow. Journey livened up by an American sergeant swilling copiously from a large bottle of crème de menthe, which he generously passed around, but few of the Australians enjoyed it.

On arrival at the HQ Officers' Mess at 1ALSG wearing travel-stained greens, I was astonished to see civilian clothes everywhere. Saturday night! Same goes for all day Sunday and Sunday night, too. Apparently it's only a 5½-day-a-week war here. To bed early — better stay awake for tomorrow's general court martial on which I am to be a member of the board.

Sunday 31 March 1968

Slow start to court martial. Defending officer raised an objection to one of the charges and this led to heavy legal discussion between the judge advocate, defending officer and prosecutor. The result of it all was that the matter had to be referred back to the convening officer (the Commander of Australian Forces Vietnam, Major General MacDonald). By then the whole day had passed, so if the Commander agrees with the judge advocate's ruling we should be able to start in earnest tomorrow.

APRIL

AUSTRALIAN MILITARY FORCES

AAB — 71A
Reprinted Dec, 1964

RECORD BOOK

CONTAINING 96 PAGES

RULED FEINT

April opened with the continuation of the court martial at Vung Tau, which brought moments of hilarity but also substantial disquiet.

Later in the month John recorded the successful pulling of the Hoa Long Dance trick, a standard practical joke on new soldiers. The joke involved seasoned warriors laying the bait by being overheard talking to each other enthusiastically about the next dance, usually the coming evening. A non-commissioned officer would announce on parade that any soldiers going to the Hoa Long Dance that night had to be out on the road in civilian clothes ready to board the vehicle for Hoa Long.

The trick would be done before the new soldiers had a chance to learn that civilian clothes were never worn at Nui Dat and that nearby Hoa Long was an insecure village of doubtful loyalty. Nor would they have learnt that Australian troops visited Hoa Long only on duty, always with caution and never for recreation. Even though the hoax had been described in detail in the Army newspaper available to all, the prospect of a good night out in the company of a girl contined to suck the new man in.

PAUL HAM

★

*Today I hear that the rice mill in Hoa Long bears
a large poster announcing 50–50 dancing on
Saturday nights. Apparently a passing infantry
patrol has fastened it on, and the local people,
few of whom can read, have left it alone.*

★

Monday 1 April 1968

Some progress, but not much, made at the court martial today.
Charges were read out and three prosecution witnesses were called.
Charges against the former Officer Commanding the R&C[1] Centre
at Vung Tau in 1967 were: (i) stealing public property; and (ii)
receiving stolen property, knowing it to be stolen. The prosecutor
alleged that the accused had lived with a Vietnamese girl during his
stay in Vietnam from February '67 to February '68, and had set her
up in a new house, furnished with army equipment which he had
stolen or received. The charges being as above, the court was
therefore not concerned with any moral issues, but simply with the
theft or receipt of a few items of furniture and cutlery. The
proceedings bogged down many times on matters of legal detail
and little was achieved today at all.

---

[1] Rest and convalescence. Troops were entitled to five days R&C leave in Vietnam and
five days R&R (rest and recuperation) leave overseas. R&C could be broken; R&R had
to be taken in one hit.

Tuesday 2 April 1968

Again not much progress made, thanks to an unbelievable number of delays due to legal tactics. The prosecution case undoubtedly exists, but is not being presented well and the defending officer, Major Fergus Thomson (Legal Corps), is obviously in his element, being both an excellent lawyer and a superb actor. Every time the prosecution attempts to present evidence, Fergus jumps up and objects, or more cunningly, contrives to have the judge advocate himself object. The court is then cleared while the legal aspects are debated and the objection is usually upheld.

A typical example occurred when the prosecution wished to present a document as evidence. The defence objected on grounds of irrelevance. The objection was upheld and the court not allowed to see the document. Meanwhile, I had been able to read sufficient of the document, from several metres away while it was fluttering in someone's hands, to see that it seemed highly relevant to the case. It was a signed statement given by the accused to his Vietnamese mistress. The more that comes out at this trial, the more amazing it is that about six to ten other (and more serious and easily proven) charges have not been laid against the accused. I cannot understand this.

The highlight of the day was a visit to the accused's mistress's house in Vung Tau. Three visits were necessary, each with a different witness, to prove to the board (and to the defence) that all witnesses were referring to the same house. Drove through Vung Tau township — very bright and lively but not at all attractive or clean-looking — then through an untidy hamlet on edge of town. Got out of vehicle and walked along winding laneway between houses for about 50 metres and came to the house in question. Children everywhere, shouting gaily, 'Uc Dai Loi [Australian soldier], hullo, mate!' Obviously a well-trodden Australian path. One little boy was wearing trousers made from Australian khaki polyester fabric, complete with a permanent crease down one side.

Local people were much excited at the sight of this impressive party: one lieutenant colonel (board president), five majors (two members of board, three Legal Corps officers — the judge advocate, prosecutor and defending officer), and four captains (two members of the board, the accused and his escort). One youth smiled knowingly at us and said, 'Fuck-fuck?' He looked most surprised when we went away again after only three minutes, obviously reluctant to believe that the whole lot had been serviced so quickly. He was even more surprised when we all returned twice more to the house within the next hour.

Everyone seemed most friendly and many people, especially the children, greeted the accused with delight. The little children were pretty charming in both manner and appearance. One grandmother held up a child to wave to us. The child looked more European than Asian. The grandmother was wizened, almost toothless, and had betel-nut juice trickling down her chin from each corner of her mouth. Her hair was grey and in the style of a flat-top crew cut. At her feet was a male dog with swollen, bleeding genital organs — even the dogs have VD! Not the most attractive or romantic setting to keep a mistress in, but nevertheless a most interesting visit, and the children were indeed delightful.

Rest of day spent with witnesses in court and with legal delays. The president (Lieutenant Colonel Dunn, Medical Corps) appeared to lose his temper at the Legal people, stormed at them briefly for obscuring justice with legal garbage, and stormed out. The board followed, and found him just around the corner, convulsed with laughter! What with Lieutenant Colonel Dunn as president, and Majors Malcolm Van Gelder and Peter Douglas ('A gentleman is one who gets out of the bath to piss in the basin') on the board, and Fergus Thomson as defending officer, one never knows what will happen next, and despite the delays, interest never flags. Altogether a most interesting day, despite slow progress of trial.

Wednesday 3 April 1968

Back to the old routine. After 15 minutes, the prosecution sought to produce a roll book as evidence. Objection! OK, clear the court while the Legal people consider the matter. After all, says the judge advocate, I don't know what it is until I've seen it and I can't see it until it has been tendered and it can't be tendered until all legal implications have been considered. It is quite beside the point that the entire court can see at a glance that it's a roll book. The legal aspects must all be sorted out before anyone is allowed to know that it's a roll book, so out we all go again while the legal fists start swinging again. Matter settled in 20 minutes, so we go back in, this time for five minutes before the defence desires to make a submission which will apparently tie the court up for the whole morning. So out we go again to wait until the afternoon. Finally resumed at 14.00 and got through the afternoon with few more delays.

It becomes more and more amazing that more charges have not been brought against the accused. It also begins to look as though the prosecution case is collapsing. The case itself may be strong enough but it is being presented in a strangely inept way. A good regimental officer could do better. This view is supported by Lieutenant Colonel Dunn, who is a doctor and considers the prosecutor (Legal Corps) to be 'out on his feet' and medically incapable of his job. However, as board president, he is powerless to bring his medical advice to bear. Meanwhile, the accused, giving evidence himself, appears to be sailing dangerously close to perjury. For sure someone is fibbing under oath. The further we proceed, the more tangled things seem to become. So we come to the end of the fourth day.

The stealing charge has been thrown out by the judge advocate on the grounds that there is no case for the defence to answer, leaving only the receiving charge. The prosecutor has now finished and has not presented a strong case.

Barbecue at 102 Field Workshop tonight. Quiet and most enjoyable evening with Major Max Tinkler and his officers. Very pleasant group here, unlike the less hospitable HQ 1ALSG crowd across the road.

Thursday 4 April 1968

Unexpectedly, no more evidence for the defence was produced this morning. Prosecuting and defending officers addressed the court. Judge advocate then directed that findings of not guilty to the stealing charge (having told us yesterday that the prosecution had produced no case for the defence to answer) and not guilty to the 'conduct to the prejudice of good order and military discipline' charge be returned (as directed on the opening day, last Sunday). He then summed up all the evidence for the sole remaining charge of receiving, explained what elements were required to prove receiving stolen property and left us to it. From his instruction we were bound to return a verdict of not guilty, and did so, having absolutely no choice in the matter.

The receiving charge could not be proved because one cannot receive stolen property from oneself, and the accused, under oath, had given evidence (*after* the stealing charge had been dismissed) of virtually having committed theft. Oh, so simply and cleverly done. Full marks to Major Thomson, the defending officer. Legal justice may have been done, but to those outside the courtroom and unaware of the fine legal points, justice will certainly not *appear* to have been done.

Captain Freeman, the accused, was very cheerful afterwards. No one else was. At lunch, the members of the board kept to themselves and munched moodily, myself included, while the three Legal Corps officers were just plain tired and in no mood for levity. Altogether the trial has been most interesting and most unpredictable throughout the whole five days.

During the late afternoon, the trial now over, a lot of information, which may not be recorded here, came my way concerning Captain Freeman himself and did him no credit. In considering the verdict, the board indeed did not believe Captain Freeman, but was powerless, since evidence just didn't exist to prove the receiving charge. Captain Freeman was very perky at dinner and wanting to buy everyone drinks. I couldn't bring myself to accept. Neither could anyone else on the board, nor could the prosecuting officer. It was just too much after his blatant admission of theft (once safe to do so) in order to escape the receiving charge. I am somewhat depressed by the whole affair which is a whack in the eye for every honest NCO and soldier in the Australian forces in Vietnam.

Went to post some postcards late in the day. The conversation at post office went like this:

'Do you have a special forces concession rate for postcards?'

'Yes, but I don't know what it is.'

'I think it's three cents. Would you check it, please?'

'Yes, it is three cents.'

'May I have 10 three-cent stamps please?'

'No, you'll have to put five-cent stamps on them.'

'Why?'

'We don't sell three-cent stamps.'

'Why not?'

'The smallest stamp we sell is five cents.'

'Then how do I take advantage of the three-cent concession rate?'

'Sorry, can't help you.'

'OK then, forget it. Now may I have some 13-cent stamps for these overseas postcards please?'

'Don't sell them either. You'll have to use 15-cent stamps.'

'Well, how about stamps of smaller denomination adding up to 13 cents?'

'We only sell five-, six-, ten-, 15- and 30-cent stamps because the smallest money here is five cents.'

'But couldn't I buy stamps in bulk; for example, five or ten 13-cent stamps at a time?'

'Sorry, can't help you.'

'Well, I'm not giving the post office $0.34 excess postage for these 17 postcards. What do you recommend?'

'Sorry, can't help you, but why don't you write to someone in Australia for this?'

Apparently the Army post office isn't much more helpful than its civilian counterpart.

Majors in the US Army wear a badge of rank, a big gold oak (?) leaf something like this but bigger, on the collar of the shirt, not on the shoulder as we do. It looks like a big headlight. Today I saw my major friend from the NZ Army who loves being saluted wearing a US Army headlamp on his collar, in addition to his normal crown on each shoulder. It would seem that this is an attempt to avoid being mistaken for a second lieutenant again by types like me.

Friday 5 April 1968

Strong wind during night. Fine sand everywhere by morning. Hair and face full of it. Such is the hazard of life on the beach front at Vung Tau. Up early and off to catch a plane back to Nui Dat at last. No sooner back at Nui Dat than away again — off to Ba Ria on a shopping run, my aim being to buy a farewell gift for WO1 Percy Long who goes back to Australia next week. Normally a mug is presented, but Perce says he's got stacks at home and he dare not bring home another because his wife thinks he's an alcoholic as it is.

Travelled with Survey Troop members through Hoa Long — ominous and silent as usual. Shootings have become so frequent that our infantry are usually patrolling in Hoa Long all the time now. Went to Ba Ria and fixed up the laundry and met Madame Minh Ha at last. Madame looks about 45 and is well groomed and very pleasant to talk to. Her French is clear and easy to understand, and we chatted for about ten minutes or so. Her daughter is now in France with her husband and children, and Madame hopes to visit them this December but does not relish the prospect of a European winter. She has invited me for dinner, either Vietnamese or French style, whichever I prefer, whenever I can afford the time, which is most kind of her. I would like to take this invitation up.

After some minutes at the laundry, we went into the town centre to do some shopping. Bought a few nice pictures on silk and we shall give two to Perce. Like all town markets, everything imaginable was on sale — beads and trinkets for the tourist, army badges, war medals (including those not yet issued to the Australian Army), clothes (most poor quality), rubber contraceptives with red forked tongue at the end, and even a shop selling complete sets of dentures. Bought additional pictures, smaller than Perce's but attractive, for only 25 cents each and was amazed to see ghastly rubbish selling for several dollars. Returning through the road block at Hoa Long we saw a couple of Australian military police taking three Vietnamese men in black pyjamas into custody; one MP had three confiscated grenades in his hands.

Fair bit to do back at Nui Dat, including the operational report for March, which has lagged because of the court martial.

Saturday 6 April 1968

Today it was announced on parade in 104 Signals Squadron: 'All personnel wishing to go to the Hoa Long Dance tonight are to fall in outside the orderly room at 17.30 hours. Transport will be leaving from there. Dress is civilian clothes.' (Civilian clothes are never normally seen in the Task Force.)

Well, about five men duly turned up at the orderly room in civilian clothes at 17.30, all being recent arrivals in Vietnam and unaware of the significance of Hoa Long as a hotbed of Viet Cong activity, although only a mile away from the Task Force — in fact, six Viet Cong were killed there early this morning by a New Zealand patrol in an ambush.

'Where's the transport?'

'Bad luck, fellers, you've just missed it. Tell you what, though — there are so many on the truck that it'll take them a while to get through the checkpoint. If you go for your life, you might catch them there.'

Off they set at full speed, and in civilian clothes, down the road until they passed a line of their mates who ceremonially presented arms as they went by. Thus ended the Hoa Long Dance.

Barbecue this evening in our canteen as a farewell for Percy Long, who leaves us next Tuesday. We have three American sergeants staying with us for a few days, and Staff Sergeant Killebrew (Reproduction Section, 66 Engineer Company, Long Binh) said a few words to convey to Perce the best wishes of all his friends at Long Binh. Altogether a very pleasant evening. To bed very early.

Sunday 7 April 1968

Up at midnight for the midnight to 08.00 shift as duty officer at the Task Force Command Post. In direct contrast with my last spell on 29 March, this time nothing at all happened, so I completed the monthly operational report. Returned to Survey Troop after breakfast, did a few routine tasks, went to bed until mid-afternoon.

THE TASK FORCE HEADQUARTERS COMMAND POST

The Task Force Headquarters Command Post was the coordination centre for the Task Force for operational matters. It was manned 24 hours a day by an Operations officer, usually a captain and usually referred to as the duty officer, assisted by a couple of signallers. They occupied half of a room, divided by a big ceiling-high partition which was all map. The huge master operations map overlaid with all current tactical information took up that entire partition and the duty officer's desk faced that wall.

Immediately behind that big partition was 'Arty Tac', the Artillery Command Post, manned by the artillery field regiment, also with an officer and a couple of signallers. Arty Tac had its own master operations map on the reverse side of the Command Post map wall.

The Command Post and Arty Tac were the only offices which always operated around the clock. The nearby Task Force Headquarters offices, which managed operations, intelligence, air liaison, personnel, supplies, etc, normally operated during the day only.

The Command Post was in contact with all operational activities outside the Task Force base. If a patrol encountered enemy, this was reported immediately. Artillery support might be needed, or casualties (or possibly the whole patrol) might need to be extracted by air. Together the Command Post and Arty Tac would take what action was necessary. In a more serious and complex situation, the GSO2 Ops (a major) or the GSO3 Ops (a captain) would also be present, if available. Only in more extreme circumstances would the Task Force Deputy Commander or the Commander himself be there for any length of time.

The jobs of the GSO2 Ops and the GSO3 Ops were very demanding and did not include running the Command Post themselves. However, they were responsible for the smooth operation of the Command Post, which included briefing the duty officers. As part of their responsibility, the GSO2 Ops and the GSO3 Ops looked in on the Command Post from time to time and became involved when fighting got heavy and more hands were needed.

The duty operations officer was rostered for an eight-hour shift, during which time he could not leave the Command Post, except when relieved temporarily for a meal, though that did not apply to the 24.00 to 08.00 shift, who had a late breakfast at 08.00.

The duty officer's full-time job was to run the Command Post. But the Army in its wisdom posted only two duty officers to the Task Force Headquarters. Two men clearly couldn't do 12 hours on, 12 off, seven days a week, without sickness or leave, so others had to be brought in from elsewhere in the Task Force Headquarters and from neighbouring units on a part-time basis. These officers were carefully trained. Two officers did the 16.00 to 24.00 shift together — one was an experienced duty officer and the other was his assistant duty officer. The latter was a learner under instruction. When deemed sufficiently experienced and competent — and there were those who didn't make the grade — the new duty officer would be allowed to handle the 24.00 to 08.00 shift — always the quietest — on his own. When the GSO2 was satisfied that this officer was ready for more responsibility, the officer would then be rostered on the more demanding 16.00 to 24.00 shift and would help train new assistant duty officers. The part-timers were rostered only for either of the two night shifts.

The 08.00 to 16.00 day shift was strictly for the 'professionals', namely the two officially posted duty officers and one or two other officers with the right background and training. Captain Noel Sproles, my Survey Troop Second-in-Command, was one such. He did not have an operational background, but was trained and had gained experience in Nui Dat to the right level. My services were also sought as full-time duty officer, but I declined on the basis that the Survey Troop had to have at least one officer and I was already assisting part-time in the Command Post anyway. However, I did do the 08.00 to 16.00 shift once or twice to help out.

Monday 8 – Tuesday 9 April 1968

Two members of the Troop got into trouble from drinking too much so I have put them on the dry for three weeks in one case and one month in the other. This is a serious and severe punishment but is an effective means of getting across the message about drinking. No charge goes on the men's records but it is now a chargeable offence for them to consume alcohol during their dry or for anyone to supply them with alcohol. Accordingly, all nearby canteens have been notified.

Heard two sequels to the Hoa Long Dance: apparently 104 Signals Squadron regularly catch all their newcomers this way and this is usually a monthly occurrence. The last bag of victims included a CMF captain who was here on a one-month visit from Australia. Today I hear that the rice mill in Hoa Long bears a large poster announcing 50–50 dancing on Saturday nights. (It was at the rice mill that the vehicle shooting mentioned earlier on occurred.) Apparently a passing infantry patrol has fastened it on, and the local people, few of whom can read, have left it alone.

Also heard today of a recent incident at Holsworthy where the anniversary party of 5th Battalion was held. Early in the morning a few officers were still in the Mess after everyone else in the camp had staggered off to bed. Some bright type opened all the doors and windows of the Mess and turned the magnificent super hi-fi stereophonic record player on — this equipment being a new acquisition and the pride of the Mess. They turned the volume up full, it being a machine capable of tremendous noise with very little distortion, and played a sound-effects demonstration record. And so the whole battalion was woken to the appalling din of an express train roaring through the camp, no one knowing which way to leap lest he end up under it. I think a similar plot is being hatched for the Task Force here.

Wednesday 10 April 1968

Very quiet day. Got many outstanding minor jobs cleared up. Still no rain, but weather now very humid — lightning flashes at night.

Thursday 11 April 1968

The Minister for the Army (Phillip Lynch) visited Nui Dat today. He arrived with a great entourage of about eight officers of assorted ranks from major general to lieutenant and a couple of civilians (Secretary of Department of Army and Minister's private secretary). Amongst the entourage was Lieutenant Colonel Russell Lloyd, whom I knew from Duntroon and Western Australia. Was pleased that he took the trouble, amidst a large gathering, to seek me out and say hullo. Seven courses for lunch! And jam! (No jam for weeks.) In vain I hunt for a second lieutenant willing to remark in the Minister's hearing that this feed will have to see us through the next week.

In the afternoon a big panic at Task Force HQ. We must have a new board listing all Task Force units for the Commander's conference today (Minister to be present). Old one has some amendments on it but still looks tidy and a new one is in preparation and will be ready next week. No good, must have a temporary one now. Job requires:

ABCDEFGHIJKLM

in this type of lettering (i.e. big enough to be read anywhere in the room) and we have only two men who can do it quickly — Sergeant Eric Clutterbuck and myself. Eric's at Long Binh, so I do it myself, to the relief of all the other draughtsmen, none of whom could do this work. Only took an hour to do the whole board, about 2 metres long and 1 metre wide, but I'm not impressed with all the fuss to get this done in such a hurry so the Minister wouldn't have to look at an amended one. It should have been thought of a week ago, not left until three hours before the conference. However, this lack of foresight is pretty normal.

An interesting situation occurred this morning. We were sending a field survey team out to the village of Ap Suoi Nghe, just to the north of us. We had been told that we would have the assistance of a bulldozer for clearing (from the Engineers), a section of infantry for protection, and transport, all to be at our office by 08.00. We were ready by 07.45, the infantry arrived at 08.00, but no sign of bulldozer or transport. Repeated phone calls, plenty of apologies and promises, but no result for about one and a half hours. The surveyors fidgeted continuously and displayed some annoyance at the delay, but the infantry just sat down and waited, obviously used to such mismanagement. Perfectly happy, they sat and read books (ready in pocket for such emergency), or slept, or cleaned weapons, or just watched the world go by. Their composure was indeed remarkable.

Friday 12 April 1968

More survey work at Ap Suoi Nghe today and this time some action. Shots were fired. All Australian troops carried out ambush drill immediately and managed to stop just in time to avoid killing three Vietnamese in ARVN uniform, presumably genuine ARVN soldiers shooting birds. This goes on all the time but every now and then an ARVN soldier turns out to be a Viet Cong in disguise. Two Australian warrant officers were killed near here only three months ago by VC in ARVN uniforms.

Unfortunately, casualties today. Last year the Australians put in a big minefield running from Dat Do down to the coast at Lang Phuoc Hai. All minefields should be covered with observation and fire but this task was taken over by the ARVN. The result is that the minefield has become a Viet Cong asset. It is their main supply of mines to use against us. It boosts VC morale because they fly flags etc in it. So now the Engineers have to take the mines out again, and there exists a real danger that the VC have moved some.

Today our infantry was following a one-day-old tank track through the minefield, believing it to be mine-free. Bang! Two killed and five wounded. The VC had put mines in the tank tracks last night and we walked right into the trap.

Saturday 13 April 1968

More survey work at Ap Suoi Nghe and more action. An ARVN versus Viet Cong clash occurred beside the survey party and the air and undergrowth were thick with machine-gun fire for a short while. Grenade launchers were also used. Result of the action in terms of casualties to either side was not known; however, it was frighteningly close to our party.

Rain tonight for about half an hour. Fall was only light. Ground was dry by morning but much dust had settled.

Sunday 14 April 1968

Warm, sunny day — last night's rain has cleared the air. Also an accident last night in Task Force: a soldier shot himself dead with a pistol, a Colt 0.38. Probably not suicide; more likely pretending to play Russian roulette, not realising that cylinders of Colt 0.38 and Smith & Wesson 0.38 rotate in opposite direction.

Took swimming party to Vung Tau. Hoa Long villagers sullen as usual. Saw the sign outside the rice mill — it does exist and it's a big sign painted on metal. It reads:

HOA LONG DANCE HALL

50–50 DANCING EVERY SATURDAY NIGHT.

GROG, GIRLS, GAIETY — THE THINGS HOA LONG

IS FAMOUS FOR!

The locals think it means off limits.

Went to Vung Tau township to get permission from local and US authorities to enter an out-of-bounds area and visit the Cap St Jacques lighthouse area to inspect the survey mark there. Then drove up a steep, rocky road to the top of the hill above Cap St Jacques, about 150 metres high. A magnificent view over the beaches, swamps and town of Vung Tau. Had a look at the old French fortifications, now being destroyed. The most southerly hill houses a group of huge coastal guns of 24cm calibre (built in 1898 and installed in 1902). Their barrels are about 8 to 10 metres long; and the breech and recuperation mechanism is colossal. Recuperator springs are made of metal as thick as a man's wrist. The hill is honeycombed with caves and tunnels — even a railway track for ammunition supply, and underground water tanks. Extensive heavy blasting has destroyed much concrete work but has done little to the huge guns. The effort to install them at this lofty point must have been immense.

Drove back down again. Stopped once or twice for photos. We had to be careful where we trod because much of this hill is a minefield. Drove along the western beach front, past many colourful kiosks along the beach side of the road. Most of these kiosks possess beds upstairs for use by bar girls and customers. Drove north along the coast road, right around the hills of Nui Lon and back again to Vung Tau. Most interesting route indeed.

The highlight of the road was a pretty little beach just below Nui Lon itself. Many people were there — all Vietnamese, but not like any others I've seen so far. These people were all clean, well groomed, well dressed. Most were having picnics. The whole appearance, attitude and behaviour was 'different'. Apparently this is a resort for the rich people. It certainly did look attractive and so did the people — of all ages. Only 1 kilometre further on and we were back in fishing villages again, and in some places the stench of putrescent fish carcasses was very strong. Of interest along the road just south of the nice beach area was a grove of young eucalypt trees.

Then to 1ALSG and had a hamburger for lunch at the Peter Badcoe Club. Went swimming, then shopping at the American PX at the Vung Tau airfield. The Vietnamese girl at door of PX insisted that I leave my pistol at the door. Not likely! Our Belgian 9mm pistols are attractive both to Americans and Vietnamese. Under her astonished eyes, I quickly unloaded and stripped it, put all parts in different pockets and gave her the useless butt. On coming out I collected the butt and assembled the weapon. This caused considerable excitement — especially the last three movements: (i) aim gun at roof and release working parts to fly forwards with a crash; (ii) whack on a fully loaded magazine; (iii) fire trigger, still with barrel skywards. Obviously many people were expecting a bang not a click. Waved goodbye to stunned audience and departed.

Returned to Nui Dat. Mario Apfelbaum (corporal, screen printer) and John Rolfe (corporal, photographer) have arrived at last, after being delayed several weeks at the personnel depot in Sydney. They replace Bill Snelson and Lindsay Rotherham, who left a month ago. Practical joke perpetrated tonight to initiate the newcomers. They were put on a fictitious picquet roster and duly manned the weapon pit with an automatic rifle, wearing steel helmets and flak jackets, staring out into the scrub. The gun had no bolt in it but they didn't know this. They were under orders not to fire (they couldn't anyway) without permission from Corporal 'Willy' Williams. Someone tossed a smoke grenade nearby at about 23.00, causing Mario to race out of the pit and into Willy's tent to inform him of the action. At this point I stepped in and stopped the show, since things were now going too far — people can get hurt with smoke grenades. Anyway, all had a bit of fun, even the victims. No rain tonight.

Monday 15 April 1968

Travelled by Iroquois helicopter to Long Binh at 08.00 and spent day with 66 Engineer Company on miscellaneous matters. Visited PX during afternoon. While there siren sounded. MPs ran into PX shouting, 'Red alert! Clear the PX.' This meant imminent attack and had never occurred before during the day. Everyone scattered to the vehicle park. The result was a Le Mans start — but with one difference — at Le Mans, all vehicles are heading more or less in the same direction. Here, vehicles all started up and headed at full speed in all directions. The vehicle park was unsealed and dust arose everywhere. Chaos was complete, with roaring vehicles appearing from the dust storm and disappearing in a flash. It was like the Keystone Cops — tremendous action at high speed, utter confusion, but no smashes.

Raced back to 66 Company. Went into operations office. Lieutenant Skip Skoglund had his feet up on the desk, reading a newspaper, obviously completely unconcerned about the red alert. I found he didn't know about it. He grabbed a phone and we then learnt that no attack was expected — there had been a short circuit in the siren electrical system!

Went back to PX and finished shopping. Did some trading in the evening with the Americans and got some very useful items. Slouch hats are excellent currency, and I have brought quite a few old ones with me, handed in from 7th Battalion in exchange for new ones prior to going home.

Tuesday 16 April 1968

Went to Saigon by jeep with Captains Joel Cain and Paul Woodbury to attend a Vietnam mapping and survey conference held at the ARVN Topographic Company office at Tan Son Nhut. Traffic heavy all the way. Saigon and outskirts much more peaceful than last time (13 February). Saw a car (Citroën 2CV 'ugly duckling') with Parisian numberplates, driven with great skill and high speed by a woman (no doubt French).

Present at conference were about eight US officers (ranks from colonel to lieutenant), three ARVN officers (ranks lieutenant colonel to lieutenant), one Vietnamese civilian, and myself. The Vietnamese were all either the ARVN Topographic Company at Tan Son Nhut or the National Geographic Service (NGS) at Da Lat. The conference was dominated by Colonel Colvocoresses from Mapping and Intelligence, US Engineer Command, Long Binh, and the only others ever to get a word in edgewise were Lieutenant Colonel Dien and Major Ruyen, both from NGS, Da Lat. Conference was very entertaining, but I got little of value from it.

Several hours now remained before catching the plane back from Saigon to Nui Dat. Went with Joel and Paul to the big PX in Cholon, reputedly one of the biggest in Vietnam. It was indeed huge. There were separate self-service shops, each as large as a modern Australian supermarket, for each of the following types of goods: (i) general merchandise; (ii) food; (iii) liquor; (iv) hi-fi electrical equipment. There was also a snack bar, a gift shop, and a car sales shop (available only to American purchasers). Bought quite a few items I hadn't been able to get anywhere else. Had lunch at snack bar. Too crowded for us all to sit together so we split up. I finished up with two elegant and attractive girls for company. I listened to their language — a tongue I have never heard before. They then spoke to me in English and I later found that they were Korean and here for a year — presumably on office duties or canteen staff. I have seen quite a few Republic of Korea army people (usually called ROKs) around in Vung Tau and Saigon. From all accounts they are magnificent troops. Their appearance and behaviour is very impressive.

Drove further through Cholon, a region of much violence a couple of months ago. In some places complete city blocks have been smashed to bits and barely a single wall is still standing. Less extensive damage is widespread. Went with Joel and Paul to a steam bath and massage parlour which they usually visit when in Saigon. This place was allegedly respectable and very clean, unlike its Vung Tau counterparts, which in most cases are brothels, and this place certainly looked clean. We got changed and went into the steam-bath room. The heat was intense and perspiration copious; however, it was not unpleasant. I strongly suspected Paul and Joel tried to 'burn me off', but stopped when it was apparent that they were suffering and I was not. I gather that they took our swanning major here a few weeks ago and that he soon encountered difficulty in breathing, and quit. Being a lover of heat, I was in a pretty good position to outlast Joel and Paul and had no trouble doing so.

We then went to individual cubicles for massage. This took about three-quarters of an hour. The girl massaged body and limbs, and rubbed on a volatile, scented fluid which had a sharp, cooling effect. She spoke halting English and no French. Conversation went like this:

'How old are you?'

'Thirty-two.'

'You married?'

'Yes.'

'You have babies?'

'Yes.'

'How many?'

'Two.'

'Two boys?'

'Yes.'

'How old are they?'

'Six and one.'

'How long you married?'

'Eight years.'

'Ah, a long time, eh.'

No comment.

I asked her age — 20 — but conversation beyond this was not easy; her English just wasn't good enough. I gather from Joel and Paul that the above questions are standard. Looking at my identity discs, she asked, puzzled, 'You American?'

'No.'

'Ah, Uc Dai Loi?'

'Yes.' Much excitement as the news was called to masseuses in other cubicles. Obviously Australians are a novelty here.

Many of the girls were singing together — quite pleasant to listen to. Total time spent in massage parlour was about one and a quarter hours. Cost: approximately $2.50. Afterwards I certainly felt clean and fresh, but hardly any more so than after a normal shower. Did not experience the feeling of invigoration that everyone else is so enthusiastic about. Certainly did not gain $2.50 worth of freshness! What then is the appeal to so many others? Of course, many massage parlours offer sex as well, but this costs a lot more. Perhaps, having a clear head and a reasonably fit body to begin with, I had less to gain from a steam bath and massage than some others.

Drove through Saigon to Tan Son Nhut to catch the plane to Nui Dat. This time I saw some very attractive parts of Saigon that I didn't know existed. Some nice parks, some large city buildings and some large city shops — all these, legacies of the French, had once been lovely, and even now, despite some deterioration, are still quite attractive. Many wide streets with trees also enhance the city's appearance. Traffic busy, bicycles everywhere and many Honda light motorbikes. Altogether, Saigon is not as unattractive as I had at first thought, and if the buildings and people could be cleaned up just a little, it would be a nice city.

Joel Cain came back with me on a one-day visit to Nui Dat.

Wednesday 17 April 1968

Routine tasks today, plus playing host to Joel. Heavy rain for about half an hour a few hours before dawn. The first real rain. Ground dry soon after dawn but less dust now. Day fine, 85°F.

Thursday 18 – Friday 19 April 1968

Joel returned to Long Binh Thursday morning. Gathering in canteen in evening for Private Reg Miller, Corporal Graeme Williams and Sapper Stan Stephens (also known as Sapper Wojtowicz and as Sapper Wheelbarrow), who return to Australia. Quiet two days of routine work, including session as duty officer on Friday night. Temperature generally 85°F, humidity 100%, clouds around. The wet must be close now.

Saturday 20 April 1968

My services have been requested as defending officer at a court martial by a soldier from the far end of the Task Force. It seems I have a useful reputation, despite the fact that I've only once ever defended anyone, and that man is still serving time in the boob. It remains to be seen whether Task Force HQ allows me to accept this — it all takes so much time.

Interesting to hear of political hullabaloo in Australia over the 'harsh' treatment by the government of an Army officer arrested on arrival for having sent 'a few harmless souvenir captured pistols' through the mail. Little do the politicians know of the fearful explosives (including a claymore mine) which were sent.

Heard of the court of inquiry into last weekend's fatal pistol accident being under way but sadly hampered by inadvertent interference. Apparently one of the first to arrive on the scene of the accident was the company sergeant major, who set about tidying up the mess with crisp efficiency — 'You two take him to the doctor, you clean up the blood and scrub the floor, you tidy up the furniture, you give me the pistol,' etc etc. The military police did not thank him when they arrived at this immaculate scene.

Temperature stable. Most days are 85°F and nights 80°F. Humidity 100%.

Sunday 21 April 1968

Very hectic today. Something big obviously in the air. Several panic jobs demanded in negligible time.

Monday 22 April 1968

Reason for urgency now made known. Main Task Force elements are to deploy against the Viet Cong some 50 kilometres away. Task Force HQ will go too. Movement to take place in a few days' time.

Despite pressure of work, we managed to get down to A Squadron 3 Cavalry Regiment for a game of volleyball before dinner. Took our own referee this time and won 2–1.

Afternoon cloudy, but still no rain.

Tuesday 23 April 1968

Overcast and humid all day. Finally some light rain in the afternoon and evening. Somewhat disappointed with the performance of several officers in the Task Force HQ. Operational situation is changing rapidly, with plans being made and then shelved. Result: many officers are getting very excited and issuing many instructions without stopping to think. This, in turn, costs other people time they can ill afford to lose.

I saw several instances of this today and one of them affected us. Mario Apfelbaum, our screen printer, had to work just about all night to do a rush job. The rush could have been avoided had one major stopped to consider questions I asked him twice during the day only to be told, 'No, carry on as I told you.' Have received apologies since, but that won't help Mario much.

Viet Cong attacked Ba Ria, Long Huong (just west of Ba Ria) and Vung Tau last night. They used mortars landed by sampan near Ba Ria and heavy (122mm) rockets fired from Long Son Island (north of Vung Tau). Rockets landed in the USAF base at Vung Tau and caused plenty of damage — two killed, 18 wounded, four Chinook helicopters disabled, one Caribou aircraft destroyed, two Bird Dog light aircraft disabled, and four garbage trucks killed in action. This is bound to shake up the complacent life in Vung Tau.

With the main fighting elements of the Task Force moving up north, the Viet Cong might well attack those remaining at Nui Dat.

It will probably take the enemy about four days to realise that the force here has been seriously weakened, and then anything could happen. Apparently a major Viet Cong action is building up in all areas, much as it did two or three months ago, but due to the heavy February casualties, this VC attack will probably not be as strong.

Meanwhile, panic reigns as everyone tries to get organised to go north. Watched Mario in action on the screen press tonight. A delight. Swift, efficient and stylish in action. It is a pleasure to watch such a skilled craftsman.

Wednesday 24 April 1968

Finished printing at 02.30 this morning. Mario's eyes were in a pretty bad way from the turpentine fumes, and my eyes were sore after about an hour's exposure. Mario had seven hours, so he can have today off. Sapper Peter Dew assisted him and he needs a rest day too. Peter's effort was a record-breaking one. He returned in the morning from a week's R&R leave in Australia, did a full day's draughting and a night's printing.

Today fairly busy, but most of yesterday's panic has died down and people have stopped dashing in all directions and shouting. Noel Sproles is going out into the field with the Task Force HQ as a Command Post duty officer, which means they will have three this time, as against two for Operation Coburg in February. Two duty officers are hardly enough for the 24 hours in a day. Noel's departure will leave only one officer with the Survey Troop, but with WO2 Spike Jones coming back from Long Binh tomorrow, this should not cause undue difficulty.

Another rush job this evening — this time the draughtsmen are on the night shift and the printing needs to be done tomorrow. Finally to bed at 22.00 and have to be up at 24.00 for the midnight shift at the Task Force Command Post. Bit short of sleep after the late job last night.

Thursday 25 April 1968

Things fairly quiet in the Command Post. At about 06.00 or 07.00, a lot of things began to happen, but no crises of a really major nature — just a whole lot of minor things all happening at once.

Quiet evening, except for excessive artillery shells being fired directly overhead. Noise was so loud that one or two shots actually caused pain to ears. The echoes crashed around the distant hills for up to 30 seconds. Main elements of the Task Force went north today — helicopters aloft all day. Anzac Day today went almost unnoticed in an otherwise very busy day.

Friday 26 April 1968

Life quieter with the main Task Force elements away and fewer people about. Much artillery noise tonight. Intelligence information has indicated that a big Viet Cong attack is building up, probably for 1 May. Occasional grey clouds seen, but still no rain, apart from the one night shower about a week ago.

Saturday 27 April 1968

Officers' Mess very quiet at lunch with so many men away, so livened things up by translating our usual dull, unimaginative menu into most extravagant French. Slipped menu onto a vacant table and awaited results. Party soon arrived and sat down. Faces sorely perplexed and puzzled as they scanned the menu. A steward was summoned to explain the situation and was, of course, equally dumbfounded, but agreed that hamburgers were indeed available, though he couldn't vouch for them being 'à la cuisine Johnson' as advertised.

Not much news yet of action further north, apart from a report that one Australian was killed and two wounded by an artillery shell thought to be from friendly forces. Unfortunately, both friendly and enemy shells hurt. During the past four days, 1st Battalion, newly arrived for a second spell in Vietnam, has been conducting minor operations within 20 kilometres of Nui Dat and has had some 12 to 15 enemy contacts — all of them unsuccessful. Probably the most embarrassing occurred when a nine man fighting patrol sprung an ambush with claymore mines and rifles on what were thought to be Viet Cong, but were found to be animals. Despite the fire power, the animals escaped. Meanwhile, a New Zealand patrol from 2nd Battalion had a night contact, fired only nine rounds, and killed three out of three Viet Cong.

Late afternoon very dark due to heavy cloud gathering, but no rain. Much flashing in sky at night but not possible to be sure whether lightning or artillery.

Monday 29 April 1968

Again fairly quiet, despite reports of big enemy build-up. Went to see visiting concert in the morning — party of nine from Western Australia, including an instrumental trio (good), a ventriloquist (excellent), an MC/leader/singer/instrumentalist (very good), a folk-singing male and female duo (good), and two female singers (poor). Saw little of the last two and plenty of the rest.

Highlights were Ron Blaskett, the ventriloquist, who was absolutely brilliant (Dummy: 'You moved your lips that time, mate.' Master: 'I didn't.' Dummy: 'I saw you. One more move and you're out of this show.') and conducted a wonderfully involved argument with his dummy on the subject of ventriloquism, making us wonder just who was pulling whose strings.

The MC, Peter Willie Harries, sat at a tiny portable electric organ and sang the best rendition of 'Uc Dai Loi Cheap Charlie' (tune: 'This Old Man') I've yet heard. He followed it up with the 'Nui Dat Blues' (tune: 'Botany Bay') and the show-stopping 'Rottnest Island National Anthem' ('. . . Just pull the twine', to the tune of 'I Walk the Line', with apologies to Johnny Cash). Altogether it was an excellent concert — much better than the last one, and this one was a success without the ribaldry from the audience which made the last concert so entertaining.

Afternoon spent on routine tasks and in a working party in our Survey Troop lines, ensuring drainage clear for the wet etc. To bed early — have to be up at midnight to be duty officer.

Tuesday 30 April 1968

Up at midnight. Shift quiet — just a few minor matters. Very heavy rain at 05.50 for about a quarter of an hour. Back to the Survey Troop and then to bed at 10.00.

MAY

AUSTRALIAN MILITARY FORCES

AAB — 71A
Reprinted Dec, 1964

RECORD BOOK

CONTAINING 96 PAGES

RULED FEINT

During May, the Task Force was involved in a clash against a North Vietnamese regiment 30 kilometres north of Saigon. Over two nights, 63 Australians were killed or wounded, the biggest casualty number for a single battle in Australia's Vietnam campaign. The Battle of Coral, as it became known, was a near-disaster, as a result of poor intelligence and poor liaison with the American forces stationed nearby.

The battalion to suffer most was 1st Battalion. On its return, the possibility of bringing out stripper Sandra Nelson to raise morale was mischievously raised by John. Sandra Nelson was a stripper making a name for herself at the Paradise Club in Sydney's Kings Cross. She had previously applied unsuccessfully to travel to Vietnam — where she had myriad admirers and could guarantee publicity for herself. While authorities might have gained the approval of the troops if they had allowed her to perform, they would almost certainly have faced opposition from the guardians of public morals at home.

PAUL HAM

★

The conference was conducted with decorum until the subject of concerts came up. Any questions? To liven things up I tossed in a frivolous one. 'When's Sandra Nelson coming up?'

★

Wednesday 1 May 1968

Heavy rain this morning, continuing until about 08.30. Mud everywhere. Much sun, high humidity. Ground still muddy at the end of day, despite the heat.

Attended Canteens conference in the afternoon. Some extraordinary things happen in departmental circles. For example, until now all goods have been surcharged 10% in case of possible loss due to war. No such loss has occurred at any time in Vietnam, so the 10% surcharge has now been withdrawn — meaning all goods must be insured instead, which puts 7% back onto the price again! Another example: 60% of the regular loads on SS *Jeparit* from Sydney to Vung Tau are canteen supplies. Most of these are bought and then mailed to Australia. To save this great waste of money, the armed forces want to make it possible for men in Vietnam to buy electric frypans and other goods in Australia and to deliver in Australia. It can be arranged by Canteens resources, but the government won't allow it, and so the waste continues.

Thursday 2 May 1968

While relieving duty officer in Command Post at dinner time, an RAAF aircraft reported six cattle north of Nui Thi Vai, and requested permission to shoot them up. Our conversation went like this:

'Did you say cattle, i.e. cows?'

'That is affirmative.' (No RAAF people are capable of a simple yes or no.)

'Why do you want to shoot them?'

'Because they're Viet Cong cattle, that's why.'

'How can you divine the political beliefs of a cow when you're in an aircraft and the cow's on the ground?'

'If we don't kill the cattle, the Viet Cong will eat them, so let's get in first.'

'What, and kill the poor beasts in case someone else does? Fair go mate.'

'May I engage them with machine-gun fire?'

'No. Leave them alone.'

'What! Are you Viet Cong or bloody RSPCA?'

At this stage a more senior officer enters the Command Post. 'What's the fuss about?'

'RAAF want to shoot up some cattle, alleged to be of Viet Cong sympathies.'

'Can't they find anything better to shoot at?'

'Apparently not.'

'Oh well, if that's the best they can do, let them have a go.'

'Hullo RAAF! Permission granted to engage cattle with machine-gun fire.'

'Ha! Am engaging the enemy now.'

Next day RAAF reports the successful slaying of two cattle — killed in action. Missed the other four.

Meanwhile, 1st Battalion has had its 25th enemy contact since arriving in Vietnam three weeks ago. Result: one Viet Cong killed in action, and two Australians wounded — one in action and the other accidentally shot himself while in the Task Force base. Most of the battalions start badly, but none have ever had 1st Battalion's atrocious luck. When its first VC kill was announced, a relieved cheer went up.

Overheard in the Officers' Mess: 'Tonight's the night.'

'Nonsense. I bet you a beer we don't get attacked tonight.'

'Bet we do.'

'OK, you're on. Now let's define what counts as an attack. Any round falling within the perimeter of the Task Force base constitutes an attack, except for accidental discharge of weapons by our own troops within the base, OK?'

'Agreed.'

'No, wait on. Anything coming in from outside must be fired by enemy, and hostile intent must be proven. All rounds landing within the perimeter and fired by the 1st Battalion, regardless of intent, shall be deemed, for the purpose of the aforesaid agreement, not to have fallen nor to count. OK? My personal belief is that our 1st Battalion is our greatest threat. Agreed?'

'Agreed'.

Fortunately, no attack occurred.

Friday 3 May 1968

Up at midnight for duty officer shift at Command Post. All quiet except for a few minor incidents. A man was reported at 02.30 to be on Kangaroo helipad heading east. Rang the Provost Detachment which is located at the east end of the helipad. 'Command Post here. A man has been reported to be on Kangaroo pad heading your way. Better watch out for him.'

'Very good, sir. Could you give me a description of the man please?'

(Oh, you wonderful clot of a civilian cop, you!) 'A black figure on black ground in a black night. Any help to you?'

'Thank you, sir. We'll watch out for that man.'

They never found him — probably because they thought that white or yellow men didn't count.

Saturday 4 May 1968

With the Task Force main HQ away, we are now getting well ahead with our normal mapping work, which is satisfying for the draughtsmen and printers, but there is less for the surveyors to do.

Task Force due to return tomorrow, now that the expected major attacks have not eventuated. The reason for this is believed to be the defection of a very senior North Vietnamese Army officer to the Americans. He supplied details of all the major VC attacks coming up. Unfortunately, two American press men, sworn to secrecy, leaked the news to USA and to the world — and of course to the VC. So knowing that we know their plans, they called off all attacks.

Went to the pictures tonight — Peter Ustinov in *Romanoff and Juliet*. First 20 minutes were excellent but then I was called out. Emergency. Task Force going further north and not coming back as expected. Big VC attack expected. Maps needed in a hurry for new area of interest — well to the north of Highway 1, which runs east from Bien Hoa to Xuan Loc. Up pretty late at night while people change their minds many times in deciding what they want. Same trouble as a fortnight ago — people not stopping to think before acting. Finally to bed at 00.30, after a strong exercise in patience.

Sunday 5 May 1968

Heavy rain this morning but only for 15 minutes. A few panic demands for maps but otherwise a quiet day. Strong cool wind in late afternoon — most unusual.

Monday 6 May 1968

Quiet day — perhaps the lull before the storm. Two battalions of Viet Cong (about 1500 men) are believed to be in the vicinity of Dat Do and there is fighting going on there at the moment. Our 1st Battalion has had several more contacts — with no result. Meanwhile, the Americans at Blackhorse had a fight with Viet Cong only nine miles north of here. Result: three Americans killed, one ARVN killed, 91 Viet Cong killed. The VC force was heading south, down our way. The most likely targets seem to be Dat Do, Long Dien, Ba Ria and Nui Dat, in that order.

Tuesday 7 – Wednesday 8 May 1968

Busy days — routine work plus many minor tasks due to change in area of operations for the Task Force.

Thursday 9 – Friday 10 May 1968

Flat out on preparation of defence for court martial that has been tossed my way at very short notice. Down to Vung Tau by helicopter at lunch time. Trial started at 14.30 and went for ten minutes before I chucked a two-hour spanner in the works by submitting that one charge laid did not disclose an offence against the Army Act. Much legal palaver and delay ensued. Charge reframed. Charges were:

1. Conduct to the prejudice of good order and military discipline in that the accused was found standing beside the open refrigerator of HQ 1ATF at 00.20 hours on 22 April 1968 by Private Jamieson.
2. Conduct to the prejudice of good order and military discipline in that he assaulted Private Jamieson at 08.15 hours on 22 April 1968.

The true story was that the accused was caught red-handed raiding the refrigerator by the duty picquet, who reported the matter. At the time, the culprit threatened to smash the picquet's head in. Later the following morning, the culprit carried out his threat in front of several witnesses and the victim had to go to hospital for an operation on a badly fractured nose. The accused was utterly and completely guilty of both charges. Nevertheless, I got him off the first charge. However, the second one was a bit too hard to toss and he got 28 days' detention and a $40 fine. He was rather unhappy about the whole affair.

To get the accused off the first charge I had to make a big mess of the prosecution and did so. The prosecutor (Captain John Rhodes, a really shrewd, experienced and quick-witted man, whom I know well) handled his side of things brilliantly. However, there was little he could do about it when I was cross-examining the chief witness for the prosecution, Private Jamieson, himself. After one to one and a half hours in the witness box, Private Jamieson had contradicted himself hopelessly several times and hardly knew black from white, and so the prosecution was somewhat embarrassed for reliable evidence. This was not a nice thing to do — Private Jamieson seemed to be a decent and honest man and an excellent soldier. The accused was a nasty piece of work (with eight prior convictions) and the other witness for the defence was even worse. I had previously expressed my conscience troubles to the Legal Corps people but was assured by them that it was not for me to decide the guilt or innocence of the accused, but to defend him to the best of my ability (which I did) and to leave it to the court to decide his guilt or innocence (which it did).

The prosecution case was presented well, and in view of all the witnesses, the prior threats, and several other indisputable incriminating circumstances, there was little I could do about the second charge, though I certainly tried.

The trial started on Thursday at 14.30 and finished at 17.00 on the Friday — quite a lot of time for a simple case with only two prosecution witnesses and two defence witnesses, including the accused. On Thursday night, the accused and the other defence witness went absent without leave into the town of Vung Tau — and were caught. On top of this, the defence witness also faces another charge for five days' absence without leave the previous week, and he is up to his neck in strife over debts he can't pay, owing over $100 on a gambling debt and over $200 to an American major who gave him the money to buy a tape recorder in Hong Kong the previous week (the purchaser returned penniless and with no tape recorder). What a mess! He was to have gone home to Australia for discharge next Monday, but has now been stopped.

Visited HQ 1ALSG Mess on Friday night for their 'happy hour'. It was happy all right — girls everywhere and hands all over them. First feeling was of annoyance, but on second thoughts, why shouldn't they who have the opportunity to enjoy themselves do so? So easy to be jealous. Girls were mainly Australian, New Zealand, US nursing sisters and Red Cross workers.

Did not stay at 1ALSG Officers' Mess, but at 1 Australia Field Hospital. Very pleasant company there — including two ex-Survey Corps men, John Lambie and Bruce Daniel, the latter being a World War II veteran, who later took up medicine, became a doctor and is now second-in-command of the hospital. The hospital has several specialists, including pathologist and surgeon, with the result that it has more full colonels than second lieutenants.

Saturday 11 May 1968

Went over to HQ Company and looked up Private Jamieson, the honest witness in the previous two days' court martial in Vung Tau. Complimented him on all he had done and expressed regret at my involvement in this whole unpleasant business. Having had his nose smashed after bravely doing the right thing, he was then publicly humiliated by an officer in a court martial when presenting evidence to the best of his ability. I felt unable to justify my actions as defending officer. I know what I did was legally correct, but at the same time I believe it to be both militarily and morally wrong, and this troubles me.

All I could do was apologise to Private Jamieson, assure him of my personal respect for him and leave him puzzled as to why 'justice' operates this way.

Sunday 12 May 1968

Got washing and a few odd tidying-up jobs done. Met a soldier during the afternoon who had left Vung Tau (where he belonged) in uniform and without weapon, caught the local Vietnamese bus to Ba Ria, attended a Buddhist church service there just for fun, then hitched two lifts to Nui Dat. We sent him back to Vung Tau on the emergency medical helicopter making its end-of-day routine run. Fortune favours the drunk!

Monday 13 May 1968

Forward elements of Task Force moved yesterday and today, from a position about 60 kilometres north of Nui Dat to a new position

about 30 kilometres to the north-west and about 30 kilometres north of Saigon. With only a couple of infantry companies and some artillery in the new position, a North Vietnamese Army battalion mounted an assault in the early hours of this morning. The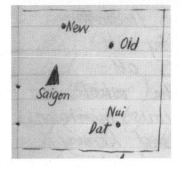
gun position was partly overrun. A gun and some mortars were lost but later regained. Ten Australians (mostly 1st Battalion) were killed and 25 wounded, several seriously. Fifty-four of the enemy were killed, mostly by the artillery firing horizontally over open sights straight into them. Plenty of excitement for 12 Field Regiment, this being their first month in Vietnam. The battle lasted from about 02.00 until 08.00, and not much action has occurred since.

During the day, the Australian strength in the area was increased to two battalions (1st and 3rd) and the Task Force forward HQ is there too. With the forward HQ are Noel Sproles as Command Post duty officer, Dallas Leary (our cook), and Sapper Dominic Yau (Survey Corps, but with Intelligence as an interpreter).

Day fairly busy with routine tasks and many map demands. Heavy but brief storm late in the afternoon. Much lightning and thunder amidst the usual deafening firing of the artillery. To bed early — on the midnight-until-dawn shift in the Command Post tomorrow.

Tuesday 14 May 1968

Up at midnight. Fairly quiet session with little action. Forward HQ is having difficulty maintaining communications due to the heavy rain that is falling there. Further news on yesterday's major action: apparently most of the enemy casualties were not caused by artillery after all (much of the flechette ammunition proved defective), but by the helicopter gunships and a Spooky, all equipped with mini-guns.

With the whole area lit by flares, the murderous mini-guns with their torrents of bullets caused heavy casualties. Most of the Australian casualties were caused not by shooting but by fragmentation from enemy rockets and mortars. I hate to think how we could manage without the overwhelming air support we possess.

To bed by 09.30 and up again at 12.00. Visited Ap Suoi Nghe, just north of Nui Dat, in the afternoon. It looks neat from the air but awful from the ground. For each home, the Australians put in four corner poles and a sloping galvanised-iron roof, each whole structure being about eight metres square. Timber and old ammunition cases were provided, and the Vietnamese added their own walls, floors etc. Some have done very well indeed, others much less so. A friendly atmosphere though, and small boys everywhere, ranging from Sun, or Soon, the cigarette-smoking nine-year-old leader of the push, down to Stalky, a two-year-old who never wears any clothes. Stalky is a nice kiddie and so is Charlie, who is a lively four-year-old.

The Survey Troop has been subdividing blocks of land for agricultural settlement by the villagers, and many of these children have been lending useful help by carrying equipment, acting as chainman on the forward end of the survey tape (a five-year-old boy is reputedly excellent at this), or by driving a Land Rover (most of them can do this, and one eight-year-old can drive the bulldozer). Their nicknames were given by Sergeant Grant Small; he has named all the others (including a couple of girls) Fred.

Had a quick look at the survey work and returned to Nui Dat. Quiet evening. No rain since yesterday, but atmosphere humid and dark.

Tonight a newspaper from home reported the deaths of four Australian newspapermen a week ago in Saigon — shot by Viet Cong. They'd been at Nui Dat off and on for the last few months and I'd seen them often in the Mess, especially Mike Birch from Western Australia. I'd thought only yesterday that I hadn't seen

Mike for a week or so. Now I know why. Their deaths were their own fault, though. They saw a gunship shooting up Viet Cong, so drove right up to the Viet Cong for a ringside seat and got shot.[1] Hardly surprising — and hardly a 'VIET CONG ATROCITY', as screamed the news headlines in Sydney.

Wednesday 15 May 1968

Caught up on a lot of minor tasks that needed doing. Made another attempt to ascertain the progress of spectacles for Sapper Peter Dew. He broke his only set in January and the medical system has still not been able to supply him with a new set. At present it looks as though a wait of a further five weeks is necessary. This really is a disgraceful situation, especially when the man concerned is a draughtsman and needs his glasses for his work.

Thursday 16 May 1968

Much action for the Task Force people north of Saigon today. Their position was attacked in a most professional manner by a regiment of three North Vietnamese Army battalions. The 1st Battalion bore the brunt of the attack, but the Task Force HQ and the Engineers got hit, too. Australian casualties were remarkably light — only nine killed and 17 wounded and, considering the fearful volume of fire from artillery, Spooky and several helicopter gunships, enemy casualties were light also, with only about 40 killed. The fighting raged from 02.40 until 07.00. The Task Force HQ received 60 to 100 mortar bombs and rockets in its area alone, so it is remarkable that only one

[1] I later found out these journalists had specifically been told not to go to the place where they were killed. — JB

man was killed there. The wires from the Command Post to the Signals bunker were cut twice. Life must have been pretty desperate for a while there. Noel Sproles and our cook, Dallas Leary, must have been in the thick of it. That makes the second major attack on the Task Force in four days. The second attack was much stronger, but so was the defence, so casualties were similar on both occasions.

At 10.30 today, an American jeep was ambushed on the road between Ba Ria and Vung Tau, quite close to Ba Ria. The vehicle received 25 bullets from a submachine gun, but no one was hurt. I've been expecting something like this to happen for a long time along this stretch of road, and can only wonder that it hasn't happened before this.

Today Long Dien was under Viet Cong control for several hours, and quite a lot of fighting went on. From Nui Dat we were able to watch an air strike being made on Long Dien. One does feel sorry for the poor villager or farmer caught up in all this conflict and carnage.

Warm, humid night. Artillery pounding away as usual.

Friday 17 May 1968

Little action for the Task Force today — a welcome change from yesterday. Fighting still continuing in Long Dien and this has already cost the lives of the village chief and Major Sanchez, the senior American adviser there. This action is involving US and ARVN forces only, not the Australian force.

I analysed several after-action reports today and made an interesting observation. A standard pattern seems to emerge from most actions involving up to 1000 men. A typical casualty list from such an action is 20 VC killed in action and five of our troops killed in action, if little or no air support is involved. A typical casualty list from a similar action where a light fire team (a pair of helicopter gunships) or Spooky lends support is 100 VC killed in action and five of own troops killed in action. It is not unusual for *several* hundred VC to be killed in the same action, if the murderous mini-guns are above the battle. Day or night, it makes no difference — the night is illuminated with flares. It is becoming increasingly obvious to me that our average enemy casualties/own casualties ratio of 10/1 throughout the country is largely thanks to the hail of lead from the airborne mini-guns. When they are present, the ratio is often as high as 20/1. When absent, it drops to about 3/1. Intelligence figures indicate that Viet Cong enlistments plus infiltration from North Vietnam is roughly equal to the kill rate of enemy. This makes one wonder where we'd be without the mini-gun and our complete air supremacy.

Viet Cong losses are being replaced with more young boys and women, as well as old men; also more untrained enemy are found. The enemy appears to be scraping the barrel for replacements, but the effective strength remains as high as ever, so no end to the conflict is in sight. The recent attempts by President Johnson to halt it all seem, in the main, to be meeting with approval from South Vietnamese people, press and government, though there are mixed feelings in some quarters where it is felt that South Vietnamese interests may suffer. However, the man in the street and on the paddy field wants a stop to all the fighting, regardless of political sacrifice — anything to stop the bullets whizzing past.

Our clerk, Peter Smith, had his first helicopter ride today, as an assistant on a Psychological Operations leaflet-dropping mission.

Sergeant Grant Small is applying for a commission and I am doing all I can to help him get it. His education is only at Queensland sub-senior level, but in his case this is not a limiting factor — he has so many other attributes. He and George Gruszka (now a captain) are the finest NCOs I have ever known and should make excellent officers (as George Gruszka has already done).

We made a dyeline copy of the sketch map of the area occupied by C Squadron 1st Armoured Regiment, here today. Unfortunately, the transparency (which bore no lettering or figures) was fed into the dyeline machine wrong side up, thus producing a mirror-reversed copy. The second-in-command of the squadron, Captain Don Campbell, a new arrival in Vietnam, took it back to the squadron to mark it up with additional information. He spent hours trying to orient himself on this back-to-front map. Too new to the area to spot the obvious trouble, he finally admitted defeat and sought help. We gave him a good one, and the other one now hangs on the wall in their HQ, boldly marked: 'KNOW YOUR AREA BACKWARDS!'

Saturday 18 May 1968

Up at midnight. Things quiet as usual in the Command Post. Have never had a session remotely like my first one when everything was happening at once. Listened to the Texan pilot from *Dr Strangelove* on the Tarzan Raisin radio net and was kept entertained by his voice. He seems to be the radio operator at Sector HQ at Ba Ria. I must tape-record his voice sometime. After going through two field wireless sets and one miniature tape recorder, his words would almost certainly be undecipherable, but nothing could disguise the extraordinary quality of his voice.

I practise my languages where possible. I use French whenever I can with Vietnamese people, and while in the Command Post I am learning to speak both American and RAAF. My progress with American is slow — I don't have the right nose, but I'm mastering the drawl, and can now make myself understood. RAAF is an easier dialect — all that is required being a limited vocabulary of specialised jargon, a flat tone of speech and very primitive grammar. One must never say a simple yes or no — everything is 'in the affirmative' or 'in the negative'. 'Affirmative' is also used in a quantitative adjectival sense to indicate some, few, much, many, positive, lots; and 'negative' is used in the same sense to indicate nil — e.g. 'negative results' means that nothing happened.

Yesterday the Survey Troop received a superb Swiss-made Fi-Cord miniature tape recorder/dictaphone. Survey Directorate in Canberra has decided we need it. The general consensus of opinion here is that there is a greater need for the Swiss secretary shown with it in the handbook. We cannot see any useful employment for this elegant instrument in our work here and only wish we had scored, if not the secretary, the 2-gallon can of acetone we've been in desperate need of for one and a half months now. The Fi-Cord has stacks of accessories, including a lapel microphone (but we have no button holes or lapels on our combat shirts); a bugging device for telephones (tempting one to ring the Command Post duty officer and request him to smile, being on *Candid Camera*); a luxury leather travelling case with handle of softest kid; a suede travelling case (for the front seat of the car); stethophone and foot controls (for use by the absent secretary). The whole instrument with its accessories is a lovely piece of Swiss workmanship, and it's a shame to have it here where conditions are so harsh on such equipment. For the time being, all we can do is to pack it away as carefully as we can and count it at each annual stocktake.

Returned to the Survey Troop from the Command Post after breakfast and got about two and a half hours' sleep before lunch. Then out in the field into heavy vegetation west of Ap Suoi Nghe village, near Nui Nghe hill, for a reconnaissance of tomorrow's land-clearing operation to create agricultural plots for the villagers. Took Sergeant Grant Small and Second Lieutenant Brian Watt (Civil Affairs Unit) with me and met Captain Bob Slater, OC, of the Australian Land Clearing Team. Had a look at the ground and had a brief discussion. All seems OK for an early start tomorrow. Party will consist of myself, Ted Morris, Grant Small, Steve Wood and John Hunter.

The area is not secure from Viet Cong activity, so we have been allotted two Centurion tanks to provide protection. Normally we get a section of infantry, but with the big operation on at the moment beyond Saigon, there's a shortage of infantry. Heavy rain at Ap Suoi Nghe turned everything to mud this afternoon, and movement of bulldozers and tanks has created a real morass. The track to Nui Nghe runs through swamp and is almost impassable. We could easily get bogged tomorrow.

Prepared gear during evening for tomorrow's job — my first field survey job since the work in the Yampi–Broome–Great Sandy Desert region in 1962! How easily does one get out of touch. Swapped my pistol for a submachine carbine, the pistol being of very limited use in an emergency. To bed early, being rather short of sleep from the night before.

Sunday 19 May 1968

Very heavy rainstorm at 05.00 for an hour or so. Two inches of rain fell. Sheets of water roaring everywhere.

Up at 06.00 and off to Ap Suoi Nghe. Most fruitful day. Big D8 bulldozer smashed down and pushed aside tangled scrub and bamboo ahead of us while we marked out blocks of land of 1 hectare area. We pegged out 26 such blocks during the day, and did about 4000 metres of theodolite and chain traverse[2] in the process. Very little protection was afforded by the tanks, and I gather that the infantry (our usual form of protection) are no better. The armoured personnel carriers, however, are usually good.

[2] A theodolite is an instrument mounted on a tripod, for measuring angles in the field. Chain traverse is a way of surveying across country with a series of straight lines of measured length. — JB

Ideally, a protection party should clear an area of enemy before we move in, and then be positioned so as to keep the area secure during the job. The tanks just did not keep their minds on the job, and they let us get ahead of them all the time. We were in a hurry to get through a big job today, so we ignored the tanks and just kept a sharp watch out for enemy ourselves. A couple of shots were fired within 300 metres of us at one stage — probably ARVN shooting birds. We saw no one. The job was fairly tiring (working in old rice paddies overgrown with dense bamboo) but interesting. Back at Nui Dat by 17.00 after an uneventful but productive day.

Monday 20 May 1968

Hot and humid as usual, but the ground has dried out reasonably well after yesterday morning's soaking.

The Civil Affairs Unit was very pleased with yesterday's work. Probably more of the same work to be done tomorrow and on subsequent days. This will provide an extra 80 blocks ready for allotment as requested by the Vietnamese Government.

The whole Task Force area was inspected by the Commander this afternoon at quite short notice, no one knowing quite what to expect. The Survey Troop was very high on the list and he spent about 50 minutes there — looking at defences, condition of weapon pits, condition of ammunition, tidiness of general area, condition of vehicles, any loose stores. He found two drink cans (both tossed by other units) but didn't comment, and little else. The vehicles and ammunition stood up well to very close scrutiny. Thank goodness. Fortunately, a few dreaded questions weren't asked, these being:

1. What is in that sea crate?

(True answer: Booze.)

2. What do you sell in that canteen?

(Again: Booze.)

3. Where did you get the timber to build this furniture?

(Answer: The previous owner didn't nail it down.)

Fortunately again, he simply admired the cabinetwork in the tents without querying its origin. As soon as he left, I rang about six or more other units lower down the inspection list and warned them of the main points the Commander appeared to be looking at. My advice proved to be reliable and I earned some gratitude as a consequence.

Stood in as duty officer at the Command Post at dinner time while duty officer went for dinner. A Sioux helicopter with pilot and observer sighted six Viet Cong between Nui Dat and Xuyen Moc. Apart from a 5.56mm M16 rifle carried for own defence in event of emergency ditching, the helicopter (a reconnaissance aircraft only) was unarmed and could not engage the enemy. An armed helicopter was immediately despatched from Nui Dat, and a light fire team of two mini-gunned fighting helicopters was requested from the American camp at Blackhorse, some 30 to 40 kilometres away, but only a few minutes' flying time.

Meanwhile, the unarmed helicopter attacked! The observer, firing from the dodging helicopter, hit and killed two VC with his 0.22-inch rifle while the VC scattered. Fire from several weapons, including one automatic weapon, was returned, and the helicopter was hit twice, fuel pressure dropping to zero. Pilot made a desperate bid to get to Xuyen Moc and made it. With the help of a mechanic flown over from Nui Dat, the aircraft was repaired, and returned safely to Nui Dat the same night, after an eventful game of aerial cowboys. The two VC killed were never verified. The pilot came close to court martial for disobedience of instruction, which nearly cost us an aircraft and exposed several other people to risk of VC attack. The pilot had recently won a Distinguished Flying Cross, and this saved him from court martial.

Tuesday 21 May 1968

Up at midnight for the Command Post duty officer shift until 08.00. All units seemed to be seeing things. Flares, searchlights and machine guns swung into action to deal with this. Several hundred shadows killed in action, several rubber trees wounded in action. No other enemy, though. Eventually everyone settled down.

Then It Happened. There was a Tremendous Bang. Half the people in the Task Force base area awoke. Machine-gunning could be heard in the far distance to the south. Then in came the news. The Vietnamese Popular Force (PF — part-time soldiers, and to some extent dominated by Viet Cong) sprang an ambush on 20 Viet Cong in the middle of Hoa Long village. Several claymore mines were detonated simultaneously to trigger the ambush, giving rise to this colossal explosion. The PF then opened up with a heap of automatic weapons. And the extent of the carnage? No casualties at all to either side! I now realise that it is true that the VC and the PF can have a heavy clash with forces larger than company size, no casualties being incurred on either side, as happened on Long Son Island about a fortnight ago. With close relatives on both sides, this is to be expected.

To bed at 09.30 and up for lunch at 12.00. Routine work — map checking — during afternoon. Saw water truck today bearing the painted sign: 'H$_2$O au Go Go'!

Divisional Intelligence Unit went rabbiting in Hoa Long today and found some burrows. In one of them they caught the Hoa Long Viet Cong chief, their biggest catch ever. They also caught a female VC intelligence agent whom they have been hunting for a long time. This really was a rich haul.

THE SURVEY TROOP CANTEEN

Part of the story of the Survey Troop canteen is given in the excellent book by Survey Troop soldier Bob McMillan-Kay on his experiences as a corporal in the Survey Troop from December 1968 to December 1969, Vietnam — A Technical Tour — with the 1st Topographical Survey Troop. In telling what he knew of the 'New' Canteen, Bob McMillan-Kay writes, 'There was certainly more to it than that . . .' Bob is dead right!

The Survey Troop Canteen, established in 1966, was very important as the social and recreational centre for the Survey Troop soldiers. For the officers and senior NCOs, the Task Force HQ Officers' Mess was available only a couple of hundred metres away and the Task Force HQ Sergeants' Mess was just across the road. But for the corporals and sappers of the Survey Troop, the Task Force HQ Company Canteen was less convivial.

A marquee was erected in the Survey Troop lines and was well furnished, complete with shelving, wood panelling and other attractive décor, thanks to the energy and ingenuity of the soldiers of the Troop. But it had to be for recreation alone, since it also had to be dry. The recreation tent could not have liquor because the Troop was too small to be allowed to have its own wet canteen (or boozer). For beer the Survey Troop soldiers still had to go to the HQ Company Canteen.

In 1967, thanks to the Survey Troop second in command, Lieutenant Keith McCloy, who had a mate in the Australian Services Canteens Organisation (ASCO) Detachment at Nui Dat, a clandestine beer supply was set up in the canteen. Although strictly illegal, it was controlled by a formal committee, with a sergeant appointed as supervising officer. It was well run and it all looked official, though of course it wasn't. This arrangement went on happily for a year or so and we routinely drew our weekly beer ration without any mishap.

By late 1968 I'd gained a pretty good understanding of how things worked in Vietnam. I figured enough men had changed over by now, and I counted on the memories of those remaining now being dim. So I planned my next move carefully. I submitted a formal complaint to ASCO that our recent Regimental Audit had revealed that we hadn't been receiving our ASCO disbursements for our canteen trading, despite the well-kept records showing all our canteen trading and all our ASCO beer purchases going back many months. Everything I said was perfectly true.

It worked brilliantly! And beyond all expectations too. Not only did we get a humble apology for the oversight, but we also got a whacking payment to catch up the entire disbursement backlog! The excuse given by ASCO was that for some unaccountable reason we were not on the list of canteens, however they were pleased to inform us that that error had now been rectified! I had only sought to legalise the illegal. The money was an entirely unexpected (and very nice) bonus!

So we were now official (and richer)! But the marquee was suffering in the tropical climate and sooner or later would have to be replaced. So we invested in a new canteen building which, thanks to the Survey Troop's enterprising driver, didn't cost a lot!

Late in 1968, an extremely heavy vehicle stopped outside the Survey Troop at Nui Dat and Lance Corporal Rocky Camps walked in to see the Officer Commanding. 'Where do you want the new hut, sir?'

'New hut, Rocky?' I replied, slowly and warily.

'Yessir. Where do you want it?'

'What new hut, Rocky?' I asked, now deliberately stalling for time.

'The new hut on the truck outside, sir.'

I looked out the door, and there's a complete army building on the back of a US Army low-loader idling with a thumping rumble so heavy I can hardly think. And this is at a time I really need to be thinking! 'Where's it from, Rocky?'

'The Yanks at the French Fort gave it to me, sir.'

Panic gripped me but I tried not to show it. What has Rocky traded for this? Do we still have our printing press? Or our process camera? At least the beer's safe — Rocky would never have traded that! But what?

'Rocky, why did the Yanks give you this?'

'They like me, sir. They reckon I'm a good bloke!'

'Yes, I'm sure they do, but why?'

'They just do! But they've got to have their truck back sir, so if you'll just tell me where you want it, I'll get them to unload it.'

That was an easy decision. There was only one place in our entire area where a building this size would fit. Unloading commenced while I made a frantic check of the Survey Troop to see what was missing. Nothing! We were safe! Well, for the moment anyway. And this building would make an ideal new canteen.

By now the initial shock was wearing off, and I was thinking I ought to be behaving a bit more graciously. 'Thanks, Rocky, it'll make a beaut new canteen and the fellows will be really happy.'

'Yessir, that's what I figured. OK for the Yanks to have a drink before they go back?'

'Sure! And thanks, all of you!'

We were still in the wet season, so it only took a fortnight or so for long grass to grow around the base of the new hut and it looked as though it had been there forever.

Then along came the Staff Officer, Engineers, from AFV Headquarters in Saigon on his periodic visit to the Task Force. This officer was known in Nui Dat as the Town Clerk, always tramping around the Task Force with rolled plans under his arm, checking them against what exists on the ground. 'Hey! When did this building go up?'

'Dunno, Charlie, it's been there for years! Look at all the growth around it!'

'Don't bullshit me! It's not on the plan!'

'Well, I can't help that, Charlie, I didn't draw that plan.'

'Aw, come on! You know what I mean!'

'No, I don't, Charlie. Don't you remember what you learnt in

Map Reading at Duntroon? When the map and the ground don't agree, it's the ground that's always right!'

'Well, I don't care! That building's gotta go! It's under power lines.'

'OK, Charlie.'

Another month passed. The Town Clerk returned.

'Hey! I told you blokes that building had to go!'

'Sure, Charlie! But we haven't had time.'

'Bullshit! It's a month since I told you to get rid of it.'

'Now come on, Charlie. You know of all the combat operations we've had to support in the last month. We've been flat out day and night doing more important things than taking a building down just to make your map look right. Why don't you change your map?'

'OK, OK. But it'd better be gone by my next visit!'

A quiet bit of research revealed that Charlie was due for return to Australia in January 1969. Only another couple of months to go. Further delaying tactics might just do the trick. On the Town Clerk's next visit, the excuses for non-removal of the building were even better than last time. And my carefully rehearsed sincerity almost had him believing that we were really most anxious to comply with his request, but the fortunes of war had simply been too much for us. And I was a major now, so of course I was truthful!

Come the visit after that, Charlie had gone home and we had a new Town Clerk. 'Hey! When did this building go up? It's not on the plan!'

'It's always been there. Just look at all the banana trees and all that other growth around it. I don't know what you're on about. Charlie never said a word about it the whole time he was here!'

Brow furrowed and shaking his head, the new Town Clerk walked slowly away, amending his map as he went.

Wednesday 22 May 1968

An Amenities conference in the afternoon and I went along to represent the Survey Troop. The Amenities system functions poorly. We've been trying for five months to get four chairs for our recreation tent — but without luck. Other units with other needs can't get them satisfied either. Amenities and Canteen services are pretty weak, really, though at least the new Amenities officer (Lieutenant Paul Parsons, NZ) is a great trier.

The conference was conducted with decorum until the subject of concerts came up. Any questions? To liven things up I tossed in a frivolous one. 'When's Sandra Nelson coming up?' (Sandra Nelson, of the Paradise Club, Kings Cross, Sydney, is a publicity-seeking showgirl who wants to come to Vietnam to entertain troops but has, she says to the press, been refused permission even to go at her own expense, ostensibly because she is officially disapproved of.) My question, as I expected, caused an uproar.

As the noise subsided came the big surprise. Bronx Honner, an infantry major representing 1st Battalion in which he's a company commander, jumped to his feet saying, 'And why not? I believe she wants to come, and the troops want her here, so why isn't she coming?'

'Aw, hell, who'd want to look at her?'

'Just about the whole of 1st Battalion who look like surviving the current operation, that's who!' Argument subsided. 1st Battalion's casualties having been heavy in the last week.

'OK, gentlemen. Would Sandra be welcome?' General consensus of opinion was that this was putting the case very mildly.

'OK then. Proposed by 1 Topographical Survey Troop, seconded by 1RAR, that the Sydney entertainer Sandra Nelson be invited here with a concert party. However, gentlemen, I doubt that the Brigadier would approve . . .'

Bronx leapt to his feet again. 'What's he got to do with it? This is for the troops, not him! What's more, 1st Battalion should be the host unit for her day here, and we'll invite the Survey Troop along too!'

Here, with coat hanger, is an early photo of the lady in question. A giant enlargement of this photo is pinned up in a prominent place in the Survey Troop, and is (once they get used to it!) regarded with some affection by its members. Sandra appeared on the cover of the New Year's issue of the *Bulletin* in January '68, but in slightly more conventional attire. The Survey Troop was delighted to hear later in the day of the possible visit by Sandra, even though it is most unlikely to eventuate.

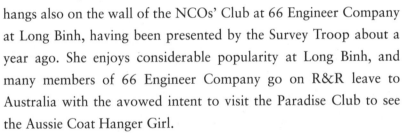

This same photo, also greatly enlarged (thanks to big camera facilities at Long Binh), hangs also on the wall of the NCOs' Club at 66 Engineer Company at Long Binh, having been presented by the Survey Troop about a year ago. She enjoys considerable popularity at Long Binh, and many members of 66 Engineer Company go on R&R leave to Australia with the avowed intent to visit the Paradise Club to see the Aussie Coat Hanger Girl.

Quiet day today, apart from the entertainment at the Amenities conference. The Brigadier may, indeed, be displeased, but the fact remains that of all Australian entertainers who could visit Vietnam, Sandra Nelson would undoubtedly be the most popular with the most people. Thinking seriously about it, I have no objection to the Survey Troop or myself being named as the originator of the suggestion — as far as I can judge, such a visit would raise morale a lot, and this is the sole purpose of concert parties. She needn't take her clothes off — just being here would be a boost to the morale of most soldiers.

Thursday 23 May 1968

Lost a friend today. Major George Constable, the Officer Commanding 161 Recce Flight, was killed when his plane went down in flames and crashed. No other details known at this stage. I'd known George since 1956. He was almost due to return to Australia.

Sapper Peter Dew, one of the livelier characters in the Survey Troop, had a disaster today, but rather an amusing one. Suffering from a tropical wog, his bowels demanded relief. He went to the latrine and was annoyed by the tiny flies which, with the onset of the damp weather, were more numerous than usual. So he dropped suitable fuel into the latrine, lit it and retired. The resulting explosion, and subsequent fire and smoke, had the desired effect on the flies but rendered the latrine uninhabitable for a long time, thanks to red-hot seats and clouds of smoke. So Peter returned to work while things cooled down.

At this stage he began to experience acute internal discomfort, so he lit a cigarette to take his mind off the problem — and coughed! Roaring a string of oaths, he fled to the latrine, running bowlegged, and with a brown stain on his trousers. Still cursing, he ripped his trousers off and hurled them down the latrine, announcing that he would consider returning to work when supplied with a new pair of trousers. This was done. I'm still waiting for the necessary loss and damage report to come in — it should make entertaining reading!

Today the Mess farewelled three officers — two RAAF officers and one USAF officer (Captain Jay Cappell, possibly the most likable member of the Mess, thanks to his friendliness and exquisite sense of humour — the man who could twitch a muscle at the corner of his mouth at the perfect instant and send a whole conference of officers into gales of mirth, the Brigadier included). One of the other officers was Flight Lieutenant Phil Hubbard, an iconoclast who never wanted to come to Vietnam, who hates Americans, loathes Vietnamese, detests the Army, and despises all Australians who don't come from Frankston, Victoria. Phil is not renowned for his broad-mindedness, tolerance and tact, and a large crowd had gathered in the Mess, eagerly awaiting his farewell speech. But to everyone's amazement, he spoke simply and sincerely, and actually praised the Army. We were all stunned. Phil had never been known to speak like this. He spoke of how much he'd learnt etc etc, and concluded with '. . . and in all sincerity, I firmly believe that *every* RAAF officer should spend at least a year of his career with the Army'. He paused for effect — then suddenly his face contorted and he snarled, 'WHY SHOULD I BE THE ONLY BASTARD TO SUFFER!'

Have had no rain for about a week now; despite some good attempts, the wet still hasn't arrived and is more than a month late.

Friday 24 May 1968

Day seemed quiet enough until atmosphere was filled with the haunting melody of the theme music from the film *Dr Zhivago*. It came from no direct source but seemed to be all around. Then we realised it came from the sky. An American Bird Dog aircraft equipped with loudspeakers for Psychological Operations was circling high above us and serenading the Australian Task Force. The tune changed to 'Tie Me Kangaroo Down, Sport', and then the plane fled before we could do anything typically crazy — like shooting it down. This livened up the morning and reminded us all that it is Empire Day — or is it Commonwealth Day? Never mind, it's not a holiday right here. Apparently a previous joke performed frequently last year by the Americans was to make like Mr Whippy and buzz the Australian Task Force for an hour or so with 'Greensleeves' playing incessantly! Obviously this wore pretty thin, because it hasn't been done for months.

Heard that George Constable was shot down by small arms fire[3] while flying fairly low. From the suddenness of the plunge into the ground, it is more likely that he, rather than the aircraft, was disabled by the shooting. The aircraft exploded on crashing and was burnt out.

Our cook, Dallas Leary, came back from the forward area today. He had a most unpleasant time during the attack eight days ago. Many mortar bombs landed within a few metres of his pit. Many of our casualties were from bombs actually landing in pits and killing the occupants, the density of the mortar fire being high.

Saturday 25 May 1968

A visit this morning by Army Public Relations to prepare an article for press release on the Survey Troop. Not wildly enthusiastic about this sort of thing but it seems to be a necessary evil, so I accepted it with a good grace. Several photos were posed for, and we ensured that Peter Dew's mighty walrus handlebar moustache was photographed from favourable angles. The PR men were most pleasant and we gave them every kind of help.

Sunday 26 May 1968

Up at 23.30 for the Command Post midnight shift. A few things happened — six men from the Engineers reported absent without leave in Vung Tau, and a vehicle, possibly from the 2nd Battalion,

[3] Later suspected to be 'friendly' fire from a South Vietnamese Regional Force post. Someone was annoyed by the low flying of the plane on a reconnaissance mission, so, just for sport, he shot it down. No action can be taken. — JB

was seen moving around the Task Force HQ area with lights on. Apart from these minor incidents, nothing until 04.00.

At this stage the forward elements of the Task Force received a heavy mortar, rocket and ground attack on their position, some 30 kilometres north of Saigon. No report came through till 05.00 because everyone was too busy fighting, calling for casualty evacuation or for air strikes; however, I could hear what was happening by listening to the radio conversation going on at the forward end. The fight only lasted an hour, costing four Australians killed and 15 wounded, and then the Spooky and light fire teams (helicopter gunships) moved in to work over the area with their mini-guns.

I got kicked in the pants at 07.00 by the staff officer handling operations at the forward end for not having woken up the captain handling operations at this end at Nui Dat at 04.00 to tell him of the attack. Of course I had considered this, but since we were not involved at this end, were powerless to help (not even a red phone to Dial-A-Prayer), and nothing had happened that couldn't be told to anyone in 20 seconds after waking in the normal course of events, I had decided that to wake the captain would have been an unnecessary act of panic. He's short enough of sleep as it is. Seems I guessed wrong! Or maybe I had guessed right, but the major at the forward end, surfacing after a night full of bombs, was viewing the world somewhat sourly. Do I carry my No-Panic-Whatever-The-Situation too far? Perhaps, but I haven't faced enough crises to be sure.

One rocket scored a direct hit on the tent of the chief supply officer coordinating ammunition, rations and other supplies.[4] He was underground at the time, so although he's intact, he needs a new tent and will be hard pressed to continue his work without

[4] Major Kevin Gurney. His trunk and his camera inside were wrecked, and subsequently went to the Australian War Memorial in Canberra. — JB

paperwork and an office. Bombs also landed within a few metres of the forward Command Post.

Things were quiet by dawn and I returned to the Survey Troop at 09.00. Went to bed at 10.00 intending to get up for lunch but slept through until 15.00 — disproving the theory (which I don't subscribe to) that it is not possible to sleep in 95°F heat, 100% humidity, daylight, and amidst constant helicopter landings right next door and artillery firing overhead.

More fighting up north during the day, but fortunately not serious. Still no rain. Despite constant threats, the wet monsoon has not arrived and is now more than a month late. Still, I don't mind the heat and humidity, and I prefer dust to mud — definitely a fair-weather soldier.

Heard this evening that Noel Sproles's shelter was ripped through with 14 shrapnel holes in this morning's mortar and rocket attack. Since he's still alive to talk about it, he obviously managed to get underground first.

Rain beginning to fall in evening. Spectacular lightning discharges all around.

Monday 27 May 1968

Apparently the film *Tammy* was shown last night to the complete disgust of everyone. All that need be done now to bring everyone to the brink of revolution is to show *Pollyanna*. Surely more suitable films for soldiers can be selected than *Tammy*?

Quiet day. Several jobs in but none of them major tasks or urgent. We've nearly completed a sign for the Divisional Intelligence Unit — Eric Clutterbuck's been drawing it. It is several feet long and bears the Intelligence Corps badge and the inscription in Gothic script. It looks so good that it has been suggested that we keep it and give our own sign away instead.

The fuss and palaver over the Prime Minister's visit next month (8 June) is commencing already.

Threatened rainstorm this afternoon did not eventuate. Much lightning, thunder and wind during evening.

Tuesday 28 May 1968

The forward elements of the Task Force were again attacked early this morning — this makes four major attacks since they moved to the location 16 days ago. Most of the attackers seem to be North Vietnamese Army units moving back northwards from Saigon to reorganise, prior to making fresh attacks on Saigon.

Weather broke at 21.00 — heavy rain storm, Hollywood style, with sheets of rain brilliantly floodlit by incessant lightning. Then light rain throughout whole night.

Wednesday 29 May 1968

Completed minor routine tasks, then down to Luscombe airfield for a concert. The concert party was from Sydney, consisting of compere-impressionist, two female singers, a family vocal group (two brothers and sister), plus drummer and electric organist. The general standard was awful. It started off with eight songs from one female singer — what a dragon! Couldn't sing, grating personality, three or four days' growth under arms, face leathery and heavily made up, sleeveless dress displaying sticking plaster on arms. Ugh. Didn't think she'd ever get off the stage. Could hear quiet messages being passed around audience: 'Mum's the word!'

The second singer was a Maori in her thirties — a big improvement on the first singer, but still hardly what the doctor ordered. Her message of '. . . and we think you guys are doing a great job, and all the girls at home think so and miss you . . .' cut no ice at all with the hardened warriors in the audience, who responded with growls of 'Get ya gear orf, luv.'

The family group were passable — they were a folk-singing group obviously modelled on Peter, Paul and Mary, and The Seekers. The girl, Helen Driessen (yes, Dutch), had obviously copied the style of Judith Durham of The Seekers very closely, and was blessed with plenty of ability also. Thanks mainly to her good voice, their rendition of the spiritual 'We Shall Not Be Moved' was the highlight of an otherwise poor concert. Although not extremely good-looking, at least she was young, and consequently appealed much more to the audience (mainly 21-year-old national servicemen).

Although the concert was weak, it came brilliantly alive in the last 60 seconds in an utterly unexpected way. The performers invited soldiers from the front row up to sing with them. About six went on stage, some willingly, others (including a weather-beaten sergeant) less so; however, once on stage they all joined in happily. Then, from a fair way back in the audience, one man was seen advancing reluctantly towards the stage under heavy pressure from his mates. A slim, very dark and very handsome man, he came up on the stage and immediately looked very shy and nervous, taking off his bush hat and wiping his shirtless body with it. The Maori woman noticed him, and went to lead him into the centre of the group.

Suddenly it became apparent that the shyness was all an act. He continued to play shy, with bursts of confidence and nervousness in turn, eyeing a girl on stage, looking away, embarrassed, looking back, starting to pat one, stopping, shocked at himself. He completely stole the show, and all attention focused on him, the whole audience standing on its feet and roaring with mirth and appreciation at what was obviously an act of polished, professional skill. His gestures, his facial expressions, and the use of his eyes were subtly timed and just perfect. This was no ordinary soldier acting the goat, but a professional performer in his element and displaying more talent than the rest of the show. The compere's act had been that of a rock-ape by comparison.

The Maori and Dutch girls joined him and lent support to his miming. At this stage the Dutch girl kissed him on the side of his neck. The audience roared at the nonchalant manner in which he received the kiss, turned his expressionless face to the girl, pointed to his lips, scored another kiss, and immediately went rubbery at the knees, his feet dancing to the music all the time he was on the stage. I don't know who this man was,[5] but I'm sure he has been a professional entertainer and a remarkably clever one — probably another of our highly skilled national servicemen. He made the whole concert worthwhile in just 60 seconds.

Some new buildings are going up for the Task Force HQ Officers' and Sergeants' Mess kitchens. One small building houses garbage cans awaiting collection. The building is identical to a city bus shelter, though lacking the seat running around the wall. On it someone has put a notice which reads:

BUS STOP. HAIL DRIVER.
TIMETABLE: Buses leave 10, 11, 12.30, and hourly
until 21.30 for Bondi, La Perouse, Long Bay.
Saturday night special for HOA LONG DANCE
departs here 19.30. One-way trips only.
Please pay as you enter.

---

[5] Discovered later he was from 2nd Battalion and returned to Australia with that battalion a few days later. — JB

This notice has caused much amusement, and so have many others on vehicles, for example, 'NUI DAT CITY COUNCIL' on the garbage truck. Another good one is the big sign on the main building of the Light Aid Detachment of the Royal Australian Electrical and Mechanical Engineers, which deals with vehicle services and repair; it reads 'BRIGGS' AUTOS, Rover Dealers' — Captain Daryl Briggs having been the recent Officer Commanding. Another one is outside the Provost compound where Vietnamese prisoners are held for interrogation. It reads 'Dicky Bird Motel, Bed & Breakfast, 24-hour Room Service, Hot & Cold Running Maids', having taken its name from Sergeant Bird of the Provost Section.

Noel Sproles returned to Nui Dat this afternoon, glad of a rest after 33 days as one of the duty officers with the forward elements of the Task Force, and having been under fairly heavy mortar and rocket fire four times.

Discovered that while lying in bed I can see the lighthouse at Cap St Jacques. Astonishing but true. From my bed in a tent in the middle of a rubber plantation I can see this light, which is about 30 kilometres away to the south-south-west.

Thursday 30 May 1968

Up at midnight and into the Command Post. Very quiet. Nothing of significance happening. Practice alert held. Siren sounded. Many amusing results. Survey Troop slept peacefully on, unable to hear siren above the noise of generators next door. Soldiers attempted to wake officers in Task Force HQ officers' lines: 'Wake up, sir! Alert! Better get into the pit!'

An RAAF officer opened one eye and said sourly and with utter disbelief, 'You *must* be kidding,' closed his eyes and returned to sleep.

Meanwhile, in HQ Company, the cook said, 'What do we do?'

Answer: 'Get into your pit!'

'But what about the early breakfasts we're cooking?'

'Never mind. Leave them and get into the pits. If *they* want a bloody practice, *they* can bloody well have one,' this decision being made by the Company Sergeant Major, a seasoned veteran, now on his second tour in Vietnam — the redoubtable K.F. 'Buddha' McDonald.

Then an officer appeared, walking nonchalantly through the imaginary enemy fire: 'Where's my early breakfast?'

'Sorry, sir, but all cooks are in the pits. There's an alert on, you know. I suggest you help yourself to a ration pack. You should have one in your own pit!'

Slept from 10.00 until 12.00, then up for lunch and to get packed. The Survey Troop plus a few other minor units (44 men in all) are going to the newly constructed beach annex to the Peter Badcoe Club at Vung Tau, to rest and relax for two nights and a day. Due to poor administration within the Task Force, hardly anyone knows of the existence of this facility, so I had no trouble arranging the visit.

We drove down without incident in a seven-vehicle convoy and settled into absolutely luxurious quarters by 17.00. Nice rooms and furniture, a lovely dining room and charming service from Vietnamese girls. The girls were very genteel — a tremendous contrast after our well-meaning but clumsy and dirty (not their fault) stewards at Nui Dat.

Some of our soldiers went (illegally) into Vung Tau during the evening, but were relatively safe because the leaders of this activity were two military police chaps from Nui Dat. Trapped in Vung Tau after the curfew (21.00), they had some anxious moments on the return trip, but were not caught by the White Mice (Vietnamese police). Passed the ROK compound with some trepidation — the

Koreans are apt to shoot at shadowy figures in the bush — when suddenly a voice said, 'G'day mate!' A Korean sentry had spotted them and was perfectly used to Australians sneaking back after curfew!

Friday 31 May 1968

A wonderful, lazy day in most comfortable surroundings. Played chess in the morning with Captain Geoff Boscoe (Officer Commanding Divisional Intelligence Unit), who is my room-mate here and a personal friend. The other officer here for the day is Lieutenant Garry Swan of the 1ATF HQ Light Aid Detachment. Garry showed us a flimsy pair of pants he'd found under the bed in his room this morning. He thought they must have been accidentally dropped from a heap of laundry by one of the girls cleaning his room, so rather than act as Prince Charming and find a Cinderella to fill them (as suggested by me), he laid them out on the coffee table in the middle of his room so that the owner could recognise them and take them.

Later in the day, while Garry was swimming, there was an unexpected inspection of our quarters by Lieutenant Colonel Peach, Commanding Officer of the Forces Amenities Unit, and an entourage of about five, perusing the new quarters in use by troops. They went into Garry's room for a small conference. I walked past and saw them situated thus:

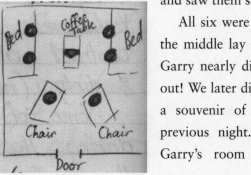

All six were seated, talking, and right in the middle lay these highly feminine pants. Garry nearly died of fright when he found out! We later discovered that the pants were a souvenir of one soldier's activities the previous night. He had planted them in Garry's room while Garry was having breakfast, and the girl tidying his room thought they were a souvenir and left them there. They were still there when Lieutenant Colonel Peach and his party left.

Geoff was visited today by Dai-Uy (Captain) Trung, Officer Commanding 10 Military Detachment, ARVN, a powerful and much-feared man — but very friendly to us. He brought Geoff some Vietnamese rice sweets — rice boiled to a brown jelly and wrapped skilfully in large leaves to give it the required tetrahedron shape. Quite pleasant when dipped in sugar. Trung's wife made them. Easy to carry, each wrapped tetrahedron was tied by a grass string to a central knot. The folding of the leaf around the jelly to mould it is obviously a job requiring considerable skill.

Heavy storm after lunch. Visited American PX and craft shop. Bought a Ferrari slot car for David and a radio for myself — got a National R397 (12 transistors, four diodes) for $25. It is specially designed for powerful and sensitive short- and medium-wave reception.

Went into Vung Tau for a Chinese meal with Geoff and Alan Cunningham (Intelligence officer at 1ALSG). The meal was nice but have had better meals for much less money in Sydney and Melbourne. Vung Tau is very lively in evening — girls everywhere and many of them looking very pretty. Trung told me earlier today that the people of Vung Tau are not popular elsewhere in Vietnam because they're getting rich while everyone else is getting shot up. Early to bed after a most enjoyable day.

JUNE

AUSTRALIAN MILITARY FORCES

AAB — 71A

Reprinted Dec, 1964

RECORD BOOK

CONTAINING 96 PAGES

RULED FEINT

In June 1968, Prime Minister John Gorton visited the Australian Task Force HQ at Nui Dat. VIP visits to the Task Force often caused much work. Tour itineraries had to be arranged, those visited had to be briefed, and briefings had to be prepared for visitors, just for a start.

The Survey Troop was often called on to assist, a typical example being to design and print the covers for the briefing notes to be handed out to the press accompanying the Prime Minister and his wife. This latter task offered the Survey Troop scope for mischief.

PAUL HAM

The 'Souvenir Programme' joke backfired to some extent because I failed to anticipate all possible responses. Apparently the PR officer noticed 'Price 20c' and said, 'This is wrong. It's a free handout.' Then he saw the condom advertisement and said, 'What's this for?'

Saturday 1 June 1968

Returned to Nui Dat this morning, with everyone unanimous in their approval of the facilities (including speedboat and surfboard) we've been using for the last day. Elbowed off the road by a large troop convoy: HMAS *Sydney* arrived at dawn today with most of the 4th Battalion aboard. The troops went to Nui Dat by road convoy, complete with tracked armoured personnel carriers bristling with aerials and guns, and above it circled a light fire team of two Iroquois helicopters, together with a third (Sioux) helicopter for visual reconnaissance. Altogether quite an escort.

There was some shooting in Cat Lo, north of Vung Tau, last night and the PF was called out this morning. Several hundreds of them lined the road, all in black pyjamas and black berets. Despite the smiles, they had an ominous look about them, and their alleged close association with the Viet Cong is not hard to believe. We were greeted at one point along the road by a boy of about ten, who shouted 'G'day, wankers!', while grinning from ear to ear, hitting himself on the back of his head with one hand and pretending to masturbate with the other. They mature early in this country!

Back for lunch at Nui Dat after this lovely break for a day. Routine tasks during the afternoon and the Survey Troop had a barbecue in our own area for the benefit of Sapper Bo Hucker, our assistant screen printer, who returns to Australia in a few days' time for discharge at completion of his national service. Sorry to see Bo go; he's been such a good and cheerful worker.

Sunday 2 June 1968

Up at midnight for spell until 08.00 in the Command Post. Am now doing this duty every third night, and it is becoming a little difficult to run the Survey Troop, especially without a second-in-command. Very quiet in the Command Post, nothing unusual happening at all. Back to the Survey Troop after breakfast. Routine minor tasks and to bed at 10.00.

Up again at 12.00 and spent half an hour trying to catch a snake. Snake is four feet long, slim and grey, and lives under the boards beneath my bed. Can't get at him easily. He's been seen by other chaps in the Troop prior to this, and at least we know where he lives. Set a rat trap outside entrance to hole and baited it with meat, but ants ate meat within an hour.

Went down to Ba Ria during the afternoon to attend a farewell party given by US Navy Seabees team before returning to USA. The Seabees are engineering construction people and have worked with us, clearing land for our survey subdivision work at Ap Suoi Nghe. Pleasant party. Saw several delightful Vietnamese children there and played with some of them. Finally dragged our chaps back to Nui Dat — it took three-quarters of an hour to get ten men into Land Rovers!

Annoyed during evening by drunken sergeant from 1st Battalion wanting maps urgently. His whole attitude was most provocative and offensive — he really was looking for a fight. He made a few remarks that I just couldn't let pass. The same man, sober, gave Sapper Ray Lawson a very hard time about three weeks ago. Altogether a most unpleasant, overbearing, aggressive man, always looking for sources of complaint where none exist. He left here and went to the Task Force HQ Sergeants' Mess bar for more beer and to complain to any warriors who'd listen. Unfortunately, he picked Spike Jones and Ted Morris, and started to complain about Survey people not caring for or understanding the needs of the fighting soldier. Spike and Ted, both of whom did a year in Korea in the infantry (and Ted served in Malaya as well), were hardly sympathetic. Spike said, 'I was in 1RAR myself 14 years ago. Where were you?' A fist fight nearly developed but was fortunately avoided.

Monday 3 June 1968

Went to Ba Ria with the laundry run today. Visited Madame Minh Ha and chatted with her and her younger daughter, Marie, who is an economics student at Saigon University. Spent about 20 minutes there. Marie's French is better than her mother's; she doesn't speak rapidly and is easy to understand.

Did some minor shopping in Ba Ria market and took a few photos, including one of a shop which sells dentures! Bought a Vietnamese Campaign Medal for about 45 cents. Although the Australians have been fighting in Vietnam for several years now, the Australian Government still hasn't struck and distributed any medals — however, cheap ones can be bought in the markets here.

Visited the Catholic Convent orphanage to hand over some paper for writing, and met the mother superior, Sister Augustine, a most charming woman. She showed me over the

Sister Augustine at Nui Dat in 1970 with Brigadier W. G. Henderson, the Task Force Commander.

orphanage (900 children in all). The children were all cheerful and fresh-faced. I had a close look at their work, and as far as I could judge they seemed to be one to one and a half years ahead of Australian children. The five- and six-year-olds were doing beautiful writing and sums with totals up to 20. I watched several in action, and their writing was both neat and fast. In honour of my visit, one class sang 'Frère Jacques' in Vietnamese, clapping hands in time as they sang. Had a drink with the mother superior afterwards and we chatted for a little while. It's good to get practice at French again. Took several photos of the children. Lieutenant Fred Greenway (original name Groenewegen), a linguist with our Intelligence Unit, comes here each Sunday to teach English (with Dutch accent) to the orphanage teachers. Fred speaks Dutch, English, German, French, Vietnamese, and is very popular here.

Stopped on the outskirts of Ba Ria to hand in and collect dry cleaning at the Saigon Laundry there and saw Cuc (or Cooc), reputedly the prettiest girl in Ba Ria and also the reason for Saigon Laundry's booming trade — half the Task Force puts clothes in for dry cleaning just to look at Cuc. She certainly is very pretty and her English is reasonable.

Back at Nui Dat I was confronted with the sergeant from last night. This time his attitude was fawning — he wanted a favour done. Fixed him up OK. Also had a few things to say concerning his behaviour last night (of which he had no memory). Told him that I had not reported him to the Acting Commanding Officer of 1st Battalion (Bronx Honner) for coming here to make trouble, and that I had not reported him to the Command Post for drinking in the Sergeants' Mess after gaining permission for an emergency vehicle trip solely to pick up maps, and that my reason for not doing so was that I considered him to be in a condition in which he wasn't responsible for his actions. I also expressed the hope that he be as tolerant of the failings of other people (I know he's not) as I was of him. He is now under a tremendous obligation to us. He has behaved very badly and we are still falling over backwards to help his battalion, so his own position has been seriously weakened and he knows it. Problem solved.

Two conferences this afternoon concerning the Prime Minister's visit next Saturday. Entourage is colossal — 37 reporters alone (even the Wodonga *Sentinel* must be represented), and about seven or eight women. Have seen the menu. Glad I'm not footing the bill. Famous last words! Just who is footing the bill? Have sneaking suspicion it will be the Mess members.

All unit commanders are to ensure that all men know the Prime Minister's name — apparently one or two of the infantry battalions have had some trouble in this regard. When put to the test, the Survey Troop not only knew the PM's name but knew that the Task Force Commander's name was Ron. I noticed that the PM's entourage includes Milton Osborne, whom I knew at primary school and again in national service in 1955. The official list, although this is a military occasion, does not show his military rank, namely lance corporal (retired).

We have to do some map checking in Hoa Long tomorrow, in the same area as where the Viet Cong village chief was caught a couple of weeks ago. Hoa Long is not a safe place at all, so we are taking a machine-gun group with our two-man party. I'm also going and will carry a radio in direct contact with the Task Force HQ Command Post (where Noel is duty officer during the day). Not terribly happy about the radio — the Viet Cong need them badly and it makes a man a good target — but better to be with it than without it.

Tuesday 4 June 1968

Started work in Hoa Long at 08.30 and completed our task by 11.00 without incident. The machine-gun group contained three men, two rifles and one machine gun. They moved ahead of the survey party (Ray Lawson and John Hunter) by up to 100 to 150 metres. The survey party made their own progress. I kept close watch and directed the gun group's movement so as to provide maximum security for the survey party. This task was done in a fairly quiet area of Hoa Long and did not involve a great deal of risk at all. However, more work must be done in the more dangerous areas of the village later on, and a lot of care will be necessary.

Spent afternoon on routine tasks. Excitement in evening: grenade and small arms fire occurring on the Task Force perimeter, but only a very minor attack.

To bed early to get some sleep before getting up to go on the Command Post midnight shift again.

Wednesday 5 June 1968

In Command Post at midnight. Things very quiet. Task Force attacked during night — preliminary bombardment of one grenade, followed by a ground attack by three to four Viet Cong! Brave — or foolish? Anyway, attack failed.

Omitted to mention an item of interest concerning yesterday's job in Hoa Long. Visited ARVN compound before starting so as to let them and the US advisers know what we would be doing. They warned us to watch for Viet Cong, but if we saw armed people in black pyjamas not to shoot them unless they were carrying enemy weapons or unless they shot us up first. Reason was that a South Vietnamese Popular Force group was patrolling through Hoa Long at the time and is ostensibly (one can never be sure) on our side. If they have Bren guns, or American M1 carbines, we mustn't shoot unless shot at, but if they're carrying Russian or Chinese weapons they're definitely Viet Cong and we can have a go at them. All very confusing — very hard to identify black weapons carried by people dressed in black, while waiting for them to shoot first. Anyway we only came across guns and black pyjamas once, and fortunately recognised a Bren gun amongst a large number of unfamiliar weapons. Even more fortunately they didn't shoot at us, either!

Attended to a few routine tasks before going to bed at 10.00. Up at 12.00 for lunch — then more routine work during the afternoon, getting minor jobs out of the way so the monthly operational report can be tackled without interruption.

Heavy rain during afternoon — the first rain for about a week. Wet still has not come.

A darts competition tonight — Survey Troop versus Task Force HQ — a home match for us and held in our reception tent. To our surprise, the Survey team won. I played chess with Mario Apfelbaum, the Survey Troop champion. Had him almost beaten, but made a blunder and got whacked. Quite a lot of interest in chess. Two more games were in progress when I left.

Thursday 6 June 1968

The forward elements of the Task Force returned today, only to discover what the rear elements have been worrying about for the last week, namely the Prime Minister's visit on Saturday.

The Survey Troop has had to do a few jobs for the visit, including the printing of some maps and also a cover for the information handout to the press. The Army Public Relations officer can be a rather stupid man, is rarely sober, and is a pain in the neck to all who have contact with him. Fortunately, I rarely do. We are doing this press handout cover for him, and although four days ago it was promised for today, he has rung twice a day every day to ask if it was ready.

This situation invited certain attention, so we printed double the number of covers required, overprinting one lot with some additional information, namely 'SOUVENIR PROGRAMME' and 'Price 20c' on the front, and a contraceptive advertisement on the back. These overprinted covers are now sitting in the PR officer's 'IN' tray. I doubt that he'll find them as funny as did those officers in the Task Force HQ who have seen them already. With only one and a half days to go until the PM's visit, he will probably fly into a panic as he sees his Great Moment thrown into jeopardy.

Listened to the opening hour or so of the First Test in England this evening transmitted by Radio Australia, but then Radio Peking jammed it with the 'Thoughts of Chairman Mao'. Light but steady rain this evening.

Friday 7 June 1968

Lively day today. The 'Souvenir Programme' joke backfired to some extent because I failed to anticipate all possible responses. Apparently the PR officer noticed 'Price 20c' and said, 'This is wrong. It's a free handout.' Then he saw the condom advertisement and said, 'What's this for?'

One of his staff explained that the printing firm (us) was getting a fee from the contraceptive firm and that this sort of thing was normal for souvenir programmes. He accepted this (!) and then rang me: 'PR officer here. The maps are fine and the covers are fine, but what's that price doing there?'

'Oh, you mean the 20c?'

'Yes.'

'Oh, is it wrong? Should it be 30c?'

'No. There shouldn't be any price. We're giving them away.'

No . . . he must be joking. Best to carry on. 'Well you can still

1st AUSTRALIAN TASK FORCE

SOUVENIR PROGRAMME

INFORMATION BRIEF

Visit by the Honourable J.G.Gorton M.A., M.H.R.,
Prime Minister of Australia

8 June 1968

PRICE : 20¢

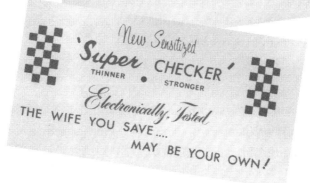

New Sensitized
'*Super* . CHECKER'
THINNER   STRONGER
Electronically Tested
THE WIFE YOU SAVE....
MAY BE YOUR OWN !

give them away, sir. It'll make them feel good, getting something for nothing.'

'Yes. I suppose so. But have you seen the back of the programme?'

'Oh, you mean the commercial?'

'Yes. There are ladies in the party.'

'Well, you could stick some paper over it — but why worry, the product advertised affects women too.'

'Yes, I suppose so. They'll have to do then. But I didn't realise that I'd agreed to this going on it.'

What! Don't tell me he's quite serious? Better keep playing along and see. 'Well, I thought you and Operations staff had decided it. We accept our tasks from Ops.'

'Yes, OK. We'll get them sent out — they'll be OK.'

Never once has he objected to the words 'Souvenir Programme'; he apparently thinks this was agreed to by him. At this stage he began to think that the price and the advertisement were funny and that the 'Souvenir Programme' would be a big success. Meanwhile, I rushed the real covers to his office. He looked at them in surprise, then back at the others and asked, puzzled, 'Well, what are these then? Is this a joke?' This was just too good to be true.

But then came the real panic. He decided that the 'Souvenir Programme' covers were better than the real covers and ordered his staff to prepare them for distribution to the Prime Minister, Mrs Prime Minister and all the press. I thought he was kidding, but Operations staff suddenly realised he was serious (what a man to trust with public relations for the Task Force) and got very edgy: 'Don't do it. Give them all to us till all the press have gone. Take my word for it that the Brigadier will slay you if one copy reaches a civilian.' This stopped him in his tracks abruptly, remarkably so for a man who claims the Duke of Edinburgh and the Queen as close personal friends ('Whenever we're in the same city, Philip and I look each other up and go out drinking together').

By dinner time, everyone in the Task Force HQ Mess seemed somewhat amused. The story had spread rapidly and officers have been hunting desperately for 'Souvenir Programmes', now collectors' items and worth considerably more than 20c. I seem to be something of a minor hero for having perpetrated the best practical joke in the Task Force since the Hoa Long Dance. However, the PR officer is not speaking to me and has reported my insulting behaviour to the Deputy Commander, Colonel Don Dunstan,[1] of the Task Force, who thought the whole business hilarious and now has his own souvenir 'Souvenir Programme'. I didn't mean to cause this humiliation, but he did to a large extent bring it on himself.

Apart from all the above nonsense, today was a fairly quiet day and I got much further with the operational report. Visited the Australian PX, hearing that there were a few toys for sale, but the few toys there were very cheap and nasty indeed.

More rain today. The ground is beginning to remain damp for longer periods.

Saturday 8 June 1968

Prime Minister's visit was a success and nothing went wrong. The PR officer, almost sober, is speaking to me again, and is delighted now at yesterday's effort with the 'Souvenir Programme'. Although under strict orders from Operations staff to keep all copies locked up until all civilians have departed on Sunday, he has already given them away to the press representatives, who of course are thrilled with them — so he is now very grateful to me for providing the opportunity to make a big fellow of himself (until the Brigadier finds out!).

[1] Later to become Chief of the General Staff and Governor of South Australia. — PH

Highlights included a visit by the five ladies in the party to 8 Field Ambulance (the Task Force hospital), this visit being essential because 8 Field Ambulance has one of the two women's toilets in the Task Force. While there, they visited the four patients. Three of the four patients were in hospital with venereal disease so these men were coached during the morning in the symptoms of diseases which could be discussed more readily with ladies; e.g., tonsillitis, damaged knee cartilage, gastroenteritis, suspected stomach ulcer — anything but the embarrassing (for the visitors) truth!

Saw the Prime Minister at lunch in the Officers' Mess but never spoke with him — things were too rushed for him to have a chance of meeting any but the most senior officers. I didn't mind, since I got landed with the most attractive member of his entourage during lunch. This was Major Dien — personal nurse to Madame Ky, wife of the South Vietnamese Prime Minister — a female Vietnamese Army officer with a sensational Vung Tau beach girl figure in a really smart colourful uniform of blue-grey cloth (short, tight skirt and jacket) with red and gold badges. The spectacle of her crossing her legs while seated in the Mess was equalled only by the spectacle of several heads meeting with a ringing clash on the opposite side of the room. She was beautifully groomed and obviously well educated — spoke very good French and English and has lived for more than ten years in France. She is married and has a family of her own, but by the look of her I doubt that she does much work in the home. Altogether the most pleasant company I've had for lunch in a long time. Many of the Professional Lovers in the Officers' Mess would have muscled in and taken her over, but kept their distance because the conversation was in French and I made sure it stayed that way.

Have identified that snake who lives under my bed — a krait, which is rather a deadly snake but, fortunately, not one of the swifter strikers. Obviously, I'd better be pretty careful with him anyway. To bed early — have to be up at midnight.

Sunday 9 June 1968

Up at midnight and into the Command Post. Not much activity at all. To bed at 10.00 and up again for lunch. Had hoped to get afternoon off for odd tasks (e.g., washing) but several minor office jobs were necessary, and all I did was to cut Grant Small's hair and have him cut mine.

Very heavy artillery during evening. Enemy attacked an SAS patrol, which was extracted by helicopter while artillery opened up on enemy. Every gun in 4 Field Regiment was firing — first time I've known this happening — and the din was tremendous.

Monday 10 June 1968

Went with Steve Wood, Bill Black, Ray Lawson and John Hunter on a field trip to Ba Ria, Long Dien, Dat Do, Phuoc Loi, Hoi My, Lo Gom and Lang Phuoc Hai, and back along the same route. This route is very insecure and subject to enemy action, so we did not travel alone, but joined a convoy from the Civil Affairs Unit who were going along it to give civil aid in the form of medical treatment at Hoi My and Lang Phuoc Hai. There has been a lot of shooting in Long Dien recently, and only last night four people were killed in Lang Phuoc Hai during an attack by a Viet Cong platoon. It is considered desirable for us to appear in Lang Phuoc Hai immediately after such action, since our disregard for the Viet Cong will (we hope!) inspire the villagers, whereas if we didn't appear, the Viet Cong would be encouraged.

Fascinating drive through the countryside, mostly dead flat (rice paddy) with rice now beginning to grow, and land turning green at last. Quite attractive view, vaguely reminiscent of Holland — flat green land, straight road along a causeway (or dyke) and green extending to small villages on horizon.

THE ONE-MAN MAP OF BA RIA

Military maps are the product of a team effort by many people with different technical skills. But in the Vietnam War a remarkable achievement occurred, unique in the history of the Survey Corps. One man made a standard military map all by himself. That man was Sapper Bill Black, a field surveyor in the Survey Troop.

This map was of Ba Ria township and environs at scale of 1:10, 000 or 1 centimetre to 100 metres. It was the third or fourth map in a series of town maps that the Survey Troop was steadily producing, but only on an opportunity basis, commencing in 1967 with the map of Lang Phuoc Hai village.

There was no immediate operational demand for these maps. They were produced to cater for a contingency which could arise at any time, and, if never used by the Australian Task Force, they were something useful that could be handed over to the local authorities when we left Vietnam. Also, by producing detailed town maps when opportunity permitted, the troop's highly trained technicians were able to keep their more advanced skills in practice.

After the initial settling-in period in Vietnam in 1966–67, the Survey Troop's field surveyors were those who most often found themselves looking for work. This was how Sapper Bill Black, a field surveyor, came to be doing the field work for the compilation of the Ba Ria map. Using air photos and the existing smaller scale base map, Bill did the necessary field checking on his own and compiled the initial draft of the Baria map.

His map compilation was of such a high standard that not a lot of specialist draughting effort was needed to draw the final map ready for printing. With the draughtsmen all under much pressure to meet deadlines and Bill still short of work, he was given a bit of guidance by the experts and was then left to himself. A good penman and a quick learner, Bill produced a fine map.

Having got the map this far all by himself, it seemed a pity to stop there. Under the supervision of Corporal John Rolfe, Bill now did the photographic processing to make the stencils for the screen printing of a multi-colour map. Finally, under Corporal Mario Apfelbaum's supervision, Bill did all the printing, sheet by sheet, one colour at a time.

The result was a most visually attractive map, and a fitting tribute to the man who had produced it all by himself. Truly a unique achievement!

Passed through Long Dien on the way. The village is badly scarred and has obviously been shot up badly during and since February.

Our first stop was the ARVN post at Dat Do. Children were everwhere in the ARVN post itself — soldiers have married quarters inside the compound, and wives and families have free run of the place. Married quarters consist of one room in a long sand-bagged bunker. Hardly luxurious, but perhaps safer than in the village itself. Children appear to get in the way a lot, but no doubt they disappear very quickly if any shooting starts.

Saw the ARVN lockup for recalcitrant soldiers. If anyone goes absent without leave or gives any trouble they toss him in the lockup for a few days to straighten him out. Just outside the compound is a big ditch about 2 metres by 20 metres, and about half a metre deep with a liquid mess, which is about 50% natural drainage and about 50% sewage from the compound. This liquid is a bilious green and slightly effervescent. The stench is very powerful, even by Vietnamese standards. In this cesspool is a barbed-wire cage about 2 by 2 metres and about 1 metre high. The wrongdoer is stripped naked and shoved in this cage for a few days. Exposed to the sun all day, insects all night, and filth all the time, he cannot lie down or stand up, and must sleep while sitting down and leaning against the barbed-wire sides — hardly very comfortable. The Viet Cong are luckier — they get killed.

Drove on through Dat Do and down to Phuoc Loi and to Hoi My where we stopped for the medical assistance to the villagers to be set up. It took a couple of hours to treat everyone. In the meantime our survey party closely examined all back lanes, to check our maps and amend them where necessary. This gave us a really close look at several out-of-the-way places and was most interesting. Being unusual, our visit attracted a lot of attention, particularly from children — which was reassuring, since the absence of children can often mean the presence of Viet Cong.

Saw a truck containing several corpses coming north from Lang Phuoc Hai — presumably victims of last night's attack.

Went from Hoi My to the ARVN post in the minefield at Lo Gom. Again families living in very primitive style in the tiny compound. Played with several of the children for a while, and played jacks with one child's mother and got beaten. Children played marbles, jacks and with crickets. They kept crickets in a grass-lined tin and got the crickets to fight against each other. Even tiny children of two were doing this with great seriousness. They were pretty good at marbles, firing not with the thumbnail, but with the marble held against the ball of the longest finger pulled back by the other hand. This method yielded plenty of accuracy, and, when the occasion demanded it, tremendous power.

Departed from Lo Gom, almost driving over a grenade held from striking by a hair-fine wire. Noticed the grenade at the edge of the road only as we passed it, and missed it by about 10 centimetres on my side. Rather too close. Drove to Lang Phuoc Hai, a fishing village on the coast. Very densely settled and dirtier than most villages. Rotting fish and human excrement everywhere, especially along the beach. Apparently the communal toilet gets flushed each spring tide and one is due soon. Again we had a good look along all the back lanes. Chief activities of locals were sleeping, talking and weaving fishing nets from white nylon line. The finished fishing net was a most attractive product. Again lots of children — a fair indication that things have settled down, luckily, after last night's Viet Cong attack here. Living space was crowded — noticed one living room full of bed (just boards), table, assorted fowls, one pig, and one Lambretta bus, the whole room being smaller than my tent (5 metres by 5 metres) at Nui Dat.

Visited a local shop. John Hunter bought a woven mat for his tent and we all bought cool drinks (bottled!). Also visited village office to obtain additional information for our map. Although dirty, Lang Phuoc Hai was interesting and we were sorry to leave. The village people were friendly also.

Drove back to Long Dien and Ba Ria. All quiet in Long Dien, the scene of shooting almost daily at the moment. Stopped at Ba Ria for a pineapple drink made from fresh pineapple and crushed ice and syrup, all pulverised in a blender. Product delicious and twice as cheap as Coca-Cola. Back at Nui Dat by 16.30 after an absorbing day in places the Task Force very rarely visits.

Tuesday 11 June 1968

The krait showed up again today, this time amongst Noel's personal gear in our tent, and Noel got a nasty fright. However, the snake had disappeared between the boards by the time he had grabbed his gun. Noel spent the afternoon boarding up likely entrance routes for snakes. The snake doesn't seem to bother about me, so I don't bother about it either, but Rocky Camps in the next tent is dead scared of it and avoids our tent by as great a margin as possible.

There are also some very large spiders about and some giant centipedes, the latter being relatively easy to catch. There are scorpions here too, but I have found none in my tent yet.

Still no rain, despite threatening skies.

Wednesday 12 June 1968

Odd incident last night. An American soldier in the US artillery battery at Nui Dat received a Dear John letter, got drunk and decided to kill himself — no, better still, let the Australians do it. Got fully armed with battle kit, steel helmet, flak jacket, weapon — the lot. Quite illogical to be armed and armoured, but then, he was drunk.

Set off for the perimeter wire, expecting to be challenged and shot. Nothing happened. Went out through perimeter wire. Still nothing. Never mind, the Viet Cong can kill me instead of the Australians.

Went through the scrub to the main road running north to Duc Thanh. Still nothing. Followed road north for a kilometre or so, bringing him very close to an Australian patrol. Again nothing. Walked back to the perimeter, expecting certain death, but still nothing. Entered perimeter safely, now enraged after having walked a few kilometres and still being alive. Decided to drag Task Force Commander out of bed by scruff of neck in middle of night and let him know just what sort of a useless outfit he was running, so headed for Task Force HQ. Missed Commander's hut in the dark and entered the artillery side of the Command Post (Arty Tac) instead. Despite night being quiet, and half the people being asleep, within one or two seconds the artillery staff cleared out. The sight of this battle-hungry figure with murder in his eyes, rifle at the ready and bayonet fixed was enough to cause a mass evacuation through doors, ventilators, louvres etc.

The American then went from this office into the Task Force Command Post. The duty officer was the imperturbable Captain John Mark, who was on the phone at the time. John looked up and said, 'I'm on the phone to II Field Force HQ and it's pretty important. Sit down for a minute,' indicating a chair. Soldier sat down and to John's horror drew his machete from its sheath. John finished call, put down phone and said calmly, 'Now, what's the trouble?' Soldier explained the trouble with the whole Australian Task Force. 'Well,' said John, 'you and I will need to put in a big report on this. We must do something about it. I suggest you get some sleep now while I draft the report and you can come back and check it in the morning. OK?' It was OK by the soldier. 'Righto then. Do you know your way back from here — will you be OK?' Muttering something about being as safe as houses in this goddamn outfit, he set off for bed, and the Arty Tac men returned from the shrubs. As a result of all this our defence is now being tightened.

Mick Rice, our new assistant printer, arrived from Australia yesterday evening. After a disturbed night, artillery being unusually heavy, he went to Dat Do today with a medical team simply to get a look at the country he had just entered. He arrived at Dat Do at the same time as a company of Viet Cong were attacking the town. The medical team waited in the ARVN compound while the ARVN returned mortar fire and prepared to despatch a ground force — but no one wanted to go. It took three hours before the force could be forced, virtually by whip and gun, to go out. They went out, immediately occupied a safe position with good all-round cover, and remained there, unable to see or shoot, until things quietened down.

American advisers were furious and wanted to withdraw all US aid — generators, pumps, troops etc. This certainly was not an impressive performance, and it's no wonder the Americans sometimes get tired of giving mountains of aid and losing their own lives for people who so willingly take the easiest way out, even if it involves the proverbial sale of the proverbial grandmother. The only reason that civil aid is remaining is that the Viet Cong want it stopped. Altogether it was a very lively first day for Mick Rice. He said very little about it when he got back, no doubt fearful that we 'veterans' would dismiss it all as being quite normal — which it wasn't: the Survey Troop doesn't normally get involved in fights with the Viet Cong.

A couple of Intelligence bulletins make it apparent today that the Viet Cong are preparing for a very heavy six-month harassment of South Vietnamese civilians and Allied forces. Saigon is to be the chief target, and 20 battalions are already in position to strike from different directions at different times. Locally, Ba Ria is a prime target. Yesterday, Saigon post office received rockets, and this morning Tan Son Nhut airport received the same. Rocket attacks are now being made in daylight hours, despite the fact that it's harder for the VC to escape in daylight. Ba Ria has been mortared twice in the last few days also. The Viet Cong aim is to demonstrate to the world that they control the country, this being considered important for the duration of the Paris peace talks (which will probably last into 1969) and until the US presidential election in November '68. So there will be continuous strikes on Saigon and provincial capitals, and the Viet Cong and North Vietnamese Army together definitely have the capacity to do this.

Heard today that every single one of the villages we worked in the day before yesterday (Phuoc Loi, Hoi My, Lo Gom, Lang Phuoc Hai) was attacked by the Viet Cong within the next 24 hours. And yet these places looked so peaceful and quiet when we were there (only a few hours after the previous attack on Lang Phuoc Hai). This is alarming because we still have work to do soon in Hoa Long, Long Dien and Dat Do, and one of these days a visit by us could well coincide with a VC attack. Only today an Australian vehicle was shot at (again!) while passing through Hoa Long.

Urgent need for some special Intelligence maps, so I must go to Long Binh tomorrow morning.

Thursday 13 June 1968

Helicopter trip to Long Binh. Noel heading south for five days' leave at Vung Tau, well earned after his efforts with the Task Force HQ, some of the time being under enemy fire.

The usual fascinating flight of 25 minutes. Country now greener from the rain already received. Warmly welcomed by Joel Cain and Skip Skoglund at 66 Company. Hospitality always magnificent there. Got all the maps and information I was after, and visited Mapping and Intelligence at US Army Engineer Command Vietnam a couple of miles away. Also visited the PX and bought a Remington

Streamliner typewriter for Ken Lyons, commanding elements of the Survey Troop back at Randwick, at cost of about $37. From the mapping point of view, this was a very useful day indeed.

Played a strenuous game of volleyball in the evening for a full hour with only four men on each side, and spent evening with several of the American officers, one of whom was a very attractive Nursing Corps captain. It was entertaining to watch two of the party competing for her attentions. We were all in Joel Cain's room, which he has just done up and decorated. Another officer who had heard of the renovations dropped in to have a look. His gaze slowly swept the room, most impressed, then he noticed the girl (the first one ever seen in 66 Company), his jaw dropped and he stared in stunned shock for about five to ten seconds while everyone else was silent also. Then he recovered himself and his jaw, and finished his scan of the room. He looked at Joel, then at the girl, and then said to Joel in solemn awe, 'You *do* have a lovely room!' and left, still dazed. He certainly meant what he said.

Friday 14 June 1968

Awoke feeling fitter than did most others — sample comment being, 'Ah feel as if de whole Chinese Army has walked frew ma mouf — and barefoot, too!' Had a close look at the technical side of reproduction at 66 Company and hope that it may be possible to introduce some innovations (e.g., scribing[2]) to 1 Topographical Survey Troop, but plenty of consideration is needed.

Could not get a space on the US helicopter to Nui Dat, so went by road to Tan Son Nhut to catch the Australian Caribou plane.

[2] Hand engraving an image printed on an emulsion coating on a transparent sheet (thus directly creating a negative transparent image and eliminating a photographic process). — JB

Many soldiers all along the route — first time I have seen them actually on the ground in fire positions. Still, no action occurred and we reached Tan Son Nhut safely. Had some trouble overtaking other vehicles — there would always be another vehicle overtaking us at the wrong moment. Situation remedied by passenger signalling with an American submachine carbine (the Grease Gun) at arm's length. Those behind got the message and stayed back.

An uneventful flight to Nui Dat. On landing a US lieutenant on board said to me (the only passenger getting off): 'Where are we?'

'1st Australian Task Force, Nui Dat.'

'Is this an Australian camp?'

'Yes, can't you see the kangaroos?' There were several vehicles in sight bearing the normal red kangaroo marking.

'WHAT! Say! Where are they?'

'Over there under the rubber trees — they're everywhere!'

'You guys bring 'em with you?'

'Yes. Never travel anywhere without them.'

'Say! This is great! Ah never thought ah'd see kangaroos here!'

My last view of the plane showed the officer with his nose flattened against the window looking out for 'roos.

Back at Survey Troop, the 'IN' tray high, including letter from the Director of Survey. Apparently Grant Small is not acceptable as an officer, since this would be unfair to others who've been rejected — and so the situation continues. This is terribly disappointing, both to Grant and myself. The army will probably lose him now. I cannot see why we don't stop the rot somewhere, instead of using past blunders as a justification for perpetrating more.

Heavy rain tonight. Grass growing and ground getting damp now.

Saturday 15 June 1968

More rain. Busy day today. Spent it catching up on backlog.

Sunday 16 June 1968

Many minor jobs to attend to. Several heavy rainstorms. Washing nearly dry just as each storm struck. Seems that the wet is here at last.

Monday 17 June 1968

Flat out today until 22.00 trying to get a whole stack of miscellaneous tasks out of the way. Made good progress but plenty more still left to do. Violent storm at 18.00 — easily the heaviest yet, and it lasted for several hours. Torrents of water everywhere and tents full of refugee insect and reptile life.

SAS had another successful action day today. Their small two- and three-man patrols have killed over 20 Viet Cong in the past five days from only three contacts — more than the entire rest of the Task Force has achieved in the past three weeks. SAS have a deservedly excellent reputation here but, of course, get no publicity at all since this would increase the VC price on their heads and would possibly reduce their effectiveness.

Rain so heavy that I had a shower in it outside my tent rather than get towel drenched while running to the shower block. Most of the other chaps did the same.

Tuesday 18 June 1968

Awakened early by earth shaking from bombs dropping. Air strike by B-52 bombers going on a few miles away on a Viet Cong base camp. It seemed as though the falling of these shattering bombs would never stop. Strange sensation at this distance — very little noise at all, but heavy concussion could be felt.

Day hot and humid. Storm in afternoon. Water everywhere, mainly from last night's heavy storm.

Summoned by my immediate boss, the GSO2 Operations, an unpredictable man and not easy to work for. He produced a crude sketch on tracing paper, heavily folded and crumpled. He then pulled a crumpled ball of tracing paper out of his waste bin and untangled it. I recognised the latter as the Survey Troop's last printing job for Operations.

'Look at this. These don't remotely fit.' (Small wonder, a crumpled sheet of tracing paper never resumes its original dimensions.)

'Of course they don't. You don't seriously expect them to, do you?'

'Yes. It's your job to see that they do.'

'Now, wait a minute . . .' and I explained the problem.

'OK, OK, but look here, the shape is different.'

I agreed, but explained that the original was so badly drawn that its register marks misfitted by up to 500 metres, and pointed out that we had redrawn lines to conform to the obvious natural features in the vicinity.

'You have no right to assume that! Men's lives depend on the position of that line! See that signature on the trace? That means it's 100% correct, so don't you go changing it!'

'Sir, the decision to change it was made by your staff, not by me.'

'Well, they were wrong. Now here's another job. Go and do it properly.'

I took it away and fitted the trace to the map. Same trouble as before. The crude sketch wouldn't fit; it seemed obvious that several lines belonged elsewhere to conform to obvious natural features. So back to the GSO2 Ops.

'Sir, I know the signature means that this is 100% correct, but don't you think there is a possibility that this line should go there, not here?'

'Of course, any fool could see that!'

'OK then, how about this line, and this, and this?'

'Let's see, these should go there and there and there, and you can follow the trace for the rest.'

'How about this one here? Surely there isn't a barbed-wire entanglement running across the middle of Bien Hoa airfield?'

'God, no, let's shift it off.' Seizes pen and alters line with heavy fist. (Men's lives depend on this!)

Generally, though, with a few exceptions, the officers in the Task Force HQ are both competent and always willing to help. I'm a little unfortunate that my immediate boss (who is now writing my confidential report on which my promotion depends) is somewhat erratic, but this sort of thing does occasionally happen and must be taken in one's stride. My main concern at the moment is to see if anything can be done as regards Grant Small's commission. I think he will leave the army next January, now that he is not acceptable as an officer, rather than having to bite his nails for years and then accept a quartermaster's commission. He wants a direct commission now, or nothing, and in my opinion and Major Stedman's (his former boss), he is strongly deserving of one. He will be a great loss if he leaves.[3] I must write again to the Director of Survey, but doubt that it'll achieve much.

[3] The Survey Corps declined to commission Grant Small. He left the Army shortly afterwards and prospered in his new career in property and development. The Army did him a good turn! — JB

To bed early to get a couple of hours' sleep before the midnight shift in the Command Post. Night humid, bed very wet with perspiration by midnight.

Wednesday 19 June 1968

Sky clear at midnight but air still very humid. Must be another storm just around the corner. Very little action occurring, so the midnight to 08.00 shift was quiet. To bed at 09.30 and up at lunch at 12.00. Afternoon busy with minor tasks. Humidity very high but no rain.

Thursday 20 June 1968

Kept busy all day with many minor tasks and one rush job. Again no rain despite frequent threats.

Friday 21 — Saturday 22 June 1968

Many routine tasks to get well ahead on before going to Hong Kong on leave next Tuesday. Amenities conference on Friday. The formal application to invite Sandra Nelson to entertain Australian troops has been equally formally rejected. Have been told that General MacDonald (Commander Australian Forces Vietnam) not amused. Met General MacDonald later same day in connection with mapping and found him most affable, despite his wide reputation for ferocity, so must assume lack of amusement over Sandra Nelson to be at a much lower level.

Survey Troop received a letter from a girl from Williamstown, Victoria, wanting a 'Digger in Vietnam' to write to her. 'He must be attractive, single and from Victoria. My statistics are bust 40 inches, waist 26 inches, hips 41 inches, and I enclose a photograph.' Photo was of a moderately attractive girl in her late teens. Letter was read out on parade. Caused much amusement but no takers.

Heavy rainstorm in late afternoon continued into evening. Muddy torrents and lakes everywhere.

Sunday 23 June 1968

Duty officer in Command Post from 16.00 until midnight. Several minor incidents, enough to keep me constantly busy. The GSO2 Ops came in several times (as expected, this being my first time on this shift) to give me a hard time, but his attempts were fairly half-hearted (he has given most others a really torrid time) and all he did on his final visit was to raid the supper.

1st Battalion surrounded by moving lights on all sides — probably Viet Cong to the north, and Australian drunks homeward bound to the south, east and west. Ordered the apprehension of all the latter and the observation of the former.

A New Zealand gunner blew his brains out this afternoon. So many accidents occur on Saturday nights and Sundays that it's obviously due to grog. (The party habit is a hard one to kick, even though this is a seven-day-a-week war.) Major James, Officer Commanding 8 Field Ambulance here, also states this. He is a remarkable man. He is a doctor, has no feet and has the Military Cross. He was originally an infantry officer and a Royal Military College graduate. In Korea he won the Military Cross and had his feet blown off in the same action, and was invalided out of the Army. He then studied medicine and rejoined the Army as a doctor, now with artificial feet and able to walk without any limp at all. He is a great inspiration to all those soldiers here who get badly wounded. Being an excellent doctor and a very likable man as well, he is a tremendous asset to the Task Force.

Monday 24 June 1968

Woken by the Psychological Operations voice aircraft warning the population in Vietnamese of the insecticide mission about to be flown. As the voice aircraft flew over the Australian Task Force, it changed its tune to 'Tie Me Kangaroo Down, Sport' and then to 'Puff, the Magic Dragon'. The latter had an ominous ring to it, since Puff the Magic Dragon is an alternative nickname for Spooky, the fearsome DC-3 (or C-47) bristling with mini-guns.

Spent day finalising minor matters before leaving for Hong Kong tomorrow. Got packed during evening, problem being to restrict everything to an absolute minimum so as to leave maximum space for loot on return trip.

Heavy rain in afternoon.

Tuesday 25 June 1968

Up early at 05.30 and down to cash office to draw US currency and then to airfield. Travelled to Saigon in a USAF C-123 — even less comfortable for passengers than a Caribou. Watched another C-123 take off immediately before ours. It ran off the end of the strip but got airborne before it hit the barbed wire just beyond. Ours took off OK. As engines hit full power, a blast of noise and wind and a stinging handful of gravel hit me in the back of neck. Windowpane missing, so had most interesting flight with head out of window only 2 metres from starboard propeller. Fascinating to take off with head in the wind as plane charged along strip.

Country now quite wet and green. Bomb craters everywhere, mostly full of water. Rough landing. Bounced high, regained control of flight and had a more successful second attempt (although roof fitting then fell off). Used about 3 kilometres of strip before we landed properly, but still had 1 kilometre to spare, thanks to the size of Tan Son Nhut. Those of us going on leave then waited for three hours at the RAAF shack at Tan Son Nhut. No chairs — just dirt outside and concrete inside. Then to the US transit camp, Camp Alpha (Stalag Alfa would be a better name, since it is devoid of amenities and people so often wait there for hours on end). Sweating humanity heaped everywhere. Finally to airstrip at 16.00 to catch Pan Am charter plane to Hong Kong.

Quick flight to Hong Kong of only one and three-quarter hours. On the plane were more than 100 servicemen, mainly US Army. Much disappointment all round at appearance of air hostesses, quite the most unattractive lot I've ever seen. Perhaps Pan Am considers that servicemen on R&R are their least fussy clients and can therefore be given the worst. Maybe so, but there is surely a limit. Sagging stockings, double chins, scruffy hair, but at least the meal was good. Landed with a wallop at Kai Tak — roughest landing I've ever experienced in a big aircraft — aircraft slewed across strip but soon settled down. Customs officer climbed aboard and said coldly in very English English, 'This is your last chance to hand in any prohibited items. As you leave the plane the amnesty ends. You will be searched in the customs office. If you have any prohibited items in your possession there, you will be arrested.' We went through customs. Sergeants and above walked straight through. Corporals and below were searched very closely. No arrests. Bus to R&R centre for a very good briefing — many pitfalls were mentioned. 'Don't let her health problem become yours . . .' 'Running out of money is not confined to sergeants and below . . .' etc.

Finally to Hotel Imperial, Kowloon, by 21.00. Had shower, first decent one for about six months, got changed into civilian clothes, also for first time in six months, shoes feeling strangely light on the feet. Paid hotel bill in advance and went out for walk in streets. Lights bright and garish. Shops all along Nathan Road — main and minor side streets full of bars. When coming to hotel from R&R centre, girls in bright mini-skirts had come running from bars to edge of road, squealing and blowing kisses to bus and hurling cards through bus window. Cards all have maps on back. The Horse Shoe (Whore's Shoe?) Bar card also indicates a suitable hotel and has been endorsed by the girl who threw that card. Walked along Mody, Cameron and Carnarvon Roads, lights ablaze, girls everywhere, touts everywhere trying to sell everything — mainly girls, pornographic films, suits and shirts. However, none were objectionable — a vast improvement on Port Said! Stopped at a news-stand to buy a magazine (July's *Playboy*, available in Hong Kong on 25 June!). The bookseller immediately offered to provide a girl.

'No thanks.'

'Sir, you don't understand. This is very respectable place. Only very high-class call girls. Guaranteed clean. Very beautiful. Cost HK$150 (A$22) for short time, HK$250 (A$36) for all night.'

'No thanks.'

'Sir, this is very high-class place. You just come and see for yourself. No entrance fee.'

'OK, I'll have a look. Pay nothing if I don't like. Understood?'

'Yes, sir. This way please.'

I followed the man along road and into doorway with bright sign, 'Mambo Room Guest House', outside. Up stairs and into foyer,

complete with desk and receptionist, a youth of perhaps 16. Along corridor and into room, one of several. Room was obviously designed for purpose to which it is put. Bed surrounded by mirrored walls on three sides. Furniture as shown, plus an air conditioner. Wall-to-wall carpet; pictures on walls. Kleenex dispensers near bed, one pink, one blue. Obviously much trouble had gone into furnishing rooms. Girl, dressed in street clothes, looked very clean, neat and attractive.

Said, 'No thanks,' and price came down to HK$100 (A$15) immediately. Departed at this stage and was given a card 'to pass onto a friend'.

Was immediately propositioned by a tout offering girls for only HK$25 (A$3.50), this being the starting price! This must really be worth seeing! Followed man down alleyways, over garbage cans, up stairs to first floor of a grimy building and into a private apartment. A family of about eight grubby people sat around a tiny table eating soup and rice, children and cats eating off floor. Tout spoke in Chinese. Two young and untidy girls looked up from soup, nodded, smiled briefly and returned to soup.

Said, 'No thanks,' and prepared to depart.

'I take you to much better place.'

'OK.' Down stairs, along alley to another road, and up more stairs to another private apartment, this one a little larger than the last. Bunks all around the wall of the one main room, roughly screened by curtains. Several girls present. Soup again. One girl was really pretty and well dressed. Others distinctly rough. At this stage came a disturbance behind curtains and two people emerged: a drunken American pulling up trousers and a girl, both arguing. The girl spoke hardly any English and the American was too drunk to be coherent, so the argument was somewhat confused. Apparently the American considered that the girl had not rendered the service required and was demanding his money back. Girl was refusing. The tout and a couple of girls moved closer to join in. Rather than risk involvement in a brawl in a Chinese brothel, I left at this stage.

No sooner back on street than was offered a blue movie show by another tout. Price cheap, so accepted offer after beating it down further. More alleyways, more garbage cans, more stairs, another private apartment. Through to back room to join audience of one Chinese and two Indians watching flickering, scratched movies projected onto a blue (!) wall. Watched four 10-minute reels totally devoid of plot, and then departed. Films were amusing rather than erotic. By now it was midnight so went back to hotel.

Wednesday 26 June 1968

Busy day shopping. Visited a recommended tailor for measurement for two sports coats, one pair of shorts, one pair of shoes. Salesman turned out to be a Melbourne Technical College student of same time as myself. Within an hour, I had met another ex-Melbourne Tech student, who recognised me in the street as Australian. Changed money at bank. Bank door patrolled by amiable Oriental giant with large shotgun and very short barrel slung over shoulder.

Went to the modern shopping centre in the Kowloon Ocean Terminal and was most impressed. Met Grant Small there and we had lunch together. He is staying with his wife (arriving from Australia tonight) at the Mandarin Hotel in Hong Kong. Found an exotic food and wine shop. Bought a Suchard raisin au cointreau chocolate block, and two miniature liqueurs — Bols Blackberry and Marie Brizard Mandarine. The chocolate didn't last long. Surprised by poor quality of toys. Looked for something for David and Peter, but the only good toys I saw were Toltoys, made in Australia.

Caught Star Ferry (one every few minutes) across to Hong Kong Island, visited Portuguese Consulate and handed in passport for a Macau visa. Not supposed to go to Macau,[4] but I think I can keep out of trouble. Went to China Fleet Club and visited US Navy Purchasing Branch there. Lots of luxury goods at very reasonable prices: cameras, sound equipment, typewriters, perfume, furs, silver, clothing etc, all most plentiful. Returned by ferry to Kowloon. Did further hunting for toys but little luck.

Had dinner in hotel — lovely five-course meal for HK$8 (A$1.20). Seated at adjacent table were two Australians and two Hong Kong harlots. From conversation overheard, the Australians were an infantry machine-gun group. The two men were more interested in drinking and swapping war yarns with each other than in the girls, much to the girls' annoyance.

'Stop drinking or you be no good in bed!'

'Don't you worry, beautiful. I'm built like an RPG-7.'

'Please, what is RPG-7?'

'It's a big Chinese rocket bomb. If it hit you in the box, you make no more money!'

The machine-gunners and the girls remind me of the tale of the USAF sergeant on R&R leave in Bangkok recently, told to me by a Survey Troop man there at the same time. The sergeant left his Bangkok hotel once during his five days there, and that was to walk 200 metres to buy cigarettes. On arrival he chartered a taxi for his whole five days' leave, the taxi man's sole job being to produce two girls twice a day for the whole five days. The sergeant would select one each time, and then select another about 12 hours later, and so

[4] Macau was under Chinese communist influence, and banned at that time for Americans. Australians were using the US forces R&R Leave system, which banned travel to Macau and purchase of any goods of Chinese origin. — PH

on. Actually, it would seem that perhaps 5 to 10% of all men on R&R spend their leave this way. On second thoughts, perhaps 20 to 30% is nearer the mark. I have noticed that it is rare for anyone returning from five days in Hong Kong, Bangkok or Taipei to be capable of any work on their first day back. Hong Kong is now pushing Vung Tau hard for being the major source of venereal disease casualties.

Took stock of expenditure so far and planned to purchase a train for David. Quiet evening tonight in contrast to last night's explorations.

Thursday 27 June 1968

Another busy shopping day. Delightful just to window shop, especially in ivory shops, with their elaborate and intricate chess sets, some of which cost up to A$1000. Most ivory looked unattractive (to me) as domestic ornaments, but were interesting to study closely in a shop.

Visited the Scandinavian shop and had a look at the many lovely products there. Although many famous houses were represented, and there were several items from Denmark's Den Permanente, there was very little in the way of furniture (chairs, lamps etc) for which the Scandinavian nations are justly famous. Nevertheless, the ceramics, stainless steel, glassware and jewellery really were a treat for the eyes. The shop is run by a middle-aged Swedish lady — very talkative (even *I* could hardly get a word in edgewise!) and full of information. Learnt quite a bit from her including the 'inside story' of how Georg Jensen gained his royal appointment in Denmark (through money and family influence!).

Visited tailor for first fitting of clothing. Met Grant and Beth Small there, Grant also there for fitting of clothing. Went with them to the China Fleet Club. Bought a mink shoulder cape for Yvonne, having already priced others elsewhere in Kowloon. We then went back to the Mandarin Hotel to view the sumptuous splendour in which Grant and Beth are now living. All doormen are huge turbaned, red-jacketed Indians. Lobby full of rich Americans. Luxury shops and showcases (including Georg Jensen!) everywhere. Grant and Beth's room luxurious.

Returned to Kowloon for dinner at own hotel. Beautiful view over whole harbour and Hong Kong city as sun was setting and lights coming out. Very nice meal in lovely surroundings. Could even see the cable tram running up and down the Peak. Lights everywhere. Even the water lit by reflection of the many small craft on it.

Friday 28 June 1968

The most wonderful day for a long, long time. Went across harbour early to Hong Kong Island. Picked up visa from Portuguese Consulate and camera (having been cleaned) from China Fleet Club, and headed for wharf to catch the hydrofoil ferry to Macau. Was expecting trouble here, since there is a lot of fuss at the moment over the hydrofoil services and a strike was threatened today. Found that there are two services, one Hong Kong-owned — blue and white ships flying the Union Jack; the other owned by Macau Casino — red ships, flying no flags but bearing Portuguese names (*Guia*, *Penha* etc). The blue ships are striking and the red ships are running. Bought ticket and went aboard the hidroplanador *Guia*, a sleek red vessel, for my first ride by hydrofoil, having gone through the Hong Kong emigration formalities with no hitch. I was the only European aboard the vessel. I noticed one Japanese, and everyone else seemed Chinese. The ship could carry about 100 passengers but barely 20 seats were filled.

Slow run to edge of harbour then full power on, resulting in a sensation not unlike an aircraft taking off, and we streaked westward for one and a quarter hours over about 40 or so miles of water, passing many lovely islands on the way. Weather fine and water blue. Water quickly became brown as we crossed the mouth of the Pearl River and headed for Macau. Landed, went through customs and started to walk to the main town centre. Taxis stopped everywhere offering lifts. 'No thanks, I like walking.'

'Impossible. It takes one hour to walk there.'

'No thanks.'

Only took 25 to 30 minutes to walk the one and a half miles to the town centre and a delightful exercise it was. Walked along the waterfront promenade to the edge of the town and then headed into the residential area. Lisbon all over again but this time a quiet, tidy, restful Lisbon. Lovely trees and small parks, graceful and stately old Portuguese buildings, many in excellent condition. An atmosphere of complete quiet and tranquillity. People quiet but friendly. Vast change after the bustle of Hong Kong to find such a placid and attractive town. On edge of city area, more Portuguese-style buildings became apparent. To be surrounded by such graceful and aged charm and tranquillity was a delightful experience, especially following on so soon after the guns and squalor of Vietnam. Macau, with its sleepy grace, seemed the proverbial Land of the Lotus Eaters in comparison, yet efficiency seemed to lie just beneath the surface — perhaps due to Communist Chinese influence. Macau certainly looked better organised than Lisbon, the latter being inefficient and chaotic to a marked degree.

Strolled down the main street (Avenida de Almeida Ribeiro), into the city centre. Atmosphere immediately became Oriental and busy, Chinese characters and bright colours everywhere in this narrow colonnaded street. Shops were mainly jewellers — gold everywhere. But times are not as good as they once were. Twice as I entered shops, youths sprang to fuse panels to switch on display-case lights. Many shops but few customers in the jewellers' shops. Tourists most conspicuous by their absence. I saw *none* all the time I was in Macau.

Wandered into the main store in the Avenida de Almeida Ribeiro and did some shopping. This shop was the Companhia de Produtos e Produções Especials da China, and things were very cheap. Bought a couple of beautifully cut wooden fans inlaid with ivory for Yvonne and Beth Small (who's taking Yvonne's fur to Australia for her). The fans, made of sandalwood, have a delicious and fragrant scent. Also bought a record of songs in praise of Chairman Mao Tse-Tung sung by the Peasants' Amateur Cultural Chorus of Ho Pei province, together with the words (in Chinese) for sing-along sessions. Record cost A$0.60, and fans A$2 each. Same fans cost A$7 in Hong Kong, and goodness knows how much more in Australia.

Came to end of the Avenida de Almeida Ribeiro and had a look at the casino, a vivid and beautifully carved structure floating in the bay. Did not enter, but admired its ornate carving from the bank. Glimpses through door showed its interior to be opulently furnished. Walked through back streets and came to the main post office. Bought postcards nearby and despatched several. The stamps were beautiful.

Macau Casino, afloat in harbour.

Wandered further through cobbled and stone-paved back streets, much like Lisbon's but cleaner, past some old churches and other graceful old buildings, then down to the waterfront immediately south of the post office and watched the children playing under the shady trees along the promenade. Nearby was a most attractive statue marked 'Jorge Alvarez', in honour of the founder of the colony in 1513.

Walked along promenade to headland and viewed the mighty Casino de Lisboa, a huge and elaborate cylindrical building under construction. Nothing has been done on this project for some months.

Following political troubles and disturbances in Macau during the past two years, the tourist flow has dwindled desperately and construction of a super casino no longer seems a wise investment.

Visited the Communist Party bookshop and bought some posters, badges and a copy of the *Sayings of Chairman Mao* (with a vivid red plastic cover, in English — foreigners gladly catered for), all for A$0.40. Everyone in the shop was most courteous and friendly. Walked back along the promenade to the hidroplanadores to catch the boat back to Hong Kong. Of course, my visit was too short to gain anything but a superficial impression, and one or two things did indicate that much lies beneath Macau's sleepy façade; however, I found the graceful charm and tranquil atmosphere in Macau delightful — truly a fascinating little outpost of Europe in the heart of Asia.

Travelled again on the *Guia* and went back to Hong Kong, although reluctant to leave Macau. Again, no other European passengers on the *Guia*. Could not recall having seen any Europeans on Macau, save for one or two soldiers near the San Francesco Barracks, who looked Portuguese but in smarter uniforms than those of the Portuguese Army. The barracks was a large white-painted stone structure and looked most impressive. Did see several dark-skinned people looking much like Portuguese-Africans (from Angola, Mozambique etc). English not much spoken on Macau; French not at all; Portuguese only a little. However, English plus a little Portuguese plus use of pen proved adequate for all situations. Met a Dutch-speaking Indonesian at one stage. Swift trip back across the Pearl River mouth to Hong Kong. Very sorry to leave after such a lovely day.

Found out later that Macau has indeed fallen on hard times. Few tourists go there and Hong Kong residents almost never go there — too dangerous for them. Macau is a gateway for Chinese products to the outside world, but the market seems to be decreasing. Meanwhile, bodies are being washed up on the shores of Hong Kong and the New Territories, having come down the Pearl River from Canton. Something pretty ghastly is going on in Canton, but nobody knows what, and China isn't talking.[5]

Saturday 29 June 1968

Finished shopping. Foolish to deny that I had a wonderful time in the Märklin shop, where I bought model train for the family. Did shopping for several other people in Vietnam.

Caught Peak tram to the Peak. Lovely view all over Kowloon and Hong Kong. Took a few photos, my first in Hong Kong, although I took photos everywhere in Macau yesterday in an attempt to record its very real charm.

Had dinner with Grant and Beth Small, watching the lights come on all over Hong Kong Island, then packed up ready to leave in the morning after four wonderful days in a clean and attractive environment. Macau already seems like a dream.

Sunday 30 June 1968

Up at 05.30, away from hotel at 06.30, on plane by 07.30, and back to Saigon (ugh!) before 09.30. Had to declare to US officials that I carried no items of Communist Chinese origin. No inspection, fortunately. Spent day in the ghastly Camp Alpha before catching late afternoon Caribou plane to Nui Dat. Nui Dat full of the din of artillery as usual. Oh, for the peace of Macau!

[5] This was at the time of the Cultural Revolution. — PH

JULY

AUSTRALIAN MILITARY FORCES

AAB—71A
Reprinted Dec, 1964

RECORD BOOK

CONTAINING 96 PAGES

RULED FEINT

The cordon-and-search operation was a routine procedure for troops in Vietnam. It involved the coordination of several units, and security was vital. Stage one required infantry troops to surround a village at night preventing anyone moving in or out. First thing in the morning, a 'voice aircraft' would fly over a village, instructing villagers to take what they needed for the day and proceed to a checkpoint at one end of the village. Once there, villagers would receive health checks, medical and dental treatment, food and drink, shelter and general care for the day. Importantly, they were also vetted for Viet Cong association.

Once the village was cleared of people, a search party would move in to search the village for Viet Cong in hiding, stores, caches of arms, tunnels etc, with the security cordon remaining around the perimeter of the village the whole time. When the search was over, the cordon would be dismantled and everyone would go home.

Sometimes things didn't go as planned.

PAUL HAM

★

A really major blunder today . . . the voice aircraft
made its flight today — a day too soon — thus
giving the whole show away.

★

Monday 1 July 1968

Day spent picking up the threads of the job at Nui Dat.

Tuesday 2 July 1968

Up early and off to Long Binh by helicopter for liaison visit on many matters that have cropped up. Attended a formal dinner in the evening in honour of the changeover of the Engineer Group commander. Dinner was pleasant, brief, and the food excellent. Mess still recovering from the ravages of a recent visit by 1 Field Squadron, Royal Australian Engineers. Serves them right for hosting such a wild bunch. However, things were quiet tonight with no one wanting to play rugby indoors.

Wednesday 3 July 1968

Went to Tan Son Nhut for conference with US Army Engineer Mapping and Intelligence, the ARVN Topographic Company, and the National Geographic Service (NGS) of Vietnam. Many matters pertinent to Australia were discussed and several other items of interest were raised. NGS has fallen on hard times. All their technicians are being drafted into the army (as infantry), so they're running out of surveyors and photogrammetrists. Also, I feel that the Americans are pushing more sophisticated equipment onto them than they can use, for example, $60,000 worth of Wild A7.[1] NGS needs stacks of advice and technical assistance to get A7 aero-triangulation work started from scratch. This is right in my own field, although I've done none since 1965, but I will (I hope!) have left Vietnam long before the A7 arrives and their big problems really begin. The Americans have also been pushing Tellurometers and Wild T3 theodolites onto NGS. Two T3 theodolites have given trouble (not sure what, but it sounds as though they've been misused). Action: nothing, except to sit down and wait nine months for the annual visit of the Wild mechanic! Two Tellurometers have given trouble (no break in the cathode ray tube circle). Action: nothing, except to wait for the next conference and ask the Australians to fix it for them. I know they're up against it, but this lack of initiative bodes ill for the future, and I grieve for the lovely A7 to go the same way in about a year's time.

Visited the Mapping, Charting and Geodesy Branch in Military Assistance Command, Vietnam (MACV), the overall military command in the country at Tan Son Nhut and went back to Long Binh after lunch. No need to visit the PX, having just returned from Hong Kong, the biggest PX of them all. Heavy rain late in the afternoon. Quiet evening and to bed early.

[1] A Wild A7 stereoplotter (measuring 8 cubic metres) enables an operator to create maps from photographs, and needs strict temperature and humidity control to preserve accuracy. Theodolites and Tellurometers, field survey instruments, use optical and electronic methods respectively. — JB

Thursday 4 July 1968

Up early to travel by road to Tan Son Nhut to catch plane to Nui Dat. Drove through Saigon for third time in two days. Noisy and dirty as usual. Normal garbage disposal system is to dump refuse in street for collection by truck at some future date. Garbage collection has suffered badly during Saigon's current and past troubles. Result: garbage piles are up to 3 to 4 feet high and up to 50 or 60 feet long. With stagnant slush all round, it can be smelt a long way away. Dogs scavenge, children play, and adults pick through it. In many cases, blocks of several houses are cut off from the street by these huge piles of domestic waste. However, amidst the squalid buildings the garbage does not attract overmuch attention. Some parts of Saigon city that I have seen are attractive, but most of the city has suffered cruelly from the ravages of war, administrative inefficiency, corruption and complete apathy. This situation seems to be deteriorating further as the NVA and Viet Cong pressure on Saigon intensifies.

Flew back to Nui Dat. Did a few minor jobs and then went by Sioux helicopter to do an aerial reconnaissance over Long Dien, in order to provide evidence at a court martial tomorrow concerning the completeness of a map. This helicopter was armed with grenades and two M60 machine guns. Long Dien is still dangerous and the pilot wouldn't go there until one inoperative gun had been fixed. Finally took off. Did the job in only half an hour. A most interesting flight there and back — the Sioux with its clear bubble and no doors afforded such a lovely view of everything. Map correct.

Friday 5 July 1968

By plane to Vung Tau in morning for court martial. Spent day in court martial building waiting to give evidence but was not called. The accused faced five charges. I am required for evidence on the third charge. The first charge took all day today — the offence being absurdly trivial, namely not tidying his tent when told to do so. Still, I had a welcome rest while waiting, and as usual at Vung Tau, stayed at 1 Australian Field Hospital and enjoyed the company very much.

Saturday 6 July 1968

Back to the court martial building to wait again. Called at 10.00. My evidence — that I had checked a map and that it was complete — took barely five minutes to give. Then waited until 15.00 to catch a plane back to Nui Dat, having spent two days plus the aerial reconnaissance on Thursday to present this evidence. Meanwhile, the Survey Troop struggles on with Noel in the Command Post, Spike Jones ill, and Grant Small still on leave.

SAS had an enemy contact yesterday — a four-man SAS patrol killed 14 Viet Cong and suffered no casualties. Also last night an American vehicle containing an adviser, four US civilians and a Vietnamese girl proceeding south along Route 15 from Bien Hoa towards Ba Ria was stopped by the ARVN outpost and advised for good of health not to proceed further but continued on. This morning their shot-up vehicle was found. All occupants had disappeared.

Sunday 7 – Monday 8 July 1968

Two busy days catching up on backlog of tasks.

Tuesday 9 July 1968

Able to start on last month's operational report today. Vung Tau court martial over at last after six days. When asked who won, the president of the board (the one and only Major Alec Weaver) stated proudly, 'I did!' After finding the accused guilty of very serious charges indeed, including deserting his post while on active service and, on another occasion, sleeping on post while on active service, the board retired to consider sentence.

Weaver: 'What's the maximum we can give him for this?'

Judge advocate: 'Death.'

Weaver: 'What do you think we should give him?'

One member of board: 'Thirty days.'

Weaver (to judge advocate again): 'What is the mean between 30 days and death?'

Eventually it was decided that Death + 30 days all divided by 2 = 115 days, and so the accused was awarded 115 days in the boob at 1ALSG, a very heavy punishment to undergo, though not so heavy in view of the offences, which could have cost others their lives. On the lighter side, it may be deduced from the above equation that 200 days in the boob is rated as the equivalent of death!

There has never been a dull moment in the Task Force since the irrepressible Weaver arrived about a month ago. I do my best to keep things lively, but it is impossible to keep up with Weaver, who has swiftly assumed the role of court jester and Master of the King's Revels. The Army is full of legends about this extraordinary man — eccentric, very fast of thought and speech, and with a rare flair for attracting attention with something highly spectacular and unexpected.

A Prussian who came to Australia prior to World War II, Weaver's first language is German, but he speaks many European languages plus Japanese, Korean and Vietnamese. He only speaks to me in German and I attempt to give as good as I get.

Had a talk with the doctor, Major Digger James, today. Too many people in the Survey Troop are getting venereal diseases lately, and we have won the Task Force Yellow Shield[2] for the second successive month.[2] No obvious reason for this — no more opportunities than usual, and no greater carelessness than usual. Seems to be just bad luck plus the usual lack of care plus increased incidence of VD in Vung Tau and Bangkok.

We have scored 25% as a unit for each of the last two months. Our nearest challenger is 12 Field Regiment (artillery) with 5%. Being such a small unit, we need only two cases and we're into double percentage figures, but even allowing for this, our score is high, so Doc James has agreed to come over for a discussion with everyone tomorrow.

Promoted Peter Dew and Paul Alderson to corporal today, both well deserved. One result of this is that Paul's swim shorts may no longer be removed while swimming at Vung Tau and handed to the nearest girl (usually a Vietnamese beach girl or an American nurse) by anyone below the rank of corporal. Apparently this is a standard occurrence on every swimming trip to Vung Tau (and is usually done by a sergeant — Eric Clutterbuck — so doubtless it will continue to be a regular event despite Paul's elevation to NCO ranks). Both Peter Dew and Paul Alderson enjoy considerable popularity within Survey Troop, so the promotions have generally been greeted with enthusiasm.

[2] A mythical trophy won monthly by the Task Force unit with the highest incidence of VD. The VD score was calculated from the number of monthly cases expressed as a percentage of total unit strength. Cases that were hard to cure and required continuous treatment could be counted in each month over a period of several months. We made light of it, but it really wasn't a joke, which was why I called in the doctor. — JB

Wednesday 10 July 1968

Up at midnight for Command Post duty until 08.00. Quiet session. Strike made by B-52 bombers about 15 to 20 miles away at 05.00 on the opposite side of the Nui Thi Vai hills. Heard and felt it here. Seemed as though bombs would never stop dropping. The B-52 bombers are based at Guam in the Pacific and do not land anywhere in Vietnam but just fly here for raids. These huge planes drop their colossal bombs from the staggering height of 30,000 feet, i.e. 5 to 6 miles up, and are neither seen nor heard from the ground by the casual observer. The only indication of their presence is the sudden eruption of the ground in a long, heavy series of violent explosions, as the unseen bombs land. Their bombing from this great height is controlled by electronic navigation aids and is supposed to be very accurate — it'd need to be!

Back to the Survey Troop and to bed by 09.00. Up again at 10.45 hours for talk with Troop by Major James on venereal disease. A very worthwhile talk and discussion resulted. The doctor had no axe to grind but simply stated the facts: this is what happens; in so many per cent of cases these complications occur; the future effects of this are . . . etc. He appealed solely to reason and not to emotion, and also handed out a lot of sound advice to those who have obviously been careless recently. His direct and straightforward talk gained an excellent reception and obviously jolted quite a few. His language was simple and his understanding of his audience was deep, and I think he may well have planted several useful thoughts in quite a few heads.

Drove to Vung Tau with Grant Small this afternoon to meet Major Ruyen of the NGS and to discuss the Vung Tau city map to be compiled by the Survey Troop and printed in Australia by the Royal Australian Survey Corps. Rained heavily on the way down and we got soaked in the open vehicle, but dried out again in the sun before we got to Vung Tau. Went to the rendezvous address only to find it was a deserted bar on the beach front in an area strictly out of bounds to all servicemen. Decided that something was wrong and then out from the bar came Major Ruyen. At this moment American MPs closed in on us. I told them to report us to the Australian MPs and to send the Australian MPs down here, and off they went. Suggested to Major Ruyen (who was not in uniform) that we try a different place for our conference, and accompanied him to a deserted classroom of a school where his field party was camped. A very pleasant spot. No MPs, and lots of attractive children. Our conference was conducted most amicably. Left Vung Tau in late afternoon and got caught in another rain storm.

Had a 15-minute game of football (no rules) with everyone on the Artillery oval. Everyone exhausted after 15 minutes flat out. Final score: Survey and Admin (3 tries, 1 goal, 4 behinds, 1 wounded in action) drew with Drawing and Reproduction (1 try, 2 goals, 2 behinds, 1 home run). Much fun had by all. Will probably have a similar session once a week from now on — as long as the ground is soft.

To bed early, having had little sleep last night.

Thursday 11 July 1968

Heard today that the occupants of the vehicle shot up last Saturday (6 July) were American entertainers. One or two escaped by feigning death after being wounded; the rest were killed. The driver, who survived, is being court-martialled.

A 122mm rocket site within firing range of the Task Force area was found today. An air strike went in and it no longer exists, fortunately for our peace of mind.

Today an ARVN convoy was ambushed by the Viet Cong between Ba Ria and Vung Tau. A 2½-ton truck was blown up by a command-detonated mine. Three men were killed and 12 wounded. As a result of this, only armed convoys may travel along this road for the time being — no more isolated vehicles, such as Grant Small's and mine on the same road about 15 hours previously.

Another SAS victory, this time five enemy killed out of six. Outside major battles, the tiny SAS patrols continue to kill more than the rest of the entire Task Force put together. Must be embarrassing for the Task Force when compiling press releases, since SAS successes are prohibited from mention.

Artillery very heavy tonight — guns firing right over our heads.

Friday 12 July 1968

On duty in the Command Post from 16.00 until midnight. Very hectic session. Everything happened at once and kept happening: an emergency medical evacuation to be organised; a big operation starting just east of the Long Hai hills; and everyone on tenterhooks and wanting to fire artillery everywhere, including the Vietnamese artillery, some of which is notoriously inaccurate.

Received no help at all from the assistant duty officer. I don't think he's fully fit for this. No use letting him do anything, I soon discovered. Too much time lost checking everything and sorting out the problems. He didn't even try to be useful. Found out later he's been here two or three months, has applied for discharge, and that his resignation is being accepted and that efforts are being made to accelerate his discharge. Just my luck to have him as assistant duty officer on a night like this. Shakes one's confidence in the officer appointment system somewhat (especially when Grant Small is unacceptable!).

161 Field Battery (NZ Artillery) had a bad night. They wanted to test-fire their M79 grenade launchers. Not really permissible at such short notice, but after taking appropriate precautions I granted them ground clearance to fire, as long as they warned all their neighbouring units and gained ground clearance from them too. The resulting flood of phone calls and mortar reports into the Command Post from just about the whole Task Force showed that 161 Battery didn't tell the neighbours. Not only that, but they never asked for air clearance to fire, and they never let their own Regimental HQ know. All told, a series of bad mistakes, but fortunately nothing serious occurred. Surprising that this should happen with a unit which is not new here. Doubtless the axe will fall tomorrow.

Meanwhile, 1st Battalion made three errors with normal operating procedure, which caused delays when time was vital. Had many misgivings when people got rude, but subsequently found out to my great relief that the fault was not mine. Things got lively at midnight — again everyone wanting to fire artillery in all directions at once, regardless of requirements for clearance to fire. New duty officer coming on at midnight was relatively inexperienced, so playing the Great Veteran, I remained there until 01.30, when things began to settle down again. Then to bed.

Saturday 13 July 1968

Quiet day. Got operational report for June completed. Latest I've ever finished a monthly report, but have had rather a lot to do since end of last month.

Rainstorm in the afternoon. Wet monsoon not as wet as expected — rain only seems to come every two or three days, rather than every day. Ground usually dries once or twice a week, though the lower lying areas remain perpetually sodden.

Short of sleep so to bed early. Listened to Test cricket on the BBC until frequency jammed by Peking.

Sunday 14 July 1968

Omitted to mention that during my hectic evening in the Command Post on Friday, on one occasion when things were quiet for a few minutes a group of officers entered — Lieutenant Colonel Latchford, Major Weaver and two US Army colonels. 'Is this the Australian HQ?' Alec Weaver demanded aggressively in German.

'Pardon. Je ne comprends pas. Mais parlez-vous français, monsieur?' I counterattacked immediately.

'Ach! Gott in Himmel! Was ist das hier?' roared Weaver.

'Voici le dernier poste de commande français de la Résistance contre les Viet-Minhs. Vous êtes bienvenus à l'Indo-Chine Française,'[3] — which was the quickest answer I could produce.

Weaver pounded the nearest desk in simulated rage and launched a torrent of angry German, concluding with a demand to stand to attention and Heil Hitler before him. With equal anger I pounded my own desk and refused point-blank in French, and insisted that it was against our orders to use or understand any language but French. Eventually Colonel Latchford managed to control his laughter and get a word in edgewise to ask how things were going. I answered his straight question with a straight answer, in English but in very slow, deliberate speech, with a heavy French accent and very clumsy grammar. I could see from his impassive face but twinkling eyes that he had been hoping for some such response.

[3] 'This is the last French Resistance command post against the Viet Minh. Welcome to French Indo-China!' The Viet Minh were the pro-communist guerrilla fighting force against the French in the 1940s and 1950s. They were succeeded in the 1960s by the Viet Cong. — PH

Colonel Don Dunstan

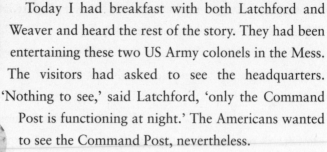

Lieutenant Colonel
Kevin Latchford

Major Alec Weaver

Today I had breakfast with both Latchford and Weaver and heard the rest of the story. They had been entertaining these two US Army colonels in the Mess. The visitors had asked to see the headquarters. 'Nothing to see,' said Latchford, 'only the Command Post is functioning at night.' The Americans wanted to see the Command Post, nevertheless.

'OK,' said Weaver. 'Let me lead the way, it's a bit tricky, and many nations are represented here,' knowing that I was on duty and could speak German. He thus set the stage for the show that followed, but was not expecting me to respond in French. Just before Weaver walked in he had said to the Americans, 'Do you understand German?'

'Yes, we've both been posted in Heidelberg,' replied one.

The resulting nonsense completely confused the Americans, which was precisely the intention of Latchford and Weaver. They then went out. 'I'm sure the Australian Command Post is around here somewhere,' Weaver said, but the Americans had had enough. They then drove their blacked-out jeep the few hundred metres to the Civil Affairs Unit (Commanding Officer of which is Latchford; second-in-command is Weaver). Weaver acting as navigator said, 'Turn right here through the minefield and follow the vehicle tracks.'

'Ah cain't see no vehicle tracks,' said the American colonel.

'Never mind,' said Weaver. 'Go ahead anyway, I think this is the right direction and we haven't had any accidents in this minefield for months!' Of course, no minefield exists inside the Task Force area, but the Americans didn't know that. I gathered this morning that these two colonels won't quickly forget their first night in the Australian Task Force! One of them is the Chief of US forces in the province!

Caught Weaver myself this morning. Persuaded him that paludrine anti-malarial pills were ineffective if swallowed whole, since they then went through the system unassimilated, and that they should be crushed in the mouth first.

'Mein Gott!' said Weaver as he chewed his pill. 'These are vile!' (He wasn't far wrong either — they're the bitterest thing I know.)

'Oh, it's only the first 100 that taste bad, sir,' I responded.

I also tried to persuade him to swap his watch to the other wrist daily to avoid skin rash, but he woke up at this stage. He then tried to catch Lieutenant Colonel Latchford, who had arrived, and quoted the doctor as authority for his advice. 'Look, you clot,' said Latchford, 'I have three-quarters of a mile of intestine to assimilate that silly little pill. What the doctor really said was not to chew your watch up!'

At this stage Colonel Dunstan (Acting Task Force Commander) walked by and said, 'Do you people know there's a war on?'

'War, war?' said Weaver. 'On the Lord's day? Impossible!'

'Can't fight a war today,' said Latchford. 'This is my day of rest.'

'Same here,' said Dunstan, 'but I think I'll go and ease my conscience and read a war book!'

Otherwise a very quiet day. Managed to get some letters written, and assembled a slot car — a Chaparral II, at scale 1:24. I hope to race it some time on the track at 104 Signals Squadron. I also have a Ferrari Berlinetta but will leave it until back home next year to assemble — too good to assemble and race here. Sorely tempting though, based on design considerations alone; this Ferrari is the best (i.e. most stable, most powerful and fastest) car of any I've seen here.

Monday 15 July 1968

Quiet day. No new jobs. Catching up on many old ones. Much rain in evening. Nice to have a day without much pressure at all.

Tuesday 16 July 1968

Five new jobs in, including two big ones to be done in negligible time. Managed somehow, thanks to sterling efforts by all concerned.

Some success by the Task Force today, but also some setbacks. SAS lost one of their most successful patrol commanders today; Lieutenant Simpson lost both of his feet and part of his legs when a booby trap was set off near him during a patrol north of Lang Phuoc Hai. A Squadron 3 Cavalry Regiment also had a casualty — one of their RAEME mechanics, Craftsman Borlace (alias Bootlace), was killed and four others injured when a mine was command-detonated beneath an armoured personnel carrier. John Rolfe, Mick Rice and I all knew Bootlace, a cheerfully noisy character of very long, slim build.

Printing in progress late this evening. Pressure of work will now be high for several days.

Wednesday 17 July 1968

Frantic day today. Demands for map printing coming in from all directions, mostly duplicating each other. We've responded to panicky (or 'flexible') demands for the last 36 hours to the best of our ability and are one of the few units to come out of this scramble well. We have met all demands and made no mistakes, though the load on our printers has been heavy. Was rather angry with an Intelligence captain on the Task Force HQ who rang early this morning to wake up Mario Apfelbaum to ask if the printing would be finished on time. We've never failed yet, and Mario badly needed his sleep. That captain will not wake Mario up again.

A really major blunder today, quite separate from all the above. A cordon-and-search operation planned for tomorrow has had to be cancelled, although it involved the Task Force, ARVN, national police and goodness knows who else. The voice aircraft which commences the operation by telling all the village people what's going on and what to do made its flight today — a day too soon — thus giving the whole show away. A gross bungle, and the captain concerned will probably be sacked as a consequence.

Today it was also discovered that yesterday's operation near Lang Phuoc Hai had been blabbed to all who cared to listen to a drunken soldier in a Vung Tau bar on Sunday. Very hard to keep drunks silent, of course, but this man should never have known the things he knew and spilt.

Went to Van Kiep, just east of Ba Ria, to have lunch in the home of Dai-Uy (Captain) Trung, commander of 10 MID, who is a friend of mine, and Captain Geoff Boscoe (Trung's Australian counterpart, Officer Commanding 1 Divisional Intelligence Unit here). First Vietnamese meal I've had and it was delicious. Certainly not tasteless — an often heard criticism. Trung has married a good cook. Altogether a delightful and enjoyable lunch. Returned to the panic at Nui Dat.

Duty officer in Command Post from 16.00 to midnight. Quite busy at times, but had a much better assistant duty officer this time (the linguist Lieutenant Fred Greenway). The GSO2 Ops has apparently decided that I have made the grade, so he is now most affable and this makes life easier. He gives everyone he meets hell at first but eases up on those of whom he approves. Also the Survey Troop light shines at the moment amidst the day's disasters, although the credit belongs to Mario Apfelbaum and Mick Rice, rather than to me.

While I was in the Command Post, an SAS patrol had contact with an enemy force. One enemy was killed and two wounded, and one SAS man wounded, and it was necessary to arrange immediate extraction of the patrol by helicopter.

A road convoy of ours had an accident near Long Binh this evening. An armoured personnel carrier had steering and brakes failure and careered off road into a shop in Long Thanh. No one hurt, but it must have made an awful mess of the shop.

Thursday 18 July 1968

Was seized at lunch today by senior officers to make French conversation with a visiting writer, a former French general in Indo-China. A very interesting man to talk with. He remarked that the Australian and US forces in this province are now located in exactly the same places and strengths as the French about 15 years ago, even with a company outpost at the Horseshoe near Dat Do. His implication was quite clear — that we, too, are fighting a losing battle in Vietnam.

Emergency during afternoon. Liaison officer needed by Task Force HQ to dash to Saigon, collect important intelligence information from Australian Forces HQ, and dash back. All normal liaison officers already busy so I went instead. Helicopter waiting. Wonderfully interesting trip by air. Got several good photos. Landed inside Free World Forces HQ Building compound and collected information — mainly huge rolls of photos. How on earth could I eat all this if the plane ditched on return trip? No worries though. Beautiful view on the way back over all the land and swamps from height of 5000 feet. Country everywhere terribly pockmarked from shells, bombs etc. Flew over a very old airfield, reputedly the first the Japanese built outside Japan during World War II. Coming back to Nui Dat, we auto-rotated[4] down from

[4] Auto-rotation is when the engine power is shut off, the helicopter falls rapidly (often very frightening for the inexperienced) and the main rotor 'free wheels', being spun by the air passing upwards through it. This prevents free falling. — PH

5000 feet to about 50 feet very rapidly, altogether a most interesting ride and a very pleasant break from normal work.

Friday 19 July 1968

Concert this morning, so went along with about two-thirds of the Survey Troop. Most popular concert ever. Wild enthusiasm from audience. Performers not up to the high standard of the West Australian party compered by Peter Willie Harries a couple of months ago, but was a wild success because of its two girls, Yvonne Barrett and Pat Carroll, both of whom have been to Vietnam before and have a good idea of what the troops like. The former, a short-haired blonde, appeared in a mini-dress with no sides, the front and back panels being joined by wide panels of half-inch nylon mesh. Beneath the mesh the only clothing visible was two thin pieces of elastic, one at chest level, one at hip level. Her singing and dancing were greeted with tremendous enthusiasm. Movie cameras, zoom lenses, binoculars appeared from everywhere. Couldn't hear a word she sang, but this didn't appear to matter.

The second girl was very slightly less spectacularly dressed (or undressed), being content merely to spill out of the top of a very low-cut neckline. Girls set out to give audience an eyeful and succeeded admirably. The rest of show was weak though. At end of the concert, the scrum of stage-door johnnies packed down tightly behind the girls' dressing room. Behind the scrum were parked several Land Rovers covered with soldiers with cameras and zoom lenses. Some soldiers were on the shoulders of others and the vehicles were covered with tottering towers of swaying humanity and photographic equipment.

Back to work after lunch. As a result of Wednesday's bungle, Captain Col Swain has been sacked and is being sent to the

Reinforcement Unit as a training officer. It is harsh treatment. As the Psychological Operations officer it was his job to task the voice aircraft to fly that mission. But as far as I'm aware, no check was made that the message delaying the cordon-and-search operation by one day had got through to Col Swain and been acted on. So I remain unconvinced that the fiasco was entirely his fault.

On the lighter side, it must be hard to create a more massive security breach than to fly an aircraft with loudspeakers over the enemy to inform him in his own language of our intentions for the following day.

Col Swain's departure and the transfer of another officer to the Cavalry Squadron has exacerbated a serious shortage of Command Post duty officers at the Task Force HQ. I have been asked to take this on full-time, together with Noel who has done no Survey work since April. But the Survey Troop must have at least one officer at least part of the time, so we will continue as we are, with Noel full-time in the Command Post and me every third night.

Meanwhile, the 'Souvenir Programme' PR officer has returned permanently to Australia for medical reasons — deafness. I hadn't noticed he was deaf, but apparently the Brigadier has! No rain now for several days.

Saturday 20 July 1968

Two conferences today as well as higher than usual demands, and on duty in the Command Post from 16.00 till midnight. Pretty frantic scramble all day, to tell the truth. Command Post duty only moderately busy.

Sunday 21 July 1968

Quiet morning. Got washing and some cleaning up done, then went down to Ba Ria this afternoon for dinner at Madame Minh Ha's with Sergeant Snow Dighton (Ordnance, Task Force HQ) and Captain Tommy Thompson (Quartermaster, Armoured Squadron), both of whom have a lot to do with laundry matters. Was kept flat out interpreting between French and English, and Madame's French isn't always the best, but really enjoyed myself, as did the other two. Lovely meal — asparagus soup, meat and salad, Cantonese rice, fried shrimp flakes, and coffee and fruit. Both filling and delicious. Local fruit unusual but also delicious — quite unlike any other fruit I have ever seen or tasted.

Driving back to Nui Dat late in the afternoon sunlight after such a pleasant occasion reminded us all of a normal Sunday outing at home. While aware that we could encounter enemy at any time, it was still possible to dissociate oneself from this and to appreciate one's surroundings. The rice is now growing in the paddies and is a beautiful, fresh shade of green. Most grateful to Madame Minh Ha for making such a pleasant day possible.

Still no rain but lightning all over sky. It was continuous. At any given instant part of the sky was lit. Have never seen such a display before.

Monday 22 July 1968

Busy day. 104 Signal Squadron rang up to express their delight at a map we had printed for them — underground cables overprinted in blue on a pale grey base map. They were really pleased with the result — so much so that they gave us another job.

Weather broke in late afternoon — hours and hours of rain. Plenty of lightning but less spectacular than last night. Also plenty of action today. No less than ten enemy contacts by different elements of the Task Force. None major, but several enemy killed nevertheless. Meanwhile, more youths are kidnapped from villages to make up the losses. What an unhappy country this is.

Tuesday 23 July 1968

Normal work heavy. In Command Post also from 16.00 until midnight. Action very hectic, so much so that I did relatively little — control of artillery, air strikes, troop movements, casualty evacuation being handled by the Task Force Commander, the GSO2 Ops and the Acting GSO3 Ops. Several separate actions were occurring simultaneously and three separate casualty evacuations were necessary. In one case, about 20 enemy were in a well-defended bunker position and were being hit with everything possible — with artillery, air strike and ground attack to follow tomorrow after about 24 to 25 hours' 'softening up'.

In the midst of it all, a soldier cleaning his rifle in the Task Force base area accidentally shot a man in the next tent — another casualty evacuation required, but the victim, shot in the head, died as the aircraft arrived. These deaths always seem far more tragic than any in action.

I took a back seat and handled all the routine matters — such as the gunshot accident — while the GSO2 and GSO3 did most of the work. The Commander sat back and read a *Kid Rawhide* comic,[5]

[5] I hadn't known Brigadier Hughes was a *Kid Rawhide* fan, but when I asked him about it later he told me there was nothing else to read in the Command Post so he picked up the signaller's literature which lay ready to hand. — JB

but dropped it now and then to make a decision. Things worked fairly well.

The fighting settled down round about 22.00 hours and the last couple of hours of my shift were a lot quieter. Just as well — I've never known things to be so hectic.

Wednesday 24 July 1968

Went to Ba Ria with the laundry run and bought a few things in the market there. Weather fine after yesterday's rain. A film about VD, *The Choice Is Yours* (RAF production), was shown this evening. Poor film — it undid some good work done by Major James. Film was most unreal and unconvincing. It invited ridicule and provoked antagonism because of its clumsy attempts to moralise. Expected something much better than this.

Thursday 25 July 1968

Busy day and a lot of rain. A few rush jobs came in. Another big operation going on at very short notice; however, I think we can cope OK, as usual.

Took my slot car down to the 104 Signal Squadron's track this evening and gave it its first trials. Not a bad car at all. Made several adjustments to it. Didn't race it. Just did several circuits to get feel of track and car. Car is a bit too big and fast for this track. Rarely used more than half power.

Friday 26 July 1968

Yet another major operation in the offing and several maps to prepare for printing. Mick Sokil returned from a visit to Long Binh with a stack of 1050 maps — an unbelievable load for one man. It's a wonder the helicopter pilot let him aboard.

Was given my annual confidential report to read and sign. It was a surprisingly good report — a rather useful thing to get from a man in such an important position as the GSO2 Operations of the Task Force. Even though I find him volatile, he must be well regarded to be put in this key job. He offered his congratulations for the standard of my work both as commander of the Survey Troop and also as a Command Post officer. I was particularly pleased about the latter aspect, since nearly all the credit for the former is not so much due to me as to the quality of the men in the Survey Troop. It is not widely realised outside the Survey Corps that a Survey unit with good men and a poor commander can function more effectively than an infantry unit in the same situation. Anyway, this confidential report did a lot for my morale.

Found out today that the 'Souvenir Programme', complete with contraceptive advertisement, which we printed for the Prime Minister's visit, was shown to the Task Force Commander a month or so ago, and that he was quite amused by it and has his own souvenir copy. Being unsure of his reaction, I would have hesitated to give it to him myself, but apparently the Deputy Commander knew he was on quite safe ground and drew his attention to it.

Heard yesterday that a major evacuated from Vietnam on medical grounds (to save the embarrassment of sacking him) has convinced the doctors in Australia that he is fit, and is now on his way back to Vietnam, since he considers his services indispensable to the Task Force! This has caused much consternation at this end, leading to urgent correspondence from here through medical channels, and his return to Vietnam is being blocked. Apparently the doctors in Australia will be better briefed next time.

Saturday 27 July 1968

Heavy load of printing today, with another major operation about to start, but Mario Apfelbaum and Mick Rice kept well ahead of the battalions' demands.

At 01.30 this morning I saw the lights of four helicopters circling many kilometres away, probably over Long Dien. Could see no shooting but the aircraft were certainly behaving like hovering gunships. No report later of any action but something was obviously happening. No rain now for two days, but plenty of cloud and lightning.

Highlight of the day at Commander's conference:

Colonel Dunstan (Deputy Commander, referring to a major project that has been running for months): 'When will such-and-such construction work be complete?'

Major Petrass (Engineers, nice fellow but a renowned procrastinator): 'Well, I can't actually give you a definite date, sir.'

Colonel Dunstan: 'Well I'll give *you* one then — Monday!'

Sunday 28 July 1968

Sunny morning so did washing. During morning went for an interview with Military Secretary (Brigadier Whitelaw), who is visiting the Task Force for three days. Spent five to ten minutes with him discussing my career, which seems to be much more secure since I have been on active service. Found him most friendly. He will apparently be conferring with the Director of Survey.

THE PARABLE OF THE PANGO

I had a long session with the Officer Commanding 198 Works Section one morning at Nui Dat, pleading desperately for his ditch digger, known as a 'pango', to dig a new pit for our noisome and almost overflowing latrine. It would have been barely twenty minutes' work and we needed it badly.

Major Bill Petrass put his arm around my shoulder and laboriously led me step by step through the diabolical difficulties of being the Deputy Commander Royal Engineers in the Task Force. It was all a matter of priorities, explained the genial Obstacle Bill, and his Works Section had all this work ahead of them (a wave of the arm in the general direction of a huge board on the wall with fine scribble all over it), and the pango was booked up months ahead for all these tasks (pointing with the finger this time), if it didn't break down under the strain.

But since I was such a fine chap and my poor unit was in such desperate need, he could see his way clear to use his power and not start me at the bottom of the colossal queue. He would give me accelerated priority for the pango, which would get the Survey Troop to the top of the list in no less than four months. He couldn't guarantee it of course — fortunes of war and all that — but he'd do his absolute best, and really, four months was extremely good in these troublous times when he had all these problems to contend with and I really ought to be very grateful for the big favour he was doing me. After all, there was a war on.

Crestfallen, I trudged back to the Survey Troop, wondering how I could confess my dismal failure to my troops. Nearing our lines I almost fell into the freshly dug latrine trench. Huh!!!???

'Who dug this?'

'Ask Rocky, sir.'

'Rocky, who dug this?'

'The pango sir!'

'Yes, but how?'

'Easy, sir. I just asked the pango driver to stop on his way past — only took him a few minutes!'

Live and learn. Obstacle Bill had scratched his head and offered every excuse in the world as he ran his chinagraph pencil all over his meaningless task board, never getting anywhere, while the pango driver (and other junior Works staff, no doubt) did jobs in accordance with their own priorities established by mateship at lance corporal level. Oh, so simple! And thanks, Rocky, well done!

Survey Troop soldiers' tents, with gravel paths laid by Rocky Camps.

Went with Geoff Boscoe to 10 MID at Van Kiep for lunch. Very pleasant visit, and another delightful meal cooked by Dai-Uy Trung's wife. Tony Hammett was there, too. I hadn't realised that Dai-Uy Trung was such a close friend of Tony (Major, 1RAR, 1968), as well as Jake O'Donnell (Major, 7RAR, 1967–68) and Bob O'Neill (Captain, 5RAR, 1966–67), all close friends of mine too.

Returned to Nui Dat as passenger in an Intelligence vehicle. Eyebrows soared in surprise when we returned to the Survey Troop and saw a Vietnamese civilian Lambretta in our car park. Neat, clean, in excellent condition, its registration current, everyone wondered what it was doing there. The explanation was an anticlimax. It is

looked after and run by a couple of our Cavalry Squadron men, who found it in the bush during the heavy fighting in May and have the Task Force Commander's permission to use it for local transport within the Task Force base area. Took a photo of it before it returned to the Cavalry Squadron.

Monday 29 July – Wednesday 31 July 1968

Three days preparing maps of patrol zones for the Task Force. First two days spent referring back to the GSO2 and GSO3 Ops all matters that were not clear. 'Now let's see, what's the trouble? Ah, yes, just as well you noticed that.' And so back to square one of the snakes and ladders board. Finally, I identified all their errors for them and we could go ahead and draw up the map for printing.

Stung on arm by wasp. Nasty big, red fellow with pincers in front and sting in tail. Red puncture on arm surrounded by small white patch and much larger reddish area about 5 centimetres across. Didn't hurt as much as I expected from such a fearsome-looking creature. Inflammation disappeared within a couple of hours.

AUGUST

AUSTRALIAN MILITARY FORCES

AAB — 71A
Reprinted Dec, 1964

RECORD BOOK

CONTAINING 96 PAGES

RULED FEINT

The Australian-built village of Ap Suoi Nghe was the new home for several hundred South Vietnamese people forced to move there by Australian troops. Their former homes, in a Viet Cong-controlled area, were destroyed. Ap Suoi Nghe was a depressing place, of dismal, linear design, set on a dusty plain. The Viet Cong murdered several of its village chiefs and deputy chiefs, until nobody would take the job. In August 1968, John's unit was involved in surveying the village area.

PAUL HAM

★

Arrived in Ap Suoi Nghe, but no children would
come near us. Very strange, because they're
normally swarming all over us immediately we stop,
especially our particular friends.

★

Thursday 1 August 1968

Unlucky day for the Task Force today — two bad accidents. A D8
bulldozer in the Land Clearing Team received an enemy rocket while
working. The rocket blew up the 'dozer, which was still burning this
evening. The driver received multiple wounds but is in hospital in
satisfactory condition. Also an armoured personnel carrier from the
Cavalry Squadron full of infantry soldiers ran over a mine today.
The explosion hurled the 12-ton vehicle plus its occupants right into
the air, and backwards in the direction it had come from. The APC
was destroyed, the driver killed, one other died of wounds, and six
others badly wounded. Major Blue Keldie, the squadron
commander, told me later that it was the largest anti-tank mine he'd
heard of. It must have contained at least 100 pounds of TNT or
plastic explosive. The explosion was absolutely tremendous and it
was most fortunate that casualties were no worse. It is suspected
that this enormous mine had been there for a long, long time and
been forgotten about until we stumbled on it by accident.

Minor incidents during evening on the Task Force perimeter.
Wire cutting heard on the southern perimeter, and several shots
were fired into the western perimeter from outside. The men on the
western perimeter (American artillery) fired back with everything

they had, and have since been told not to shoot and give their positions away unless they have a definite target to shoot at.[1]

Friday 2 August 1968

In Command Post from midnight to 08.00. Finally to bed at 9.30 and grabbed a couple of hours' sleep before lunch. Found out that we have lost the Task Force Yellow Shield for July and are down in third place with 10% VD incidence, behind Canteens, 20%, and the American Artillery, 13 per cent. Both of our two casualties were from sexual contacts prior to the doctor's talk earlier in July.

To give an idea of the magnitude of this problem, here are the statistics for the Task Force (about 4000 to 5000 men) from the Task Force monthly report for July, now being circulated:

Casualties: 1 officer; 111 other ranks.

Diseases: 58 gonorrhoea; 54 non-specific urethritis.

Origin: Vung Tau — 80; Singapore — 11; Bangkok — 9; Hong Kong — 4; Ba Ria — 2; Xuan Loc — 2; Long Binh — 1; Saigon — 1; Taipei — 1; Tokyo — 1.

Units: 3RAR — 34; 2/35 Artillery Battalion (US) — 13; 1RAR — 9; 1 Field Squadron RAE — 8; 1 Armoured Regiment — 8; 12 Field Regiment RAA — 7; 3 Cavalry Regiment — 5; 2SAS Squadron — 5; 4RAR — 5; 104 Signals Squadron — 3; HQ Company — 3; 5/42 Artillery Battalion (US) — 2; Canteens — 2; Survey — 2; 52 Supply Platoon — 2; 53 Signals Battalion (US) — 1.

---

[1] The Task Force artillery was augmented by two batteries of US artillery to provide heavy and medium artillery support which Australia lacked (with only field artillery, which is 'light'). These two US batteries were Battery A of the 1/83rd Artillery Battalion and Battery A of the 2/35th Artillery Battalion. — PH

Some surprises amongst these,[2] especially Xuan Loc. No one from the Task Force has been there, except for a tank from the Armoured Regiment, which I'm told broke down a couple of months ago in Xuan Loc with a damaged suspension for a few hours — plenty long enough for the transmission of social diseases. Ba Ria is also a surprise, since no one goes there except on duty, but I have heard of soldiers on laundry visits to Ba Ria trading two apples for a quick session around the back of the barn, and one soldier was charged for stealing Army property after trading a crate of apples for a longer session. He won much unpopularity for raising the price and ruining the market.

The overseas centres all involve R&R leave. A large party from the 3rd Battalion spent a rest day (rest?) at Vung Tau recently, no doubt contributing to the large scores for both the battalion and Vung Tau. The battalion figure is much less startling, though, when alternatively shown as only 3% of the unit strength. Vung Tau is pretty pestilential these days. It used not to be so bad when the Australian hospital at Vung Tau treated any Vietnamese girl who sought treatment. However, this was stopped by the mayor of Vung Tau (dependent on votes for his position), who forbade such treatment on the grounds that it was insulting, since 'everyone knows there is no prostitution or VD in Vung Tau'. Our medical authorities have estimated the VD incidence amongst Vung Tau girls to be 100% and Saigon 98%. These figures apply to girls to whom servicemen have direct access and physical contact, not all of whom are necessarily prostitutes.

Meanwhile, other problems occur. There is much talk of a most spectacular case of homosexuality occurring in the canteen of the RAEME Workshop of the Armoured Squadron last Sunday afternoon in front of a large audience. As a result, three men face a general court

[2] Figures include all cases treated during the month regardless of when the infection was initially contracted. — JB

martial. It appears to have been quite the most sensational floor show I've ever heard of. Seems unnecessary to make all this fuss, though. All concerned were drunk and had accepted a dare. A few weeks on the dry for everyone would probably have been more appropriate.

Saturday 3 August 1968

Another busy day. More incidents on the Task Force perimeter last night. It does seem that our defences are being systematically probed. Many things point to major activity throughout the country late in August, and it is distinctly possible that we could be on the list.

Task Force Commander, Brigadier Hughes, summoned me in a big hurry today. The 1st Battalion, about 20 kilometres north-west of Nui Dat, wanted to call down artillery fire, but didn't dare do so because they weren't sure of their position to within 2 kilometres and suspected that the map was wrong. Quickly grabbed photos and checked. Map was wrong — a cleared area had been shown in the wrong place. Found out that the map had been prepared (in 1967) not from air photos but by sketching from a Cessna circling high in the air. Under those circumstances it's a good effort, but we'll have to produce better than that and produce new maps from photos. Much work ahead.

Survey Troop visited by Task Force Deputy Commander, Colonel Dunstan, to look at progress on the Task Force defences plan we're working on. This large-scale plan of Nui Dat (scale 1:2500 or 1 centimetre to 25 metres) is to show every weapon pit in the Task Force, all main weapons, and the arcs for fire for all machine guns. Classified Secret, it will have a very limited distribution and no copy is to go outside the Task Force perimeter. From Colonel Dunstan's remarks, it seems that the Task Force could be needing this map very soon.

Meanwhile, Intelligence has located (thanks mainly to SAS long-range patrols) a Viet Cong regiment about 20 kilometres north of us. Surreptitious preparations are now in hand to wipe it out. No chance of a security leak on this one — hardly anyone knows of it yet — but there could be a heavy fight within the next week. Things do appear to be warming up all around us.

Heavy rain today, perhaps the heaviest I've seen so far.

Sunday 4 August 1968

Saw the Commander this morning on a mapping problem. First time I've needed to take any matter directly to him, but it was a pretty serious one and he gave it pretty close attention and agreed to the course of action I'd recommended. Problem was that some serious errors have been discovered during the past fortnight in maps produced by the Survey Troop in November last year. In one case, a company of infantry narrowly missed getting blown up by our own artillery because the map was wrong. In another case, an infantry battalion (1st Battalion yesterday) fortunately called for a check of the map before calling for the guns to fire. Anyway, we've now got our own course of action planned, the first task being to obtain good photography.

Remark of the day:

Scene: Officers' Mess at lunch.

Steward: 'Sweets, sir?'

Officer: 'What have we?'

Steward: 'Combination dessert, sir.'

Officer: 'What's it a combination of?'

Steward: 'Thursday's, Friday's and Saturday's!'

Got washing done between rainstorms and checked maps prior to printing. Cleared up office and did other odd jobs, including a complete clean-out of tent. Removed all mould and spider webs. The wildlife here has defeated me. Not only do I have to share my quarters with a snake over 1 metre long, but on checking the rat poison bowl I find that the rats are nesting in it. This is adding insult to injury.

Went down to Van Kiep in late afternoon to 10 MID for a farewell party for Chanh, Dai-Uy Trung's second-in-command, who is now to be promoted and is to take over 3 MID, stationed about 200 kilometres to the north-east of here. Chanh has been the interrogation chief of 10 MID and is also the most fluent English speaker in the detachment. Also at the party were Brigadier Hughes and several other Task Force senior officers. Trung and Chanh and one other ARVN officer brought their wives, all of whom were charming. Also present were several of the district chiefs, one of whom (Thieu-Ta Thuong of Long Dien) spoke excellent French — the best I've yet encountered in Vietnam. Not surprising, since he's French-educated. Meal was simple but delicious: meat rolls in rice paper, mint and meat rolls, crab soup with rice. Taste was lovely and we all ate well, and the Commander obviously enjoyed himself, too.

On returning to Nui Dat, I stopped off at the Cavalry Squadron with their second-in-command, Tony Larnach-Jones, who was also returning from Van Kiep, and dined with other friends — Blue Keldie, Brian Kollias and John Crossman — before heading back to the Survey Troop lines.

Land mine casualty.

More mine accidents occurred today. Another D8 bulldozer has been damaged and also a Centurion tank. Only four of the Land Clearing Team's seven D8 'dozers are operative. Saw the APC that got blown up on Thursday 1 August. Pretty big mess. Whole of front blown off.

Saw photos in *Life* magazine of weapons handed in to police in USA. The guns included a double-barrelled aircraft machine gun.

Photo also showed a shop advertisement for a fearful-looking gun labelled 'Nigger Getter. This gun carries a nigger back guarantee' — the gun was an automatic heavy-gauge shotgun with a barrel only a few centimetres long. The USA obviously still has a long way to go in its campaign to stamp out violence.

Meanwhile, Biafra starves to death, with several thousand dying daily, while Britain flies in not food but firearms. At least the aid I've sent to a friend there has reached him, but of another friend I've heard nothing since their terrible war started last year. My Nigerian friends are on both sides in this Biafran war and they are friends with each other too. Vietnam is bad enough, but other countries are in an even worse plight.

Monday 5 August 1968

Caught up on a lot of odd jobs and hope to tackle our monthly report tomorrow.

Things are getting lively around us. The Task Force had 13 enemy contacts yesterday and more again today. Today we also had our second visit in 48 hours from the Deputy Commander, Colonel Dunstan, to have a look at the Task Force defence plan we are preparing. Seems highly probable that within a few days we shall be playing Tonight's The Night, a game we haven't played for a few months. A major assault on the Task Force position is not likely, but we could receive heavy rocket and mortar fire, and this would certainly shake us up a lot.

Meanwhile, preparations are in hand to destroy the enemy regiment to our north. Are we too late? Our Intelligence experts think so. One has vowed to commit unspeakable acts of self-degradation in the Officers' Mess before a large audience if more than one local guerrilla is caught in the pending attack. We are also waiting ten days before we hit the enemy, and it seems likely that there may be no enemy in the area by then — they never wait long in the one spot. We are also waiting for B-52 bomber strikes etc to be organised. This delay may have cost the opportunity to destroy an enemy force equal in size to all the casualties inflicted on the enemy by us during the last couple of years. Will be interesting during the next few days to see how things turn out and to see who's right.

Now, two to three months later, considered thoughts are emerging on the heavy fighting in May at fire support base Coral. The general consensus of opinion is that our movement to Coral and our handling of the first few days was fearfully unsound, and it was only by a fluke that the complete Task Force HQ wasn't wiped out. Anyway, we got away with it and enemy casualties were severe. It was complete luck that our casualties were so light, but more enemy casualties would have occurred had not our press and radio informed the enemy so promptly as to what strength we had. Until then, the enemy hadn't realised that we were not Americans or ARVN. On finding this out, the enemy tactics immediately changed. Without this knowledge, it seems certain that the enemy would have continued to attack for much longer and would have suffered very heavily, once the initial period of confusion was over. Easy to be wise after the event, but many valuable lessons have been learnt — we hope.

Heavy rain each afternoon now seems fairly regular. The wet is at last settling down, but it's now August and there should only be two or three months before the dry begins again.

Tuesday 6 August 1968

Went out to Ap Suoi Nghe village with Noel Sproles, Grant Small, John Hunter, Ray Lawson, Captain Peter Thomas (Public Relations) and a civilian journalist from AAP-Reuter. The purpose

A standard hut at Ap Suoi Nghe.

Sergeants Ted Morris and Grant Small with 'Sapper' Gung at Ap Suoi Nghe.

Captain John Bullen receiving help.

Sapper John Hunter and Sergeant Grant Small resting while their job is done for them. Captain Noel Sproles in background.

*Sapper John Hunter
and his survey class.*

*A keen Ap Suoi Nghe surveyor,
who is genuinely at work here.*

*Other enthusiastic
surveyors at
Ap Suoi Nghe.*

of our visit was to allow the press to see us in action surveying land using the Vietnamese children we've trained as survey assistants. Many of the children are very good chainmen indeed, especially Gung, a seven-year-old Montagnard.[3] We have taught some of the children elementary English and they make remarkable progress.

Arrived in Ap Suoi Nghe, but no children would come near us. Very strange, because they're normally swarming all over us immediately we stop, especially our particular friends. Viet Cong nearby? Absence of children can often be a warning sign. Finally, after much coaxing, some of our best friends joined us and we then surveyed a line with them.

The children were wonderful. Gung and his friends displayed remarkable professional competence — laying out the tape, applying tension, marking the ground, driving in the picket, painting it, moving on again and carrying the equipment. They also understand the theodolite, and how to use the optical plummet to plumb it over a ground mark. They can set ground marks and pickets, too, and can use the theodolite to wave the chainman on line. Most impressive for five- to eight-year-old youngsters. One apt pupil was a nine-year-old with a baby on her hip. A pretty child, she was most interested in the theodolite and its use.

The press people got all the photos they wanted and we then went down to the store for a drink and played marbles with the children and got badly beaten. Grant Small is wonderful with children and they all adore him.

Returned to Nui Dat. Saw last week's blown-up armoured personnel carrier again. We all had a look and took several photos. Found out during the evening that the Viet Cong attacked the South Vietnamese military post at Ap Suoi Nghe, only a couple of hours after we left. Now we know that our suspicions were correct — the Viet Cong were indeed in the vicinity this morning.

[3] The Montagnards were the tribal people of central Vietnam — PH

The big operation to wipe out the enemy regiment to our north has now been cancelled. Don't know why for sure but obviously the enemy must have moved away. Did the enemy know that we knew he was there? Or did he move simply because it's unsound for him to stay any length of time in one spot? Whatever the reason, we were too late. Meanwhile, 300 enemy have been seen moving into the Long Hai hills, so we could be moving back there again ourselves.

Wednesday 7 – Thursday 8 August 1968

All battalions are back in the Task Force base area and intensive patrolling, more so than ever before, is being carried out. This is because of the very real threat that Nui Dat could be subjected to heavy rocket attack at any time within the next couple of weeks, and the fact that strong patrolling will make it harder for the enemy to establish rocket bases close to us. Meanwhile 1st Battalion and the tanks and cavalry are on standby for the defence of Ba Ria if necessary.

Rained Wednesday night and Thursday morning. Unusual to get morning rain.

Friday 9 August 1968

Tried to get monthly report for July completed today amidst a heap of minor matters and failed. Up late at night instead.

Signal came to Task Force HQ from Australia today pointing out that the following eight officers (there followed a list of seven majors and myself) are due for promotion to major (substantive rank) in 1968, and requesting recommendation or otherwise. The signal also listed qualifications held for promotion to major. Much to the amusement of the A Branch staff and myself, out of the whole eight officers, I'm the only one fully qualified for promotion to major and also the only one who is still a captain!

Twenty-one patrols went out tonight. Easily a new record, beating the 15 that were out a week or so ago. (In normal times there are only six to eight patrols out at night.) In addition, there is a company of infantry, a troop of tanks and a troop of cavalry just north of Ba Ria waiting in case any trouble starts there. On top of this, the rest of 1st Battalion is standing by to assist if necessary. Obviously enemy activity very close to us is seriously expected.

Saturday 10 August 1968

My birthday today — yet another in an unusual place (Gibson Desert 1961, Broome 1962, Singapore 1963, Lago Maggiore and Simplon Pass 1964, Paris 1965, and now a Michelin rubber plantation in Vietnam 1968).

Really hectic day today — flat out all day. Managed to get monthly report completed. Pat Cox, our quartermaster sergeant, goes on R&R leave tomorrow, and with one day to go, three days' worth of loose ends suddenly were found. Much sorting out to be done at short notice so straight into the job goes Grant Small — untrained but capable, competent and reliable at absolutely anything.

Found snake skin sloughed recently in our quartermaster store by rather large snake (about 2 metres long).

Farewell party for Doug Bosher in evening, our first changeover for about three months. Best party here yet. Very lively and happy, thanks to some most entertaining visitors. Major Bruce Daniel, second-in-command of 1 Australian Field Hospital, Vung Tau, was visiting Nui Dat, and came to the party at our invitation. A World War II member of the Survey Corps, he served in the Royal New South Wales Lancers after the war while he studied medicine. When

In front of the Survey Troop.

qualified as a doctor he transferred to the Medical Corps (Citizen Military Forces) and is now in Vietnam on full-time duty. A tremendous wag, he was a colossal hit with everyone. His mimicry, sense of humour and old Survey songs from the war endeared him to all, but he achieved one great distinction by becoming the new Survey Troop beer-can pushing champion, by defeating the local champion, John Hunter, on his home ground. The object of game is: toes behind line, empty can in each hand, then down on all fours, hands supported on ends of beer cans. Then place one beer can as far forward as possible with one hand, while fully supported by the other hand. Then spring back off the supporting hand in one clean jerk to finish behind the line without falling forward. Any floor contact at all forward of the toe line earns disqualification. To win at this, height, strength and agility are essential. John Hunter, aged 20, had all three and beat Grant Small, who's extremely agile and strong but lacks height. Then Major Daniel, who'd been in the Survey Corps before John Hunter was born, beat all comers.

Also present were Woody and Blue, a couple of drivers from HQ Company and a very lively pair, indeed. These two produced their specialty act — race calling. Acting as radio announcers they went non-stop for about 20 minutes. They called two races (the Hoa

Long Welter and the Dat Do Dogs) and kept up a continuous flow of commercials, tips for next Saturday's races, interviews with trainers etc. Their act was excellent. Meanwhile, Dallas Leary, our cook, who bets on anything that moves, and runs a book on most Australian races each weekend, was calling prices for the races Woody and Blue were calling.

Also invited to the party was Private Garry Self, an Officers' Mess steward known to all as Gazza. Although a pleasant and most amusing character, Gazza upsets many officers because of his scruffy appearance and his clumsiness. A national serviceman from Hobart, and always willing to burst into song — usually 'Rule, Tasmania!' — he is very happy-natured and has a great reputation as a rich character. At the party tonight he also contributed to the entertainment, never being short of the right remark at the right time. I heard for the first time the true story of The Soup. A fortnight earlier I had heard of a steward being charged for spilling a plate of hot soup over Major Peter Murray in the Mess. Tonight I found out some additional facts, viz:

1. Major Murray was most unpopular with the stewards.
2. Gazza deliberately tipped the soup over him.
3. He was fined $10.
4. He collected $25 in bets.

Gazza announced at the party that in two weeks' time he was returning to Australia for discharge at the end of his national service. He then stated his intention to drop more soup in the right places and said to me, 'Who don't you like in the Mess, sir? You name him, and I promise you, he will wear it.' I declined to name anyone, so Gazza then said, 'OK sir. If you're too chicken then I'll pick one myself.' Gazza proceeded to name an officer who, he declared, 'will wear it!'. Actually this officer is also unpopular with the stewards and is therefore an automatic choice but I guess this is his problem, and I'll keep right out of it.

Major Bruce Daniel was saying to Gazza, 'You're just the man I need! Come down to Vung Tau and work in the HQ 1ALSG Mess and I'll give you a great long list to work down for me!'

Party finished at 22.00 after a most entertaining evening indeed.

Sunday 11 August 1968

I am required for Board of Court Martial at Vung Tau next week, immediately after I return from Long Binh. Court is being held for the second of the two members of the Armoured Squadron Workshop homosexuality case. Last week's vice trial resulted in a warrant officer being reduced to sergeant and receiving a severe reprimand. Next week a craftsman is being tried for his participation in the proceedings. Since no one, including witnesses, was sober, it promises to be a rather interesting tangle of contradictory evidence, especially since last week's court martial gave all the witnesses a practice run for this week's! Meanwhile, Charlie Squadron 1st Armoured Regiment has been nicknamed Cecil Squadron. But not in the presence of the Armoured Corps!

Found out today that Cuc, the charming girl from the Saigon laundry in Ba Ria (see back to 3 June '68), is engaged to an Australian second lieutenant, who will be leaving the Army when his national service is completed. He's a nice fellow, and Cuc is very sweet — but she's never been outside Vietnam and is still learning English (mainly from her fiancé). I fear that the transition to Australian life will be a greater shock than she or her fiancé realises, and he has hardly had any real chance to get to know her well.

Dominic Yau, a Survey Corps corporal who is an interpreter with the Intelligence Unit here, also intends to marry a local girl. She is from Vung Tau. Few of the normal regulations apply here, because Dominic Yau, although in the Australian Army, is an Asian himself, and holds Asian nationality, a fact which provoked Australia-wide publicity when it was first discovered three or four years ago. He had been in the Army a year or so before his citizenship became widely known. He and his fiancée are both professional interpreters with a great deal in common. Also they are both fluent in Chinese, Vietnamese and English. Unit commanders are required to discourage soldiers from marrying local girls, and to point out the obvious difficulties arising from such unions. But Captain Geoff Boscoe (commanding the Intelligence Unit) and I both think Geoff should be giving his blessing to this union, which he proposes to do.

Lots of B-52 strikes tonight — earth shaking and heaving frequently. The bombs are felt more than they are heard. Our intensive patrolling is being maintained, as we desperately seek information on enemy movement, and there's a lot going on all round us. A regular regiment from the North Vietnamese Army is in the province for the first time ever, and is heading this way. Not certain yet whether it's heading for us or the civilians of Ba Ria. Same applies to a rocket battalion, also known to be heading this way. Looks as though everyone is in for a lively time in the next few weeks. Meanwhile, this very night, things flared up in Long Dien, and 3rd Battalion rushed in with tanks and armoured personnel carriers. Things look nastier than they have for a long time.

To bed very late at end of a busy day. Artillery pounding steadily all night, B-52 strikes also felt.

Monday 12 August 1968

Up early to catch helicopter to Long Binh. While climbing aboard, I noticed another helicopter about 50 metres away, aflame all over, so I drew the pilot's attention to it and immediately found myself without a helicopter to get into — he wasted no time deciding that he didn't want to carry passengers and disappeared very smartly. The blazing helicopter was an American gunship, one of a light fire team of two US Army gunships which had just landed at the refuelling point. The second gunship also cleared off smartly.

The burning one was a spectacular sight — completely enveloped in flames and black, oily smoke, with its blazing main rotor still whirling (for a time anyway). Knowing the gunship to be fully loaded (it was just coming on duty) with thousands of rounds of mini-gun ammunition and about 40 rockets, each of which has a lethal range of a lot more than 50 metres, I went quickly to the edge of the helipad and lay in a shallow depression about 100 to 150 metres away, together with the other passengers for Long Binh. All the crew of the burning aircraft except the pilot were outside the helicopter when it ignited. The pilot had two seconds to get clear. He made it.

The blaze was enormous for 10 to 15 minutes. The flaming main rotor swung more and more slowly as it sagged and collapsed. Then the mini-gun ammunition began to explode. Multiple bangs and crackling could be heard. Tracer bullets went everywhere, making a spectacular fireworks display of white flashes away from the huge ball of rolling orange flame and the heavy black smoke. Then came a loud explosion — the first rocket — and a gleaming metal cylinder about 1 metre long went streaking horizontally out from the inferno, bouncing and skidding over the helipad towards the road. It stopped at the edge of the road and lay there, smoking, having not yet exploded. Men in the vicinity scattered madly, leaping into ditches and behind vehicles, but it lay there in full view, still smoking. More explosions. More rockets snaking and fishtailing over the pad and still not exploding. Soon the area was strewn with live rockets, some on the helipad, some beyond it.

Then it came! The bang was deafening. I cannot recall having heard a greater explosion at close quarters. Angry metal screamed overhead. Stones flew. Hard objects bounced along at great speed.

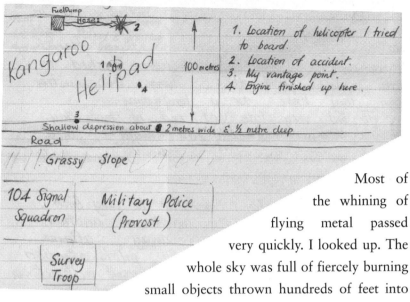

1. Location of helicopter I tried to board.
2. Location of accident.
3. My vantage point.
4. Engine finished up here.

Kangaroo Helipad

FuelDump

Hazard

100 metres

Shallow depression about 2 metres wide & ½ metre deep

Road

Grassy Slope

104 Signal Squadron

Military Police (Provost)

Survey Troop

Most of the whining of flying metal passed very quickly. I looked up. The whole sky was full of fiercely burning small objects thrown hundreds of feet into the air. There was no part of the sky where blazing debris could not be seen. Got to feet and dodged those pieces coming down on me — could see them easily thanks to the flame on them. Dropped down again as something else exploded and sent more metal aloft. Looked at the wreckage. It had gone. The whole aircraft had been blown to pieces in the big explosion. Fuel tanks, I thought at first, but I was told later that it was the propellant charges of one whole pod of rockets — the warheads themselves never exploded. The pieces of the destroyed helicopter had been scattered up to half a kilometre away from where it started. The largest remaining piece was about half of the motor, and it had landed about 60 metres away.

Then the early rocket that had finished up beside the road exploded and hurled its warhead out horizontally. It hit an RAAF vehicle which was stupidly passing by, didn't hit with its business end leading, bounced off, landed in the Provost lines and disappeared in the long grass, still having not exploded. More rockets leapt about. One flew spinning into the air and headed straight for the Survey Troop. In mid-flight, its own propulsion started up and deviated its course into the Signals Squadron instead. One man was hurt. A rock about 20 centimetres across was hurled in a very flat trajectory for about 200 to 250 metres into the Provost lines. It crossed the road at chest height — it was slow enough to be seen, but probably too fast to be ducked — luckily no one was near it.

All this time there was the crackle of bullets; however, they attracted little attention beside the flying rockets. At this stage gawking bystanders began to appear. First came a stupid Provost sergeant walking straight along the road. He came up and said, 'You'd better move on, sir, it's very dangerous here.'

I, still lying down, said, 'Yes, and if you'd seen the rockets crossing the road just before you came, you wouldn't be standing up and talking.'

He said, 'I saw them,' in an attempt at nonchalance, but spoilt the effect by attempting to light a cigarette with hands that trembled too much to put the flame to the tobacco. He then headed off down the road towards safety.

Then up came the Deputy Commander, the GSO2 Ops and the Aide to the Commander. Despite two more bangs and swishes as two more rockets skated aimlessly across the pad, across the road and into the long grass, they continued strolling along the road. They asked what was happening. I, more comfortable lying down and out of the direct path of shrapnel, told them. They continued to stroll about. I stayed put, having warned them. Bang! Another rocket across, and it stopped on the road right beside the Aide who, yes he really did, casually leant over for a closer look at the smoking lethal cylinder. I thought, if that rocket goes off — goodbye! But it didn't. Then another rocket came straight at us. I was safe as it whizzed overhead. Colonel Dunstan and the GSO2 were not, but it missed them. The GSO2 shoved a corporal aside in his leap into the ditch for safety. The corporal leapt in after him, his boots landing on the GSO2's head! The GSO2 emerged from the ditch, pronounced the situation dangerous and abruptly ordered everyone to depart.

Just then the padre arrived in a Land Rover. Bang! Another

rocket! Padre and others leapt behind vehicle for protection. Bang! This time a rocket behind the vehicle, and everyone raced round beside the vehicle. Blam! Off went the first rocket. People were jumping everywhere trying to find a protected part of the vehicle. Looked like the *Keystone Cops*. Eventually they turned the vehicle around and headed off. I went with them, and on to the Task Force HQ to arrange to go on another ride to Long Binh.

Cannot understand the recklessness of so many people. Very fine for officers to display courage to inspire men in face of enemy, but when no enemy present, surely the main aim is to use common sense and take precautions to reduce casualties to a minimum. To me, lying in the shallow, but fully protected, depression, the antics of the 'brave' were entertaining, but could easily have been tragic.

Returned to helipad at 10.00 to catch other helicopter and had an interesting flight up Route 15 to Long Binh. Arrived at 66 Company just in time for a farewell ceremony for Colonel Colvocoresses, the head of Mapping and Intelligence, the superior HQ of 66 Company. Brief and pleasant ceremony. Everybody likes Colonel Colvo (as everyone calls him, even he himself). They presented him with a plaque bought from Cheap Charlie of Bien Hoa, a local Vietnamese shop and reputedly the original 'Cheap Charlie' of Vietnam. Despite this it was a nice plaque.

Visited Mapping and Intelligence and while there I traded an old Australian slouch hat (thrashed to death by 7th Battalion) for a parachutist colonel's cap to send home. Visited the PX to do some shopping. Also visited 517 Terrain Detachment who make special maps showing cross-country going etc.

Spent pleasant evening talking with old friends Bill Brogan and Skip Skoglund and met some new faces: Lieutenants Ken Steward and Sam Entriken, and Warrant Officer Glen Swarthout.

Have never heard such heavy B-52 strikes as today's. Bombs falling all afternoon — mostly on outskirts of Saigon.

Tuesday 13 August 1968

Conference at 09.00 with Mapping and Intelligence (US Army) and NGS. Interesting conference, and several matters cropped up in which I was able to assist. One or two humorous incidents occurred too, viz:

'We need to send our survey party *there*!' (pointing to map).

'But, Colonel, we cain't do it. That's the most insecure area in the whole country!'

'Insecure? Goddamn it! The greatest concentration of American troops in the country is there!'

'Yes, Colonel, and have you considered why the greatest concentration of American troops is *right there*?'

Brave talk indeed from a captain to a colonel! But then it was the captain who commanded the survey troops who looked like facing this particular task.

After the conference I went, with several of the others, to have lunch in the Mess of the Commanding General of the US Army Engineers in Vietnam. There were only 14 of us altogether. The food was simple but beautifully prepared and delicious. Stacks of

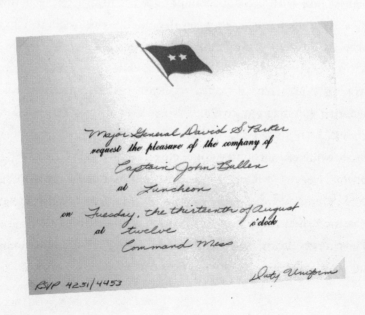

crab! Food served by two extremely attractive Vietnamese girls. The General picks them well. Altogether a very enjoyable meal.

Returned to 66 Company. Traded another slouch hat from 7th Battalion, this time for a Montagnard crossbow and a quiver of five arrows. Can't take it to Australia, due to Department of Agriculture regulations, so will give it to the Survey Troop canteen for decoration. Very nice little weapon — beautifully carved and very powerful.

Dinner in evening — a farewell dinner attended by all US topographic officers in Vietnam, given in honour of Colonel Colvo who goes home tomorrow. Several officers are newly arrived from USA and I made some good friends.

Promotion seems relatively fast in the US Army. Met one man my own age who was commissioned a year after me and who has just been promoted to lieutenant colonel. All of them seem to reach major within six to eight years of being commissioned. My length of service as a captain alone is, to their amazement, longer than some of them have taken to be commissioned as a second lieutenant and rise to the rank of major. Pay, rank for rank, is about twice that of the Australian Army.

Met Colonel Maberry, Colonel Colvo's replacement. He spoke of previous experiences with Australians, notably Spencer Snow on the survey of New Britain in 1954.

Wednesday 14 August 1968

Up early and down to helipad. Caught helicopter back to Nui Dat. Helicopter travelled direct, and did not follow the road as they usually do, so I saw more of the country for the first time. Back at the Survey Troop, did miscellaneous jobs and caught plane to Vung Tau in afternoon. Settled in at 1 Australian Field Hospital; as usual, made most welcome. Have been down so often for court martial work that I am regarded as a regular visitor and have been told that I can always have a bed there.

During the evening, a couple of other friends arrived from the HQ 1ALSG Officers' Mess to warn me that Peter Mazengarb, the HQ Company Commander, was uttering loud threats in the HQ Mess to have Captain Bullen dragged out of the hospital and paraded before him in his office in the morning. Reason was that he had reserved accommodation for me (not at my request), and I had stayed at 1 Australian Field Hospital instead (although I had informed HQ Company I was doing this). Typical Mazengarb, a champion grizzler. I remember him from 13 National Service Battalion at Ingleburn 13 years ago.

I've arranged accommodation at HQ Company on three previous visits to Vung Tau, and three times Mazengarb has bungled it and foisted me onto some other Mess in 1ALSG at the last moment. So now I go where I'm welcome. Mazengarb has just now been promoted to temporary major, which bothers me not at all since I'm two years senior to him as a substantive captain. Am looking forward to tomorrow's encounter with him. Was proposing to tell him a few facts about himself and his HQ Company and what he could do with the lot; however, my hosts have advised me to say only that I'm at the hospital as a guest of the Commanding Officer, and if Mazengarb has any objection he can see Colonel Watson about the matter. Will accept this advice. Colonel Watson obviously welcomes the confrontation. Should be a lively day.

Thursday 15 August 1968

Court martial lasted barely an hour. A staggering thing happened. The accused pleaded guilty, apologised for his despicable act, and threw himself on the mercy of the court, and got 90 days in the slot.

He was charged with having 'committed a disgraceful and indecent act . . . ' Was defended by an RAAF flight lieutenant legal officer brought specially from Malaya. Apparently the accused wished to plead guilty. Don't know why. I wish I could have defended him. It would have been the easiest defence I'd ever had, once I'd persuaded him to plead not guilty. Reasons:

The act, with regard to the circumstances (which were extraordinary), was not indecent.

1. No sexuality at all was even alleged.

2. All witnesses for the prosecution had been drunk at the time and their evidence was worthless. Had the accused pleaded not guilty, the prosecution would have had to prove guilt, and could not have done so.

3. The accused should have been found not guilty of the charge laid. He was indeed guilty of drunken stupidity, but he had not been charged with that. Sadly, I was unable to convince my fellow board members, whom I felt were swayed by prejudice more than by evidence. They viewed the incident as homosexual and to be treated with severity. So I took my only option and formally dissented from the finding and sentence. The whole affair should have been settled within the squadron and should never have come to a court martial, but too many people got too excited and spiteful over it.

Visited PX in afternoon. Bought a few minor things including some instant coffee and Pream instant milk.

Several officers down here from the Task Force this evening. Seems as though the Task Force may get hit by the enemy tonight. Movement all around Nui Dat, including part of a rocket battalion. Seems likely that enemy will attack Ba Ria, after having first bombed the Task Force to create confusion amongst the forces most likely to protect Ba Ria. Didn't hear from Mazengarb all day.

Friday 16 August 1968

Caught early aircraft back to Nui Dat. Task Force was not attacked during night but several other places were, including Blackhorse, an American camp about 20 kilometres north of us and about the same size. The attack consisted of mortars and rockets only, but further to the north a Vietnamese village just east of Xuan Loc and beside the big mountain Nui Chua Chan got an awful hiding from bombs and rockets, and received a ground attack from a Viet Cong battalion as well. Xuan Loc was also hit.

Tonight is the second anniversary of the first major attack on the Task Force base, two nights prior to the battle of Long Tan. Everybody prepared for attack.

Saturday 17 August 1968

Quiet night, apart from our own artillery pounding incessantly. Urgent job to be done today but no problem with it.

Had lunch at Madame Minh Ha's at Ba Ria on occasion of the departure of Captain Tommy Thompson, Quartermaster of the Tank Squadron, for Australia next week. Food as usual was delicious. Am slowly mastering chopsticks. Am very popular with Madame Minh Ha because I can interpret English–French and vice versa for her. Her brother, a captain in the police, was there too. He also speaks reasonably good French. The highlight of the meal was crab and asparagus soup.

After leaving Madame Minh Ha's we delivered freshly cleaned uniforms to the tank crews stationed around Ba Ria. The Australian Task Force has a battalion of infantry and two troops of tanks around Ba Ria ready for instant action, in view of the present enemy threat.

I then went to 10 MID at Van Kiep to attend a small farewell party that the detachment was giving in honour of Geoff Boscoe, the commander of the Task Force Divisional Intelligence Unit, who goes home on Monday. It was a very simple party, but even the Phuoc Tuy province chief came. 10 MID gave Geoff a lovely lacquered wood dressing-table box, with inlaid mother-of-pearl and an inscription plate. Dai-Uy Trung, the 10 MID commander, made a very nice speech. Dai-Uy Trung is a pretty tough man. He is widely feared by the Viet Cong, who have placed a high price on his head. 10 MID does most of the interrogation of prisoners and this also gives ground for fear. Trung's previous post was as chief of police in Da Nang. He has survived three mine or grenade explosions, one of which cost him the sight in his right eye. He wields considerable power in the land, yet is of gentle and friendly manner — to Australians, anyway! He is obviously very sorry to see Geoff go, since they have done a lot of dangerous work together and have had a lot of success, and have also become very close friends. I admire Trung, a true patriot.

Returned to Nui Dat and got caught in a heavy rainstorm, which developed into the heaviest rain I've known. It lasted for several hours, and everything was flooded. Whole trenches and weapon pits were filled. Tent floors were awash. Water everywhere. Eased up near midnight.

Sunday 18 August 1968

Viet Cong entered Ap Suoi Nghe last night and cut throats of the village chief and his deputy. Same thing happened six months ago. I wonder if there are any more citizens willing to assume responsibility when this happens — it being the Viet Cong's aim, of course, to eliminate those willing to accept responsibility and help

Madame Trung, Dai-Uy (Captain) Le Ba Trung, and Captain John Bullen.

people. This will have set back the effectiveness of civil aid to Ap Suoi Nghe a great deal.

The murder of the few citizens who are willing to do their best to help organise a little refugee village is a terrible thing. I wonder how many people will hear of this in Australia. It is tragic that this sort of thing attracts so little publicity, while our press and politicians rant and rave over water being given to a Viet Cong agent to make her talk.[4] The Vietnamese killed her the next day anyway. Senses of values do indeed get distorted in war, and it seems that sometimes the further one is from the war the more distorted is one's view. However, this latest affair is a heavy blow to the long-suffering refugees in Suoi Nghe.

Attended a small party at the Divisional Intelligence Unit for another farewell to Geoff Boscoe from all people in the Task Force associated with him. Geoff has done a wonderful job here and a lot of people turned up, even the Task Force Commander, Brigadier Hughes. All of 10 MID came, and Dai-Uy Trung brought his wife — who does not look like the mother of eight children, which she is. An American major came from Long Binh, together with Chanh, the commander of 3 MID. Geoff received many lovely gifts, easily the largest collection I've seen at a farewell in this country. The province chief sent two beautiful gifts, one for Geoff and one for Geoff's wife. Madame Trung also gave Geoff a couple of gifts for his wife. Nice to see Geoff's wife recognised — Geoff's been in Vietnam since April last year.

Afternoon quiet but evening busy. Top Vietnamese sources have given urgent advice of the fact that the enemy intends to attack Vung Tau and Ba Ria and other targets tonight. It is expected that the Task Force will receive rocket and mortar attack tonight to divert

[4] The water torture case mentioned 14 March 1968. — PH

attention from the probable ground assault on Ba Ria. Overheard Brigadier Hughes ordering a second casualty evacuation helicopter to be standing by tonight, along with the usual one at Vung Tau, in case we get casualties at Nui Dat and the helicopter gets hit before it can leave Vung Tau. Briefed all members of Survey Troop on action to take in event of attack, hoping that all precautions will prove unnecessary. Found when checking radio and phone communications that HQ Company hasn't even been warned of the serious situation and that neither their phone nor radio is working properly, nor do they have any instructions as to what to do in an emergency. Sorted their mess out as best I could and suggested they get hold of their commander and ask him what was going on.

To bed early in case sleep is lost tonight if we're attacked. Can feel B-52 bombs landing a long way to our north.

Monday 19 August 1968

Some action nearby — a bit of grenade throwing on the perimeter wire but nothing serious. Meanwhile the alert continues for another night at least.

Tuesday 20 August 1968

Quite a lot of close machine-gun fire from midnight until 02.00 but nothing to show for it later. Again no attack on us. Found out today that many business people in Ba Ria (including Madame Minh Ha) went to Vung Tau two days ago to avoid any attack, and have now returned. The attack was expected at 02.30 this morning — rockets, mortars and a ground assault on Ba Ria and Long Dien, and rockets and mortars on Nui Dat to keep us from rushing immediately into Ba

Ria and Long Dien. However, something serious obviously went wrong and the attack did not eventuate. Rather surprising, actually; the local Vietnamese people are usually pretty reliably informed. Although the residents returned today, the alert continues, and with the exception of 1st Battalion guarding Ba Ria, all forces are in the Task Force base area or patrolling around it.

The Survey Troop was challenged to a volleyball match today by the Task Force HQ Officers' Mess. Although eligible to play for either side, I played with the Survey team. We won three games to nil. Noisy night. Much artillery and some machine-gun fire.

Wednesday 21 August 1968

Still no major action around us but we're all on the alert and every effort is being made to gain information on enemy intentions.

Thursday 22 August 1968

The Battle for Long Dien burst forth today — the heaviest village fighting in the province since Tet (first week in February '68). 1st Battalion with tanks and APCs fought all day. About 100 Viet Cong were in Long Dien, all in small groups, moving and striking quickly throughout the whole town. Civilians everywhere. What a tangle to work out who is enemy and who is friend. Even the 'friends' are hardly friendly in these circumstances. Our tank crews were instructed not to fire the tanks' main guns — fair enough, really, as a few shots from those deadly 20-pounders, with their high velocity, would make an awful mess of the town. As it turned out, the tanks were requested to fire late in the day and did let off a couple of canister rounds. Heavy rain and wind all day. Fighting eased at end of day. The final score was 11 Australians wounded, 36 Viet Cong killed and an unknown number of Viet Cong wounded; two of the Australian wounded are seriously ill, but are expected to recover. We could have committed a greater force to Long Dien, but did not, since it was strongly suspected that this was just a feint by the enemy and that the main attack would come elsewhere.

Meanwhile, Dat Do had a hard time, with the Viet Cong locked in combat with the ARVN and US advisers for a while. The fighting in Dat Do was on a much smaller scale than in Long Dien, but friendly casualties were a lot higher in Dat Do and the enemy suffered less.

Altogether a busy day for the Task Force, trying to liberate Long Dien, protect Ba Ria and work out which way the enemy will jump. To bed early — in Command Post from midnight.

Friday 23 – Sunday 25 August 1968

Fairly quiet session in Command Post from midnight until 08.00. Things livened up a lot after 07.00, but it was apparent that yesterday's savage fighting in Long Dien will not be repeated today.

Duc Thanh, just north of us, was mortared last night and a large ambush (usual result — no Viet Cong casualties, no ARVN casualties) occurred in Ba Ria. Otherwise, very little happened.

The 3rd Battalion went to Long Son Island by air today to search the island for rocket sites, which could pound both Ba Ria and Vung Tau, and are believed to be there. Little was discovered, however.

Meanwhile, the alert continues and all our forces remain in or close to Nui Dat, ready for fast action anywhere. We know the enemy is all around us in considerable strength, but cannot work out what he will do next. We suspect

USAF B-52 bomber

he feels the same way about us and is keeping out of the way and watching us closely to observe our reactions. One thing is sure: although he has not yet launched his main attack, he meant to do so before this, but things went wrong. It is thought that the major upsetting factor has been the incurring of serious losses from B-52 bomber strikes within the past fortnight.

The mighty B-52 bombs are indeed frightening — they certainly frighten us if they land within 25 kilometres of us. We get used to the shooting of small arms and to the pounding of artillery, but the shuddering of the ground, hills, buildings etc from B-52 bombs is a chilling experience. We never see or hear the bombers. We never hear the bombs fall. Suddenly one 'feels' what is happening and wonders just when the tortured earth will stop heaving.

Meanwhile, in the stand-off the unfortunate civilians in Ba Ria are urgently filling sandbags. No rain on Saturday or Sunday — most unusual.

Monday 26 August 1968

Quiet day. Got a lot done — now almost up to date. Still no rain.

Tuesday 27 August 1968

Concert in morning. Poor show — the second-worst this year. The troupe consisted of Eddie Mendoza (an aging North English comedian), The Prestons (a folk-singing couple from Wollongong), two female singer/dancers, and a rhythm section of three. Highlights were:
1. The folk-singing — this couple was good, but nowhere near as good as The Seekers, whom they were emulating.

2. Eddie Mendoza's joke about Admiral Lord Nelson and the corduroy trousers. (All his other jokes were feeble, old, or had been done better by previous concert parties, but the one on Nelson wasn't bad: 'Prior to the Battle of Trafalgar, HMS *Victory*'s masthead lookout reports French frigates on the horizon. Admiral Nelson orders "Battle stations" and sends for his cutlass. The lookout then reports lots more frigates approaching. Nelson sends for his scarlet tunic so that, if he is wounded, the blood won't show and thus dismay his men. The lookout reports an even larger fleet of French men o' war approaching from another direction. Nelson now sends for his brown corduroy breeches.')

3. One of the girls who couldn't sing, looked even worse, but had good legs and was prepared to display all of them.

4. Comments from the audience. Samples of the latter:

   Eddie Mendoza: 'And now I'd like to do an Italian piece.'

   Corporal Peter Dew's voice from audience: 'Wouldn't we all!'

   Eddie Mendoza: 'I meant on my piano accordion.'

   Peter Dew again: 'Don't get caught in the bellows, mate!'

Generally the audience was faster off the mark than the performers. Another example:

   Girl in mini-dress standing with legs apart at edge of stage while singing into microphone suddenly notices a soldier from front row who has his head on the stage floor between her feet looking upward through his camera with telephoto lens. Girl stops singing and looks down: 'Hey, that's a bit rude isn't it?' Soldier (cheerfully): 'I don't mind!' and continues to aim and fire camera up her dress.

Altogether it was a weak concert, though not quite the weakest.

Looks as though the next few days will be very busy. Noel is on R&R leave in Hong Kong and Spike Jones goes into hospital tomorrow for examination of a suspected stomach ulcer. The supremely capable Grant Small is now acting as second-in-command of the troop.

Played volleyball in the late afternoon for Officers' Mess versus RAEME Light Aid Detachment and we won the match. I played a much better game than usual and contributed a lot towards the result. It was really a pretty untidy and disorganised affair, but I got plenty of exercise, which was the main thing.

Heavy rain in evening after four dry days.

Wednesday 28 August 1968

Much minor action immediately to the north of Nui Dat. Nothing serious — just a few road blocks and a bit of shooting and mortaring — no casualties. Route 2 finally cleared as far as Duc Thanh, after a minor APC operation. Busy day and late night to catch up.

Thursday 29 – Saturday 31 August 1968

Three fairly quiet days. Not much enemy action, but large enemy forces are still known to be near, so our own forces are still patrolling very actively and standing by ready to leap into Ba Ria or any other towns. The casualty evacuation helicopter is still standing by nightly at Nui Dat, in addition to the usual one at Vung Tau.

Received a Father's Day card from home today. This is the second Father's Day card from the children since I was re-posted, leaving the family at Wodonga. I hadn't really realised until now that I've been away from home for well over a year. Rain now intermittent.

SEPTEMBER

AUSTRALIAN MILITARY FORCES

AAB — 71A
Reprinted Dec, 1964

RECORD BOOK

CONTAINING 96 PAGES

RULED FEINT

Encounters with bar girls in Saigon or Vung Tau were almost inevitable whether a soldier sought their company or not. Many girls touting for 'Saigon teas' were farm girls working to send money home to their families, some earning double what their fathers might earn from labouring on the land. Bar girls had perhaps even more to risk in a liaison than a soldier, with pregnancy a very possible consequence as well as VD. Besides infection, bars also posed other risks. Australian Army charge sheets contain many accounts of fights with locals and US soldiers. The slightest provocation triggered bar brawls, a few spilling out onto the streets and drawing huge crowds. Dealing with drunken soldiers was an occupational hazard of the Australian and US military police, who could be surprisingly patient with the offenders.

PAUL HAM

★

'I want to be completely cleared,' said the drunk.
'I'm not drunk and I want you to put me through
all your sobrite . . . sobrity . . . sobritery, tests.
You know the ones I mean.'

★

Sunday 1 September 1968

Urgent job in morning. Probably our fastest ever. Drew it up and had it dyelined and delivered for distribution in less than two hours. Eric Clutterbuck was at Vung Tau today and we have no other draughtsman capable of swift free-hand work, so I did this one myself. Job passable but not excellent. I'm badly out of practice at draughting and was just getting good as I finished.

Overheard an amusing story in the canteen in the afternoon: '. . . we'd arranged to shack up for the weekend so I bought a heap of French letters from the chemist on Friday. The chemist said to me, "Onto a sure thing, eh?" I said, "You bet I am!" and then left. When I came around to pick her up that evening, her father opened the door. Gawd! Would ya believe it? The chemist!'

Father's Day today. Smokes handed out to all married fathers from the Father's Day Council of New South Wales. I gave mine away to some of the unmarried fathers who were protesting vociferously against this discrimination.

Gazza, the Mess steward, has gone home to his beloved Tasmania. He spent his last week stalking his officer target around the Mess with several plates of soup, but could never catch him away from the Brigadier's side. When asked by another steward why he didn't let it fly anyway, he is reputed to have replied, 'I may be a fool, but not that big a fool. I've hurled a lot of soup in my time and my vast experience informs me that a lot of fall-out occurs and a few other people wear it too, and I do want to catch that plane home!'

No rain today. Is the wet breaking up early perhaps?

Monday 2 – Wednesday 4 September 1968

Busy time getting many tasks completed prior to downing tools for a day to visit the beach annex of the Peter Badcoe Club at Vung Tau. Noel and I are both going, together with half the Survey Troop, so no loose ends must be left to cause difficulty while we're away. Ted Morris is now on R&R leave, Spike Jones is in hospital (suspected ulcer), so is Eric Clutterbuck (neck X-ray after a knock while swimming at Vung Tau last Sunday), so Grant Small is now in command.

Easy trip down — there are 72 of us in all, since I am in command of a large group of minor units, including one or two with a reputation for bad behaviour. Got ourselves settled in. Many went on leave into the town of Vung Tau. No one got into trouble. So far so good. Had swim in evening in the new swimming pool.

Thursday 5 September 1968

Went for a swim in the morning and then to the American PX for shopping but bought little. Very tempted by a Remington 550 cordless shaver for worldwide use (90 to 250 volt) for only US$24.50, but decided to leave it for the time being. Bought a Vietnam colouring book for David and a couple of minor items, plus a small red book called *Quotations From Chairman LBJ*, which goes rather well with *Chairman Mao's Thoughts*, which I bought in Macau a couple of months ago. I find myself more in tune with President Johnson than Chairman Mao. I can relate well to Chairman LBJ's 'Don't spit in the soup, we've all got to eat!'.

Went into Vung Tau township this evening on leave for the first time since arriving in this country some seven months ago. Only spent two hours but found it quite interesting and entertaining. Most shops were open but there was little to buy — mainly cheap souvenirs at not-so-cheap prices. Vung Tau's main attraction is obviously its night life. Girls everywhere — some on the streets but mainly in the bars, which are just everywhere. Some girls are attractive, others are less so; some have charming manners, others less so. Walked past all the bars and salesmen along to the Grand Hotel, reputedly the main night-life centre. Entered the bar there and almost tripped over the neckline of the first girl inside the door. Despite the clutches of an equally voluptuous girl, who put her arms around me from behind, I made it to the bar itself and then paused to take stock of the situation. One bar, double-seated booths, dull lights, soft music, and girls and servicemen everywhere. Some servicemen were talking together, but mostly they were paired with girls. Some couples were embracing, others just talking.

I joined Peter Smith, our clerk, the only Australian I recognised there, and we watched the world go by for a while. The system is that a girl joins a man, and if he buys her a 'Saigon tea' (a thimbleful of champagne, lemonade or tepid water for about $3) she stays with him and they talk and she is most affectionate until the $3 is considered expended, and then another Saigon tea must be bought for the situation to continue. While I was with Peter, several girls came up to talk to us; all spoke English, some also spoke French, and most were both beautiful and charming. None, however, stayed very long once they realised that neither of us was buying (Australians do have a reputation for being Cheap Charlies

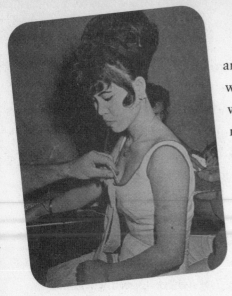

and very tight-fisted — and small wonder, since no one can compete with the Americans at showering money about), although quite a lot of body contact occurred to help persuade us to buy their company and perhaps a lot more later. The bar was fairly crowded, so the girls were able to exploit this easily, pressing themselves against any unaccompanied man. Peter and I were watching one girl with a really beautiful smile who was with an American. She smiled at us a few times. We smiled back and soon had the American to contend with, he believing we were trying to steal his girl. We calmed him down, but then he became very friendly, and this was worse. He told us some of his Heroic Adventures In The War, but then his girl, bless her, dragged him away.

Then a fight broke out. A drunken Australian was trying to punch a bar girl in the face and was expressing his feelings freely: 'Fuckin' slope-headed bastards! Filthy noggie sluts! . . .' etc. She seemed pretty angry, too. I intervened, having first taken care to ascertain the winning side and join it. I grabbed the Australian and hauled him out of it. He was so drunk I could have done it one-handed. Got him out of the way and cooled him down.

'Those fuckin' slopes! I fuckin' hate 'em.'

'Yeah mate, yeah. But don't let them get you down.'

'Lemme go! I wanna puncha slant-eyed bitch inna mouf!'

'No, mate, later on. Let her go for the moment. Stop here and have a smoke.'

Peter came good with a cigarette and we managed to cool him off. The bar girl was rather annoyed with me and said so. 'Why you stop fight? I can look after myself. I beat him easy.'

I explained as best I could. 'Sorry 'bout that, but this man heavy-weight champ of Navy. Last fight he pull whole hotel down. You leave him with us.'

Meanwhile, another man put his arm around the girl and headed her to a booth while Peter and I steered the drunk in the opposite direction.

Another girl appeared. 'You have man here speaks French?', the word having apparently spread. Someone pointed me out. She came over, obviously interested. She asked a few questions. I answered vaguely and put questions back at her. She came from Bien Hoa; she had two children; she didn't like Vung Tau (work too hard); she hoped to return to Bien Hoa soon; she had a daughter, Julie, now aged two — would I like to see photo?

'Yes please.' Her photo showed a 100% American baby, with 'Anthony James, aged 6 months' written on back. I suspect it may have come from an American wallet. I didn't believe a word she said, but she was very pleasant to talk to. However, after a few minutes, someone who would buy her drinks entered the bar and she joined him instead.

Spent about an hour in the Grand Hotel and then wandered back to the marketplace to catch the leave truck back to camp at 20.45, curfew in town being 21.00. Arrived back at market five minutes early so wandered into a bar for a look. Girls were much less attractive than at the Grand Hotel, but one or two looked very pretty. One sexy creature came up and said, 'You come out the back with me?'

'I'd love to, beautiful, but not enough time.'

'You have five minutes, that's plenty of time!' Escaped to market again and caught truck with all the drunks back to camp.

Friday 6 September 1968

Up early and packed ready for return to Nui Dat. Not all members of our 72-man party looking healthy. Many very seedy from alcoholic and/or sexual excesses of previous day, and a few had been picked up by the MPs while trying to sneak back into camp this morning after breaking curfew for all-night sessions with girls in Vung Tau. The main culprits were from the Task Force Garrison Military Police and 8 Field Ambulance. The Survey Troop came through unscathed. Leisurely drive back to Nui Dat. Spent afternoon catching up on routine tasks. As expected, all has gone very smoothly with Grant Small in command for the past two days.

Invited to A Squadron 3 Cavalry Regiment for dinner, so went along after work. To my surprise, it turned out to be a big affair with the Task Force Commander and goodness knows who else there, too. The purpose of the gathering was to present plaques to those Task Force units who had done a lot for the Cavalry Squadron. Presentations were made to Task Force HQ (received by the Commander), the 1st, 3rd and 4th Battalions (received by their Commanding Officers), 12 Field Regiment Royal Australian Artillery and Royal New Zealand Artillery, 104 Signals Squadron, and, to my complete astonishment, 1 Topographical Survey Troop. Couldn't figure why such a minor unit was being acclaimed along with such major units, but a lot of nice things were said about us anyway. A very nice plaque too. Altogether a most pleasant and enjoyable gathering, but I had to leave early and scamper back to the troop for our normal evening parade, where I handed the plaque over to the men who really earned it, so it can be mounted in the Boozer (which has on many occasions offered hospitality to members of A Squadron 3 Cavalry Regiment).

No rain for several days.

Saturday 7 September 1968

Not much drawing or printing possible today due to the Engineers working on the rewiring of our area — a much-needed task, too. The wiring here has been an electrician's nightmare. For example, in our printing room alone we have three motor-driven vacuum pumps (two for vacuum frames and one for the printing press) one arc lamp, one electric 5-gallon water heater, one heavy-duty air conditioner and a lot of normal lighting. The arc lamp alone draws 70 amps. The main cable to the building is a 55-amp cable. The other day we had everything on at once and blew out the circuit breaker in the main Task Force generator, hence the rewiring now in progress!

Fair bit of rain today but not the usual brief and heavy downpour. Weather is definitely changing pattern now. To bed early; in Command Post tonight.

Sunday 8 September 1968

Up at midnight and into the Command Post until 08.00. Night very quiet with little happening.

Heard details of nasty accident the other night while I was at Vung Tau. An SAS patrol far to the west near Route 15 had a night clash with a 24-man Vietnamese PF patrol and scored a heavy victory. Was the PF's fault, but most unfortunate just the same.

The PF's American adviser knew of the presence of SAS somewhere in the area and had been advised to stay clear, but he overlooked this rather important piece of information and led his PF patrol straight into the ambush laid by the ten-man SAS patrol. The SAS patrol was armed to the teeth and poured forth such a ferocious volume of fire that the American adviser reported his 'enemy' as consisting of one company plus mortar support; i.e. well over 100 men. An understandable misjudgement. In the heat of battle at night, a host of automatic small arms with automatic M79 grenade launchers attached would have easily created the illusion of a much larger force.

The battle raged for over an hour. Confusion aggravated by poor map reading. An incorrect location reported by the PF gave the initial impression that there were two separate enemy contacts occurring at the same time in different places almost a kilometre apart. At one stage, the SAS patrol was the target of mortar fire from the PF post at Lang Phuoc Hoa. Eventually the awful truth dawned and a 'friendly' clash was confirmed. Finally, a cease-fire was called and the wounded evacuated by helicopter.

Amazingly, casualties were much less than they could so easily have been. At least seven PF soldiers and their American adviser were wounded, some of them seriously. Everyone very sorry, and although the matter is of course being officially recorded, it is otherwise being quietly suppressed. There were no Australian casualties, and the PF and the Americans, being in the wrong, naturally don't want to shout about it. All a terrible mistake and the losers have learnt the hard way.

I noticed in the Cavalry Squadron's Officers' Mess yesterday that all their Playmate pin-ups have disappeared, and found out that this was done by order of General MacDonald, Commander, Australian Forces Vietnam, when visiting Nui Dat recently. This autocratic act has annoyed a lot of people for many reasons, viz:
1. This is the home of the Cavalry Squadron, not of General
   MacDonald.

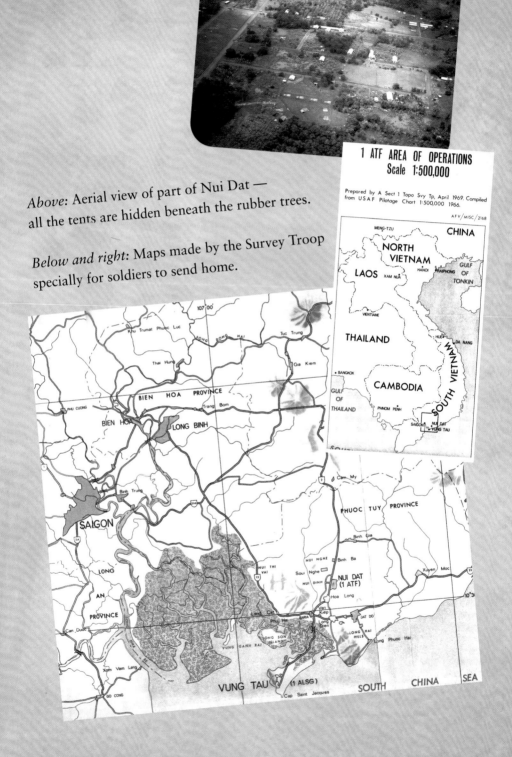

Above: Aerial view of part of Nui Dat — all the tents are hidden beneath the rubber trees.

Below and right: Maps made by the Survey Troop specially for soldiers to send home.

1 ATF AREA OF OPERATIONS
Scale 1:500,000

Prepared by A Sect 1 Topo Svy Tp, April 1969. Compiled from U S A F Pilotage Chart 1:500,000 1966.

AFV/MISC/2168

Top: Hercules 'Spectre' gunship at Tan Son Nhut,
7 November 1968. *Above*: Chinook helicopter at Vung Tau.

Below: The Playmate count on the draughting hut wall shows
the Survey Troop to have been in Vietnam for 24 months.

Above left: Stage-door johnnies await their prey at Luscombe Bowl; *above right:* Yvonne Barrett on stage; *right:* Rocky Camps pushes his luck with Pat and Wendy Sullivan.

Below: Symbols of the Vietnam War. Life and war coexist as combat troops go into action past men of peace today, or perhaps boy scouts on a hike tomorrow.

Top: Turret of tank protecting the Survey Troop at Ap Suoi Nghe, 19 May 1968. *Above:* Huey gunship destroyed at Kangaroo Pad, 12 August 1968. Its motor is burning at far right.

Below: A healthier gunship on Kangaroo Pad.

'Spooky', alias 'Puff the Magic Dragon', on the ground with multi-barrelled guns visible, and at bottom, in action at night, firing 300 rounds of 7.62mm ammunition per second.

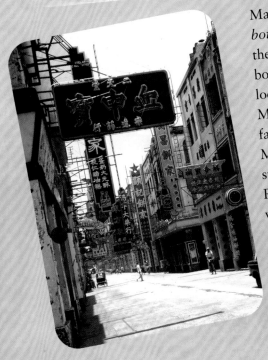

Macau, 28 June 1968. *Top to bottom*: Wrapping paper from the Communist Party bookshop; lunch at home for a local resident near the floating Macau Casino; park scene not far from the ferry terminal; Macau's main commercial street, the Avenida de Almeida Ribeiro, contrasting strongly with Hong Kong's hectic bustle.

Two business cards from the heaps showered into the bus by excited girls blowing kisses in Hong Kong, 25 June 1968.

View down the Victoria Peak tramway, over Hong Kong and across to Kowloon. Kai Tak airport is at upper right. This cable-hauled tramway, ascending 400 metres, was built in the 1880s.

Top to bottom: Military Payment Certificate (60 per cent actual size), the military money in Vietnam; the Survey Troop mascot, a Vietnamese dragon; lunch menu at the Pacific Officers' Club, Vung Tau, 28 November 1968.

Below: Captain Bullen's original diary notebooks, front and (inset) rear.

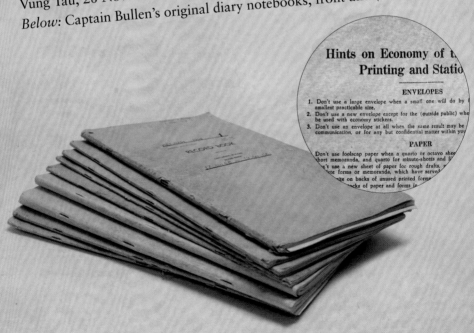

Hints on Economy of t
Printing and Statio

ENVELOPES

1. Don't use a large envelope when a small one will do by smallest practicable size.
2. Don't use a new envelope except for the (outside public) whe be used with economy stickers.
3. Don't use an envelope at all when the same result may be communication, or for any but confidential matter within you

PAPER

Don't use foolscap paper when a quarto or octavo shee short memoranda, and quarto for minute-sheets and fi
Don't use a new sheet of paper for rough drafts,
lete forms or memoranda, which have served
ite on backs of unused printed form
ocks of paper and forms in

2. The pin-ups were arranged in a rather attractive display and it did enhance the appearance of the Mess.

3. Everyone else thought the Mess most attractive until General MacDonald on his first *and only* visit to it. General MacDonald's autocracy is renowned but I didn't expect it to extend this far.

Command Post livened up at dawn as an operation by the 4th Battalion got under way, and several enemy were encountered and shot. No casualties of our own, so no emergency procedures needed to be organised. About 07.00 the GSO2 Ops came in, determined to make trouble — as the beast usually does before it's been fed. Had a torrid couple of minutes but I had all the answers, so he quit and went and ate someone else instead. Ah well, he goes home next month and is being promoted to lieutenant colonel, so someone else will then have to bear the brunt before feeding time. He came back again after breakfast and was perfectly amiable. Left Command Post myself shortly after 08.00 and had breakfast. Then back to bed till lunch time.

Urgent drawing and printing job in afternoon, but got it done OK without complications. The GSO2 Ops was delighted with it and will probably remain tractable for several days now. The job was done very fast — drawn and printed in four to five hours from start to finish with 110 copies screen printed. In addition, job was very accurate, better than most — mainly because I drew the original myself, rather than the GSO3 or GSO2 Ops, who always turn out a draft that is very hard for our draughtsmen to work from.

Quiet evening so to bed early to catch up on sleep.

Monday 9 September 1968

Got a lot done and very nearly finished the monthly report for August in one day. More favourable comments on last night's printing job, so I passed them on to all the men who did it. Engineers are still rewiring our buildings so not much drawing and printing was done today.

Much strong wind — most unusual — and no rain until a short burst late in evening. Had a lot of booster injections today — cholera, plague, smallpox and typhoid. Body aching all over, so early to bed.

Tuesday 10 September 1968

Ghastly day, thanks mainly to typhoid, I think. Struggled through until mid-afternoon, by which time body aches and headaches had become so severe that I had to lie down. Had a feverish couple of hours' rest, perspiring profusely, but then felt much better and got up for dinner. Met Steve Hart at dinner, the new Officer Commanding 547 Signals Troop, who arrived today. Nice to see Steve again, having not seen him since Germany in 1965.

Wednesday 11 September 1968

Much better day. No ill effects remaining except for sore arm. Got several minor tasks completed.

Heard 1 Australian Civil Affairs Unit referred to as 1 Australian Piranha Unit. Wondered why. 'What!' said my informant. 'Haven't you ever gone into the Mess for a meal only five minutes after it's started and met the Piranha officers marching out, all in step, leaving an array of bare tables behind them?' Yes, I had noticed this, now that it was mentioned.

Being rather taken with this name for the CA Unit, I passed it onto another friend later on in the day. He, a veteran of 11 months here, and due to go home, replied, 'Didn't you know? They used to be called that when I first came here and they were even more voracious then!'

Tragedy today. Paul Alderson has been stopped from going home next Tuesday. He is required to give evidence at a court martial in the middle of October concerning the accuracy of a map he drew. He now has to wait in Vietnam at Her Majesty's pleasure for about five weeks or so. I made all the arrangements for Paul to go home about a month ago, when the Legal officer promised me that Paul would not be required for this court martial. Chased around everywhere today, and even presented Paul's case to the Chief of Staff at HQ Australian Forces Vietnam in Saigon, but no luck. Paul has to stay here. Very bad for morale for this to happen at such short notice. Doubly unfortunate that it has happened to one of our best and most conscientious men, a man thoroughly deserving of favourable consideration.

My argument to all whom I've accosted is that the checker of any survey work is more responsible for the quality of the work than the man who did it in the first place. This is standard Survey Corps policy. Thus, the commander of a mapping unit (and ultimately the Director of the Survey Corps) is responsible for the accuracy of all maps produced by that unit. Therefore, if anyone is to testify in court on map accuracy, it should be the unit commander — i.e. me. The Task Force HQ and the Chief of Staff at Saigon appreciate all this but are powerless because it is a legal matter and the Legal Corps view reigns supreme. My esteem for the Legal Corps sinks even lower.

Steady light rain all evening. Most unusual. Normally we get short, heavy showers.

Thursday 12 September 1968

Very busy day. Had plenty to do, then a lot of visitors came along and I finished up getting very little done.

Much amusement today over an unfortunate accident. An officer of justifiably wide renown for his sexual exploits handled the 50-calibre gun on his armoured personnel carrier in the Cavalry Squadron incorrectly, with the result that a round exploded before it was fully in the firing chamber. Apparently the head space on the weapon was incorrectly adjusted and was excessive. He is now in hospital at Vung Tau while they extract shrapnel from his testicles. 'Couldn't happen to a nicer bloke!' is a comment I heard many times today, said each time with a broad grin.[1]

Steady light rain for most of the day today. Weather is most uncertain at the moment.

Likelihood of attack on the Task Force seems to be decreasing for the time being. Quiet night tonight with relatively little artillery.

Friday 13 September 1968

Quite a busy day and several minor matters cropped up. Finished printing the Dat Do map today and it looks a very attractive job — five colours. Checked the new (third edition) Nui Dat map and it will be printed next week. Noel, Grant and John Hunter have been busy for several days assembling storage racks in the new map store, which will be a real beauty when completed.

Not much rain today, weather very humid as usual.

Announcement of postal strike in Australia caused much annoyance here. This is the one thing that upsets people more than anything else, even enemy action. The PMG[2] is held in unbelievable contempt by everyone here. Same applies to the Amalgamated

[1] Heard later that some of the brass fragments could not be safely extracted surgically, so the patient now has the nickname 'Jingle Balls'. — JB
[2] Post Master General, as Australia Post was then known. — PH

Postal Workers' Union, in the eyes of those who know where the blame really lies.

Last night the US Army lost a Mohawk reconnaissance aircraft into the sea off Lang Phuoc Hai — the crew of two were lost. Cause of crash not known but the subsequent search-and-rescue aircraft received anti-aircraft fire, and so did other reconnaissance aircraft later today. To avenge this, several air strikes went in this morning, the aim being to teach people not to shoot at US aircraft. One target received two air strikes at different times, so life was pretty grim around Lang Phuoc Hai.

US Army OV-1 Mohawk.

The Mohawk is an interesting aircraft. Designed for air strikes initially, it is used solely for reconnaissance. It is fast and very quiet (has turbo-props), and is rather elegant in appearance. Its motors buzz rather than roar. It is very easily distinguished by its silence in flight, its three-finned tail and its auxiliary wing tanks.

Saturday 14 September 1968

The Mohawk aircraft which crashed on Thursday night was on a sensor mission, and only a parachute and a first aid kit have been found. It is thought to have been shot down but no definite evidence exists.

Desperately busy day today. Had to produce 20 maps in two hours, each drawn up with a lot of information, and each consisting of four maps joined together. No time for printing; they had to be hand drawn. Two men cut and joined maps, while two more did the line work and I did the lettering with felt-tipped pens. Went flat out and we just made it. I used up four felt pens on the job in only two hours, which gives an idea of the pace. Hope we don't get many jobs like that one.

New and major operation is on at very short notice, involving both the 1st and 4th Battalions. Noel is required to go forward with the operation for about ten days, starting tomorrow. Spike Jones goes on R&R tomorrow, and I go to Long Binh on Monday for a conference, so Ted Morris will be in charge of the Troop with Grant Small as second-in-command.

In the midst of this afternoon's frantic rush to draw the maps, the new Public Relations major arrived with an Australian politician in tow, who wanted maps to take home to Australia. Pushed a couple at them and pushed them off pretty quickly.

Meanwhile, operations continued and we had a bad day. Three Australians and one New Zealander were killed, six Australians were wounded, a tank had its track blown off, and two enemy (North Vietnamese Army) were killed in three clashes not far from Nui Dat. Can't win 'em all.

No rain today at all, but humidity still very high.

Sunday 15 September 1968

Bad road accident in the Task Force base area (speed limit 15 mph). Several men badly hurt — one leg nearly severed and other serious injuries. This could result in further beer restrictions.

Again no rain, again high humidity.

Monday 16 September 1968

Up early to catch the plane to Long Binh. Got into helicopter, which flew about 100 metres across to the refuelling point, scene of the Great Explosion last time I went to Long Binh. As we landed beside the refuelling point, one passenger, a US soldier, lit a cigarette. Persuaded him to put it out! Finished refuelling and headed north-west. Interesting trip and as usual I managed to win an outside seat. Landed at Bearcat camp on the way to deliver papers to the Thai Army HQ there — probably same place where Noel is at the moment. Went on to Long Binh.

To Saigon in the afternoon with Joel Cain. City a mixture of the very rich and the very poor — not easy to understand the tremendous extremes. Saigon is a city in a war, yet some magnificent commercial buildings are going up. Had a good look at a huge block of shopping arcades — a gigantic and modern shopping centre, complete with bowling alley, ice rink, steam baths etc. Seemed to belong more to Hong Kong than to Saigon. Had a look in some shops but bought nothing — prices were not cheap by Australian standards. In the street I saw many art stalls, but the pictures were crude and garish.

Went to a restaurant for a very nice Chinese meal. While at dinner we were joined by one undesirable youth and later two prostitutes. The youth was obviously out to have a meal at our expense and professed great love for the USA. We tolerated him for a while but made it plain that we were not buying him dinner — whereupon he parted his hair to show us a small scalp scar which he claimed was an enemy bullet wound. Joel immediately jumped to his feet, opened his shirt and displayed a huge and most impressive 'bayonet' scar on his stomach (actually the result of an operation when four months old). The Vietnamese youth then opened his own shirt to show us what looked like an appendectomy scar. Fortunately, this was as far as the war wounds display went.

The prostitutes were moderately attractive but not sensationally so. The one who sat next to me told me her name was Helen; she was 24 (she looked about 17); she worked to support her family; she had only been working for two months; she worked for the restaurant; and her job was to talk to the customers. 'They all say that,' said Joel.

Returned to Long Binh after a thorough check of the parked jeep for booby traps, grenades in petrol cans etc. In the evening there was a farewell party in the Mess for a major leaving the next day. A very lively evening was spent. Interest was displayed in minor games and tests of agility, so I showed them the game where one places a beer can out as far as possible and springs back off the second can held in the other hand. Although I was about 3 feet short of the record set by Major Bruce Daniel at Nui Dat a month ago, I managed to come second against the Americans, being finally defeated by a 6-foot lieutenant. Their technique was poor — a short man such as myself should never be hard to beat. They then produced several other similar games:

1. Heels against wall, keeping legs absolutely straight at all times, place a beer can as far forward as possible and resume erect position without bending knees or shifting feet or touching floor with hand. (I couldn't do it.)

2. Kneel on floor, place forearm on ground with fingers extended, then with elbow against knee and arm straight forward, place cigarette packet upright on ground and touching fingertips, so packet is now at a measured distance of forearm plus hand from knee. Then place hand behind back, lean over, knock packet over with nose and resume erect position. This can be made more difficult by placing the packet further away, say one packet thickness at a time. I got to three packets away before finding it impossible, but by then I had won.

3. Push a beer can as far forward as possible with hand through legs from behind. I lost very badly at this one.

Much mirth during this last game. Susie, the Vietnamese girl behind the bar, was invited to participate. A most attractive girl, Susie is tremendously popular with everyone in the Officers' Club. She is extremely pretty and moves with rare grace — not the ungainly waddle one sees so much of — and speaks with much charm. Immediately that Susie came from behind the bar, George Caporale, the Reproduction Platoon commander, raced for his room to get his camera, figuring that he'd get a pretty good view of Susie. While he was away, just about the entire club went to one end of the bar, facing Susie, expecting her skirt to ride up high. Then Susie, to get more freedom of movement, swiftly hitched her skirt up over her hips — displaying a trim pair of outdoor shorts![3] Never had there been such a colossal anticlimax. Everybody laughed, including Susie, who knew she'd fooled everybody. Susie then began to push the can forward and the flashgun of George Caporale's camera went off, George not knowing that the finished product will prove somewhat disappointing. More mirth, George not fully understanding why.

Finally to bed, very late after an evening in lively and most entertaining company, which included one or two gifted natural comedians.

Tuesday 17 September 1968

Down to Saigon again and to Tan Son Nhut for the conference with the NGS and HQ US Army, Republic of Vietnam (USARV) at the ARVN Topographic Company office. Very crisp and brief conference

---

[3] Thought for the day: why does Susie wear outdoor shorts under her dress? Does she expect foul play in the Officers' Club? Answer: Yes! Found out later that she and one of the officers regularly go to Saigon for a day's 'shopping', which they spend within the walls of one hotel room! — JB

— only 58 minutes instead of the usual two to three hours, thanks no doubt to the return to USA of Colonel Colvocoresses, who was never at a loss for words. But we miss this immensely likable man, who cared so much for this poor country.

Drove past Saigon golf course and saw a burly American golfer carrying one golf club and a cigar. Behind him struggled his tiny Vietnamese caddy, staggering under a big golf bag and a machine carbine. Drove through Saigon streets, huge heaps of domestic refuse everywhere, some of it being scavenged by animals and people of all ages, and in one place a front-end loader was trying to clear it, but making little impression.

Returned to Long Binh and discussed several technical matters with men in 66 Company. During afternoon a shot was fired from a 0.45 pistol by a 66 Company soldier who has been involved in fraud, doesn't pay debts, doesn't support his family, and generally speaking is in a heap of trouble and is about to be court-martialled. This unauthorised discharge of a weapon is the last straw, and the whole legal machinery is about to be set in action against him. Due mainly to bad debts right around the world and to attempts to draw pay in two places at once, this man faces discharge and possible gaol.

It never rains but it pours. After dinner, two Vietnamese prostitutes were found in the camp and the military police took over. They had apparently been smuggled into the camp in a truck by two sergeants (one from 66 Company[4] and one from HQ 79 Engineer Group). Both girls looked dirty, and one girl had very unpleasant sores on her arms and legs. I went down to the MP station with Joel for the interrogation of the Vietnamese girls and the sergeants. While there, a dishevelled and intoxicated sergeant was dragged in by two MPs and shoved in front of the MP duty sergeant. Before anyone said anything, the drunk presented a five-

[4] This sergeant went soon afterwards to the Officer Cadet School. He also received the Bronze Star for his meritorious service in Vietnam. — JB

minute address for the defence. The MP duty sergeant tried several times to get a word in edgewise but failed. Knowing of the fearsome reputation of the American MPs I was expecting to see the drunk get hit behind the ear and dragged out by the heels. But no. The MP duty sergeant smiled patiently and kindly, and then said in an unbelievably friendly and gentle manner, 'Yes, sergeant, that'll be OK, now off you go and get some sleep.'

But no. That was not good enough. 'I want to be completely cleared,' said the drunk. 'I'm not drunk and I want you to put me through all your sobrite . . . sobrity . . . sobritery, tests. You know the ones I mean.'

'No, sergeant,' said the MP duty sergeant. 'There's no need for that, no one's accusing you of anything. It's pretty late, so hop off and get a bit of rest.'

But no. Still not good enough. 'I insist on being exonerated,' argued the drunk. 'I know I'd be safer to keep my mouth shut, but there's an important principle at stake here . . .' etc.

I was expecting the drunk to be knocked senseless any second. But no. The MP duty sergeant displayed extraordinary tolerance and eventually persuaded the drunk to go away and go to bed. It was a wonderful display of human understanding, and I marvelled at the tact of the MP duty sergeant, who handled the situation so perfectly and whose only subsequent comment on the matter was a brief glance skyward and a quiet smile to the audience.

Meanwhile, interrogation continues out the back and the girls were stripped and searched by Vietnamese women police as well, hardly a pleasant task in view of the sores — and the fact that both apparently had syphilis. This all took a lot of time, and it was not until 03.00 that the girls had been handed over finally to the Vietnamese police. This was the third time these particular girls had been caught in the camp and they seemed to think it was all a bit of a joke. Finally back to 66 Company and to bed about 03.30.

Wednesday 18 September 1968

Quiet morning at 66 Company rudely shattered by the rasping roar of a couple of mini-gun bursts from a gunship aloft not far away. First mini-gun I've heard for about six months, but the sound is utterly unmistakable — and horrible. Only two bursts, and things then settled down again.

Had intended to go with Joel to Saigon and Tan Son Nhut for technical visits to mapping staff in Military Assistance Command Vietnam and Combined Intelligence Center Vietnam, but could not do so due to unexpected legal complications with the court martial case from yesterday. Went with Joel and First Sergeant Crunkleton to consult the CID at Bien Hoa. CID most efficient and helpful. Members are military but do not wear uniform, so that rank and identity are concealed. Drove through Bien Hoa town and the neighbouring villages of Bui Tieng and Vinh Cuu. First Sergeant Crunkleton, a new arrival in Vietnam, is most unimpressed with Vietnam and finds it basically squalid. Joel finds the country beautiful and rich. I agree that a few attractive places do exist but they are not typical.

Saw two interesting things in Bien Hoa: (i) my first train in Vietnam, slowly shunting goods wagons; (ii) a dump of drainage piping bearing the markings 'MADE IN AUSTRALIA BY STEWARTS & LLOYDS' (presumably Artarmon, NSW). Returned to Long Binh and quiet evening.

Thursday 19 September 1968

Just about to leave for Saigon once again when complications again occurred unexpectedly. A soldier in 66 Company has been shot in leg by a Viet Cong sniper while on a field survey job about 20 kilometres south of Long Binh and about 40 kilometres north-west of Nui Dat. The Survey Platoon was doing some levelling work in a cleared area in the midst of three ARVN posts — an apparently secure area, so no protection parties were employed — and suddenly bullets came out of the bush about 300 metres away. Ankle badly smashed. Casualty taken to 93 Evacuation Hospital at Long Binh for immediate surgery. The accident is worrying in that: (i) it could just as easily have happened to us on many past occasions; and (ii) it could easily happen again and is almost impossible to guard against.[5]

Finally got away from Long Binh — wow, what an eventful week they're having there — and headed for Tan Son Nhut to catch plane back to Nui Dat. Arrived at Tan Son Nhut, Saigon, too late for afternoon plane so booked on first plane tomorrow morning.

Visited the PX at Tan Son Nhut but did not find anything I needed. Went with Joel and driver to a hotel in Cholon where we booked in for the night. Walked in nearby streets. Mildly interesting and not very attractive; in fact, pretty hard on the nose in many places. Nevertheless, it must have been fairly attractive many years ago when buildings were presumably better cared for. Looked in shops. Prices all seemed very high — naturally enough, amidst a war, I should imagine. Noticed lots of items of stolen American stores and equipment for sale. Whenever we went in the streets, the smell of incense was there — Hong Kong has it too — a sweetish but rather sickly smell. If only one could record and reproduce smells, as can be done with sights and sounds, a stroll through a city such as Saigon would produce a most interesting bouquet indeed.

Watching evening peak-hour traffic, Saigon and Cholon hardly appear to be a city at war, yet a closer look soon reveals the barbed

[5] The following week, the Survey Platoon from 66 Company, this time with Thai protection, was mortared in the same location and two men were wounded. Wounds included a severed femoral artery! — JB

wire, wire-and-rail barricades, high cage-type fences etc, obviously designed to keep trouble at as great a distance as possible. Bullet and shrapnel scars are frequently seen on buildings and fences. Sandbagged guard posts are outside any building of size or importance. Blocks of old homes, at first glance being destroyed for reconstruction, are seen on closer inspection to have been blown apart by explosions. It is hard to imagine this big, seething city ever recovering its former elegance.

Returned to hotel and had a nice but expensive dinner. Joined during meal by several girls — same system prevailing as on 16 September. Declined all requests to buy Saigon teas. The girls are pretty keen to have teas bought for them because their standing with the management is good only if plenty of customers buy Saigon teas. Since I bought none, the girls didn't stay terribly long with me, and I noticed that the more attractive the girl, the quicker she moved on for richer plunder elsewhere. The less attractive girls stayed longer, apparently accustomed to putting in greater effort to get Saigon teas.

One girl stayed a long time because I was Australian, the only one around. She told me she had lived with an Australian for several months about two years ago, but he had soon gone back to Australia and unfortunately she had a baby by him. Her story is probably true, since she made no attempt to capitalise on me as a consequence to her story. The baby is now aged one and she likes him a lot, but rarely sees him because another family looks after him. Much as she likes the baby, his conception was, of course, accidental and not desired, but she regards this as an occupational hazard. The father's name is Fred (I might have guessed — every Australian in Vietnam is called Fred) and he worked in Saigon.

Meal was a Wiener schnitzel and a nice one, but was overpriced at $3. After dinner, I went upstairs to the bar and spent some time watching the bar girls shuttling back and forth supplying 'companionship' in exchange for Saigon teas and negotiating for bed-mates later in the evening. Standard prices for all-night sessions appear to be between $15 and $25. The 'companionship' they offer at the bar is pretty limited — usually by their poor English and by their lack of much in common with most soldiers visiting the bars.

Minor excitement and everyone went to the windows when a fire broke out one block away, but it wasn't a big one. To bed reasonably early — still trying to catch up on sleep.

Friday 20 September 1968

Up early to catch the plane back to Nui Dat. Morning peak-hour traffic in Saigon extremely dense, and frequent long halts occurred. Finally got to Tan Son Nhut and arrived back at Nui Dat after four eventful but rather unproductive days away.

Returned to find Grant Small in command, Ted Morris having had to go to 1 Australian Field Hospital for a lung check. Conference for all unit commanders held today. Also we collected an urgent job to join and mark up five maps for the investigation into an accident yesterday — a USAF F-100 fighter shot up 14 Australians while putting in an air strike on the enemy. Fortunately, none died, though one has a slender hold on life, having received 26 pints of blood so far — after being shot through the throat with a 20mm cannon slug. The other 13 are OK, comparatively. From the maps we drew up, it seems likely that the following happened:

Aircraft did bomb strike on enemy.

Observer aircraft checked the result of bomb strike and called for a cannon strike.

Australian ground troops, engaged in battle with enemy, used smoke for cover from enemy view.

Fighter coming in for cannon strike mistook the thrown smoke for the bombed target and shot it up.

The Australian troops were right on line with the aircraft approach path and collected the rounds which overran the target.

Seems due to a misidentification in the air — very bad luck for all concerned.

Found out that Noel is not at Bearcat after all, but has gone to fire support base Grey as a liaison officer with the Royal Thai Army Volunteer Forces HQ at Binh Son, which is about 40 kilometres north-west of Nui Dat. FSPB Grey has been attacked by the Viet Cong every night since the Thais (with Noel) moved in. It has been heavily mortared on each of the last four nights, and on 17 September Noel was wounded in the body and leg from mortar shrapnel. Only minor injuries so he carried on. He is the first member of the Survey Corps to become a battle casualty since World War II. He also has the dubious distinction of being the most mortared and rocketed officer in the whole Australian Task Force at the moment, having been through the savage fighting at FSPB Coral in May. Sent off the casualty notification to Task Force HQ, together with Noel's request that his parents not be informed.

Noel is not the only Survey Troop member to come under fire this week. Also on 17 September Peter Dew was in Saigon for an eye test for new spectacles and was given a lift through Saigon by US military police. On the way, they ran through a civil disturbance where bullets were flying around. Naturally enough, when a military police jeep showed up, people started shooting at it, but their aim was bad. Nevertheless, Peter had a pretty lively minute or two.

Saturday 21 September 1968

In Command Post at midnight. Night quiet around Nui Dat, but FSPB Grey received two mortar and rocket attacks. It was a pretty heavy couple of attacks, and the flares and rocket trails could be seen from Nui Dat, 40 kilometres away. Noel survived both OK. A ground attack occurred on the edge of the Thai position but was strongly repulsed. The Thais lost four killed and 19 wounded. The Viet Cong lost 32 killed. Altogether quite a savage fight.

Received bills today from Officers' Mess for Noel and myself for the Task Force Commander's birthday party held last Tuesday. While the party was being held, I was doing the rounds of MP stations at Long Binh, and Noel was under attack at FSPB Grey and was wounded by mortar fragments at that very time. Persuaded treasurer to cancel bills, certainly Noel's anyway.

Very nasty accident in 1ARU this afternoon. A man was setting up a claymore mine when it exploded. It blew him to pieces. Those pieces that could be collected were placed in a plastic bag and taken to the hospital. No one knows why the claymore blew up and an investigation is under way.

Heavy rain in late afternoon, perhaps the second- or third-heaviest downpour this wet. I had to attend a conference at its height. I had walked about 150 metres when I became wet through, despite wearing a raincoat. The rain just burst through the fabric. In the same distance my socks and boots became saturated simply from rain hitting my trousers, penetrating right through and running down my legs into my boots. I could feel my toes sloshing in water. Didn't bother to wear coat on way back — was so drenched that further rain didn't matter.

Sunday 22 September 1968

Quiet day so got a good bit done, plus some washing.

Monday 23 September 1968

Many visitors today, so got little done. We had a training session on the M16 rifle, which is being issued to us today in place of our F1 carbines.

Had to do a small field survey and also to draw a plan in connection with Saturday's fatal accident in 1ARU with the claymore. Pieces of the victim had been blown up to 175 feet away. I was shown the colour photos taken immediately after the accident, and few pieces were recognisable as human remains. The only recognisable part was the faceless head on the legless and armless body, which had been burst asunder. The sole of a foot was found 40 feet from the rest of the same foot. Investigation is checking whether Signals transmitting aerials could have caused the current pulse which set off the electric detonator,[6] and this is why our survey was necessary.

Quite a lot of rain in the evening but none of it really heavy.

Tuesday 24 September 1968

The GSO2 Ops has returned to Australia and a more relaxed atmosphere prevails. His successor is giving us three and four days' notice of Task Force operations instead of the 90 minutes to three hours that we are used to.

Noel returned today from his eventful one and a half weeks with the Thai Army and much in need of a decent sleep. His shrapnel wounds (one in the back, two in left side and two in right leg) are healing well, despite having been infected. Shrapnel came from a mortar bomb, which was a direct hit on the roof of the building

[6] Subsequently considered highly likely. — JB

Noel was in. Laughing it off, Noel says he's been hurt worse at formal dining-in nights! Seriously, though, men were killed around him at FSPB Grey.

Noel had some interesting stories of the past few days. The Thais are relatively inexperienced yet seem to be tough soldiers — and extremely savage at times. Noel witnessed several deliberate murders of enemy wounded. Both sides consider decapitation and staking of heads as normal practice. Noel had quite a surfeit of grisly sights during the week — including that of a Thai nonchalantly scooping up the brains which had fallen out of a split enemy head, and coolly tossing them into a plastic bag, which he then took away with him. Many slain enemy were only 15 years old. One marvels at their fierce dedication — many had dug graves before the battle, and all were equipped with a sash by which their bodies could be dragged should they fall in combat.

The Thais never bothered to interrogate prisoners (they murdered them instead), nor to collect and examine enemy weapons and ammunition (they dumped the lot in a pile and destroyed it). Even the Thais were impressed with the enemy's desperate determination and recklessness — but they slaughtered them in hot or cold blood just the same.

Comment of the day overheard in our draughting office: 'I thought Captain Sproles had been to the war, but he's been off on a picnic in a pleasure boat!' This being a reference to the souvenir Noel brought back — an enemy sampan paddle.

Discovered that HQ Australian Forces Vietnam (AFV) in Saigon have informed Noel's parents of his wounds despite his request that this not be done. I find that they do this every time, regardless of the wishes of the wounded man and the fact that his wounds may be extremely minor. This is done out of fear of being accused by the press of 'suppressing casualties in Vietnam', and the next of kin can go hang. Two other recent examples are:

1. SAS soldier seriously wounded. Wife informed and most upset. Soldier recovers and returns to the same dangerous duty. Wife very worried. Soldier receives very minor wounds and requests wife not be told. Wife told.

2. National serviceman with very minor injuries requests parents not be told, since father has weak heart. Parents told. Father has heart attack.

Saw Task Force Commander about all this and he is taking the matter up with HQ AFV where the problem lies. In the meantime, this is too late to help Noel's parents, so I wrote them a letter myself, since (Noel not having mentioned it in his last letter home) they must be worried badly and be wondering just what to believe.[7]

Observed a soldier returning from R&R leave in Taipei, requiring a truck to carry his loot. Loot consisted of 96 gramophone records (all 12-inch LPs at about 30 cents each), plus sound equipment, medical textbooks for the doctor, and miscellaneous goods — the most heavily laden tourist since I brought the electric train back from Hong Kong. Taiwan recognises no copyright, therefore records and books are amazingly cheap. He also brought back photos of the remarkably beautiful Eurasian girl who acted as his guide in Taipei for only US$15 per day. She spoke excellent English and saved him stacks of money by bargaining for him everywhere. Altogether he had a pretty good leave. The word soon got round and some officers in the Task Force HQ Mess asked to see the photos. The result is that a lot of people now intend to go to Taipei for R&R.

[7] I got a lovely letter back from Noel's mother, thanking me warmly for my 'promise' that no more harm would come to her dear Noel. Aghast at what she had read into my well-intended letter, I said to Noel, 'Look what you've got me into!' and firmly ordered him to lead a sheltered life from now on — for my sake, not for his! — JB

Wednesday 25 September 1968

Spike Jones, Grant Small and John Hunter went off with the Divisional Intelligence Unit to An Nhut (between Long Dien and Dat Do) this morning on a snatch-and-grab raid, in order to take known Viet Cong agents by surprise and capture them. Operation most successful. They caught 15 and no one got hurt.

Range practice today. Went outside Task Force perimeter wire for weapon practice, mainly to expend surplus 9mm ammunition, now that we must hand in our F1 carbines and get used to the M16 rifles just issued. I fired my pistol and found to my surprise that I can shoot reasonably accurately with it. Also fired both F1 and M16. The F1 is a very easy weapon for me to fire accurately with but I need a lot more practice to master the M16.

Today we became aware of a hilarious piece of mis-timing. About a month ago, Lieutenant Garry Swan, Officer Commanding the Task Force Light Aid Detachment, submitted a defect report to Army Headquarters, concerning lawn-mower motors. The motors were throwing con rods and not standing up to high-speed running as mowers. Today, to Garry's dismay, this article on go-karting with mower motors appeared in the Army newspaper. Garry expects to hear further from AHQ!

Thursday 26 September 1968

Very hectic day — busy with map overprint for next operation and all sorts of complications occurred, the worst being power failures and shortage of maps to be overprinted. 1st Battalion had depleted our stocks of the key map, not realising that they would later be receiving the same maps with an overprint for the operation. At least our new GSO2 Ops, Major Keldie, in the background was supportive.

Mario Apfelbaum and Mick Rice very busy today and were working tonight also, but had to stop when the fumes, mainly from mineral turpentine, became too strong — their effect on lungs and eyes was pretty savage.

One hears many sad tales from the Divisional Intelligence Unit these days. This unit depends greatly on the ARVN unit 10 MID at Van Kiep for assistance and information. 10 MID under Dai-Uy Trung was a real force in the land. Trung has now been gone about three weeks, and 10 MID has completely collapsed. Trung, of course, was of extraordinarily high class for such a job. While chief of police in Da Nang, he backed the wrong coup about two or three coups ago and was sent to Van Kiep for a few years' penance while his contemporaries rose to the ranks of colonel and general. However, it seems now that Trung has been forgiven and is on the way up again. Meanwhile, 10 MID without its feared and capable leader has become a hopeless rabble. It is run by a triumvirate of three lieutenants (disparagingly referred to by the Australians as the Troika), none of whom is game enough to assert his authority, lest the others strike him down. The rest of 10 MID do exactly as they like, and the Australian Task Force has been badly let down on several occasions.

Friday 27 September 1968

A rather tragic day. No less than six VD cases amongst us today. Admittedly only two were fresh cases and the other four were relapses from previous cases believed cured. Of the two fresh cases, one was from a sexual contact last April, and the other was relatively recent. The April one is surprising, but the doctor says that such late symptoms do occasionally occur, and possibly symptoms at an earlier date may not have been noticed. The four relapses are worrying, since there is obviously some difficulty being encountered in effecting complete cures. Looks as though we are unchallenged premiers for September for the Task Force Yellow Shield. No obvious explanation for these high casualties exists. If anything, sexual contacts are fewer and less frequent than during the previous year or so. It is significant, however, that we have had only one fresh case of VD from a sexual contact subsequent to the doctor's talk in July.[8]

Managed to get a fair bit done today, including one rush job for a new operation. Light rain all day today.

Party in Officers' Mess in evening in honour of visit by Director of Infantry (Colonel David Thomson) and a former Chief of the General Staff (Lieutenant General Sir Reginald Pollard). As many infantry officers as operations could spare came to the Task Force HQ Officers' Mess and it was quite a large gathering. Met many old friends: Brian Lindsay, Tony Hammett, Kim Patterson, Bill Reynolds and several others, all infantry company commanders. Most of them have been majors for well over two years now, and expressed some surprise at my own lowly rank — yet another of many incidents during the past year which have indicated that my

[8] Spoke too soon! We had two more fresh cases of VD within the next week, and two more a week later. — JB

own standing is higher outside the Survey Corps than inside it. General Pollard is a friendly soul and provided lively company during the evening, as also did Colonel Thomson (who astonished me by calling me John and greeting me with a most warm manner some ten years after last seeing me).

However, the brightest spot of the evening was provided by Major Digger James and the 4th Battalion band. The band played march music, so Digger James turned on his smartest drill and marched back and forth as a sentry on his beat. His drill was as snappy as one ever sees on any parade ground or outside a main barracks gate, despite his wooden leg and feet; it was amazing to behold. Then to everyone's delight, he grabbed the Task Force Commander and insisted that the Commander march with him also. Brigadier Hughes had little choice but to do as Digger insisted, but could not drill nearly as smartly — and neither could General Pollard, whom Digger dragged in a minute later. The music then changed to a Scottish reel. So Digger immediately did the Highland fling, a remarkable feat for a man with artificial limbs.

In another corner, Steve Zagon, an Intelligence captain of Hungarian origin, was teaching a group the 'Song of the Volga Boatmen' — in Russian. Considerately, he wrote the words down, but being in Cyrillic characters, this was of little help.

Party finished at about 21.00. I don't normally have much to do with Mess functions, but this one was most enjoyable. In fact, apart from the big disadvantage of domestic separation, military life has been remarkably pleasant since leaving Bonegilla and the Survey School about 15 months ago. Both at work and socially, there has been no shortage of good company and friends.

Saturday 28 September 1968

Reasonably quiet day and got a fair bit done. Sore ear so went to 8 Field Ambulance for the doctor to have a look. Ear full of infection and fibreglass splinters — from anti-noise ear-plugs used while shooting last Monday. Infection no problem to fix, but all the fibreglass splinters are causing the doctor some worry. After a painful half hour most have been flushed out, everyone hopes.

Into the Command Post at 16.00 to fill in as duty officer in an emergency due to a shortage of duty officers. First time I've done the evening shift for a couple of months, so it's good to get back into practice again — the evening shift always involves a great deal more work and responsibility than the midnight shift, and there is the added task of training the assistant duty officer, too. Evening busy but mostly routine matters associated with the commencement of a new operation — 3rd Battalion did an air assault into a new position late this afternoon. Finally to bed at 01.00.

Sunday 29 September 1968

Fairly quiet day — not a great deal to do. Got a few odd sewing and washing jobs done.

Several cases of malaria today, mostly from infantry battalions, including one major and two lieutenants. Despite the most stringent precautions, malaria is occurring quite a lot and is causing some worry. Have never yet had a case in the Survey Troop — just as well, since VD is causing us quite enough worry as it is.

Have just heard that we are to entertain a large concert party on Tuesday, leaving us only one day to prepare for it. Looks like a busy day tomorrow. Left washing out overnight to dry. This brought good rain.

Monday 30 September 1968

Day off to a flying start. Breakfast has never been lively since the end of the days of Dave Dawe (NZ), Fergus Thomson and Geoff Boscoe, a particularly nimble-witted trio, but things improved today. 'What's the name of that Sydney suburb where all the Jews live?' asked someone, trying to remember Rose Bay. Quick as a flash, Steve Hart replied, 'Melbourne!' *That* woke the Victorians up!

One Australian Iroquois helicopter was shot at and hit by enemy ground fire a few kilometres north of Nui Dat today, but no serious damage was done. An American Iroquois helicopter in the same region was also shot at and was shot down, all passengers being killed, including one joy-riding Australian.

All our Sioux helicopters have been grounded following discovery of fuselage cracks. We now await replacement aircraft from Australia, so it will be a long time before we have any Sioux aircraft flying again.

Rain has been regular and reasonably heavy for the past few days — maybe there's more of the wet still to come.

OCTOBER

AUSTRALIAN MILITARY FORCES

AAB — 71A
Reprinted Dec, 1964

RECORD BOOK

CONTAINING 96 PAGES

RULED FEINT

Every couple of months or so, an official government-sponsored concert party from an Australian state would visit Vietnam, the states taking it in turns to be represented. Many performers visited Vietnam several times during the war, Lorrae Desmond and Lucky Starr being perhaps the best known and most popular.

For a performance at Nui Dat, the party would be flown in during the morning to Luscombe airfield, perform straight afterwards at Luscombe Bowl, be hosted by a Task Force unit for a barbecue lunch, and be flown out again in the late afternoon. Luscombe Bowl, adjacent to the airfield, was simply a wide slope facing a simple stage with dressing rooms attached. Audiences brought their own folding chairs.

The host unit's main function was to provide and manage the barbecue lunch. The host unit also provided any other assistance that the concert party's military escort from Australia might require.

Unexpectedly, an extra concert party was recruited from enthusiastic amateurs in 1ALSG and the RAAF base at Vung Tau, and a concert at Nui Dat was planned. Major units were not seriously interested in hosting a concert party of fellow servicemen but the Survey Troop pleaded successfully for this opportunity to show how well they could do the job. The day was such a great success that the Troop was given the next official concert party — from Queensland — later that same month. This time the Survey Troop excelled itself, being the first host unit to offer an exclusive ladies' toilet, a private changing tent and showers.

PAUL HAM

Then Peter Dew wanted to have a blow on the trumpet. He used to blow a trumpet in a jazz band many years ago in Melbourne — in fact, his band had Judith Durham as a singer until they sacked her because they considered her untalented!

★

Tuesday 1 October 1968

Down to Luscombe airfield early to meet the concert party from Vung Tau. All organisation went smoothly. Very large party — 18 in all. Concert party was not from Australia, but was from 1ALSG and RAAF at Vung Tau, and consisted of one Army Nursing Corps lieutenant (folk-singer and go-go dancer), one infantry lieutenant (drummer, trumpeter and saxophonist), and a whole host of very talented people, indeed.

To everyone's surprise, this concert of amateur performers was excellent, perhaps the most talented group since the West Australian party under Peter Willie Harries. There were two bands — a rock band and a dixie band — and a variety of artists of all types. The nurse, Barbara Black, was attractive and very popular indeed. There was a good tenor singer, and one man who presented a song in Cockney, followed by 'Donald, Whar's Your Troosis?', which branded him as a Scot. He then dumbfounded everyone by reciting 'Down at Tumbabloodyrumba Shooting Kangabloodyroos' in a faultless Riverina accent. There was a New Zealand military police corporal, a big, fat Maori (with many tattoos but not Maori ones!) who sang Maori songs, played guitar, and, wearing a hula skirt of wooden beads, turned on a hilarious dance act with Barbara Black. There was an electric harmonica player. Altogether it was an excellent concert.

Had a barbecue lunch back at the Survey Troop recreation tent. Very heavy rain hit but Dallas Leary and helpers had everything very well organised and the lunch was a great success. While waiting for the rain to ease, the dixie band got the instruments out and turned on an impromptu session, to the delight of everyone. Then Peter Dew wanted to have a blow on the trumpet. He used to blow a trumpet in a jazz band many years ago in Melbourne — in fact, his band had Judith Durham as a singer until they sacked her because they considered her untalented! Peter was handed a trumpet and joined in with the band. To everyone's amazement he played magnificently and did an excellent solo passage. To play like this, without his lip in practice and not having touched a trumpet for two years, was a pretty good effort. Tape recorders came out, and much of the session was recorded.

The concert party left at 15.00, Barbara Black and two sound technicians remaining to catch a later aircraft to Vung Tau. No sooner were our last visitors away than I had to grab a quick meal and some sleep before going on duty in the Command Post at midnight.

Wednesday 2 October 1968

Quiet evening in Command Post, with just a little shooting on edge of Dat Do and a casualty evacuation to be organisd for an apparent malaria case.

Thursday 3 October 1968

Spent most of the day in the Task Force HQ. Rain during morning; afternoon fine. Weather very unpredictable at present.

Friday 4 October 1968

Lots of minor matters unexpectedly cropped up today, but were dealt with fairly easily — fortunately, since I must now go to Long Binh tomorrow for a discussion on aerial photography for Phuoc Tuy province. Hope to get up and back from Long Binh in same day. Managed to get all important matters clear before leaving for Long Binh.

Went to Her Majesty's Theatre (the HQ Company fleapit between the rubber trees) to see the French film *Un Homme et une Femme*, possibly the first film of any quality to be shown during the eight months I've spent here so far. Very good film, but although I sat in the front row only metres from the screen, it was not possible to enjoy the film fully, thanks to the American-dubbed soundtrack and the audience who hollered 'Weak as piss!' throughout the whole film. Guess this will be the last time they show a decent film.

Saturday 5 October 1968

smoke

Up early to catch helicopter for Long Binh. Helicopter late and didn't take off until 08.15; however, it travelled directly and made a swift trip. Nearing Long Binh, another aircraft not far away received fire from the ground. Two F-100 fighters arrived almost immediately and put in a rocket attack, taking it in turns to dive on the target. The explosions and the immediate spurts of smoke to several hundred feet were most spectacular. The smoke plumes were dark and sharp-edged. They appeared instantaneously, and then after several seconds, would begin to soften, spread and disperse.

Meanwhile, the jet aircraft above continued to leap high in the sky and then to swoop with great speed again. The target took heavy punishment, and from our passing helicopter it was possible to see that the aim was very accurate, with all the rockets landing in the same place. Air strikes are commonplace in Vietnam, but this was the first one I've been reasonably close to. Landed safely at Long Binh without further incident. Got a lift to HQ USARV and had a most profitable discussion. Went from there to 547 Map Distribution Platoon to get some maps. Had lunch with Joel Cain at 66 Engineer Company and then left after lunch to get back to HQ USARV (about 4 kilometres away) and catch bus to Saigon.

Swift trip to Tan Son Nhut. Got off at MACV and visited the Mapping, Charting and Geodesy branch. Gave them some information they wanted. Visited the Security and Counter-Intelligence branch to get some spectacular security posters featuring 'Peanuts' cartoon characters. None in stock so they said, 'Well, how do you like this one instead?', proffering a photo of a bikini-clad girl reclining on a beach and saying:

'The last thing I want to talk about on your

R&R leave is CLASSIFIED INFORMATION!'

I looked at it critically and said, 'The idea's excellent, but couldn't you have used a better looking girl?' The lieutenant colonel and the two majors present shuffled and looked a bit embarrassed. Finally, the lieutenant colonel said, 'Well, not really. You see, she's the boss's wife!' So I agreed that, yes, she was very good looking indeed, thanked them, and shot through before they could get their hands on my Belgian 9mm pistol, which has such tremendous fascination for all Americans. 'Say, Ahssie, thaat's a swell hand gun yuh've gaht thear!' Thefts of 9mm pistols by Americans have reached such proportions that Australians who work constantly with Americans are now issued with the American standard — the much heavier Colt 0.45 inch. It is similar in design to the 9mm but bigger and much more awkward to handle.

1 Topographical Survey Troop, October 1968.

Left MACV for the RAAF office at Tan Son Nhut, only to be told that, despite my well-organised use today of two American jeeps, one ARVN jeep, one American truck, one bus and one American helicopter, I now can't get onto an Australian plane on which I was booked yesterday, but must spend a night in the notorious Stalag Alfa instead. 'Sorry, sir, but your booking was mislaid and the plane's now full.'

'Sergeant, I'm a unit commander returning to my unit, and this in my hand is a roll of maps urgently required by the Task Force. Now let's see your passenger manifest and we'll decide who gets off the plane.'

'Sorry, sir, but we don't work that way . . .'

At that moment a hand took the map roll from me and hit me over the head with it. I looked around . . . Dai-Uy Trung! Still on his course at Saigon and heading back to his family in Van Kiep via Nui Dat for the weekend, he displayed his delight in seeing me. Following an incident about four months ago, when Dai-Uy Trung was booked by Task Force HQ on an RAAF plane and then prevented from catching it by a Movement Control sergeant who 'didn't like Afghans!', Dai-Uy Trung is now treated with great respect and handled with great care by all Movement Control people. Not wishing to displease the much-feared and all-powerful Dai-Uy Trung, it was expedient for the RAAF sergeant to do the right thing by an obviously close friend of him — so I caught the plane.

Plane late, so had a long and fascinating talk with Dai-Uy Trung, who is always interesting company. He will probably be promoted to thieu-ta (major) soon and become a district chief, or may return to 10 MID for a while to sort out the mess that that unit has fallen into since the ineffectual Troika took over.

Sunday 6 October 1968

Hoped to lie in today and catch up on lost sleep. No luck. Aroused at 07.00 because the Task Force Commander wanted me urgently. Struggled into clothes, made a couple of cursory swipes with shaver and staggered down road, wondering what on earth was happening or about to happen. Arrived at Task Force HQ and was introduced to Major General Brogan, Quartermaster General, who wanted to see me. Reason: to convey regards from cousin Arthur Bullen, Canberra, fellow tennis club member. Chatted for a few moments and then departed, as Major General Brogan was about to return home after a quick visit to Vietnam.

Played cricket this afternoon for HQ Company versus 104 Signals Squadron. Match a bit one-sided because 104 Signals Squadron had Signalman Graham Christie (opening bowler for Hawthorn–East Melbourne in Melbourne first-grade cricket) opening the bowling for them. He was quite quick but fortunately neither fit nor in form so I had no difficulty playing him until I did a few stupid things in an attempt to score more quickly. Made 20, top score in a total of 56, some recompense for the three blows to the body I took from rising balls. Despite the conditions, which were very hot indeed, Graham Christie took seven wickets for 22. 104 Signals Squadron scored 70, with Major Steve Hart scoring 29, the top score of the match. Late in the innings, one HQ Company bowler took a hat trick, with every one of the three wickets caught by the same fieldsman — fielding at point.

The match was a light-hearted affair and everyone had a very enjoyable time, despite being interrupted a few times by bursts of artillery fire, let off by medium guns only 50 metres away. The noise and concussion at such close range was tremendous. Two USAF F-100 jet fighters buzzed the Task Force at appallingly low altitude in quick succession. The noise was shattering as they screamed over us and then used their after-burners to produce a heavy explosion. Still, better during the day than right on dawn, as they did one ghastly Sunday about seven months ago.

Monday 7 − Tuesday 8 October 1968

Two very busy days. Am one of the fortunate few players not stiff from Sunday's game, but have impressive and very large bruise on hip where all three hits the other day landed. No pain though. Another late night.

Wednesday 9 October 1968

Kept very busy today but managed to get most of the monthly report done. It contains the official report of Noel's adventures as Task Force Liaison Officer to the Thais last month.

Heard about court martial at Vung Tau a couple of days ago. An unheard of thing happened. When asked with the usual legal rigmarole if he had any objection to being tried by any officers on the board, the accused staggered everyone by saying yes! The board president recovered his composure and asked whom he objected to. The accused indicated a major. When asked on what grounds he objected, the accused said that the major had been heard to say on . . . such and such a date at . . . such and such a time in the HQ 1ALSG Officers' Mess, '. . . I reckon 98% of the bastards would be guilty anyway, or they wouldn't be on a court martial,' and that this had been heard by the defending officer. The defending officer agreed that this was the case. The judge advocate upheld the objection and the major had to be replaced — furious but unable to do anything about it.

He is doubly furious because he detests the Legal Corps captain who is the defending officer, anyway. This captain has a somewhat pompous manner and is not a popular figure at all, and so the major is particularly angry at this public humiliation inflicted on him by the legal officer. The news reached General MacDonald in Saigon, who reacted with typical force and savagery. We understand that he has advised all senior commanders in Vietnam and has ordered it to be placed on the major's record that 'this officer is unsuitable to serve on a court martial'. The victim is indeed angry, but for the moment is powerless. Actually, it's a bit rough to hold against a man a chance remark made at some time or other, either seriously or in jest, by just about everyone.

Meanwhile, the defending officer has threatened to do the same to Captain John Becker (a staff officer on the Task Force HQ) at another court martial next week. Our legal man dislikes John Becker because the latter has persistently baited him ever since the legal officer came to Nui Dat. They have adjacent offices and John Becker, mischievous by nature, has always given him a hard time. John was talking with me this morning, 'Have you heard that our legal man's going to object to me next week?'

'Is he? On what grounds?'

'He seems to think I suffer from khaki encephalitis and that I'm incapable of giving anyone or anything a fair hearing, let alone a prisoner at a court martial.'

'Going to do anything about it?'

'God, no! I'm perfectly happy to be banned from court martials. Still, on second thoughts, it could be as handy an excuse as any for punching him up the throat. It's nearly 17 hours since I punched anyone and I hate to get out of practice.'

Today the court martial involving Paul Alderson as a witness was held. As a result of the efforts of the military police and our legal captain, despite my explanation of clear Survey Corps policy on the question of map accuracy, Paul has been held back in Vietnam for an extra month for this court martial. He was present today at the court martial but was told just as it started that he would not be required after all. This came as no surprise. I had foreseen this two months ago and was most upset that the Legal Corps would not release Paul when no real reason existed for keeping him. Anyway, at last the Legal Corps has agreed that Paul is not needed after all and he is now to go on the first available plane, which is next Tuesday, having served 13 months in Vietnam.

At the Task Force Commander's conference this afternoon, held in a metal-roofed hut, it was barely possible to hear what was said. Twigs, bark, nuts and other debris were raining down loudly on the roof, as if several people were hurling rubbish onto the building. An officer went outside and diagnosed the trouble — squirrels stripping the tree tops just for fun. He threw a rock at them and missed. The rock crashed back on the conference hut roof, the squirrels chattered angrily and debris continued to fall. Fortunately, it wasn't a lengthy conference.

Fine day today. No rain. Continuous and heavy evening lightning to the north. Weather still very humid, but now the storms are less regular.

Thursday 10 October 1968

Off to a flying start with a rush drawing and printing job. Took longer than expected but we still beat the deadline comfortably.

Heard today of heavy casualties two days ago. 1st Battalion and 4th Battalion in separate enemy contacts sustained four killed and 11 wounded. When a helicopter began evacuating casualties, heavy machine-gun fire riddled the aircraft, which took many hits in the engine compartment, cockpit and main rotor. Miraculously no one was hit and the helicopter could still fly. Despite a shot-up main rotor, the aircraft flew 50 kilometres to Vung Tau, where the crew landed, leapt out and into a new helicopter, flew it back to the scene and this time picked up the casualties successfully. The enemy, in the meantime, had been 'pacified' by a light fire team of two gunships. Not a bad effort by the casualty evacuation helicopter — US Army. Cost of new rotor blades: $10,000 for a start. Very lucky the damaged blades didn't fall off on the 50-kilometre run back to Vung Tau.

In view of the publicity given in the Australian press to 'atrocities' committed by Allied forces, it is interesting to note that an unarmed helicopter covered with red cross signs all over it drew heavy enemy fire, and I have heard not one single comment on this — reason being that this is perfectly normal and we all expect it. It is simply an accepted fact that the enemy shoots to kill on all possible occasions and never takes prisoners.

Meanwhile, the SAS had a contact and suffered no casualties. Enemy losses were eight Viet Cong, three oxen and three ox carts, all killed in action. This contact got the Australian Task Force into hot water with the Vietnamese and American Army authorities, since the victims were apparently innocent civilians, slaughtered by Australian bloodlust. Fortunately, an Australian took a few photos of the scene. When printed they showed unmistakable 122mm rockets (the big nasty ones) strapped beneath the ox carts. Innocent civilians? Another well-deserved triumph for the SAS. This small squadron, engaged solely on long-range reconnaissance patrolling, has already killed over 100 enemy in six months, more than some of the battalions have done.

Worked late at night on monthly report but got it finished.

Friday 11 October 1968

Quiet day despite another rushed job at short notice, completely changing the job we did yesterday. No one's fault. The tactical situation just changed suddenly and plans had to change to meet it.

A Viet Cong rice cache of 28 tons has just been found — enough to feed a regiment for a month (i.e. enough food for 40,000 man-days). This month's rice haul is now about 45 tons. Almost all this rice is readily recognisable as long grain rice from the USA which had been given out as civil aid. Some of the captured rice is destroyed and some of it is distributed to refugees — probably the same refugees from whom it was seized by the Viet Cong in the first place. After redistribution it will probably be seized again and so the game goes on. And each time a bit more gets spilt.

Strong efforts are now being made to clamp down on Australian soldiers trading Army property and food in local villages and towns in return for Vietnamese property and, of course, sex. Quite apart from the fact that these stupid people are trading their mates' food and Army property for their own selfish pleasure, they're also managing to keep the Viet Cong well stocked with food and equipment.

Back at camp, we have two more cases of VD in the Survey Troop — one from Vung Tau and one from Sydney. I give up. (But I can't.) Admittedly, there have only been three fresh cases since the

THE SURVEY TROOP LADIES' TOILET

It all began when the Survey Troop was invited by Task Force HQ to nominate men to attend a hygiene dutyman's course. At the time our field surveyors were short of work, so we could easily spare a few men to attend. I saw this as a good opportunity for a field surveyor to gain useful field knowledge so I nominated Sapper Bill Black and three others.

When Bill returned from his course, I learnt that he was now a fully qualified hygiene dutyman, a recognised Army trade. I hadn't realised he would be trained to this level. The thought immediately arose — could we put Bill's new skills to good use in the Survey Troop? Yes, indeed we could! We could have a ladies' toilet.

There was no ladies' toilet in the entire Task Force. Women rarely visited the Task Force anyway, but when they did, they usually used the toilet facilities of 8 Field Ambulance — possibly just as foul as most other latrines at Nui Dat, but at least 8 Field Ambulance did offer slightly more privacy, being in a flywire-proofed shed out the back and being harder than most to see into.

If the Survey Troop were to have a real ladies' toilet, then we could expect that the word would soon spread and female visitors who would not otherwise visit the Survey Troop would now do so. Hopefully this would lead to more visits by Red Cross workers, known to the soldiers as 'doughnut dollies'. Doing the rounds of the units in the Task Force, the doughnut dollies were attractive, friendly and warmly welcome. Also, possession of a ladies' toilet would greatly enhance the Survey Troop's bids to host concert parties from Australia, a privilege usually granted only to major units.

So Bill Black built our ladies' toilet. And it was a beauty too. I declared it out of bounds for all males, no matter how badly caught short. Its use was forbidden except for the purpose for which it had been specifically built. This way we could keep it clean and fresh — worthy of our expected visitors.

It achieved our aim handsomely. The doughnut dollies stepped up their visits and we scored two concert parties (one from Vung Tau and one from Queensland) before 1968 was out. And our soldiers' morale was boosted accordingly.

doctor's talk three months ago, but this gives little cause for complacency. Indications are that the one or two most serious cases may never be fully cured.

Very heavy storm hit us today from the south-east — very unusual indeed. Again working late in evening but have now caught up on most things.

Saturday 12 October 1968

Yesterday, Vietnamese Army units had five clashes with the enemy within 20 kilometres of Nui Dat. In each case the enemy was ambushed and there were no casualties to either side. This seems to be becoming the standard result for Regional Force and Popular Force clashes with the Viet Cong — as if a tacit agreement not to hurt each other exists (as is known to exist on Long Son Island, where many PF and Viet Cong are brothers).

Heavy fighting in Dat Do today. Regional Forces and US advisers fought two companies of Viet Cong. Casualties: one US captain killed, seven RF killed, two VC killed. RF was conducting a sweep through Dat Do when the VC attacked. RF fled, leaving their commander (the US captain) to be killed by the VC. Definitely not the RF's finest hour — and not the first time they've fled from battle and left leaders to their fate.

Farewell party tonight for Paul Alderson and Ray Lawson, who go home on Tuesday — not a wild party and we all got to bed early.

Sunday 13 October 1968

Very quiet day so had a bit of a rest for a change and did nothing except washing.

SAS jumped another enemy party yesterday and killed two out of three, and took the third person prisoner. These three turned out to be genuine innocent civilians. Admittedly, they were in an area where civilians were not allowed, and there are some strange inconsistencies in the story of the survivor, but if the benefit of the doubt is given, these people were not Viet Cong. The local information service had never let them know what they could and could not do, and where they could and could not safely go, and this cost two people their lives.

Monday 14 October 1968

Frustrating day due to frequent power failures, but situation rectified during afternoon. Much rain all afternoon.

Tuesday 15 October 1968

Ray Lawson and Paul Alderson left for Australia this morning, and Rod Offer arrived this afternoon — the first replacement so far during 1968 to arrive on time. Much rain again during the whole afternoon — weather now quite different from a few weeks ago, when a heavy downpour in the late afternoon could be relied on. Got packed during evening for a two-day trip to Long Binh and Saigon.

Wednesday 16 October 1968

Up early to catch helicopter to Long Binh. While waiting at Kangaroo pad, watched the casualty evacuation helicopter outside 8 Field Ambulance practising rough landings. Pilot cut power a few times while about 2 metres off the ground and dropped the aircraft to the ground. Its skids spread and it bounced heavily a couple of times. He also landed a few times with forward speed of about 10 to 15 kilometres per hour and skidded forward on the skids for about 5 to 10 metres. Frustrated airliner pilot? I winced to watch, but the aircraft was still airworthy at the end.

Finally, got aboard the II Field Force courier helicopter and we flew first to Bearcat to the Thai Army HQ to deliver mail. We then flew to the refuelling point. As we landed beside the fuel hoses I noticed an American passenger smoking. I motioned to him to put his cigarette out. He misunderstood, so I grabbed his arm and clarified the matter. He shrugged his shoulder and coolly took a drag. I grabbed him again and yelled at him (motor still running) to put it out. He refused. With my other hand I made as if to fist him up the throat. This message he understood, so he put the cigarette out — just as the fuel flow started. His rank — private, first class!

I was seated at edge of helicopter and had excellent view of refuelling, with aviation spirit pouring and dripping only 1 metre from me and about 1 metre from the roaring turbo-exhaust. Undid safety belt ready for wild leap (being a devout, practising coward), having already rolled sleeves down, but nothing blew up and we were soon on our way again. Have done this trip many times now, but I never tire of helicopter travel. Have now done about 30 hours' helicopter travel in Vietnam, most of it in Bell Iroquois (Hueys) of the US Army.

Arrived at Long Binh and spent the day on many tasks I had to do there — chasing up maps, TV valves, Tellurometers, training pamphlets and, of course, sufficient quantities of the latest *Playboy* magazine to go round the Survey Troop. Visited the Map Depot, 79 Engineer Brigade Group Motor Pool, 517th Terrain Detachment, 93rd Evacuation Hospital, HQ USARV, 53rd Signals

Battalion, the II Field Force PX, and of course 66 Engineer Company, where I stayed as usual. Returned a pair of Tellurometers we've been repairing for the NGS. The instruments have almost been completely rebuilt by 131 Divisional Locating Battery Light Aid Detachment of the RAEME at Nui Dat and now are working, but only just.

Celebration tonight in NCOs' Club for promotion of First Sergeant Marty Wilkerson (an old friend) to staff sergeant. Admired the club's latest acquisition, an autographed photo of Raquel Welch — with breasts and genital region fully displayed. Apparently she did not pose for this photo (unlike Sandra Nelson with the coat hanger), but posed in a bikini subsequently removed by photographic retouching of extremely high skill by someone in USARV, probably in MIBARS (Military Intelligence Battalion Air Reconnaissance Support).

Thursday 17 October 1968

Up early and got to HQ USARV by 07.30 to meet up with Mapping and Intelligence staff and go to Saigon with them. Jeep driven by Colonel Maberry himself, the Mapping and Intelligence Chief. One of the best drivers I've ever travelled with — really good understanding of capabilities of the jeep and how to handle it in the hectic and chaotic Vietnamese traffic. Took different route from usual, travelling to west and north of the main route. Saw much new country, most of it rural and sparsely settled. Mild alarm at one stage when ARVN troops were encountered — some sort of hostile activity going on. Drove through Saigon's dense morning traffic to the Office of the Chief Engineer, ARVN. Conference fairly brief. Visited Tan Son Nhut PX, the best in Vietnam, on the return trip.

Have previously noticed lots of children always beside the main road selling drink bottles of pink fluid to motorists. Had always presumed that this was some sort of drink, but realised today that it is petrol, sold by the bottle, for the hundreds of Lambrettas passing by. The fact that those petrol bottles also make excellent weapons is worth being aware of. Arrived back at HQ USARV at lunch time and returned to 66 Company. Made additional visits at Long Binh and spent some time at 53 Signals Battalion hunting for valves for the Survey Troop TV set, but this failed also. Heavy rain in afternoon. Got soaked for nothing. Attended screening of blue movie in evening. Film plotless and boring; however, audience was lively and some hilarious comments came forth, which can't be repeated here.

Friday 18 October 1968

Spent another couple of hours chasing TV valves without success, then back to Nui Dat. Hitched a ride from Long Binh to Saigon with a 66 Company officer who wanted to look up an allegedly French-speaking New Zealand girl he'd sighted in a Saigon restaurant a week ago and, if possible, spend tonight with her. I said it was more likely that she came from New Caledonia than New Zealand, and asked him if he spoke French. He said, 'No, that's why I want you along.'

He went to a shipping line office and there discovered that she was an executive. She was French but spoke fluent English, not extremely attractive physically, but was a sparkling conversationalist. She had lived for nine years in Vietnam and is now about to leave permanently — for São Paulo, San Francisco, Noumea or Melbourne — but is not yet certain where. She has three children, aged eleven, eight, five, and has just shed her second husband, a Vietnamese. Found much to talk about with her. Her prospective suitor said little except to make the odd remark in praise of the USA, and we left after an entertaining hour, Lothario having decided not to proposition her for the night because he found her 'too frank'. 'Anyway,' he said, 'it's you, not me, she wants to go to bed with.'

'What! How do you make that out? You heard all the conversation in the office.'

'Man!' he said. 'And you haven't realised what she wants? Do you have to be told these things?'

I thought back carefully and then said, 'No, mate. You're hearing what you want to hear. Nothing she said had any other significance at all.'

'Oh, man!' he continued. 'Are you ever all wrong! Don't miss an opportunity like that!'

'No thanks, mate. I don't want to get involved.'

'Who said anything about getting involved? It's sleeping with her that I'm talking about.'

'Well, anyway, I don't find her attractive — I just haven't the time or the inclination.'

'You should make it, man. I've got lots of inclination and stacks of time!' This is true. I happen to know he spends one to two days in Saigon every week following his inclinations and a large part of his time at Long Binh sleeping. His reward: he is about to be presented with the US Army Bronze Star for meritorious service in Vietnam.

Had lunch in the United Services Organization cafeteria in Saigon. Not cheap — 70 cents for a hamburger and milkshake. My companion booked a phone call to his wife and daughter at home in the USA — the Americans can do this, but I gather that it is expensive and not highly satisfactory (communication is one-way only and the speakers must say 'over' at the end of each message so that operators can reverse the direction of the call).

Went to Tan Son Nhut to the RAAF terminal. As usual, a bungle. I have grown used to RAAF inefficiency but find their accompanying rudeness harder and harder to tolerate. They make no secret of the fact that they regard the Army as a herd of extremely rough and uncouth creatures. Although I was booked on a plane, I had no movement order (this never having been required before), so they wouldn't let me on the plane. I was about to write my own movement order out, when they said it had to be done on the correct form and I'd have to go to HQ AFV in Saigon to get one. I sought the boss, an RAAF flight lieutenant. He agreed that it was a pity that I had to miss the plane because of this; however, it was not his concern, and that for all he knew I could be someone else in disguise and not authorised to travel. I produced my Army identity card with its photo, all sealed. He said it could be forged for all he knew.

This was too much. Told him what I thought of the RAAF Movements organisation in Vietnam and that I wouldn't have come from Long Binh to catch their plane if they hadn't told me I was booked on it. I apologised for causing all this trouble, since it was apparent that a great deal of trouble was involved in transporting people, and that in future I would, where possible, inflict this trouble only on the US Army, who always displayed greater efficiency, zeal and reliability. The flight lieutenant said that that arrangement would suit the RAAF fine, too. I then wrote out a movement order on blank paper, handed it over and said, 'Now, will you accept this or not?' He dearly wanted to say no, but reluctantly accepted it, and so I caught the plane after all.

Back at Nui Dat discovered Rocky Camps is in hospital at Vung Tau, having cut neck artery while shaving — or rather, trying to trim hair at back of neck with razor, hardly a very smart idea. Two more members of the Survey Troop have to go to hospital for last-resort treatment for VD, which has resisted all other treatment so far (including more than 500 pills and 20 injections).

Saturday 19 October 1968

Caught up odd jobs in morning. Attended lecture by Brigadier Maurice Austin (visiting from Australia) on Defence Force Retirement Benefits Fund in afternoon. Learnt a little on this vast and complex subject, but have a lot to learn yet.

Vung Tau received rocket attack last night — eight wounded. 122mm rockets were fired from the north from Long Son Island, not the first time this has happened.

Storm warning received. Fierce gales and rain have just hit Cam Ranh Bay, a few hundred kilometres up the coast, and are expected here tonight. Rained all day and evening but never heavily.

Formal dinner in honour of Brigadier Hughes, who returns to Australia tomorrow. Good meal (for a change!). Left immediately after meal in order to get a couple of hours' sleep before midnight.

Sunday 20 October 1968

Up at midnight and into Command Post for midnight till 08.00 shift. Very quiet session indeed — as far as the war was concerned. The heralded storm hit at 02.00 and lasted for an hour. Winds were very strong and several trees came down. Rained all night but was never really heavy.

Commander rang as usual at 06.45 to find what had happened during the night. This being his last day here I wished him many happy days of the return, and told him that all international airline pilots had gone on strike at midnight, but that, despite the weather, the *Jeparit* was ready to sail and had space for one or two steerage passengers and that I'd booked him aboard. He took the news like a man and said he was quite happy to return on the *Jeparit* — any way out of here was good enough.

His plane left after lunch and passed, by arrangement with the RAAF pilot, low over D Company of 1st Battalion. The Company Commander, Major Tony Hammett, had been dragged up before Brigadier Hughes only a few days ago because several men in D Company had been seen without shirts by the Brigadier, and there is a blitz at the moment on wearing shirts to avoid getting insect-borne diseases. As the plane swooped low over D Company today, the whole company (about 100 men) took off their shirts and waved goodbye with them. The message later came back that Brigadier Hughes was not impressed.

Monday 21 October 1968

Whole Task Force in state of great confusion this morning due to today being 'C Day'; i.e. changeover-of-currency day. All of the American military currency (which we all use) is being changed to a new series. This was announced during the morning with no notice, and no one could leave the area until in possession of a certificate that he'd handed in all his old currency. With about 5000 people in the Task Force affected, this brought everything to a standstill — a bad occurrence with operations against the enemy being conducted simultaneously — but, fortunately, 'C Day' only occurs every other year or so. The actual date is kept strictly secret so as to catch all the financial racketeers on the hop. Any Vietnamese who's been dealing in military payment certificates (MPC) instead of Vietnamese piastres suddenly finds himself with a load of useless currency, as does his military counterpart, who must prove to a board, if he has more than $250 in his possession, that he came by it honestly.

Within the Task Force, however, I found that all the Big Operators (the bookies, the crown-&-anchor men etc) had known about C Day for four days and had had stacks of time to spread their working capital around. Even the man who won $2000 at crown & anchor last night had no trouble spreading it safely around.

Now, of course, everyone is flat broke for a few days until the new MPC is distributed — so no cash transactions can occur, and the PX, post office, cash office etc are closed for business until then. Much chaos at first but things are slowly settling down and we'll be back to normal again when we get our money back in the new notes.

At this afternoon's briefing conference, the first with the new Commander, Brigadier Sandy Pearson, all representatives were asked in turn, as usual, if they had any points to bring up. As usual, few did. However, the house was brought down when Lieutenant Tony Hill, RAN, the liaison officer from 9 Squadron, RAAF, and known to all as The Admiral, stood up and announced that 'the Senior Naval Officer of the First Australian Task Force welcomes you to your new command', he being the only naval man in the whole Task Force. As the mirth subsided, his voice was heard to say: 'Score: Navy one, Army nil.'

Tuesday 22 October 1968

Frantically busy day. No less than four major tasks, all operationally urgent, hit us at once. Everybody flat out today and tonight, in order to meet our commitments before tomorrow's concert. Tomorrow should be enjoyable — we are host unit for a concert party from Australia, the first for a couple of months or so.

Oreste Biziak, our new clerk, arrived today and quickly settled in. Within three hours he was being used as assistant printer. What a day! I think it rained but I can't remember for sure.[1]

[1] If it did rain, it was the last rain for 1968. — JB

New money issued today. New notes decidedly unspectacular, but at least they buy things, and that's an improvement over the last 30 money-less hours. The 5-cent, 10-cent, 25-cent and 50-cent notes are all almost identical in design but of different colour.

Wednesday 23 October 1968

With today's job out of the way yesterday and last night, we were able to settle down and enjoy the concert today. All went smoothly and we had a wonderful day. Concert party consisted of: Wilson Irving, real name Reginald Wilson-Irving (leader and compere); Les Crosby (trumpeter); Jeff Smith (organist and accordionist); Jim Howard (drummer); George Hill (variety artist and Queensland Opera singer); Valda Scott, real name Valda Shellnack (singer); Judy Connelli, real name Judith O'Connell (comedienne); Janie Richards, real name Anne Richards (dancer).

We met the concert party at Luscombe airfield and took them to Luscombe Bowl for the concert. My first effort was to go backstage and throw out all the hangers-on who were in everyone's way. Amongst those I chucked out were two Public Relations officers and three PR sergeants. They were most upset at this, particularly at the threats I uttered, which included offering physical violence to any of them who did other than as I told them. These PR people are a menace at all concerts. They grossly exploit their privileged position; they crowd performers backstage; they block the audience's view while taking their own private photos from out front; and they send their entire staff on a one-man mission. This time it didn't happen because I got in first, and for the first time at a concert this year, both performers and audience got a fair go.

The concert was a great success, less talented than the wonderful West Australian group and, in fact, the Australian Forces group

Survey Troop sergeants' tent lines, with (l to r) Sergeants Eric Clutterbuck, Pat Cox, Ted Morris, WO2 Spike Jones and Sergeant Grant Small.

from Vung Tau last month, but probably the third best this year, thanks to the wild popularity of George Hill and Janie Richards.

Of all concert performers this year, only two who are not attractive girls have received thunderous applause here, and they are Ron Blaskett (the West Australian ventriloquist) and George Hill today. George, a butcher by trade, told yarns and sang songs with rare skill — a real Queensland bushwhacker. His yarns brought the house down, but it was his Queensland Opera singing that captivated the audience. His hillbilly songs and yodelling were simply grand.

Janie Richards was in a class all of her own. Her job was to look gorgeous and to dance. She was the most attractive girl seen in Nui Dat this year and certainly the best dancer — and small wonder. Aged only 17 and just out of school, she's been deeply involved with classical ballet since the age of five. She joined the Victorian Ballet Company but was unable to make great progress because of her lack of height, so has just recently turned to cabaret dancing instead, bringing with her a wealth of skill and experience. A tiny blonde with a ponytail hairdo and excellent figure and legs, she was a tremendous hit with the audience. Her almost child-like (and quite genuine) lack of sophistication was apparent to the audience and gave her added charm. I mentioned to her before the show (bearing in mind comments from previous audiences) that she'd probably find this audience a lot different from ones back home. She said simply, 'I've never played to an audience back home, so I've no basis for comparison. I'm completely new to this game. I was invited to come here because someone with influence saw me practising.'

Despite her inexperience with audiences, she displayed stacks of confidence and skill. She started by dancing onto the stage, stopping at a microphone, and asking, 'Anyone here from Townsville?'

'Yes!' came a voice.

'Do you know me?' said Janie.

'Ah . . . yes! You're Janie Richards!'

'Right,' she said. 'Come up here and say hullo.'

He did so and received a kiss which sent him reeling dizzily back to his seat. The audience was pretty lively but was completely captivated by Janie's beauty and simple charm. After her first dancing act, I asked her how many times she would go on stage. She replied, 'Once more.'

I said a lot of men would be pretty disappointed at not seeing more of her. 'But,' she said, 'I've only got two dance acts fully prepared.'

I said, 'With your looks you don't have to dance. You can just stand there and be looked at and you'll be the greatest hit this year.' She ultimately did this — amidst tremendous cheering.

The compere livened things up by dragging in men from the audience from time to time, notably those quick to answer back — for example:

Wilson Irving: 'Now fellows, you don't really want to see any more of Janie do you?!'

Tumultuous roar from audience through which a voice of great power and penetration could be heard: 'I'd rather look at her than you, mate!'

Wilson Irving: 'Come down here and say that!'

Voice was immediately prodded out of the audience by willing mates and proved to be owned by a big, jut-jawed infantry corporal, half-shy and half-defiant.

Wilson Irving: 'Now, Corporal, what did you say just now?'

Corporal (gaining confidence): 'I said I'd rather look at her than you. Geez, mate, you've got a face like a broken boot!'

Wilson Irving: 'OK, Corporal, you can stay here with Janie and dance with her.'

The corporal made a valiant effort but had an ice-block's chance in hell of keeping up with the twinkle-footed Janie, whose high kicks went higher than his head.

After the show we returned to the Survey Troop where Dallas Leary had prepared a magnificent lunch. Before getting started, the girls had showers and the men were taken for a drive. We were the first host unit ever to offer a concert party a shower — a necessity in this climate — and the girls were really grateful. They used our sergeants' two tents for changing, while Eric Clutterbuck, Ted Morris and Grant Small ensured that the wrong people didn't get into the act. The daily water truck arrived just as two girls, wearing nothing but towels and thongs, were walking out of the sergeants' tents towards the shower. The driver slammed on his brakes just in time to avoid knocking down a grove of rubber trees while he worked out whether or not he saw what he thought he saw. Looking completely stunned, he finally went on his way.

Meanwhile, the men were driven to the main external gate of the Task Force. The lure and danger of the unknown (to them) territory beyond appealed to them strongly. They tried to proceed but the gate sentry said, looking at all these civilians with only two soldiers, 'You can't go out like that. You haven't enough weapons. Here, have mine!' and he handed his rifle over, to the amazement of all. They went on a quick run down to the Hoa Long checkpoint and back, sufficient to give the concert party men a Taste of Real Adventure, and the opportunity (for which they were extremely grateful) to see and photograph at close quarters water buffaloes, rice fields and Vietnamese people.

We had a delightful lunch, which lasted until about 15.00. From remarks made by the concert party (some of whom have visited Vietnam before) and by hangers-on such as PR people, our hospitality was the most relaxed and enjoyable given to a concert party yet. Hope so. We might get more now that we, the first minor unit ever to host a concert party, have done so much better than many large units. The spirit of the barbecue was very happy and developed into a pleasant sing-song, which produced more yarns and Queensland Opera from George, and the following two songs from us — the only two Australian songs so far from the Vietnam war.

'Cheap Charlie'
(Tune: 'This Old Man')

Uc Dai Loi, Cheap Charlie,
He no buy me Saigon tea,
Saigon tea cost many many Pee,
Uc Dai Loi he Cheap Charlie

Uc Dai Loi, Cheap Charlie,
He no give me MPC,
MPC cost many many Pee,
Uc Dai Loi he Cheap Charlie

Uc Dai Loi, Cheap Charlie,
He no go to bed with me,
For it cost him many many Pee,
Uc Dai Loi he Cheap Charlie

Uc Dai Loi, Cheap Charlie,
Make him give me one for free,
Mama-San go crook at me,
Uc Dai Loi he Cheap Charlie

Uc Dai Loi, Cheap Charlie,
He give Baby-San to me,
Baby-San cost many many Pee,
Uc Dai Loi he Cheap Charlie

Uc Dai Loi, Cheap Charlie,
He go home across the sea,
He leave Baby-San with me,
Uc Dai Loi he Cheap Charlie

('Pee' meaning Vietnamese piastres and 'Mama-San' meaning madam of a brothel.)

'Twelve Months in Vietnam' © 1968 by 2nd Battalion,
Royal Australian Regiment
(Tune: 'Twelve Days of Christmas')

On the first month in Vietnam, my CO said to me:
    A sniper in a bushy-topped tree.

On the second month in Vietnam, my CO said to me:
    Two CBUs, and
    A sniper in a bushy-topped tree.

On the third month in Vietnam, my CO said to me:
    Three APCs,
    Two CBUs, and
    A sniper in a bushy-topped tree.

And so on, each verse getting longer, up to the final verse:

On the twelfth month in Vietnam, my CO said to me:
> *Twelve dinkum Aussies,*
> *Eleven Yanks goddamning,*
> *Ten drummers drumming,*
> *Nine new battalions,*
> *Eight VCs running,*
> *Seven Sabres strafing,*
> *Six sex-starved soldiers,*
> *Five Hershey Bars,*
> *Four gunships gunning,*
> *Three APCs,*
> *Two CBUs, and*
> *A sniper in a bushy-topped tree.*

('CBU' being an air-dropped cluster bomb unit that dispenses many small bomblets which often don't explode and when found by Viet Cong are used as mines or boobytraps.)

At the conclusion of the party George Hill presented us with a record of songs he has composed and sung about the Vietnam War. Several of us, including myself, were delighted to receive our own personal copies autographed by George. In return we presented the concert party with some samples of our work, notably our much sought-after travel poster — 'This Vacation Visit Beautiful Vietnam', depicting a rather spectacular war scene. It, and a few other items (best not described), were very well received.

Thursday 24 October 1968

Some news on the MPC change is now coming through. About $30,000,000 of the old series is unaccounted for — lost in action, mislaid, in Viet Cong hands, outside Vietnam; in fact, anywhere in the world. This figure sounds impossible, but when one hears other stories such as: (i) two Saigon prostitutes with between $10,000 and $20,000 in their possession committed suicide; (ii) a laundry in Ba Ria was left holding about $20,000; (iii) various bars and brothels in Vung Tau have suffered similarly; (iv) when in Hong Kong I met local people wanting to sell me MPC which US servicemen had passed to them; all this makes $30,000,000 seem not so impossible after all. The Viet Cong must have a lot stashed away too — and now it's worthless. Apparently the Vietnamese MPC collectors were really caught on the hop, even though the Australian bookmakers and gamblers had somehow scented everything about four days earlier.

Went to 10 MID at Van Kiep for lunch today to attend a farewell for Dai-Uy Trung who goes tomorrow to Hué as a district chief. This will win him promotion to thieu-ta (major) and is most pleasing. Many nice farewell gifts were given to him, including a set of binoculars from the Senior Province Adviser (American). I gave him a copy of Bob O'Neill's book *Vietnam Task* — the story of the 5th Battalion in Vietnam 1966–67, during which time Trung and Bob became very good friends, which made this gift an appropriate one.

Returned to Nui Dat in early afternoon with much to do, especially after yesterday. Got all minor jobs out of the way, leaving major ones for tomorrow.

Friday 25 October 1968

Heavy artillery, i.e. real heavy artillery, is to be used in this province. The US battleship *New Jersey* is off the local coast and preparing to smash land targets with its 16-inch guns. The presence of the USS *New Jersey* is a well-kept secret at the moment and is not, we hope, generally known.

The new Task Force Commander, Brigadier Pearson, held a conference with all unit commanders today. The pattern of operations is to change. No longer is the Task Force to conduct search-and-destroy operations (cynically termed 'search and avoid') here and there throughout the province. The aim now is to hunt our old enemy 274 Viet Cong Regiment. This regiment is to be tracked down, hunted relentlessly wherever it goes, and then destroyed. The next target will be the Viet Cong's D445 Battalion, an even older foe. The war is at last getting personal.

The two-can-per-man-per-day beer ration imposed by Brigadier Hughes has been removed. The new Commander rightly considers that this is for the unit commanders to handle — it is their responsibility to ensure that things don't get out of hand. Things did get out of hand before, especially with 2nd Battalion and the Engineers, and this led to the imposition of the ration system, thereby punishing the innocent along with the guilty. Everyone hopes the new system will prove successful, and that the Engineers manage to curb their wilder tendencies. During my nine months here I really have noticed that our behaviour problems have come mainly from Engineers rather than from the infantry battalions. This opinion is shared by all, including the Engineers, who appear to revel in their notoriety and endeavour to live up to it, never resting on their laurels.

Saturday 26 October 1968

The dry has come. Today was fine and hot all day, and the humidity was lower than usual. Brightest rumour of the day: the Vietnamese are about to change their piastre series in a bid to recoup last week's losses when we changed our currency!

Sunday 27 October 1968

Went to repeat performance of last Wednesday's Queensland concert. This concert was an even greater success — almost as good as the West Australian one about six months ago. The concert was preceded by a recital from the 4th Battalion Band — not marvellous. The concert proper began with a trumpet solo of 'South of the Border' by Les Crosby, which made the 4th Battalion Band's raspberries and mis-hits sound pretty weak. Jimmy Howard's drumming during 'Caravan' was easily this year's best and received wild acclaim — as did Janie Richards and George Hill again. George produced a completely different repertoire of yarns today — not only that, but none were the same tired old jokes put over by concert party after concert party. Judy Connelli hit the audience very fast and captured them with her personality and voice. George's Queensland Opera again laid everyone in the aisles. Singer, yodeller, guitarist and raconteur extraordinaire, his sense of timing was superb and the audience loved him — and also many of his quick comments:

1. Did ya hear about our new champion channel swimmer? Swam across in three and a half hours and back again in three and a half minutes — his jockstrap got caught on the pier!
2. Fixing fences on the Queensland border a bloke had an accident one day. 'That arm's gotta come off,' said the doc.
   'OK, OK,' said the bloke. 'If it's gotta come off, it's gotta come off.'

'Yeah,' said the doc. 'But it's gotta come off fast and we've no anaesthetic.'

'She'll be right,' said the bloke. 'I don't feel pain.'

'Fair dinkum?' said the doc.

'Yeah,' said the bloke. 'Never felt pain in me life. Go ahead.'

So the doc went ahead and amputated the arm and the bloke never batted an eyelid. 'Gawd,' said the doc. 'That's remarkable! And you've never experienced any pain in your life, eh?'

'Yeah, mate,' said the bloke. 'That's right — no, I lie — I have felt pain twice.'

'When was that?' asked the doc.

'Well,' said the bloke, 'I was down on the border, rabbiting one day. I'd just set and anchored the trap. I was squatting over it and covering it over when — whack — it went off and caught me fair smack in the orchestras! Wow! Did that hurt!'

'I bet it did,' said the doc. 'And when was the second occasion?'

'The same day,' said the bloke. 'At the instant I ran out of chain!'

Headed from concert, which finished late, straight to cricket match to play for HQ Company against 161 Recce Flight. 161 Recce Flight scored 119 — I had a bowl and took three wickets for six runs off three overs. This was very economical against a team of heavy hitters but was a little frustrating because I didn't bowl any spinners. Hands were perspiring too much to grip the ball tightly, so I pretended to be spinning it a lot but actually sent down nothing but straight ones with varied flight and pace. We scored 80, of which I top-scored with 23.

Their bowlers were very fast and very erratic — in fact dangerously so — but the first man to be knocked out was their own wicketkeeper! Whole match was sadly marred by appalling sportsmanship from 161 Recce Flight. We were treated to the spectacle of all 11 fieldsmen (including two captains and several sergeants) arguing with and browbeating an unfortunate umpire until he reversed what had been a perfectly correct decision. No question of judgement was involved; it was simply a question of applying the rules. The two HQ Company batsmen took no part in the argument and accepted the incorrectly reversed decision without comment — thereby emphasising the infantile behaviour of the other team. I later took over as umpire and within ten minutes had become involved in further incidents:

1. I had to tell the fielding captain firmly that there were certain decisions that had to be made by the umpire and not by the fieldsmen.
2. I had to inform fieldsmen that play could not be delayed while they hunted for and lit cigarettes.
3. I had to order three fieldsmen to stop arguing amongst themselves and to stop holding up the game.
4. The batsmen were prevented from running two byes by a fieldsman (Army rank: captain) who told them that the ball had touched the wicketkeeper on the way and was dead.

At this final and flagrant breach of the rules I bawled out the skipper of the fielding side and told him to control his team properly. I threatened to send the fielding captain (not an officer) off the field, together with those team-mates (mainly officers) he could not control. This was, of course, totally beyond my jurisdiction as umpire, but something had to be done and I was the senior officer present on the field. This, at last, had effect and I had no further trouble but it was a pretty strong clash of wills for a while.

Again no rain — day quite fine and hot. No rain now since early last week. It seems that the big storm of the previous weekend was the death throe of the wet.

Monday 28 October 1968

Many minor tasks today plus two visits to other units, and Noel away at Vung Tau on court martial duty. Visited 3rd Battalion at lunch time and had lunch with Ray Stuart. The 3rd Battalion is now getting ready to go home in about three weeks' time.

Stirred up this afternoon's Commander's conference. The new Task Force Commander has indicated that he wants his daily conferences to be more lively and entertaining — so I took him at his word. Instead of the usual, 'Survey, no points, sir,' when my turn came, I said 'Survey, sir. It has come to our attention that the Vietnamese are about to change their piastre series in an attempt to recoup last week's losses due to our MPC series change. However, there is no cause for alarm, since our printing section will ensure that the Task Force is not caught short.' This went down extraordinarily well and after the conference The Admiral was heard to remark: 'Score: Navy one, Army one.'

Had dinner at A Squadron 3 Cavalry Regiment. The new second-in-command there is Captain John Grey, a very old and good friend of long standing.

Tuesday 29 October 1968

Task Force buzzed at noon by an F-100 fighter. Most spectacular to watch as he screamed overhead and then threw plane into an almost vertical climb, commenced to spin about his longitudinal axis and within a few seconds had disappeared through a small cloud several thousand feet up.

Sapper Peter Aukstinaitis arrived unexpectedly today. He's been due (as Paul Alderson's replacement) for about two months but was delayed for a tonsillectomy in Australia and has finally arrived after five minutes' notice.

Weather humid, but no sign of rain for a week now.

Wednesday 30 October 1968

Up at midnight for midnight to 08.00 session in Task Force HQ Command Post. Taking over from the outgoing duty officer, I noticed that there were a couple of markings on the master operations map on the wall that he hadn't mentioned in our checking of the map together. The black crosses looked like artillery targets to be hit later in the night, but there were no explanatory numerals beside the crosses. 'You didn't mention these. What are they?'

'Heavy artillery.'

'Out there? But those locations are out of range of all our artillery, including the heavies.'

'It's very heavy artillery!'

'OK, then. Whose?'

'Well, we're not supposed to know, but those are the targets the *New Jersey* is hitting tonight from out at sea.'

Later in the night a minor snarl with the USAF at II Field Force Vietnam HQ (our superior headquarters). Wanting clearance to put an air strike into our territory, they begrudged the 45 seconds it took to obtain clearance from the battalion actually on the ground, and said so. However, I gather this is normal from them, although it hasn't happened to me before. I know that time is precious to a strike aircraft up in the air, but the lives of the people beneath are even more precious.

News from Xuyen Moc to our east — the district chief (a military appointment, usually a major or captain) has been killed, cut up into little pieces, and the pieces buried. Nice guys. No particular reason for the deed, except that the victim was a local VIP.

Thursday 31 October 1968

Busy day with many interruptions. Helicopter to Vung Tau late in evening was delayed due to accident during afternoon. An SAS patrol was being inserted into position by air, accompanied as usual by a light fire team of two US Army gunships. Much enemy activity was seen in the area from the air, so there was no point inserting a patrol to find this out. The helicopter containing the SAS patrol headed back while the gunships remained to shoot up the enemy. Score: the enemy lost three trucks and we lost one gunship! Aircraft was shot down. Crew survived and were rescued. An air strike then went in, ensuring that the helicopter was destroyed.

Got aboard RAAF helicopter returning to Vung Tau at end of day. Aircraft full and there was no co-pilot, so I had the co-pilot's seat which, for someone with reasonable knowledge, interest and experience with Bell helicopters, was fascinating. Good view, too. All other passengers were bad malaria cases being evacuated to 1 Australian Field Hospital at Vung Tau. They all looked very sick indeed and could barely walk to the plane. Had the plane crashed I don't think it would have worried them, they were in such a bad way. Malaria, with over 250 cases this month, has pushed VD out as the most widespread disease in the Task Force.

Three more helicopters with malaria cases came down to Vung Tau during the next hour. Many have been transferred to US Army hospitals, but there is now no more room there either, and evacuation to Butterworth, Malaysia, is now about to commence. All this is over and above the less serious cases in the Rest & Convalescence Centre at Vung Tau and the more serious cases evacuated to Australia.

Spent evening at 1 Australian Field Hospital, having presented a Survey Corps plaque to their Officers' Mess as thanks for their generous hospitality during my many court martial visits. The plaque is also appropriate because two members of the Mess, Major Bruce Daniel and Captain John Lambie, are ex-Survey Corps men.

NOVEMBER

AUSTRALIAN MILITARY FORCES

AAB — 71A

Reprinted Dec, 1964

RECORD BOOK

CONTAINING 96 PAGES

RULED FEINT

Late in 1968, a lengthy postal strike paralysed Australian mail services, bringing the Amalgamated Postal Workers' Union (APWU) much unpopularity. Defending themselves against the cry 'What about the Diggers in Vietnam?', the APWU claimed that the soldiers' mail was getting through. But suffering the same mail delays as everyone back home, the troops' morale was lowered by this untruth.

The soldiers' response was to create the 'Punch A Postie' leaflet. When a rough draft was shown to John with the suggestion that the Survey Troop might print it, he found its humour somewhat heavy-handed, and wasn't enthusiastic. However, with several of the Survey Troop soldiers very keen on it, he could see the morale implications, approved it to be drawn up properly and approached Psychological Operations to organise printing.

The leaflets were indeed a morale booster for the troops, but the APWU took deep umbrage at them — the APWU Federal Secretary going so far as to warn the Army about the union's World War II commandos and boxing champions, and declaring the whole affair to have been instigated by B.A. Santamaria's National Civic Council within the Democratic Labor Party. Finally, the Minister for the Army ordered an official investigation.

Unrepentant, John knew that his role in the affair was supported at senior levels, including by the Task Force Commander himself. But higher up, anything could have happened, especially with the Minister wanting a scapegoat. It was not for another 30 years that he found out his key protector had been the irascible Major General A.L. MacDonald, Commander of Australian Forces Vietnam. A ferocious disciplinarian, MacDonald was astonishingly benevolent in this case. He commented to a fellow officer shortly afterwards, 'I thought it was a real hoot, but, of course, I couldn't tell Bullen that!'

PAUL HAM

Friday 1 November 1968

Up at 06.00 and down to airfield to catch RAAF Caribou back to Nui Dat. Busy day, quiet evening, weather fine.

Saturday 2 — Sunday 3 November 1968

Two frantically busy days trying to get everything well ahead before leaving tomorrow to go to Da Nang (far north of South Vietnam) with the Australian Army Training Team courier run.

The Training Team of advisers scattered over the country has its headquarters in Saigon and sends mail, despatches etc round the country twice a week under escort of an officer. This is not normally done by Task Force officers but was specially arranged in my case by Brigadier Hughes before he left because Matthew D'Arcy, a close friend of mine, now lives and works permanently in Da Nang. Matthew D'Arcy did an extended tour of duty as a captain in the Training Team where he met and married his wife, a Vietnamese interpreter and daughter of a retired army general. On being re-posted to Australia in August 1967, Matthew resigned from the Army and returned with his wife to Vietnam, and is now working for the Catholic Relief Service in Da Nang.

Monday 4 November 1968

Up early to catch plane at 07.15 to Tan Son Nhut. Plane flew north to Blackhorse, the camp of the 11th Armoured Cavalry Regiment, US Army, before proceeding west to Tan Son Nhut, so it was an interesting trip. Landed at Tan Son Nhut and went by bus to HQ AFV, home of the 'Saigon Warriors', who, during the attacks of Tet in January–February '68, had to eat field rations for as long as three days and to shower from overhead buckets. These fearful hardships (and others) have been divulged recently to the Australian press by the Warriors Who Survived. This has aroused much annoyance in the Task Force, especially in the infantry battalions, who are normally on field rations for weeks at a time. In camp at Nui Dat, we all shower from canvas buckets. When battalions are out on operations they get no showers at all, nor do they draw $5 per day Saigon Allowance.

The Saigon Warrior (Captain Harry Swales), sitting beside me in the plane, was telling me about the super stereophonic sound system he's just bought with savings from Saigon Allowance. My heart bleeds for the poor Saigon Warriors stopping overnight at Nui Dat or Vung Tau who complain to Task Force men, as Harry did to me, that the visit is costing them a lot of money, i.e., no Saigon Allowance while away from Saigon!

Visited the Training Team HQ and was courteously and efficiently briefed. My plane leaves for the run early tomorrow. Went to HQ Company, AFV, to arrange accommodation and was handled with hopeless inefficiency by a warrant officer. Fortunately, he classified my case as being too hard, and passed me back to the

Training Team HQ, who quickly sorted this simple matter out. Accommodation is scarce so I'm staying in the Dong Khanh, a Vietnamese hotel (and glorified brothel) in Cholon. The overnight bill will be paid by the Australian Army.

Spent morning and afternoon in hotel writing up the Survey Troop monthly report for October, which I'd brought with me in case I got a free moment. Went for a walk for one and a half hours during afternoon. Would have liked to have taken camera, but for my first unaccompanied stroll through Cholon (which was badly shot up during Tet and is still subject to minor incidents), it seemed more prudent to leave the camera locked away and carry an M16 rifle instead. On the basis that the 9mm pistol has only limited range, accuracy and hitting power, and that just about anything at all, from minor rioting to full-scale war, can occur without warning in both Saigon and Da Nang, I've swapped my pistol for Grant Small's M16 and a great heap of filled magazines and spare ammunition. My travelling bag is fearfully heavy, but better that than wishing in the middle of a fight that I had more ammunition.

As it turned out, I had a very peaceful stroll of about 3 to 4 miles without any incident at all. I walked from Cholon to Saigon and back. The air was full of dust, grit, noise, bike exhaust, garbage fumes and an incense smell that I don't find pleasant. The incense is not unpleasant itself, but I think I don't like it because it's closely associated with a country that I feel no deep love for. I pity Vietnam's plight but, despite the pleasant climate and the enchanting children, I find that I have little real affection for Vietnam — and I realise this more strongly whenever I recall the wonderful day in Macau about five months ago.

The streets of Cholon and Saigon were busy, the people were friendly and I'm certainly quite used to the squalor, but I just cannot develop enthusiasm for this country, however hard I try. There are attractive parts of Saigon, but the war and its barricades are everywhere, and the people go their ways without displaying much interest in life (though possibly the same remark is true for any big city in the world). One can only observe that once, maybe 30 years ago, Saigon was probably very attractive, and that goodness only knows now what future lies in store.

Wrote a couple of letters before dinner. Had dinner in The Cavern, one of the several bars in the Dong Khanh. The dinner was nice, but very expensive, costing just under $5, so there goes my Saigon Allowance for the day. Plenty of attractive company for dinner, but it soon palled, the conversation being so strictly limited. Sample conversation:

'May I sit down?'

'Sure.'

'My name Lee.'

'Hullo, Lee.'

'What your name?'

'John.'

'Where you from, John?'

'Long Binh.'

'How long you been in Vietnam?'

'Nine months.'

'How old you?'

'Thirty-two.'

'How old you think I am?'

'Twenty-eight?' (She looked about 21.)

'Me 27. You no speak American? You American?'

'No, Uc Dai Loi.'

'Ah! Uc Dai Loi Number One. Cheap Charlie, eh? Hey, Cheap Charlie! You buy me Saigon tea?'

'Maybe later.'

'Why not now?'

'No money now. Maybe later.'

NUMBER ONE OR NUMBER TEN

The Army is renowned for doing things by numbers. The limited English spoken by the Vietnamese people does likewise. Everything is evaluated on a sliding scale from one to ten. 'Number One' is good; 'Number Ten' is bad. The system is greatly simplified by never using anything in the range of two and nine.

From the soldier's point of view, Number One is dry socks, dry anything, fresh food, Australian beer, a letter from home, a letter from anybody, a concert with ten girls, R&R, being short (i.e. nearly due to go home) . . .

Number Ten is mud, sodden smokes, everything that isn't Number One, Ba Mi Ba beer, no beer at all, a concert with no girls . . .

From the Vietnamese bar girl's point of view, the Australian soldier (Uc Dai Loi) is Cheap Charlie and therefore Number Ten.

'Hey, you Cheap Charlie Number Ten! You spend night here?'

'Yes.'

'You got girl to sleep with?'

'No. No money.'

'Ah, you real Number Ten Uc Dai Loi Cheap Charlie! Hey, come on! You buy me one drink for lucky?'

'Maybe later.'

'No can stay here all night, Cheap Charlie. You call me when you got money.'

This type of scene was enacted several times. It certainly livened up the meal time somewhat and the girls were very easy on the eyes, but their blatant commercial greed tended to more than counter their physical attractions. One girl, older and married, did stop and chat for a while and was quite pleasant, but the rest were hungry vultures. Still, I had to laugh when one girl taunted me with a new verse of the 'Cheap Charlie' song:

> Uc Dai Loi, always broke,
> He is just a hopeless soak,
> He try to give bar girl a poke,
> Uc Dai Loi, he one big joke.

I thought this was priceless and asked her to sing it again so I could remember it. Nonplussed for a moment, possibly not having drawn this reaction before, she finally obliged.

Departed from The Cavern and went to the Upstairs Bar. Same system. Girls possibly a little more attractive than in The Cavern, and much less willing to dally with Cheap Charlies. Watched the world go by for about half an hour and found it most interesting.

Average time taken for a girl to persuade a partner to buy her a Saigon tea: two to three minutes. Length of time the Saigon tea sits in front of the girl: one to two minutes. Time taken to drink the

Saigon tea: one to two seconds. Time taken for second Saigon tea to arrive: one to two minutes. Cost of Saigon tea: $1.60. At this rate a man can shell out $10 to $20 per hour and receive in return:

1. Conversation about as inspiring as that above.
2. Close cuddles plus a few suggestive strokes of the leg.
3. Vague promises of better things to come later (which will cost in the vicinity of a further $20 to $30).

The girls are professional in every sense of the word, and their acting is very polished. Most of them have good figures and beautiful hair, and keep their hands moving over their figures most of the time and touching and rearranging their hair. If business is slack, a couple of them will dance cheek-to-cheek by the jukebox to arouse interest.

Left bar and on way to my room met a group of five boys aged about five. The children are the real charmers of Vietnam. They all seem so bright and quick to learn and are always delightful. I showed them a few games one can play with one's fingers and this was a big hit. To bed early for early start tomorrow.

Tuesday 5 November 1968

Up at 06.00 and picked up from hotel shortly afterwards. Went to Free World Forces HQ building, collected mail and pay for the Training Team, and went to Tan Son Nhut. Took off at 09.30, my first trip in a C-130 (Hercules). Not very comfortable, but not as uncomfortable and noisy as I've been led to expect (the C-123 is the worst I've struck in this regard). Flew to Phu Cat and then to Da Nang, total flight taking about two hours. Met by member of Training Team, went to their headquarters, at 'Australia House', just in time for a barbecue lunch held in honour of pay day and Melbourne Cup. Met a few old friends I hadn't seen for many years. Also met Warrant Officer II Tom van Bakel from Eindhoven, who had served in the Dutch Army before coming to Australia.

No sign of Matthew D'Arcy, though. Story is that he and wife have left, following a big dispute with Civil Operations and Revolutionary Development Support (CORDS), which is the overall controlling body for all civil aid work in Vietnam, and the Catholic Relief Service for whom Matthew works. Cause of dispute: the National Broadcasting Company of USA visited Vietnam and interviewed Ambassador Komer, Chief of CORDS. Later in Da Nang, NBC interviewed Matthew, asked the same questions and got an entirely different set of answers. Both interviews were broadcast throughout USA on the same programme on TV. Uproar in USA! Situation aggravated by Matthew not being an American. Komer demanded Matthew's resignation and/or sacking. Boss of Catholic Relief in Saigon said that in that case he'd resign too, since he had authorised Matthew to speak and what Matthew said was the truth. End result: Komer had gone to Turkey, and Matthew has gone to Australia.

Had dinner at the local US Advisers' Officers' Club. Not as good as last night's dinner in the Dong Khanh hotel, but it was half as good and cost one-eighth as much. Quiet evening, so early to bed.

Wednesday 6 November 1968

Light rain all day. The wet here is just starting. It is amazing but true that the seasons here are the exact opposite of those at Nui Dat, Saigon and Vung Tau, only a few hundred kilometres away along the same stretch of coast. Here the six-month dry is just ending.

Visited Catholic Relief office to hunt news of Matthew. He left last Monday, the day I was in Saigon, so I only missed him by a day. No suggestion of any argument or trouble was even hinted at by the girl I spoke to.

Had quick look through Da Nang, Vietnam's second-largest city. Not much different from other large towns — untidy and not clean. However, despite the war, everyone carries on happily. Barbed wire everywhere, just the same as Saigon. Many trees in the streets. As Vietnamese towns go, it isn't too bad at all, but it is, nevertheless, far from being elegant or efficient. Was advised not to carry a weapon in the town. It was pleasant to be able to travel without a gun for the first time since I've come to Vietnam, though, my own instinctive feeling is that the Australian advisers have grown rather blasé and no longer take full precautions; however, it's hard for a newcomer to assess the situation quickly. In fact, there has been savage fighting here quite recently and I believe in being realistic, not fatalistic.

Played two games of chess with Tom van Bakel and got thrashed soundly in three-quarters of an hour and not quite as soundly in two and a quarter hours. He's a good player and I was lucky to last so long in the second game.

Many advisers were in this afternoon to collect mail etc and I spoke with most of them. Several were very critical of the way Australia is running her share of the war. Criticism of the Task Force was strong, despite their apparent lack of familiarity with what's happening there. Being from the Task Force, I felt targeted. I did attempt to explain some of the other issues involved and that the whole situation is more complex than they appear to realise, but a gentle approach got me nowhere. I found it impossible, for example, to convince a captain, commissioned for less than three years and in Vietnam for only six months, that his criticisms of the way the Task Force was being run were perhaps unjust. He being one of my hosts, I didn't argue with him but left it at that. I was surprised at the bitterness and low morale of some I met this afternoon. I hadn't expected this. As the first Task Force officer to make this courier run, and being well aware of the dangerous life that many of these men are leading, it seemed more prudent and courteous for me to shut up. Steady consumption of beer during the afternoon had impaired capacity of most to receive or dispense much logic. However, quite probably my experience here today is not typical of the Training Team as a whole. Certainly I've found the attitudes of Warrant Officers Kevin Mitchell and Ike Lever (both based at Van Kiep, near Ba Ria) very different.

The Australian Army Training Team in Vietnam leads a difficult life. There are about a hundred of them altogether, some being advisers and others administrators. Of them all, about five per cent get killed each year, and many times that number become battle casualties who survive. Most of the rest lead the same risky existence but escape unscathed. There are a few who lead a very soft life indeed. It is amusing now to look back at the Rugged Veteran act one warrant officer put on when he returned to Australia in late 1967; and one of the men here now (a captain) mentioned that he 'hadn't *had* (!) to sleep with a Vietnamese girl in five months, since there were more than enough round-eye (i.e. non-Asian) girls available'. His villa is next to the American female entertainers' villa, and he finds the supply of American and Australian entertainers plus nurses adequate for his needs. He draws a Da Nang Allowance, which helps defray expenses. But, in general, one must not decry the overwhelming majority of the Training Team who really are living dangerously.

Thursday 7 November 1968

Down to the airfield this morning to catch plane back to Saigon after a most interesting two days at Da Nang. Travelled back to Tan Son Nhut on a one-and-a-half-hour flight by Hercules. Was seated with an American concert party and found myself opposite a girl entertainer wearing an open-weave crocheted 'see-through' mini-dress. The view was intriguing, to say the least. Next to me was a guitarist from the same party. His hair was shoulder length, he hadn't shaved

US Air Force C-141 Starlifter.

for two days, his clothes were filthy and he stank.

Landed at Tan Son Nhut at 13.30 after a comfortable trip. While waiting for the RAAF Caribou to Nui Dat, I watched the planes go by at Tan Son Nhut, the world's busiest airport. All types of aircraft, both military and civil, were landing and taking off. Saw many interesting ones, especially the huge C-141 Starlifter, with its sleek silver lines and swept-back swooping wings — similar to the B-52 bomber and one of the world's biggest aircraft (though a bigger one, the C-5 Galaxy, is going into production now). The Starlifter, a USAF heavy transporter, really is big — its tail tip is 30 to 40 feet off the ground. Also saw a 'Spectre' Dragon Ship for the first time. There are only a handful of these monsters in Vietnam. This Hercules gunship makes the fearsome Spooky look feeble in comparison. Spooky, a converted DC-3, carries three mini-guns of 7.62mm calibre and about 7 tons of ammunition — frightening in itself, but Spectre has four mini-guns of 7.62mm plus another four of 20mm calibre, plus a Hercules load-full of 40 tons of ammunition. The volume of fire must be appalling and annihilating. The big aircraft is black. On its nose is a badge of a crescent moon, over which leans a grinning skeleton with a blazing mini-gun cradled in its arms.

Watched many other aircraft at Tan Son Nhut and finally flew back to Nui Dat on the Caribou. Rain fell at Nui Dat today but atmosphere is not highly humid.

Friday 8 November 1968

Very busy day catching up on work accumulated during my absence. Went to 8 Field Ambulance this morning for toe infected by ingrown toenail. Doctor decided to remove half of nail. Was halfway through job when helicopter arrived with a battle casualty — shot through the chest. So, down tools and change jobs, and then back to the toe job about 20 minutes later. No trouble — all in the day's work for him.

Saturday 9 November 1968

Another busy day with interruption for further treatment to toe. In Command Post from 16.00 until after midnight. Quiet shift but felt tired when bedtime came along. Nearly a disaster — an aircraft had engine failure, but finally got back safely to Nui Dat. By the time the aircraft landed, all the people alerted for action were ready to go straight to the forced landing site — RAAF, cavalry, infantry — and then all had to be switched off again. All other incidents were very minor.

Sunday 10 November 1968

One emergency job plus a lot of other tasks to do before leaving tomorrow for Da Lat for NGS conference on Tuesday.

Heard today that last night while I was on duty in the Command Post, a D8 bulldozer (one of the giant land-clearing 'dozers) had gone from the Engineer Squadron to the Tank Squadron and back again. No permission had been asked of the Task Force HQ; for obvious reasons this permission is essential for all vehicle movement at night.

I'm told the driver was Major Moose Kemp, Officer Commanding the Engineers, driving Major Peter Badman, Officer Commanding the Tank Squadron, home after a party. Apparently this was reciprocal hospitality following a party a week ago at the Tank Squadron, after which Moose Kemp was driven home in a Centurion tank.

Weather now fine and stable.

Monday 11 November 1968

Up early and down to helipad by 07.15 to catch helicopter to Long Binh. Helicopter had not turned up by 09.30, so went to Task Force headquarters to find out what had happened. Helicopter had not left Long Binh. Flight now cancelled. Rang HQ USARV at Long Binh to let them know of this upset to plans. Booked on plane due to leave nearby Bien Hoa for Da Lat at 10.30, I was now too late to catch the Da Lat plane.

Then it happened! Phone rang — 'A helicopter is now on Kangaroo pad. It has brought Major Payne (US Army) on a special courier run here and it goes to Long Binh in a few minutes . . .' I leapt for the door, raced to Kangaroo pad, and there, waiting to go, was a Cayuse helicopter — the Flying Tadpole — the helicopter which has fascinated me ever since I first saw one within a few minutes of setting foot in Vietnam more than ten months ago. I have always wanted to travel in one, but since it is a US Army aircraft and used only for special missions, I have never remotely looked like flying in one. This helicopter was indeed going to Long Binh and it had space for one extra passenger, so I climbed aboard the tiny four-seater and away we went.

There is little space in the Cayuse, so, without doors, I was actually seated at the very edge of the aircraft and overhanging the ground. It was very windy. Also, this very small helicopter is less stable in flight than others I've flown in, and it bounces and whips about much more during minor air turbulence. All this makes the passenger really aware that he is flying. This was the most pronounced impression I've had since the time in 1963 when I participated in a demonstration of the load-carrying capacity of the (then new) Bell 47G3 helicopter and travelled about 1500 feet aloft sitting on the external litter of a civilian 47G3 above Canberra.

The view from the Cayuse was excellent and this, together with its rapid speed of over 120 knots, provided a very interesting effect. Flying roughly at the same level as thin clouds, the clouds seemed further away than they actually were and appeared to be racing back across the landscape in spectacular and rather eerie fashion. Altogether it was an utterly fascinating and thrilling ride.

Flew to Long Binh and landed on the VIP pad at HQ USARV. Went by vehicle to Bien Hoa airfield, a few kilometres away, and arrived just in time to catch the aircraft to Da Lat. Had barely recovered from the thrill of the Cayuse ride when I saw the next plane I was to travel in — and fell in love with it — the first fixed-wing aircraft that has really appealed to me. It was a Beechcraft 'Executive' (U21) twin turbo-prop seven-seater — small, sleek and elegant both inside and out. Normally used by generals and other VIPs, this aircraft has miraculously been made available for Major Ed Wintz, Lieutenants David Sneesby and Charles Thomas, and myself to fly to Da Lat. Wow, what a day! The Beechcraft had rakish lines and engines that sounded quiet but powerful. I realised this as we sprinted down the strip, reaching 100 knots in only a few seconds. Its climbing performance was amazing. It sped upwards at almost 2000 feet per minute. In just over five minutes it had reached 10,000 feet and then levelled out to cruise at 200 knots. As to be expected in an aircraft for use by people to whom time means big money, it was fitted out with a lot in the way of comfort, navigational devices etc (including a radar screen).

The flight to Da Lat in the highlands took only half an hour. There was an anxious moment coming in to land — a helicopter flew into our path on collision course. We held course, helicopter dodged and we missed. Third aerial dodge I've experienced so far in Vietnam. Landed at Da Lat, altitude 5000 feet above sea level, surrounded by hills up to 7000 feet. This first view of Da Lat from the air gave an impression of lovely scenery and this was confirmed from the ground. Da Lat is clean — the first clean place I've seen in Vietnam. The roads wind around hills covered with graceful conifers and elegant homes. In the centre of the town is an artificial lake, about 1 kilometre across, surrounded by grassy parkland, trees and gardens. The homes display both Oriental and French influences. Even the rough cabins of market gardeners are attractive, being built from wood panels or logs rather than rusty sheet metal, like poor homes elsewhere. The people are clean, neat and well groomed. Nowhere was life squalid or crowded. The air was fresh and cool — too cool for me, but comfortable for the others (especially David Sneesby, an Alaskan). Men in the streets were wearing suits with ties — another 'first' for me in Vietnam. Western influence in dress was most pronounced. Girls wore skirts rather than the usual slacks and looked far neater than their counterparts elsewhere in Vietnam. Both sexes were mostly dressed in attractive jumpers — clean and in good condition. Flowers were everywhere — frangipani, poinsettia, flowering vines etc. It seems that Da Lat is to Vietnam what Switzerland is to Europe.

I travelled straight to my hotel beside the spacious and attractive marketplace — and saw the first clean market I've seen in Vietnam. Instead of the usual rotting fish, meat and excrement, this market smelt of fresh strawberries and flowers. Dumped bags in the Modern Hotel and went out for a walk with the others through town.

Noticed many signs in French — more so than elsewhere in Vietnam. Had late lunch (or early dinner) in a pleasant restaurant. David Sneesby and I walked around further, while Ed Wintz and Charles Thomas went to an American camp to change money. Amazed at some items in some shops — Suchard and Lindt chocolates, for example, but at exorbitant prices (five times the Swiss price and twice the Australian price for the same item). Plenty of expensive watches at expensive prices — I wonder who buys them?

Visited a Chinese pharmacy. Behind the counter, on back wall, were 120 unlabelled wooden drawers. The pharmacist, wearing white coat, checked the items listed on the prescription in Chinese characters, turned to the wall of drawers, extracted a quantity of herb, bark, seeds, dried berries or other dried animal or vegetable matter, weighed it out carefully, and added it to the growing pile on a large square of paper before him. Sometimes he threw an item, after weighing, into a brass mortar and ground it with a brass pestle. The grinding seemed to be more ritualistic than practical, ending each time with a couple of blows against the side of the mortar — thump, thump, thump, thump, ding-ding. Finally the square of paper was folded up and the parcel changed hands — presumably to go home to be converted to soup. The pharmacist made a careful check of the prescription before wrapping the parcel. How he knew what was in which of the 120 unlabelled drawers, I don't know, though I did wonder whether it really mattered, anyway.

After further window shopping, David and I had a very nice Chinese dinner. At last I'm getting the hang of using chopsticks — it's like learning to write all over again.

Went to the local cinema after dinner to see *Sexy Follie*. We didn't know in what language the soundtrack would be, but the subject was such that we didn't think this would matter. Cost was only $0.60 for the best seats. Saw previews of two coming films, *Seven Colts of Thunder* and *El Chuncho*, both of which dripped

guns and violence in heavy doses.
Both had French soundtracks. Saw
a Vietnamese newsreel, very similar
in style and content to newsreels
anywhere else. The main film had an

American soundtrack plus Chinese, Vietnamese and French
subtitles, and it was an Italian film. As expected, the soundtrack
was superfluous. After the show, the shops were all closing and
one's sense of security began rapidly to disappear, as shutters came
down, folding gates went across, barricades went up, and curfew
(20.00) approached. One then begins to notice that even Da Lat is
full of sandbagged bunkers and barbed wire — just like the rest of
Vietnam. Even the cinema had bunkers on its roof. The only
difference noticeable between the barbed wire in Da Lat and Saigon
is that flowering vines grow in the wire at Da Lat.

Returned to hotel — much noise from roof so went up to
investigate. On roof was a bar full of girls and carousing soldiers,
including two appallingly disreputable Australians who claimed to
be warrant-officer advisers from Pleiku down here for six days'
drinking and wenching before returning to the war to rest. The
captain's stars on my shoulder attracted much
attention, as well as very high prices from the girls —
who were not at all attractive themselves,
unlike the many we'd seen in the
streets in Da Lat during
the day. Girls were
asking $50 to spend
the night with them.
On rejection, they did
not lower their prices,
thus indicating that
they could probably

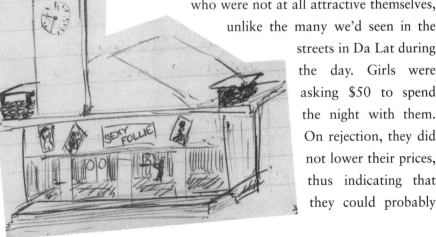

get the same amount elsewhere without trouble. Apparently they did so — within half an hour, most of the girls had gone off to rooms with the American and Australian soldiers.

Not all, though. On returning to my room I found a girl waiting for me. She wanted $25, but left when it was apparent she wasn't getting it. Same also happened to Ed, David and Charles; in fact, Charles scored three girls and Ed two. Locked door from inside, barred window and slept (as in Saigon and Da Nang last week) with fully loaded rifle right by me. Slept lightly, being woken many times by high-heeled shoes tripping through corridors and in and out of rooms. Was also woken by rhythmic creaking of bed in room above me at 23.00, 01.00 and 06.00.

Tuesday 12 November 1968

Went to American Army camp for quick breakfast of bananas and coffee, and then to the NGS building. Very interesting drive past many really attractive homes amidst scenic settings. Despite the beauty of these, the tranquil atmosphere was spoiled by the appearance of bunkers, barbed wire and floodlights. The NGS building is huge — a giant barn from the outside and a high-ceilinged monastery from the inside. It looked at least one or two centuries old, but was built in 1941. The meeting was smoothly conducted, and the NGS people spoke unexpectedly good English. The chief, Lieutenant Colonel Khai, spoke fluent English but with a French accent, not Vietnamese. After the meeting we all had a look over NGS and it was fascinating. It reminded me a lot of the Institut Géographique Militaire in Brussels — monastery setting and mixed civil–military personnel. I watched a Wild A8 stereoplotter operated by a white-coated Vietnamese. Working on the plotting table attached to the A8 was a girl in a flowing ao dai (Vietnamese women's dress). They had three stereoplotters there — two Wild A8s (Swiss) and a Poivilliers D4 (French). I soon discovered that many of the NGS people had spent two

years at the training school of the Institut Géographique National in Paris, and all spoke fluent French but with an Oriental accent. I spent about ten minutes with the photogrammetric section and was reluctant to leave. Not until now had I realised that I miss the photogrammetric work that I once did.

We returned to the main office and had a delicious Vietnamese lunch, then went for a walk to the nearby French school, the Lycée Yersin. The students were a thoroughly presentable-looking lot. The school was an attractive building surrounded by attractive gardens. The girls all wore skirts, this being unusual in Vietnam. The children were mostly aged ten to 16. Some spoke Vietnamese. Others spoke French — French French, not Asian French. Many stately homes were nearby, and we had a lovely view over the golf course on the next hill.

A man came to see us from one of the nearby homes and addressed us in perfect English with a trace of French accent, introducing himself as the dean of the school. We spoke with him for some ten minutes or so. Although his manner was so courteous as to be faintly rude, we learnt some interesting facts. Da Lat is only 44 years old and was founded in 1924–25 by Dr Yersin, a physician, who found that the highland climate of this region was of benefit to sufferers of many ailments. The main street in Da Lat, and also this high school, are named after Dr Yersin. Da Lat is strongly French. The high school is a private school, not a government school, and French is the main language. Vietnamese is a compulsory subject, and there is a choice between English and German.

The curriculum is designed to give a broad education to people who later will require knowledge and understanding beyond the boundaries of Vietnam. But why such French emphasis? Because Vietnamese culture, economy and tradition are basically French, he argued. He also neatly implied that everything worthwhile in the world was French, and that as an academic he had little time for uncouth soldiery (we were armed); but he did this in a very subtle manner and was exceedingly polite, in a chilly sort of way. While I did not share his point of view on all matters, at least I felt I could understand it.

His dismissal of the importance of Chinese influence in Vietnam's own cultural background, going back over a thousand years, was also readily understandable. Having lived in Europe, I'm only too familiar with the cherished and confident French belief in French superiority in everything.

We then went to the airstrip to catch the plane back to Bien Hoa. Had to wait a long time but I had interesting company — an ARVN master sergeant who spoke good English and French and who had a pretty serious interest in the future of his country. After he left, I stripped and cleaned my M16 rifle while waiting for the plane. This attracted an audience of 13 ARVN soldiers, rapt with interest — although they were carrying the same rifles! Was this the first time they'd seen one being cleaned? The condition of their rifles tended to substantiate this. Or was this the first time they'd seen an officer cleaning a weapon? And a three-star officer too! Most probably this was also the case.

The plane came in, smooth and fast, the U21 Beechcraft again. Another thrilling ride in this lovely aircraft. Landed at Long Binh (instead of Bien Hoa) only half an hour later, after a flight of about 200 kilometres. Drove by bus to HQ USARV, and then by truck to 66 Company to spend the night there.

Wednesday 13 November 1968

Quiet day at Long Binh. Visited HQ USARV during morning to clear up one or two matters from yesterday's conference at Da Lat. Spent rest of day on work I'd brought with me from Nui Dat and got a lot done. Atmosphere pretty restful at 66 Company these days — big change since my first visit nine months ago, immediately after the Tet attacks when this Topographic Company got attacked by two Viet Cong battalions and was saved by the helicopter gunships.

Thursday 14 November 1968

Caught helicopter from Long Binh early in morning. Got a bad scare landing at Bearcat on the way. Pilot came in far too fast to land and very nearly crashed. With years of experience (250 to 300 hours) as a passenger in various helicopters, I may not be able to fly one, but I can recognise good and bad flying when I see it. At 100 feet I knew we were coming in too fast. At 50 feet the pilot knew it and threw on full power to break our descent. As I expected, with a full load, we kept falling. Fortunately, although the pilot couldn't stop the aircraft, he kept his head and managed to change our steep descent to a more level flight. We levelled out just above the ground and about 30 metres beyond the helipad.

The pilot had been tossing the aircraft around like a sports car since we left Long Binh, but not until landing at Bearcat

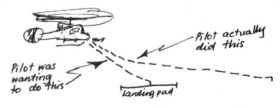

did I suddenly realise we were in trouble. Anyway, we got out of it OK. Took off from Bearcat and travelled many miles just above ground level. Went skipping just over the tree tops of the Binh Son rubber plantation (where Noel Sproles was wounded two months ago), and then finally climbed to 1000 feet (lower than the usual 2000 feet above sea level, which is considered safe from ground fire). The low-level flying was exciting but also frightening. Flying over a homogeneous mass of rubber-tree crowns, the odd tall tree is hard to pick when one is rushing at it at about 150 kilometres per hour, and we flashed past a few trees at our own altitude or higher. Had they been right on our course I think we may have had trouble seeing them early enough to climb over them. Also, with a full load, we had limited power for quick dodging. Don't know why we were doing this. Must have been either for fun or to dodge Thai or Vietnamese artillery. Anyway, again we made it safely and reached Nui Dat without further incident. Our landing at Nui Dat was very slow and cautious. Thus ended a ride packed with more action than usual.[1]

Friday 15 November 1968

Task Force operations during the past fortnight have not been conspicuously successful. 274 Viet Cong Regiment continues to elude the Task Force.

Two Australians were wounded today when a tank hit two mines in quick succession. The first mine was an anti-personnel mine, but the second was much more substantial and damaged the tank, wounding two of the crew. This happened in the Duc Thanh minefield, laid by Vietnamese and American forces. Apparently, we didn't believe they had really put mines in it (although they said they did), but we believe it now. Haven't heard what the two casualties think about it all but I can imagine.

[1] Heard later that the same aircraft *did* crash-land at Long Binh on the return trip 30 minutes later. No one hurt. — JB

Saturday 16 November 1968

On duty in Command Post from 16.00 until 00.30. Very busy session — flat out from 16.00 until 23.00, but then very quiet. An SAS patrol killed four Viet Cong. Four claymore mines were set off simultaneously — three enemy disappeared off the face of the earth, the fourth, with entrails and stomach hanging out, got away (probably to die almost immediately), and the other one escaped.

Sunday 17 November 1968

Sequel to yesterday's SAS ambush — having blown the three Viet Cong to pieces (the official report described them as 'destroyed' instead of the usual 'killed'!), the patrol set about collecting blood samples for medical analysis for malaria investigation by pathologist. Not much existed to provide a sample, but a head was found. While extracting blood from the face, an eyeball rolled and momentarily gave the SAS man a bit of a scare. However, adequate blood was brought back for analysis. The American advisers have not yet made an accusation of murder of innocent civilians as they sometimes do. Innocent woodcutters don't go into forbidden regions bearing arms as these ones did.

Went to 3rd Battalion farewell party today and found it most enjoyable. The invitation, produced by the Survey Troop, folds out to enormous length.

In addition to the 3rd Battalion officers, officers from Vung Tau and all over Nui Dat, were there — even Major General MacDonald from Saigon. Met many old friends there including Major Horrie Howard, commander of B Company, 3rd Battalion. Horrie, an old friend from Chatswood and also from Duntroon, has been awarded the Vietnamese Cross of Gallantry for his efforts in the savage street fighting in Ba Ria during Tet. He may also be awarded the Military Cross, having led his company in three major battles this year.[2]

Being handed round at the party were hundreds of leaflets —

SOLDIERS OF AUSTRALIA!
UNITE AGAINST PMG STRIKES!

PUNCH A POSTIE RTA ON

SOCK IT TO 'EM DIGGERS!

— produced thanks to the recent postal strike which held up mail for Vietnam for a week.[3] The idea came from a Signals unit at Vung Tau. We drew it up and Psychological Operations printed thousands of them. It has proved a huge hit here (and maybe in a different way in the PMG also), and stacks of leaflets have gone back to Australia — on parcels, in letters, with returning soldiers etc. 3rd Battalion returns to Australia next Tuesday, everyone armed with these propaganda leaflets, even the Commanding Officer, Lieutenant Colonel Jim Shelton. The whole affair is a huge joke here, but it wouldn't surprise me if we hear more about it — one mustn't upset civilians.

As an example, all unit newspapers here now must be censored before publication. This was because 1 Field Squadron had published a poem in their newspaper which was sent home by a man whose mother did not like its tone and complained to politicians. The Minister for the Army followed the matter up for her, and now the freedom of the Nui Dat press has been lost. The poem in question was one of a series submitted by the Poet Laureate of the Engineers,

---

[2] Major Horrie Howard was later awarded the Military Cross. — PH

[3] 'RTA' means Return to Australia, perhaps the favourite military abbreviation known to Australian soldiers. — PH

and was considered by the officers of 1 Field Squadron to be very clever. Anyway, measures have now been taken to prevent Australian front-line combat soldiers from being confronted with anything — other than battlefield atrocities, of course — which might offend more sensitive Australians who are not fighting in Vietnam.

Left 3rd Battalion party with some SAS friends and visited the SAS squadron area up on Nui Dat — on the hill itself. Was most impressed. Surrounded by bamboo, bananas and other tropical plants, it is in a pretty setting. As far as operations and administration are concerned, it is the most efficient and best organised unit I've seen in Vietnam. The operations office and signals office are really well run. The whole place looks highly efficient — and the results in the field more than speak for themselves. Spent about half an hour with 2SAS Squadron — a vast improvement on the pirates of 1SAS Company I lived among in Western Australia six or seven years ago — then headed back to the Survey Troop, after a most pleasant four-hour break.

Weather still fine and stable — it seems certain that the dry is really here to stay.

Monday 18 November 1968

Would have been a quiet day but had several visitors and got little done. Late night as a result.

Tuesday 19 November 1968

Another quiet day. Not much new work in these days, so we're getting well ahead on many outstanding tasks.

Wednesday 20 November 1968

Intrigue is afoot. Intelligence sources have discovered that a Viet Cong agent in the nearby hamlet of Ap Suoi Nghe is planning to murder another Ap Suoi Nghe villager, father of the girl murdered a month or two ago by the Viet Cong. The Viet Cong murdered her because she had a boyfriend who was a policeman in Duc Thanh and was suspected of having supplied information leading to the arrest of this VC agent (who was released since nothing could be proved). She was murdered unnecessarily — it was her father who supplied the information, and the VC now know this and intend to kill him also within the next few days. Our forces have no evidence sufficient to justify seizure of the would-be assassin, so it seems that the Province Reconnaissance Unit (PRU), a branch of the ARVN, will take this matter over and quietly revert to its original role for this one occasion.

The PRU was originally formed as a series of government-sponsored killing squads as part of the CIA-sponsored Phoenix Programme. They killed VC and others who were definite and known undesirables against whom nothing could be proved. This elimination system was successful for a while, but then got out of hand, as the victims began to include political opponents and innocent men with desirable wives etc. The PRU then became a normal Army force, the role it occupies now, and its reputation is good. However, little encouragement is needed for the PRU to assist in the occasional abrupt elimination of an enemy who could not be eliminated by other means. So, if all goes according to plan, before the VC agent kills the father of the girl he murdered, he will be killed himself by the PRU from Ba Ria, who no doubt will be dressed and armed as Viet Cong for the occasion.

Meanwhile, a newly arrived rubber plantation owner from France is under suspicion as a VC agent. He runs the Gallia plantation near Ap Suoi Nghe. Authorities are reluctant to touch him because he is

French, not Vietnamese, but many regard his nationality as being totally irrelevant and consider that we should capture and interrogate him. I have been warned to stand by to act as interpreter for the interrogation, in the event of approval being gained to capture him.

Fairly quiet day today. Not much happening with part of the Task Force up near the north-eastern corner of Phuoc Tuy province, hunting the elusive 274 VC Regiment which has obviously dispersed.

In the Task Force HQ Command Post from 16.00 until after midnight. Very quiet session apart from two incidents.

Heard that a forward observation officer from the New Zealand artillery with an armoured force in Duc Thanh lost critical codes and cipher information about four days ago. This serious security breach went four days unreported and this makes things far worse. With this information the enemy can crack our coded messages easily, and we know they are good at this.

It never rains but it pours. The Americans working with the Australian Task Force on the north-eastern border of Phuoc Tuy province had a big helicopter lift yesterday, which involved, amongst other things, 36 Conex metal shipping containers (about 2 metres x 2 metres x 2 metres) being slung under Chinook helicopters, usually one per load. Of these, no less than three were dropped due to ropes of 6000-pound breaking strain being used for 8000-pound loads. Of the three that fell, two have been found. The third is missing in heavy jungle known to be full of Viet Cong, and it contains codes and cryptograph information, plus cipher equipment (message scramblers etc). There is a colossal search on to recover this container, but no luck so far, and judging by the nature of the country it won't be found either.

I was informed that it had fallen at a distance of 3000 metres on an azimuth of 270 degrees from Fire Support Base Tiger, which means that the pilot probably said something like, 'Ah think ah might've drahpped it about three clicks west of Tiger,' being reasonably sure that he wasn't north, east or south of Tiger at the time. Anyway, this loss exceeds the other loss by the New Zealand artillery officer, but at least it was reported immediately. Nevertheless, much concern (euphemism for 'panic') has been caused, and the Americans are still pursuing the frantic, and I fear fruitless, hunt to find it before the enemy does.

An aircraft near Nui Dat received ground fire tonight, apparently from an ARVN camp. This type of thing got out of hand long ago, and has now reached the stage where our pilots expect to receive ground fire whenever aloft. The idiotic people on the ground do this for fun, just to see (they usually use tracer) how close they can get. They have been known to score hits. Particularly at night, our aircraft seem to receive more friendly fire than enemy fire these days — nothing spiteful, just good clean fun. Several times pilots have been sorely tempted to strafe camps that have fired on them for sport, but this hasn't happened yet.

Thursday 21 November 1968

The dry is now well and truly here. Dust is everywhere and the greenness of the countryside is disappearing rapidly, as the grass and leaves die.

Went swimming in the newly opened pool late this afternoon with the Survey Troop. Pool is water-polo pool size and about 1.5 metres deep. It is above ground and made of a plasticised canvas, and is much appreciated by all. We tried to play water polo but it became a sort of keepings-off, quite without rules. A player would leap from the water, take an excellent catch and drop back into the water. Applause? No, just ugly shouts of 'Drown the bastard!' and then the catcher and the ball would disappear under a thrashing mass of about ten men. Or an unmarked player near the edge of the pool would take a pass and, looking round for support, would never know what hit him, as an opponent, running around the poolside, would leap in and tackle him from above.

At one stage I tried to hang onto the ball until a few more team-mates arrived in my vicinity. Took a deep breath and wrapped myself right around the ball. Last thing I heard as I was forced under was 'There's no rank in the pool! Kill 'im!' Every time I felt air on my face I took a fresh breath. I hung on a long time in the fierce scrum but eventually lost it. Surfacing after the ball had finally been ripped off me, I found that the ferocious scrum had dragged me right across the pool. Altogether it was a lot of good fun and good exercise. Being out of condition, half an hour of this furious struggle was quite enough for the first time.

To bed earlier for a change.

Friday 22 November 1968

Today the bombshell burst in Australia. Our 'Punch A Postie' leaflet has made a big impact there, far sooner and much bigger than expected. The Amalgamated Postal Workers' Union is up in arms, and has officially protested to the Department of the Army against this 'despicable', 'contemptible' act 'in the worst possible taste' etc. Questions have been asked of the Minister for the Army in Parliament, and the usual political football is blowing up. The news first came through on Radio Australia this morning, the announcer barely concealing his glee at the Postal Union's discomfort. The news was later broadcast all over Vietnam by the American Forces Network. The American announcer made no attempt to conceal his mirth. The whole Task Force is elated at the outcome of it all, from Commander down to the bottom, and regards the affair a huge and most successful joke.

The Postal Union has made a tactical blunder: by complaining about combat soldiers being upset by mail strikes at home, they have alienated public sympathy still further, and they can ill afford this. The situation at the moment seems to be that the Postal Workers' Union is howling with anger, now that their propaganda has been unexpectedly countered by propaganda operations mounted by another government department, while the Army in Vietnam is laughing fit to kill itself and I am something of a hero — not for the first time this year — due to my efforts to lighten the grim side of the war. Doubtless further events will occur — the union is screaming for revenge — but I seem to be fairly strongly placed in this battle.

Apart from the above hilarity, today was quiet. No doubt about it — with most of the Task Force away from Nui Dat, there's a lot less fresh work for us, and we catch up on outstanding work. Felt a bit stiff in the shoulders today. No wonder, after yesterday's savage wrestling in the pool.

The lost Conex container has not been found, and little hope is now held for it. Pity. The codes in it will be pretty useful to the enemy, even though all forces in the southern half of South Vietnam have already switched codes since Wednesday's double loss.

Saturday 23 November 1968

The Postal Union matter has developed further. The Minister for the Army has requested an investigation, to be conducted by Colonel Bradbury, Chief of Staff at HQ AFV in Saigon. Everyone above the rank of captain now getting frightened. Everyone, from Chief of Staff down, thinks whole affair hilarious, but no one will admit it to anyone senior to himself. Interesting to watch the moral courage ebbing away now that it seems possible that Major General MacDonald will produce a scapegoat to appease the

Minister. Most Task Force HQ officers at my level are disgusted at the lack of moral courage amongst our more senior ranks. So Mike Nelson and I will have to ride this storm out, a possibility not worrying either of us greatly, since neither of us believes that we have done anything terribly wicked. We both decline to implicate others, but the whole affair was done quite openly, and many senior officers approved wholeheartedly at the time.

Captain Mike Nelson, the GSO3 Psychological Operations, is involved in this because the leaflets were printed on the Psy Ops multi-lith printing machine. The Survey Troop screen press was very unsuitable for this small-size and high-volume job, so the Psy Ops machine churned them out by the thousand, just like the Psy Ops leaflets they print in large quantity every other day. Mike is a very junior captain, holding only temporary rank, in fact; and the overall responsibility for the leaflet production is mine, so I'll have to protect him as far as I can. The original idea may not have been mine, but I permitted it to proceed.

Quiet day so got many tasks up to date. Four inches of rain promised tonight but none came.

US Air Force put in an air strike — bombs and all — on C Company, 4th Battalion today, the same company which collected an accidental air strike from the USAF about two months ago. Fortunately, there were no casualties this time, apart from an ankle sprained while leaping for cover. But the Officer Commanding C Company, Major Brian Lindsay, is understandably not in a forgiving mood.

Sunday 24 November 1968

In Task Force HQ Command Post from 16.00 until after midnight. Fairly quiet apart from a major contact with the enemy by 1st Battalion in the north-eastern corner of the province. Two Australians were killed, including the platoon commander. This was not one of our better days.

Monday 25 November 1968

Cloudy all day. A few drops fell at noon but no real rain.

Approval has been refused for the capture and interrogation of the French manager of the Gallia rubber plantation suspected of being a VC agent. Next move would be to thank him in the presence of a known VC agent for information supplied against the VC, and then let the VC handle the 'double-crossing' appropriately. This is being discussed light-heartedly at the moment, but could become more serious if further evidence against him accumulates.

Meanwhile the 'Punch A Postie' matter takes a new turn. Senator Wheeldon (ALP, Western Australia) has asked a question in the Senate concerning the leaflet 'inciting the troops in Vietnam to violence against the poor workers of Australia'. He misquoted from the leaflet so badly that obviously he had never seen it. The Minister for Repatriation (representing the Minister for the Army in the Senate) replied that he knew nothing about it, but that it was nice to see the honourable Senator from Western Australia taking an interest in the troops in Vietnam for the first time. Hullabaloo broke out and the Minister for Repatriation was forced to withdraw his statement and apologise.

At the same time, another newspaper has just arrived in Vietnam, and lo and behold, it has a picture of the offending leaflet, obviously different from the one which Mike Nelson and I are assuming responsibility for. This one, produced in Vung Tau about a week before we produced the more professional-looking job, has obviously caused the trouble which is rebounding on Mike and me. However, it makes little difference, since it could just as easily have been one of ours, and we are not conscious of having committed any great crime. As a matter of fact, morale throughout the Australian Forces in Vietnam has improved as a result. Instead of the usual upset here at mail strikes, everyone's had a good laugh.

This morning I was summoned to the office of the Deputy Assistant Adjutant General on Task Force HQ,

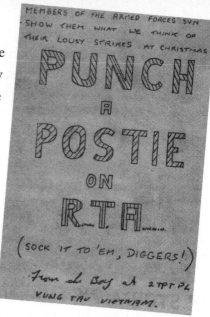

Major Bill Hoffman. Colonel Bradbury is conducting his formal investigation into the 'Punch A Postie' leaflet. Since I'm making no attempt to hide anything, Colonel Bradbury sees no need to travel to Nui Dat and is conducting the investigation by phone from Saigon.

Phone to his ear, with Colonel Bradbury at the far end, Major Hoffman started asking me Colonel Bradbury's questions. Plain sailing for a while, with Major Hoffman relaying my answers into the phone, until the question: 'How many were printed?' A simple question deserves a simple answer, so I answered truthfully: 'Four thousand, one hundred.' Major Hoffman winced, swallowed, recovered himself and said into the mouthpiece: 'Quite a few, sir.' The earpiece crackled sharply. Major Hoffman took on the look of a trapped animal. He gulped, looked desperately around his office, swallowed again, then took a deep breath and said, 'Four thousand, one hundred, sir.' Grimacing, Major Hoffman held the phone handset out at arm's length, while we both listened apprehensively to the angry squawking pouring out of the earpiece. I don't know which of us, Major Hoffman or me, was more relieved when the conversation eventually ended.

Tuesday 26 November 1968

Down to Vung Tau today for three of the five days' R&C leave due to me while in Vietnam. Caught RAAF Caribou from Nui Dat. It was about a quarter of an hour late, but despite this, it lost a further 20 minutes above Vung Tau while the pilot played Red Barons. Above Vung Tau we met another RAAF Caribou which had just taken off. We flew very close, side by side, for quite some time until both crews had taken sufficient photos of each other, and then we started playing Red Barons in earnest. Our plane chased the other as both planes dodged, wheeled, banked crazily, ducking in and out of cloud. Soon, the other plane escaped, did a few swift manoeuvres, and came in on our tail — and our aircraft then nearly turned itself inside out trying to twist away from the other. We swooped and dodged through cloud, and I thought we might well finish up wearing the other plane, but although we had one close squeak as we came out of the cloud, we escaped safely. I felt much happier when the game was over and we dropped below the cloud and landed. The passenger next to me, an Army corporal, said nothing the whole trip apart from an incessant, savage snarl of 'Fuckin' RAAF!' That's just about what all the passengers felt.

Travelled by Kombi to the R&C Centre at Vung Tau, handed gun in for safe keeping, collected room key for Grand Hotel Annexe, which is where the officers stay, and moved into the Grand — room very comfortable — complete with refrigerator (though I've no use for it). Unpacked and had lunch in the restaurant — quality high, quantity low, cost high.

Went out walking during afternoon. Wandered around main centre of Vung Tau. Looked in shops but saw very few possible purchases. Clothing shops had a few warm children's jackets made illegally from American poncho liners, but the prices were high. Bars everywhere and girls everywhere trying to lure customers in.

Went into one bar at request of girl at door. Lost popularity quickly when I: (i) wouldn't buy her a Saigon tea for $1; (ii) wouldn't go upstairs to bed with her for $7; and finally (iii) wouldn't even buy her a drink and go upstairs to bed with her for a total cost of $1. She demanded to know whether I was 'Number Ten Cheap Charlie' or whether I loved men instead of girls. I told her, 'Both!' and headed off. Had a look at five steam bath and massage parlours: four were obviously brothels; the fifth was doubtful — I suspected it was, in fact, true to label, but in Vung Tau one can't be sure. Saw some nice Christmas cards but they cost $0.60 and $0.70 each!

Finally returned to hotel after an afternoon's walk, having taken a few photos and spent nothing. Had dinner at Pacific Hotel, the big American Officers' Club at Vung Tau — quality low, quantity

This one is primarily a brothel and secondarily a steam-bath and massage parlour. The numeral '69' is used in many cases to advertise a brothel.

There are many tailor shops like this one — mostly run, not by Chinese or Vietnamese, but by Indians. Prices are not cheap.

This is not from Vung Tau, but from Ba Ria. However, the quaint wording is to be found everywhere in Vietnam.

high, cost low! Watched Vietnamese rock band playing: three guitarists, two female singers, one organist, one drummer. Noise was tremendous and could be heard more than a block away. The group wasn't bad at all; however, the big attraction was the drummer, who was unbelievably skilful — perhaps one of the very best I've ever seen — sticks twirling between fingers between beats — in fact, every trick in the book, yet never missing a beat and turning on excellent solos from time to time. The most amazing thing was that the drummer was a nine-year-old girl.

Went back to the Grand for the evening. Spent an hour in the bar watching the bar girls flit back and forth. Suddenly I saw one that looked familiar — Susie, the girl behind the bar of the Officers' Club at Long Binh a couple of months ago. She has since left, and everyone has wondered where she'd gone. I spoke with her a while. She remembered me immediately as the Australian who showed the Americans those agility games with empty beer cans. She works at Vung Tau for the sake of the extra money to support her children at Bien Hoa. Living at Vung Tau she now only sees her children about three times a month, so she's looking forward to the day when she's earned enough to retire to a less lucrative but geographically more convenient job. These bar girls work long hours — from 10.00 until about 22.00 or 23.00 in the bar, and often they spend all night in bed with the clients, so mostly they're running short of sleep, but they don't show it. Bar still very lively when I left, about 21.30.

Wednesday 27 November 1968

Had breakfast in the Grand — a French breakfast — well, almost. The menu was French, the waiter was more at home speaking French than English, the coffee was strong, the cup was big, the roll was served in a dainty cane basket; but there the resemblance ended. The coffee had that bitter flavour characteristic of Vietnamese coffee, and the roll was hard and very different from the Parisian croissant. Nevertheless, it was most enjoyable and a big improvement on Nui Dat.

Today there is warning of a great typhoon about to hit Vung Tau. It should arrive at 15.00, and the worst should hit at 01.00 tomorrow morning. Tremendous winds and four inches of rain are expected. Sky is cloudy, but the local people, with an eye to the sky, say that there is nothing wrong with the weather. They may be right. Some light rain fell during the evening — no wind, no heavy rain.

Spent afternoon preparing messages on tape recorder, a task outstanding for many months. Got a few Christmas cards written also.

Went for another walk before dinner. Hauled three Australian soldiers out of an out-of-bounds area before they got grabbed by the MPs. The average soldier just hasn't a clue what is in or out of bounds, and it's not usually his fault that he doesn't know, but this doesn't help him when he gets caught.

Vung Tau must have nearly 100 bars, each one with a fleet of girls. That adds up to a very large number of girls, all fiercely competing for cash from servicemen. Of course, most have come to Vung Tau from other places, attracted by the money. Even small boys aged five to ten solicit in the street: 'Hey sir! You want girl? I find you Number One girl for short time!'

Had dinner at the Pacific Club and then returned to the Grand. Spent about an hour in the bar there. A young New Zealand lieutenant, an infantry platoon commander, has fallen in love with a bar girl in the Grand, and tonight's his last night before returning to Nui Dat. He's a very nice fellow, and she is certainly the nicest girl there — her name is Tuyet (or, in English, Snow) and I've known of her since I first came to Vietnam, though I've only met her once before. She is very well known for being the only girl with any manners, charm and the ability to conduct a serious conversation in

English or French. Granted she is a cut above the normal bar girl, but the fact remains that she is still a bar girl. Like Susie, Tuyet has a baby in Bien Hoa to support, and comes from a very different environment from that of most foreign servicemen. Maybe this smitten lieutenant will wake up to the facts of the situation — maybe not — before it's too late. For some people, especially the younger ones, the Susie Wong legend dies hard.

Left bar about 20.00 — apart from the novelty wearing off fast, the smoke-saturated atmosphere is very hard on the eyes.

Thursday 28 November 1968

More rain and light wind but absolutely no sign of a storm, let alone a typhoon. The typhoon must have been successful enemy propaganda to keep our air movement restricted.

Had another French breakfast and enjoyed it again. Spent morning writing letters and Christmas cards. Had lunch at Pacific again — but this time a magnificent feast, and at the usual price of $0.50, too. Thanksgiving Day today. The occasion has little significance for me, but I've no objection to getting a superb feast as a consequence.

Friday 29 November 1968

Beautiful, fine weather — back to the normal weather of the dry again. So much for the typhoon! So the weather eyes of the local people prophesied much more accurately than the sophisticated meteorological know-how of the USAF — which is what I and many others had suspected all along.

Had another French breakfast. While in dining room I noticed a group of ten Australians — sleepless, untidy and partly drunk, with beer cans everywhere — having obviously been drinking from the crack of dawn, following on from heavy activity the previous night. At this rate they should be in a good old mess by lunch time — if the money lasts, which it probably will. Listening to the raucous obscenity which was drowning all other sounds in the dining room, I told them to keep the noise clean, or if they preferred to keep things rough then to keep quieter . . . they obeyed willingly enough, but I had the feeling that they'd heard this advice many times before and that they'd keep the noise under control for about five minutes before breaking out again. Oddly enough, this behaviour seems to be a peculiarly Australian characteristic. During my ten months in Vietnam I have not noticed any tendency by Americans or Koreans to create the obscene din that Australians so frequently make. As a group, the drunken Australian must be pretty much disliked by the Vietnamese, who regard it as bad manners to talk loudly.

Spent morning on further letters and Christmas cards. Packed at lunch time and got changed back into uniform and headed off to catch the plane back to Nui Dat. Flight back was thankfully uneventful.

Life has been busy in the Survey Troop during my absence — many jobs of considerable operational urgency.

Meanwhile, the matter of 'Punch A Postie' has soared to new heights. Copies of leaflets have been reproduced in most Australian papers. Three major cartoonists, including the one and only Paul Rigby, have featured the matter. Rigby's cartoon displays no love at all for the Postal Workers' Union. All this publicity has triggered off still more leaflets here in Vietnam bearing all sorts of messages, ranging from the satirical 'Pacify A Postie — Come to Holsworthy for the Love-In', to a particularly savage one, reputed to have originated from within HQ AFV itself, in Saigon. There are now so many around, that, especially in view of the HQ AFV product, action against Mike and myself becomes even less likely — except,

"... and that's ANOTHER reason for abolishing the whistle ...!"

"Oh, thank you! For one mad moment I didn't think we'd be sending a card this year!"

of course, for the fact that ours was the only one with real professional presentation and which had an official air about it.

Sky completely clear — it is now suspected that the typhoon was invented by the USAF to get a day off.

Saturday 30 November 1968

Very quiet for the first half of the day, then much frantic effort due to a major change in operational plans, resulting in much fresh drawing and printing work for us, which kept us going till very late at night.

DECEMBER

AUSTRALIAN MILITARY FORCES

AAB — 71A

Reprinted Dec, 1964

RECORD BOOK

CONTAINING 96 PAGES

RULED FEINT

Christmas in Vietnam had its problems. 'Peace on Earth and goodwill to all men' does not blend well with war. Christmas demands social activity and spreading of Christmas cheer, and both of these activities require transport which is needed for operational use. At Nui Dat distractions from warlike operations were always welcome but not when they hampered operational effectiveness, as was apt to happen at Christmas.

Christmas truces had been seen before — though only when welcomed by both sides — 25 December 1914 being an outstanding example. In Vietnam only one side observed the 'truce' — to the inevitable advantage of the enemy, who knew exactly when this literally heaven-sent opportunity was coming and determined not to waste it.

PAUL HAM

★

*Christmas preparations are now inescapably
mounting, much to the annoyance of everyone,
except perhaps the chaplains. The Australian
Government is determined that we shall enjoy
ourselves whether we want to or not.*

★

Sunday 1 December 1968

Went to Vung Tau with our weekly beach party, my first beach visit
since April. Called in at the Education Centre at 1ALSG to collect
flash gun (Toshiba electronic Strobe-lite) plus 58mm ultraviolet
filter and lens hood bought for me last week in Hong Kong by
Lieutenant Graham Pratt for my Yashica camera. Cost for the
whole lot was only $16. Visited 1 Australian Field Hospital and my
several friends there, including Bruce Daniel and John Lambie.
Went into Vung Tau, had Chinese meal (quality low, cost high), and
did some shopping, then back to 1ALSG to join our beach party.

Returned to Nui Dat in convoy full of the usual drunks,
including several drivers. This is as big a problem as ever. I have
laid charges against one driver who overtook other vehicles in the
convoy after having been ordered not to do so, forcing two
oncoming Vietnamese civilians off the road in the process. A far
stronger hand needs to be taken with vehicle commanders (mostly
sergeants), who drink themselves and exert no control over their
drivers and passengers.

Spent evening in our canteen, where we had a slide show with
Dallas Leary's new projector.

Monday 2 December 1968

A depressing thing happened today. A month ago I wrote to the School of Survey with a query concerning the allowances paid to Sapper Mick Sokil while he was at the School. Today the reply came, containing remarks I know not to be true, yet I have no choice but to accept the School's word. Then, in the last paragraph, comes a savage personal attack on myself, signed by R. Wilson Captain, for H.M. Hall, Lieutenant Colonel. This makes it plain that: (i) my letter has been interpreted as a slight against Robin Wilson; and (ii) personal animosity towards me has blinded them to any rights or wrongs in Mick Sokil's case. It is most upsetting to encounter such an attitude. This is the only time during 1968 we have asked the School for any assistance, and it comes only one month after we had gone to considerable trouble to supply a lot of material to assist the School prepare for a training course. Drafted a strong letter to Lieutenant Colonel Hall but decided not to send it since:

1. It would stir up feeling, already hostile, which could rebound against junior members of the Survey Troop doing courses in the future at the School (sadly, that sort of thing has happened before).

2. It's probably better to treat the matter with the contempt it deserves rather than let it be known that a deliberate attempt to hurt me had succeeded. I should be able to take this sort of thing in my stride.

3. I must stick to my aim, which is to do what is best for the Survey Troop soldiers in the long run. Personal feelings must not intrude on this.

But none of this helps Mick Sokil, whom I fear has become a casualty of petty spite. The School has refused to investigate his allowances further and I can do nothing more from this distance to help Mick. Worse still, the correspondence was seen by the troop clerk, Oreste Biziak, when he opened it. Oreste was visibly concerned at the tone of the letter and was embarrassed when he passed it to me. Mick Sokil also knows what has happened. Inevitably the word will get around and this will not be good for morale. Altogether a most unfortunate event.

Tuesday 3 December 1968

Up at midnight and into the Command Post until 08.00. The eight-hour shift was very quiet. To bed by 09.30 and got two to three hours' sleep. Busy afternoon with much work to do.

Wednesday 4 — Thursday 5 December 1968

Two quiet days. Wrote operational report for November, the earliest I've got the monthly report completed for some months now. Mario Apfelbaum returned from Hong Kong with a lot of loot, but a lot less than he had intended to buy.

Friday 6 December 1968

Much enemy activity last night, including the murder of the hamlet chief of Ap Suoi Nghe, the third chief of that hamlet to be murdered this year by the Viet Cong. The artillery from Nui Dat was particularly active, mostly firing at targets near Dat Do, where a fight raged for some hours — with very few casualties.

The 'Punch A Postie' episode seems to be dying down now, though not without occasional mutterings. Have heard nothing further said here in Vietnam, but we still see the odd newspaper comment in Australia. Read a letter today accusing the Army of misrepresenting facts by attempting to imply to the public that mail services to Vietnam were being curtailed, whereas (according to the good union official) no such delay had ever occurred. The truth is that a mail delay in Vietnam equal in length to the strike in Australia did occur. So far, three men in Australia have publicly made fools of themselves over this trivial affair — two union men and one politician (Wheeldon).

On duty in Command Post from 16.00 until 00.30. Pretty tired when I knocked off after midnight.

Saturday 7 December 1968

Perhaps our quietest day ever for the Survey Troop. Not so quiet on the operational side, however; and Noel Sproles found himself commanding the Task Force for a couple of hours. A battle flared up somewhere between Dat Do and Lang Phuoc Hai, involving the ARVN and Viet Cong, and the Australian Task Force was asked for help. The Commander was at a fire support base halfway to Bearcat, the Deputy Commander was at Ba Ria, the GSO2 Operations was away with the Commander, and everyone else in the HQ of sufficient seniority to do the job was either away or not sufficiently in touch with current operations to take over quickly, so Noel as duty officer in the Command Post took over operational command and organised the Task Force's rush to aid the ARVN.

All went well except for an RAAF effort that earned much contempt. Helping us was an American light fire team of two Huey gunships. Enemy fire shot a side-gunner in one of the gunships, which flew immediately to Nui Dat,

Victim's eye view of a Huey Cobra.

dropped off the wounded gunner at 8 Field Ambulance, and asked for another gunner for their side-mounted M60 machine gun. The RAAF had several Hueys at Nui Dat with crews (including side-gunners) idle, so RAAF was asked for a side-gunner. The flight lieutenant on air liaison duty at Task Force HQ muttered that he'd have to ask the Group Captain at Vung Tau and did so by phone. The Group Captain said no. On being told that this was to give urgently needed support to troops in enemy contact and fighting for their lives, he replied that he wasn't prepared to let RAAF people travel in US Army aircraft since he didn't consider their aircraft servicing to be good enough. So Noel asked 4th Battalion instead for a volunteer machine-gunner to go with the gunship. Several machine-gunners were trampled to death in the rush! And so the American gunship, with an Australian infantry side-gunner having the thrill of his life, returned to the battle. Meanwhile, the story of the RAAF's refusal to help has spread rapidly and the RAAF has sunk lower than ever in most people's estimation.

On the lighter side, the US Army has grounded a Cayuse pilot who tore the skids off his aircraft on the roof of a truck in a convoy. The best excuse the pilot could produce was that the truck had been behaving provocatively, but although he scored high marks for originality, his case was somewhat unconvincing.

Sunday 8 December 1968

Up early and down to Vung Tau as convoy commander for beach party from Task Force. Much trouble has been occurring on beach parties, with drunken soldiers behaving in appalling fashion on the return trip, including drunken drivers forcing civilian vehicles off the road and hurling beer cans at civilians with shouts of 'fuckin' noggie bastards!' etc. Had a quick talk with whole convoy before we started and gave everyone fair warning. Easy trip down.

Spent day at 1 Australian Field Hospital with Bruce Daniel and John Lambie in relaxing surroundings and then returned with convoy. Behaviour perfect — no problems at all, despite very large convoy. Suspect that previous problems have been due to inexperienced officers, mostly second lieutenants (it's unusual for a captain to command such a convoy) being reluctant or hesitant to take a firm hand in the face of trouble. I am confident in handling situations involving aggressive drunks, but it has taken many years to develop this confidence, and many newly commissioned officers just don't have the experience to cope with such a situation. Apparently today's convoy was only the second sedate convoy in recent months.

Task Force HQ officers have told me that there are only two officers who lead trouble-free beach parties — Major Alec Weaver and me. My approach is simple. I prefer to stop men getting drunk in the first place. That's a lot easier than dealing with them after they're drunk. Before we start from Nui Dat, I call for the senior NCO from every vehicle in the convoy to report to me for a roadside briefing. If there's no senior person in a vehicle, then I ask them to elect one on the spot. Having assembled my vehicle leaders, I note their names and then tell them that I hold each of them personally responsible for the conduct of all men in their vehicle and, at the end of the day, no one will be allowed to travel back in the convoy to Nui Dat unless he is in a condition to be an effective part of a fighting team if we should have the misfortune to get ambushed on our return trip. I will inspect before we leave Vung Tau, and anyone I have doubts about will be left behind and can explain to his CO the next day why he failed to return with the beach party. Of course, there are always a few who overindulge at Vung Tau, but they're not in a bad way and are looked after well by their mates. So, no problems.

I don't know what the secret of Alec Weaver's success is. I think I prefer not to know!

Monday 9 December 1968

Day started with one problem and one potential problem. The first is a probable load of VD. As for the potential problem, it is similar but comes from a very recent contact. I tried to assess the likelihood of VD having been contracted and this conversation occurred:

'But she was clean, sir.'

'They're all clean.'

'But this girl really looked clean.'

'They all look really clean.'

'But she's only new to the game, sir, she's only just started.'

'Yes, they're all new.'

'No — this girl really is new. She's not from Vung Tau. She's only just arrived in Vung Tau.'

'They've all just arrived. Where was she from — Bien Hoa or Saigon? That's where they usually come from.'

'No, nothing like that, sir. She was from Cam Ranh Bay.'

CAM RANH BAY!!!! Ye gods!!! How blissfully ignorant can one be!! 'Well, you'd better keep a close watch out for symptoms and if there's any doubt, see the doctor immediately.'

Cam Ranh Bay, the site of a big US base, is reputedly on a par with Vung Tau for the most widespread and hardest-to-cure strains of VD in Asia. On this cheerful note, I got packed and headed off to catch the Long Binh helicopter.

Helicopter went by a most devious route to avoid artillery fire, and this made the trip very interesting. Added interest was provided by the fact that the aircraft was very heavily loaded. The pilot lifted off, and hovered gently up and down a few times quite close to the ground, testing controls and checking instruments, apparently concerned about the manifold pressure. Just as I thought he was about to touch down and order some of the load off, he tilted the nose slightly forward and we went ahead at snail's pace, and then very slowly increased speed. We used up about 200 metres of airstrip before we had gained sufficient airspeed to start climbing. This was a gunship take-off. The gunships with all their ammunition are too heavy to lift straight off or to hover (except close to the ground when cushioned by their own down-draft), and need a lot of airstrip to get up sufficient speed to climb. On really hot days, when the air is not very dense, gunships can be seen running along Kangaroo pad (about 500 metres long), their skids occasionally bouncing on the ground as they try to lift off, and they use up most of the strip this way. Once aloft they can manoeuvre, but have little reserve power.

We flew north towards Blackhorse, then west to Phu My on Route 15, and then north again to Bearcat, then west across the river, then north, then east back across the river to Long Binh — a fascinating flight.

Went by truck to 66 Company and met the new Commanding Officer, Captain Bill Harkins, vastly different from Joel Cain. Bill is a real survey commander and obviously is very interested in his work and is tightening up a lot of things. Joel Cain was a big improvement on his predecessor (who, I'm told, was sacked), and now things at 66 Company are looking up further.

Spent afternoon chasing up many minor errands, which have mounted up since my last visit. Atmosphere during the evening not as relaxed as usual, due to a VC rocket and mortar attack on the adjacent unit last night only a few hundred metres away. Two men died — one from mortar shrapnel, and the other from fright, most unusual to hear of heart failure in a young soldier, but it happened.

Tuesday 10 December 1968

At midnight came another attack. It went on spasmodically until 01.00. The explosions were very heavy and rocked the building I was in. Much noise from the American answering fire could be heard, but there was no doubt which bangs were going out and which were coming in. One heard the outgoing explosions. The incoming ones were felt as well. Although the blasts shook us up a bit, the fight didn't involve 66 Company, and things soon settled down, enabling us to get a decent sleep.

West to HQ USARV for monthly conference, which was handled quickly and efficiently, and in afternoon I got work done that I'd brought from Nui Dat.

Very nice evening in Officers' Club at 66 Company — they really are a good crowd. A most energetic and enjoyable game of volleyball afterwards — first game for a long time. Court is lit, so we played late. Many aircraft came in to land nearby at and after sunset. The slim Huey Cobras looked like sleek sharks silhouetted against the evening sky above us as they came in low overhead. Quite apart from their fearful weaponry, the Huey Cobra must look frightening to the enemy. It really looks the killer that it is.

Wednesday 11 December 1968

Returned to Nui Dat immediately after breakfast. The Survey Platoon from 66 Company is putting a survey party on Nui Thi Vai, a mountain just west of Nui Dat, but some uncertainty exists as to whether a helicopter can be landed on the peak. So, to save a special reconnaissance mission being flown, I persuaded the pilot of the II Field Force courier aircraft, a Huey, to do it on our way from Long Binh to Nui Dat. I sat in the outside seat of the aircraft to ensure a good view when we came to Nui Thi Vai — and then discovered that the safety belt for that seat was missing. So with no side to the aircraft, and sitting right at the edge I took a firm grip on the seat with hands between knees. Landed at Bearcat. On taking off we flew low over the rubber plantation to avoid artillery or other aircraft, but unlike last month, we flew at a more reasonable altitude this time, namely about 100 to 200 feet above the ground, instead of at tree-top level. We climbed for a while, and then landed at Fire Support Base Julia, where the forward HQ of the Australian Task Force is at the moment. We then flew direct to Nui Thi Vai, throttled back, and slowly, almost hovering, chugged over and around the peak, the aircraft being between 5 and 20 metres from the ground most of the time. This gave us an excellent view of the top of Nui Thi Vai. The pilot and I had a very good look all over it and could pick out two possible landing zones, one right on the summit, and the other about 200 metres down a spur from the summit. As we slowly cruised around Nui Thi Vai, known to be Viet Cong territory, it occurred to me that no VC with a weapon handy could possibly pass up such a magnificent opportunity to destroy a helicopter. At that range one could hardly miss an aircraft so low and so slow — and with no other aircraft in sight to hit back. I was a bit apprehensive, since, with the aircraft tilted over to give the pilot and me the best possible view, I hadn't much chance of staying aboard without a safety belt if ground fire did come at us and happened to hit me. Anyway, although we took about five minutes and did five or six circuits of the summit and a few passes over it, not a shot was fired.

The side-gunner next to me was pretty tense and had his machine gun cocked and at the ready all the time. The pilot was obviously enjoying the welcome break from his normal routine flying. The other passengers looked puzzled, not realising what was going on.[1] I was doubly pleased that no shots came — the target had been so tempting that the absence of enemy fire was a very

[1] I heard a week later that a fellow passenger had in fact complained about the courier run being used as a recce flight. — JB

good indication of the absence of Viet Cong from the summit, which is heartening for the survey party going there.

As we left the summit, the pilot put the helicopter into a dive down the steep eastern slope of Nui Thi Vai. The Huey hit 110 knots before it made so much noise that the pilot eased up and levelled out. The Huey normally cruises at 80 knots and this was the first time I've known one to exceed 100 knots. We then headed east and landed at Nui Dat without further incident, having had a ride that was both unusual and interesting.

Returned to the Survey Troop to catch up on backlog of work. During the day, Task Force HQ told me I was now a major and had been so for a couple of days, with seniority backdated to last June. Rumours of this have been floating around for months — inevitably, having been the senior captain in the Task Force ever since I arrived in Vietnam. Speculation about someone in this position is only natural and there had obviously been plenty. Have ignored it all up till now. Twice during the last few days, however, rumours more authentic than usual have come through — so convincing, in fact, that I went to the trouble of checking them officially — and was told officially that I wasn't promoted.

As an example, the Survey Troop at Nui Dat was phoned two days ago by HQ AFV to say I was promoted, and the Survey Troop phoned this information to me at Long Binh. I phoned HQ AFV from Long Binh to check this and to get details as to date etc but was told that nothing was official, so I carried on as normal. Then, within the next day or so, up again to major, down again to captain, and up again to major — all by word of mouth alone. On the final occasion, I felt that the situation had become ridiculous. So I stated that I was continuing as captain until I had seen it in writing. Finally, I got a direct order from Task Force HQ to go and get major's badges and wear them, since I'd been a major for two days already but apparently much administrative fumbling had occurred, and I should have been told a week ago that promotion was coming. Went to get badges from the quartermaster store, only to find that there are no major's badges in the Task Force! Major John Taylor, Officer Commanding HQ Company, finally fixed me up with his spare set.

Set off to hunt and eat any majors with temporary rank, or any with substantive rank later than last June, all of whom have suddenly become junior to me. Found plenty, but they're all people to whom I've been giving a hard time for months, and if anyone has old scores to settle it's them not me, so I let them alone. All of a sudden I've become about five years senior to people like the Legal officer, and this takes all the fun out of baiting them. Now that I'm senior to them all, it seems unsporting.

Initial problem: it's hard suddenly to start calling all majors by their first names after never having done so before. Problem easily solved — call them all Fred, the standard Australian name in Vietnam.

Wonder what the Postal Workers' Union bosses would say if they were to hear of the promotion of the arch-villain of the 'Punch A Postie' episode to major within a week or so of the big stir? Given a free hand, I could well crack lieutenant general in a month or so at this rate. On the other hand, maybe best not to push my luck too far.

Second problem: whether or not to turn on the expected party in the Officers' Mess to celebrate promotion. I feel that promotion at this late stage after seven years as captain is little cause for celebration at all — however, matter quickly taken out of my hands. Rush job hit us at dinner time which would obviously keep the Survey Troop going till early in morning, so, most conveniently, back to work again. Late night, as expected, but job completed and ready for collection at dawn.

Thursday 12 December 1968

Busy day today co-ordinating activities of the American survey party from Long Binh (which includes Colin Laybutt, one of our surveyors who is working with 66 Company at present), the infantry platoon from 4th Battalion, which is securing Nui Thi Vai for them, and 66 Company itself, which is directing about five survey parties altogether. The infantry and the survey party had to climb Nui Thi Vai by foot (500 metres high) — a fearful task, thanks to very steep terrain, dense vegetation and heat — but completed their mission. About 400 pounds of gear for the survey party goes in tomorrow morning by helicopter, now that a landing pad is clear and secure.

Meanwhile, we start playing Tonight's The Night again — first time since August. Enemy uprising throughout all of Vietnam is expected tonight — same as during Tet. The Task Force is among the expected targets and never has it had less defence. All the battalions are out on operations — all that remains at Nui Dat is one company (which is standing by, ready to leap into Ba Ria in event of attack there), plus the normal supporting troops in the Task Force.

So we prepare for a lively night, mortar and rocket attacks on us being probable, and minor ground assaults to probe for defence weaknesses being possible. Out come the steel helmets, including one with psychedelic flowers and the slogan 'MAKE LOVE NOT WAR' painted all over it. Ammunition etc, all checked, ready for action.

Then at dinner time the anticlimax. In walks the ARVN liaison officer to the Task Force. He has a long-standing reputation for being where the action isn't. He is renowned for leaving Nui Dat whenever action is even a remote possibility. Now, after a week's absence, he has returned to Nui Dat on tonight of all nights. Obviously Nui Dat is considered safer than anywhere else. Meanwhile, many ARVN interpreters arrive in the Sergeants' Mess. They also are usually conspicuous by their absence at any hint of trouble. Deduction: Ba Ria, not Nui Dat, will be hit tonight. We shall see.

Friday 13 December 1968

Our ARVN liaison officer was right. Nothing at all happened. The survey party moved to Nui Thi Vai by helicopter and the rest of the day was also quiet.

The Task Force HQ had expected that my promotion to major automatically meant that I was no longer available for operations duty in the Command Post. I took the view that since I was still in a captain's posting as Officer Commanding the Survey Troop, and since the Task Force HQ was so short of captains, especially experienced ones, it didn't seem fair to leave the Command Post in the lurch. As I saw it, nothing had changed except the rank I wore so I volunteered to continue, regardless of rank. My offer was accepted with alacrity and gratitude.

On duty in Command Post from 16.00 until midnight. Tonight, things did happen. During the afternoon many suspicious activities had occurred close to the Task Force perimeter; for example, men making measurements on the ground while pretending to herd cattle. During the evening there were people all around the perimeter in small groups, never presenting a worthwhile or stationary target at any one place.

Some mortars were fired from our east, landing to the north of us, so we immediately tracked the mortar bombs with radar, fired artillery at the mortar position, and tracked our own shells going into the same spot. The mortars stopped firing immediately. This was the only major incident amongst many minor ones, activity and movement being constant throughout the evening. At midnight I handed over to the next Command Post officer, but so many minor things were happening, it was his first spell ever, and he was very uncertain and nervous, so I stayed for a while.

For about half an hour or so there had been movement within 100 metres of our perimeter under close observation by the nearby New Zealand artillery. Finally, noting that it was not moving away and that it was in the spot where: (i) we had seen people making measurements during the day; and (ii) we happened to have a defensive fire task (i.e. a target already selected and noted) registered for our mortars, ready to fire any time; I decided to hit it. 4th Battalion's mortars were to fire; NZ artillery to observe and correct the fire. The Artillery Command Post beside me leapt into action and began calling phone orders to all concerned, including a patrol. With ground and air clearance gained and everyone close to the target warned and underground, firing began at 02.00. Our accuracy was perfect. The target was covered with 32 bombs. The noise was quite impressive, since the bombs were falling only 500 metres away from our Command Post. The enemy lights disappeared immediately the first bombs landed. One bomb produced a double explosion, so apparently we did hit something worthwhile.

Not possible at this time of night to deduce the effectiveness of our mortar fire, but if, as suspected, the enemy was setting up a mortar or rocket base, he will have been severely discouraged. Meanwhile, the phones rang with countless inquiries, from the Task Force Deputy Commander downwards, wondering what on earth was happening. Reason for the consternation was that our mortar base was more than 1000 metres from the Task Force HQ and the bombs were falling barely 500 metres from the HQ — with the result that most people presumed that we were under enemy attack. Having woken most of the Task Force, I managed to soothe everyone and things slowly became quiet again. Finally to bed at 03.00.

Saturday 14 December 1968

Another quiet day. Just as well, really, because I felt tired after having had very little sleep last night. Found myself not terribly popular for having woken up and scared so many people last night by triggering a mortar attack on the enemy. Beneath the grumbles were obvious overtones of jealousy because I'd had this opportunity.

This morning's search of the impact area revealed charred fragments of a large container, a 'Ho Chi Minh' sandal, and three sets of footprints heading in hot haste for Hoa Long. Not a very spectacular contribution to the war effort when measured against the cost of 32 mortar bombs; however, maybe this action stopped us from getting mortared or rocketed, but of course this is hypothetical.

Quiet evening in our canteen with a farewell to Grant Small who goes home next Tuesday.

Sunday 15 December 1968

Very quiet and restful day. Have minor throat and sinus infection at the moment, so was quite glad to take things easy.

Monday 16 December 1968

Drove down to Vung Tau to visit American survey party at Cap St Jacques, but missed them. They are observing at night and are apparently in town during the day. Spike Jones and Grant Small came with me. We did some shopping at the Australian and American PXs and then returned to Nui Dat, stopping at Ba Ria for iced pineapple drinks. Discovered that another Army vehicle coming from Vung Tau to Ba Ria had been shot at about half an hour before we passed the same spot.

Written confirmation of my promotion finally arrived today. Also a tragic incident. Two 9th Battalion platoons had an accidental clash and shot each other up. Two men were wounded and one killed before the error was realised.

Tuesday 17 December 1968

Grant Small returned home this morning. His departure has left a tremendous gap and he is greatly missed. This is the first time I have really missed someone who has gone home from here. One could not have wished for better company, greater skill or more gifted leadership than Grant has displayed. There is now no one left who was here when I came.

Went out by helicopter to Nui Thi Vai to visit the survey party there. They have been there for four days but have done no work due to high (40-knot) winds at night. This weather appears to be normal, so goodness knows when they will finish. Surveyors were somewhat browned off, being unable to work and being defeated by the weather. By contrast, the infantry were very happy indeed. Life was quiet. No enemy to bother them. Conditions were comfortable. The weather was fine. All this added up to a very pleasant existence for them — a welcome break from their normal work.

Rush job arrived during evening for drawing and printing tonight, and despatch on aircraft at 08.00 tomorrow morning. Managed OK.

PREVENTIVE MAINTENANCE

Earlier in 1968 the Survey Troop had produced the unofficial but immensely popular 'Travel Poster', thanks to the draughting skill of Corporal Peter Dew and the printing skill of Corporal Mario Apfelbaum. Later in the year the same team eclipsed its earlier effort, again taking artwork of American origin and modifying it. This time the product was the 'PM Poster'. It too was unofficial.

Originating from a concept devised by the American cartoonist Will Eisner during his World War II US Army service, the Preventive Maintenance (PM) programme had become big in the US Army by the time of the Vietnam War, advising soldiers in the simplest terms on how to maintain their equipment properly.

To grip soldiers' interest, PM was presented in comic book style, often by Connie Rodd, a voluptuous, blonde character in overtight clothes, whose advice was often suggestively ambiguous.

Peter Dew took an illustration from a PM pamphlet on the M79 grenade launcher, enlarged it to poster size, and redrew it with a few minor modifications. The grenade launcher part held aloft by Connie was exchanged for a condom and the theme was changed to safe sex. Ever thoughtful, Corporal Paul Alderson suggested the slogan: 'The wife you save may be your own'.

The very professional-looking result faithfully copied the US Army's PM style, even down to a fake file number in the corner. A hundred of them were quietly fed into the US Army distribution system at HQ USARV at Long Binh, just to stir the Americans up. Quite unexpectedly it aroused wild enthusiasm, even as far away as the de-militarised zone on the North Vietnam border. This led to strong demands for a reprint. Confusion followed when the US Army printing company proudly went to reprint its most popular poster and then couldn't find the file for it!

In Nui Dat the PM poster was distributed through the Task Force Headquarters Registry. A copy thus went to every unit in the Task Force. Although highly popular, the poster did not please the disapproving chaplains and at least two Task Force unit commanders. The medical people, however, welcomed it enthusiastically. At HQ AFV in Saigon, the senior Australian doctor in Vietnam wanted a copy of the poster displayed in every regimental aid post in the Australian forces in Vietnam, declaring it to be the only safe sex message which really got through to the troops.

Due to its popularity the PM poster held great trading value with Americans and Australians alike, and its circulation was controlled carefully so as not to flood the market. Although a highly prized souvenir, not many came into individual possession.

The chaplains readily forgave the Survey Troop for the PM poster when they were given 200 copies of a beautifully designed and printed Christmas poster to distribute personally around the Task Force in December 1968.

Will Eisner continued to draw PM pamphlets and posters for the whole of the Vietnam war. PM pamphlets continue in the US Army today in much the same style, although Connie Rodd has retired, having been replaced by characters who dress and speak in a much more politically correct manner.

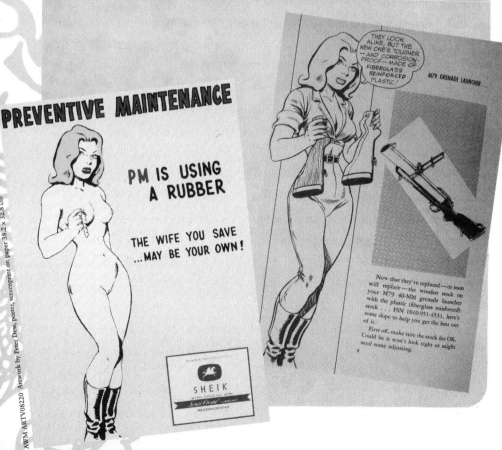

Wednesday 18 December 1968

Despite publicity in the Army newspaper in Australia, the old Hoa Long Dance trick still catches new arrivals in Vietnam. Last Saturday evening one hopeful warrior turned up at the HQ Company Orderly Room in civilian clothes and carrying a carton of Peter Stuyvesant cigarettes under his arm — in the belief that one carton was the standard price for a girl after the dance.

Thursday 19 December 1968

The survey party on Nui Thi Vai and the infantry platoon with them had a nasty fright last night. The ARVN shelled them with 105mm howitzers. No one was wounded but they were heavily shaken and showered with debris. Apparently the ARVN gunners at Phu My, a few miles to the north-west on Route 15 felt like some practice, so they aimed their artillery at the top of Nui Thi Vai and let fly — regardless of the fact that they were firing into territory under Australian control and in which activity is forbidden without clearance from the Task Force HQ Command Post. This was a very bad, though not unusual for ARVN, breach of safety regulations. An investigation is being conducted by the American advisers to the ARVN in that region, but it won't bring back the shells that were fired, and in all probability won't prevent a repetition of this incident. The ARVN reputation for irresponsibility with weapons is indeed well deserved.

Four new men arrived today: Sergeant Paddy Strunks (in place of Grant Small), Corporal Bob Kay, Sapper Rod Gilbert and Sapper Ian Wark. Otherwise a quiet day.

On duty in Command Post from 16.00 until 01.00. Busiest shift yet — was flat out all evening until 01.00. Things never stopped happening yet the situation was never quite dire enough to shout for the Deputy Commander. Several enemy contacts occurred. We incurred heavy casualties (one killed and eight wounded from a claymore mine), and casualty evacuation had to be organised quickly. A battle broke out in Hoa Long and we lent artillery support. A man with malaria and another bitten by a snake (believed to be a krait) required urgent evacuation. The Hoa Long battle raged for a while, but as usual in such ARVN versus VC battles, casualties were light.

The casualty evacuation helicopter for the snakebite case flew from Vung Tau up to Duc Thanh, then back again with another casualty. The pilot reported ground fire against his aircraft all the way up and all the way back. Apparently he provided the target for impromptu practice by every ARVN, Regional Force or Popular Force post between Duc Thanh and Vung Tau. It's indeed fortunate that our Vietnamese allies are such rotten shots. This night firing against friendly aircraft just for fun has got quite out of hand but little can be done about it — though an American fighter pilot did his best today.

> Pilot to base: 'Am receiving ground fire from [map grid reference given].'
> Base to pilot: 'That must be friendly fire from such and such ARVN camp. I will try to get them to stop.'
> Pilot to base: 'When you do, let them know that the strafing they are now receiving is also friendly.'

Friday 20 December 1968

Another fairly quiet day in the Survey Troop but made busy by a shift for a few hours in the Command Post, my first time on day duty, standing in as an emergency replacement. Things, compared to last night, were very quiet, but there had been a lot of excitement before I came on. Poor C Company of 4th Battalion has just received its third air strike in three months. Again, fortunately, no casualties. That makes three air strikes in three months by USAF on Australian troops, and the same company has worn it every time. This one was entirely the fault of the ARVN, who requested the strike on an old Viet Cong base camp, completely overlooking the fact that they had given this area to the Australian Task Force to operate in. USAF presumed that ARVN had gained Australian clearance for the strike and therefore went ahead. Embarrassing for USAF, although they weren't at fault, and considerably more uncomfortable for C Company, especially after incurring 13 serious casualties in the first strike on them last September. ARVN again are in disgrace, and again there is little prospect of improvement.

Meanwhile, the survey party on Nui Thi Vai is again in trouble, this time from the enemy for a change. A small armed party of Viet Cong showed up but escaped from the ensuing fight. This resulted in an uneasy night on Nui Thi Vai with several ambushes being set in case the VC turned up again during the night. However, a quiet night was spent.

Saturday 21 December 1968

A fortnight ago, the 4/12 US Light Infantry Battalion presented the Australian Task Force with a captured enemy bugle, highly polished and beautifully mounted on a polished board with an elegant presentation plate. Its theft from our Officers' Mess has just been discovered, and in its place was left a piece of paper inscribed 'The Phantom Bugle Thief Strikes Again'. This loss has caused much consternation — since the Task Force Commander, as yet unaware of the loss, has just invited the Commander of the 4/12 US Battalion to the Task Force HQ on Christmas Day to receive a suitable trophy in exchange — and on such an occasion the bugle's absence will be most conspicuous. The loss of the bugle has raised a great hue and cry around the Task Force HQ and nearby units. It is really a delicate situation because if the thief gets really frightened, he may well destroy the trophy to save himself from getting caught with it. Anyway, one can take consolation from the fact that if things like this can cause so much fuss, we must be winning the war.

As a result of the high winds on Nui Thi Vai, plus Viet Cong activity and ARVN artillery, plus malaria amongst the survey team on one of the other survey stations, the survey team from Nui Thi Vai is being brought in and returned to Long Binh.

Sunday 22 December 1968

At dawn this morning, the bugle was heard — somewhere in the vicinity of the USAF lines and the 12 Field Regiment (artillery) lines. A posse was swiftly mounted by the Officers' Mess president, but failed to achieve its mission.

Christmas preparations are now inescapably mounting, much to the annoyance of everyone, except perhaps the chaplains. The Australian Government is determined that we shall enjoy ourselves whether we want to or not, and has made arrangements for money to be spent (calculated to 0.01 of a cent) on each man to give him turkey and chicken for Christmas — regardless of the fact that Australians in Vietnam live on American rations all the time and have reached the stage where they can hardly stand the sight of turkey and chicken — amongst other things. If this turkey's been brought here as a special treat for the troops, then no effort is allowed to be spared in seeing that the troops get it.

It is already apparent that Christmas is imposing a colossal administrative burden on the Task Force, particularly with regard to movement by air. This seems to be extremely unsafe in view of the current tactical situation, which is most unfavourable. Everyone right down to the private soldier is well aware of this and knows that the enemy will exploit to the maximum any opportunity we give him. Christmas under these circumstances is a nuisance and is resented. The packages and mail from home are appreciated but any fuss beyond that meets with antagonism, and I can understand why. No one wants truces (for the enemy to resupply himself) or parties. Everyone would rather press on with the war and get it over with. The Christmas message, 'Peace on Earth, Good Will to All Men', just isn't making much of a hit in this environment.

Did washing and some other odd jobs, including a complete clean-out of my tent — it needed it. The dry hasn't been with us long, but the dust is really starting to penetrate into everything.

Monday 23 December 1968

Received a letter from home querying a rise in rent for our married quarters. From the dates, it is obvious that the first definite information about my recent promotion received by my family was when they were informed of a rise in rent. Some days later, I was informed of my promotion. Some weeks later, with luck, I might start receiving a rise in pay.

The Christmas administrative burden continues to increase. The RAAF just hasn't enough aircraft or pilots to meet all the demands on it for social visiting, beer hauling etc. Meanwhile, we are to have a Vietnam-wide Christmas truce from 18.00 on 24 December to 18.00 on 25 December. It is a fine old tradition of this war that during Christmas and Tet we cease fire so that the enemy may resupply and move his forces and attack us. We are still getting over the results of last Tet, some 11 months ago. I find myself full of anti-Christmas and anti-truce sentiment, and I find that most people around me think this way.

On duty in the Command Post from 16.00 until 01.00. Kept reasonably busy, but not a hectic night like the one four nights ago. Sometime after midnight I contacted II Field Force HQ at Long Binh to order a USAF air strike on a VC base camp a few kilometres from Nui Dat. The strike was to be delivered the following evening. However, they wouldn't accept it. Why not? Christmas truce! I tried to suggest that they put in the strike before the truce started and I reminded them that the truce was for 24 hours, not 25; however, they felt that such action was outside the spirit of Christmas goodwill. Bearing in mind how the enemy will celebrate Christmas, I feel that we're getting soft in the head, but I have no choice but to accept this paradoxical situation.

Tuesday 24 December 1968

Drove to Ba Ria in the morning with Eric Clutterbuck, Paddy Strunks, Rocky Camps, Rod Gilbert and Ian Wark, and went to the orphanage. A Christmas party was being held for the orphans and we went along with toys bought for the children. As always, the mother superior and the sisters were kind and charming, and the children were beautifully behaved. They responded to us with great enthusiasm. To the children, a thieu-ta (major) is obviously someone of importance, and it pleased them that I'd come. Several of the small children knew English and displayed a willingness to learn more. They had a quiet and most enjoyable little party. I was amazed when a boy of about seven gave me a piece of chewing gum, then put out his hand for the wrapper, screwed it up, went outside and put it in the rubbish bin about 20 metres away. Such tidiness is extraordinary in Vietnam, and it says much for the nuns that, despite standards outside the convent, they maintain their own standards of behaviour so successfully.

I have not met many military people in Vietnam speaking French, so it came as a surprise to hear an American sergeant speaking fluent French with the mother superior. On listening further and speaking with him, I discovered that this man was of French birth and upbringing, so no wonder he spoke French French and not American French.

Returned to Nui Dat for lunch and busy afternoon. The Officers' Mess had Christmas dinner tonight, a sensible idea. Very nice meal — for a change — and even the turkey and chicken were bearable.

Wednesday 25 December 1968

Aroused at 07.00 by Spike Jones and Ted Morris serving breakfast in bed to the entire Survey Troop. Breakfast consisted of a mug containing a 50/50 mix of hot, unsweetened, fearfully strong, black coffee and rum. This murderous brew lifted eyebrows and nostrils, laid back the ears, and made the toes curl. No one was allowed to escape, as Spike and Ted wished everyone a Merry Christmas in this never-to-be-forgotten fashion. Men soon came leaping out of bed, gasping for breath, with tears in their eyes. As he came out of Noel's and my tent, Spike sighted Mario Apfelbaum in the distance, raised the rum bottle and coffee percolator aloft, and set off after him. Mario fell onto his knees, thrust his clasped hands heavenward and pleaded, 'Mercy! Mercy! You got me already the first time you came around! No! No! Not again!' Quite the foulest and most lethal drop of coffee I've ever tasted.

Most of the Survey troop spent the morning in the canteen, recovering from breakfast. We broke open our Christmas parcels from Australia, including a small parcel of assorted useful things from the Australian Forces Overseas Fund for each man, and a large crate for the troop, containing food, light shades, electrical fittings, darts and other very useful items, from the Survey Regiment at Bendigo.

Had a quiet morning — got washing and a few other odd tidy-up jobs done. Afternoon also was quiet and I got some letters written. In the evening the Survey Troop had a barbecue. Altogether it was a very quiet and most enjoyable Christmas Day — for us, anyway. The RAAF, the Public Relations people and the Medical people (fixing the casualties from accidents due to excessive drinking) naturally have different thoughts.

Thursday 26 December 1968

Plenty of truce violations yesterday — as expected by all but the most naive. Our artillery fired no less than 15 combat missions during the 'truce', all being in support of troops fighting off enemy attacks. Very little was launched against the Australians — but then there has been no major attack on the Australians since last May. But the ARVN just to our north took quite a hiding yesterday.

Meanwhile, as a recent *Time* magazine article showed, war deaths continue to mount steadily. US forces are losing about 200 men per week, and overall US deaths now stand at 30,000. South Vietnamese casualties are quoted as 73,118 military dead, and Viet Cong and North Vietnamese estimates are 422,979 dead since 1961. At this stage, the number of Australian deaths is somewhere around the 200 mark.[2]

[2] It eventually reached 520. — PH

Friday 27 December 1968

More than half of the Survey Troop went down to Vung Tau today for two days at the Peter Badcoe Club, which should be a pleasant break for them. The consequent reduction in work and in general distraction enabled me to get well ahead in most of the tasks in hand.

In the Command Post from 16.00 until half-past midnight. Everything very quiet indeed — very little action occurring anywhere. Task Force Deputy Commander Colonel Dunstan kept wandering around, muttering, 'I don't like this at all. It's just too bloody quiet to be true.' Then the long-awaited action started. West of us, along Route 15, many minor gunfights broke out, and much movement of large groups of troops was reported. A major action seemed imminent. On request from ARVN, we fired our artillery to support the action. Meanwhile, I commenced to request Spooky to stand by, for either flare dropping or heavy shooting or both. However, at this stage it became apparent that the rapidly developing battle was between ARVN and Regional Force troops, both groups being friendly (well, on paper anyway). It wasn't obvious which team our artillery was playing for, so we stopped firing and forgot about Spooky. We never heard further from our 'allies', so presumably they got this little tangle sorted out.

Tonight Firefly flew his first mission in this province, accompanied by the usual heavy fire team. The Firefly is a variation on the Huey with normal gunship armament plus a battery of landing lights, and from all accounts produced a most spectacular night display of floodlight, tracer fire and rockets as he annihilated some enemy sampans along the coast east of Lang Phuoc Hai. (Everything, regardless of race, colour or creed, becomes 'enemy' at the moment it is destroyed by friendly forces. This phenomenon is cynically known in the trade as 'conversion by the sword'.)

Saturday 28 December 1968

Concert today. Having some work, including a draughting task to do, I stayed back allowing the others to go. From all accounts it was not a brilliant concert, so I seem to have done better by getting the draughting job done (always a relaxing occupation for me) while listening to the Test cricket on Radio Australia.

Sunday 29 December 1968

Down to Luscombe airfield to catch RAAF Caribou to Vung Tau to take up final two days' R&C leave. Less eventful flight this time — no other plane to play Red Barons with. Went to R&C Centre and then to Grand Hotel.

Spent afternoon walking around Vung Tau. More rubbish than usual in the streets and the stench was very strong. Had delightful evening meal in the Rendez-Vous Restaurant, a modern and attractive building. Many well-to-do Vietnamese families there, and also many servicemen — including a raucous bunch of six RAAF men. An American NCO climbed onto the stage and chatted quietly to the band, with whom he was obviously a friend. After a few minutes, he took the microphone and began to sing a Vietnamese song in Vietnamese. 'Aw shit!' growled the RAAF. However, the singing was good — the singer was obviously an experienced and talented entertainer and had a very easy voice. The Vietnamese in the audience obviously liked the singing — as did everyone but the RAAF. The American, a slim, dark Latin-looking type with an Italian name on his uniform, then sang a couple of tuneful popular Italian songs. This also was very well received by the locals. However, the applause was drowned by a tuneless rendition of 'Waltzing Matilda' from the RAAF. The band politely provided a quiet accompaniment for them.

Not content with this, the RAAF then sang 'Uc Dai Loi, Cheap Charlie', determined to occupy the centre of attention. They finished the song and then all shouted in unison: 'Up the old red rooster. More piss!' and held grog bottles aloft. I would have intervened, but thought it better not to since this would possibly create further disturbance and perhaps a fight, which would be worse still. So I just had to sit it out, ashamed (not for the first time in Vietnam) to be an Australian. Neither the Vietnamese nor the American looked happy.

Returned to the Grand Hotel and got an early night. Didn't bother to visit the bar — it has lost its novelty.

Monday 30 December 1968

Very quiet day. Got a lot of reading done and went for some walks. Parts of Vung Tau are almost pretty; in fact, they would be pretty but there is always something — barbed wire, rubbish etc — to mar the effect. Had meals at a couple of other restaurants, but food nowhere near as good as last night's. Again to bed early.

Tuesday 31 December 1968

Was sitting (in civilian clothes) under the trees near the Front Beach, reading, when a shoeshine boy came up and offered his services. A ragged and somewhat grimy six-year-old, he was extremely polite and very quiet and gentle of manner. I rejected his offer, but he started on one shoe just the same. I warned him, 'No money,' but he smiled, said OK and continued. As I watched him he produced a high-gloss finish in two minutes, which I felt would have taken me at least five minutes to achieve, despite some experience at this. He was good and he was proud of it. He then asked me if I liked the finish he'd produced. I had to agree. He asked if I'd like him to continue and do both shoes for 30 piastres (about $0.22). I said yes, but I only had 11 piastres with me. He said OK and proceeded to work beautifully over both shoes, and then very courteously accepted his 11 piastres, said goodbye and went on his way.

After lunch I got changed back into uniform and was waiting for the vehicle to take me back to Vung Tau airfield when the same shoeshine boy came by and politely asked if I wanted my boots polished. I said no, it wasn't worthwhile polishing work boots, and anyway, I had no more piastres. He said, 'OK, I have time, you have time, I clean boots.' I let him go ahead. He did a beautiful job with great speed. His movements were fascinating to watch — even the careful, deliberate action with which he used a small flat piece of metal to open the polish tin. When he finished I thanked him and he smiled. He went to go but I stopped him and gave him a small Australian flag I had with me (I usually have one or two). He looked at it, admired it and gave it back.

I said, 'You can keep it.'

He said, 'I don't need it,' and again went to move away. I stopped him again and this time gave him my own tin of boot polish. He was really pleased with this. We then said goodbye and he went on his happy way. Quite the most gentle and polite child I think I have ever met.

Meanwhile, the vehicle to take me to Vung Tau airfield to catch the plane back to Nui Dat didn't turn up as arranged, and I missed the plane and had to stay overnight at Vung Tau, so I stayed — as usual when stranded in Vung Tau — at 1 Australian Field Hospital. Evening was quiet but livened up later as midnight approached. Visited the Other Ranks' Club with the hospital officers, and also the HQ 1ALSG Officers' Mess. At the latter, they were having a 'Back to Kings Cross' night, and everyone was dressed as beatniks, hippies, gurus and behaving in an appropriately idiotic fashion. As a nondrinking outsider, I found the whole affair rather absurd, and watched closely the Vietnamese staff assisting with supper. I tried to gauge their attitude to the scene before them. One Australian assured me that the Vietnamese were always delighted to see Australians so happy. Viewing the same scene through sober eyes, I sensed the Vietnamese attitude to be more of puzzlement and perhaps some contempt. I think I felt much the same way myself but I was less puzzled.

Met Lieutenant Barbara Black — the hospital sister who visited us last September as a member of the excellent concert party from 1ALSG — and at her request rescued her from the clutches of a crowd of officers who wouldn't keep their hands off her body and escorted her back to the quieter environment of the Hospital Officers' Mess. (Discovered later, as I'd half expected, that Barbara's abrupt disappearance into the night in the company of a stranger from the Task Force provoked considerable — mistaken — speculation and comment!)

But the peace and quiet of the Hospital Officers' Mess didn't last for long. Just after midnight and New Year, as everyone was about to wind up the evening and go to bed, in came the officers of 17 Construction Squadron somewhat the worse for wear, and it was not until after 03.00 that we got rid of them. In the meantime, all hospital staff, tired out from an official party the previous night, had crept off to bed except for Barbara Black, Bruce Daniel (the duty doctor for the night) and myself, we three being the only ones who'd had nothing to drink. The Engineers challenged us to all sorts of indoor games of agility and balance with beer cans and cigarette packets. Bruce Daniel was handicapped with a sore arm, so I finished up beating all the Engineers at every single game with complete ease. The hospital honour was satisfied, and the Engineers were none too pleased at being beaten so easily. Of course it wasn't a fair competition — I was sober, the opposition was not. Anyway, they finally left and the rest of us got to bed at about 03.30.

JANUARY

AUSTRALIAN MILITARY FORCES

AAB — 71A
Reprinted Dec, 1964

RECORD BOOK

CONTAINING 96 PAGES

RULED FEINT

January saw the arrival of the Survey Troop's new Officer Commanding to replace John. He did not take over command immediately, but rather from Noel Sproles, acting as second-in-command when Noel went home. This arrangement enabled a smooth handover of command to be effected progressively over a few weeks.

As part of this transition, orientation visits to Long Binh and Vung Tau were arranged, the latter visit producing an amusing misunderstanding at the Grand Hotel.

PAUL HAM

Our entrance created a tremendous stir.
Two majors in uniform plus a 'round-eye' girl
was a most unusual sight in the bar.

★

Wednesday 1 January 1969

Up at 07.30 for breakfast. Despite shortage of sleep I was obviously feeling much better than many others at breakfast, and probably many others still who were not at breakfast. Travelled back to Nui Dat by road convoy during morning. Quiet afternoon and early night — much needed.

Thursday 2 January 1969

On duty in Command Post from 07.30 until 16.30 — my second time on the main day shift. This had been suggested to me several months ago but I had rejected it on the grounds that with Noel full-time on operations work in the Task Force HQ they could hardly have me full-time too, since this would leave the Survey Troop without any officers at all. However, things have now reached the stage where the Task Force HQ is desperately short of operations officers with the experience and ability to handle the full day shift when most of the action happens. They are now down to only five (including both Noel and myself) to man both the forward Command Post at Fire Support Base Julia and the rear Command Post at Nui Dat. Since work in the Survey Troop is relatively light at present, I agreed to help out.

With the Deputy Commander and many of the operations staff away from Nui Dat for most of the day, I was a bit apprehensive lest incidents occur which were outside my experience; however, nothing cropped up which I wasn't able to handle fairly easily. An SAS patrol jumped and killed seven Viet Cong, and then got attacked on three sides by a force of 70 to 80 enemy with mortar and medium machine-gun support. Miraculously, with the air full of flying bullets and shrapnel, all members of the six-man patrol escaped and we got them extracted by helicopter without further ado or excitement. About half a day later when all concerned had calmed down, they discovered that two of them had received wounds but hadn't noticed. It really was a close squeak for them.

Some rain today. Only light but nevertheless remarkable in the dry.

Friday 3 January 1969

I am now within a couple of months of going home, so have started to regain physical fitness by running and doing systematic exercise. I was surprised when I saw WO1 Percy Long doing this before he went home nine months ago but it now makes sense.

Saturday 4 January 1969

Busy day on the monthly report for December. Several minor interruptions occurred and a few new jobs came in. Quite a bit of light rain fell during the day, again most unusual. Last year's dry went from October '67 to April '68 without any rain falling at all, or even looking like falling.

The Task Force was buzzed several times today by Mohawk aircraft. 'Buzzed' is the right word — it buzzes along very quietly with its turbo-prop motors. It is always an interesting aircraft to watch and it demonstrated today much of its high performance in the air.

Sunday 5 January 1969

Very quiet morning, following an unusual and heavy fall of rain in the early hours. We have now had rain on three out of the last four days; this is extraordinary during the dry.

Played cricket during the afternoon for HQ Company against 106 Field Workshop. We won by 119 to 80. Steve Hart and I opened the batting and put on 31, the highest partnership of the match. I scored 15, caught two batsmen close to the wicket and took two wickets in two overs when bowling. However, one stroke while batting made everything worthwhile. In the opening over of the match I played my loveliest off-drive ever. Everything was perfect, foot placement, weight, timing, bat swing — completely effortless. The bat made little noise and I put no power into the shot, yet the ball streaked away at tremendous speed. The hapless fieldsman in its path about 10 metres away had no chance of getting out of the way; the ball hit him in foot, shins, arms, chest and chin and then fell forward in front of him. His team-mates warmly congratulated him on his brilliant save. Unimpressed, his reply was deeply sincere: 'Youse can all go and get fucked!' However, this one glorious drive was not a sign of fireworks to come. Although I picked up runs easily, I never repeated the effortless timing of that one off-drive. I don't know how I did it. But it was quite a thrill to achieve — even momentarily — perfection.

Monday 6 January 1969

Had hoped to get monthly report done today but never even started it. All sorts of minor matters cropped up — visitors, new jobs, administrative matters etc. Clear, windy day. Just as well there's been rain recently or the dust would be in everything. Could be more wind still to come. I remember quite a lot of wind when I first came here, round about this time last year.

Tuesday 7 January 1969

Many minor tasks to get completed before the arrival later today of Major Peter Constantine (my successor as Officer Commanding 1 Topographical Survey Troop). There was much confusion during the day as to who was arriving in Vietnam from Australia today. The Movements people finally told us that no Major Constantine was coming — much to Noel's dismay, since he goes home next week if Peter comes today. Anyway, Movements had made a mistake, Peter arrived and Noel was all smiles again. We gained two sergeants too — Graeme Birrell and Terry Linz. Had little time to greet Peter and show him around before going into the Command Post on operations duty from 16.00 until 00.30. Evening shift was fairly quiet with only one casualty evacuation.

Wednesday 8 January 1969

Sent Peter off on a reconnaissance flight for an hour to have a look at the country for about 30 kilometres around and to get himself oriented. Range practice in afternoon. I gave it a miss and minded the office. Day was pretty free from interruption and I got a lot done — including December's operational report.

Thursday 9 January 1969

Drove with Peter to Vung Tau for an orientation visit. Pleasant, easy trip down. Being commander of the Task Force convoy, we travelled at the front, collected no dust and had a slow run. Visited 1 Australian Field Hospital and the Education Centre before lunch, and toured around 1ALSG. Had lunch at the hospital with John Lambie. We wished to visit some survey stations on the Vung Tau peninsula which I hadn't visited before, so at John's suggestion we took along a hospital driver and, as a guide who had been along the new roads only recently, Lieutenant Barbara Black who was off duty today.

We drove into Vung Tau and requested permission from an American adviser to visit the most southerly station — the old French gun emplacements on Cap St Jacques itself — which is guarded by ARVN. The adviser, a US Army major, took one look at Barbara in her light sun frock, was visibly impressed and announced that, just to make sure we did gain access to the Cap St Jacques guns, he'd better come with us. I hadn't the heart to tell the major that we'd been there plenty of times before without any authority at all.

Track very heavily overgrown with bamboo, so it was an exciting ride for Barbara, huddled close against the windscreen of the open Land Rover with bamboo crashing and whipping everywhere — mostly against the three of us in the back. Had a look at the survey station near the old, massive guns — and then headed for the lighthouse hill on the same ridge. Had to search hard for the survey station, but found it on the roof of an adjacent building. At last I have visited the Cap St Jacques lighthouse, a great landmark, and which throws a thin shaft of light 30 kilometres away, into the rubber plantation, into my tent and onto my pillow.

Returned from the twin hills of Cap St Jacques down to Vung Tau. Drove past the Grand Hotel, and there, his eyes happily alight and waving to me, was my little friend of 31 December, the shoeshine boy. I stopped the vehicle and jumped out. Clearly recognising me, he ran up and gave me a great hug as I leant over. I think I was as delighted to see him as he was to see me.

Entered the bar of the Grand with Peter and Barbara to look for Susie, the girl from the Officers' Club at Long Binh whom I saw here last November, and to approach her on behalf of the Long Binh officers, who'd very much like her to return. Our entrance created a tremendous stir. Two majors in uniform plus a 'round-eye' girl was a most unusual sight in the bar, which, at that moment, contained about 20 bar girls and one solitary American who looked utterly astounded.

I soon spotted Susie, and right beside her was Snow (Tuyet), whom I'd also met last November. Rather than leave Peter and Barbara standing awkwardly by themselves, I invited Susie and Snow over and made formal introductions all round — somewhat different from the easy familiarity usually encountered in bars. We chatted for a moment and I spoke to Susie on the subject of returning to Long Binh; she seemed very interested in the prospect, since she misses her family a lot. While we were there, I noticed the other girls lining up — it seemed they thought of us as an official VIP visit or something. Anyway, business over, we soon left, after formally shaking hands all round. Snow's manners were absolutely perfect — her graciousness is in strong contrast to the many grasping harpies around. However, one should never lose sight (as so many do) that even Snow and Susie are in this game for money.

Left the bar and my friend the shoeshine boy, and went to the American PX at the air base. Did some quick shopping and returned to the hospital for a pleasant evening. Bruce Daniel said that the hospital Commanding Officer and other doctors often made hygiene inspections of the Grand and other restaurants, and that the girls in the bar must have mistaken this afternoon's visit for a hygiene inspection of them — especially in view of the fact that we'd brought an Australian girl with us. They would have presumed Barbara Black to be a nurse, which, of course, she is.

During the evening, John Lambie showed Peter and me over the whole hospital — and it is indeed a most impressive and efficient place. Also most impressive was John's own knowledge of the hospital. It is rare to meet a quartermaster knowing so much about the operational side of his unit. Altogether a fascinating evening.

Friday 10 January 1969

Left 1 Australian Field Hospital after breakfast and went back to the Grand. My little friend was waiting for me and in five minutes had polished my boots beautifully. I gave him as payment a small tin of boot polish I'd brought. He was obviously thrilled with this practical gesture and thanked me very warmly yet politely.

Peter and I then drove around the coast and to the craft shop in the American camp, then back to Ba Ria, where we called in on Madame Minh Ha, and then to the orphanage to see Sister Augustine, and finally to the drink shop for one of those wonderfully refreshing pineapple drinks: chilled pineapple, crushed ice, plus a little sweetened condensed milk, all whipped up in a high-speed blender — and at half the price of Coca-Cola. Returned to Nui Dat in time for lunch.

Saturday 11 January 1969

Morning spent on miscellaneous tasks. In the afternoon made a dash by helicopter to Long Binh and back to collect maps urgently needed for operations commencing tomorrow. Took Peter Constantine and Sapper Rod Gilbert along too. As always, a most interesting and enjoyable ride, and an unusually fast one. Spent only a few minutes at the far end, just long enough to introduce Peter to Bill Harkins, Commanding Officer of 66 Company, and to grab the maps, and then we were on our way back. As we flew over the Task Force HQ at Fire Support Base Julia, the 155mm medium guns burst into shooting beneath us, and the immediate vicinity of the guns became shrouded in dust. As we watched further we saw the flashes, smoke and dust from the shells falling some 10 kilometres away. The effect was spectacular and we saw it very well as we flew on a course parallel to the direction of fire and passed fairly close to the area of impact.

Back at Nui Dat, we had a farewell party for Noel Sproles, Eric Clutterbuck and Ted Morris, who leave next Tuesday. It was a very good evening, and the two HQ Company drivers, Blue and Woody, came along and presented some excellent entertainment. They called a race or two in their best broadcasting style (the RTA Stakes and the Hoa Long Welter), together with commercials and interviews with trainers etc. They turned on a ventriloquist act with Woody as ventriloquist and Blue as dummy, and this absolutely brought the house down.

Sunday 12 January 1969

Quiet day. Got washing and other small tasks done. In Command Post from 16.00 until 02.00. Enough things happened to fill the time pretty well — too well, in fact. An urgent casualty notification kept me going until late. Strictly speaking, these are the job of the Staff Captain in A Branch, but it seemed pointless to wake him up at 01.00 in the morning to do a job which I, already on deck, could do just as easily. Needless to say, he was grateful next morning.

Monday 13 January 1969

Air full of helicopters due to the changeover of 4th and 1st Battalions in the field. I find that not only can I distinguish all helicopters by their sound now, but I can usually tell how many there are and also whether they are climbing or diving — except that the Huey and the Huey Cobra (both with the same engine) sound the same. Quiet evening.

Tuesday 14 January 1969

Monthly conference with HQ USARV, HQ MACV and NGS today — held for the first time at Nui Dat. Made necessary arrangements in morning to prepare conference hut and then met the delegates at Luscombe airfield — Lieutenant Colonel Jonah and Major Julian Driscoll from MACV; Major Ed Wintz and Lieutenant Charles Thomas from USARV; Thieu-Ta (Major) Ruyen from NGS, and Dai-Uy (Captain) Ranh from 1st ARVN Topographic Company.

I took them on a tour of the Survey Troop and was surprised to find how interested they all were — not only in our technical work but also in the way we live, this being their first real contact with the Australian Army as a whole rather than with individual members across a conference table at an American HQ. The conference went smoothly and afterwards we had a lunch in the Task Force HQ Officers' Mess, where, thank goodness, the food

HONOURS AND AWARDS

Forty years on, honours and awards in the Vietnam War are still a vexed question. With the Long Tan awards announced in 2008, the Australian Government only fanned the flames. I have never understood why the obvious solution of a Long Tan clasp to the Vietnam Medal for all involved has never been adopted. And similarly for the battles of Coral and Balmoral if considered appropriate. Battle clasps to a campaign medal were once a standard means of suitable recognition, but have been little used since the Boer War of 1899–1902. A pity.

No Survey Troop men received awards from the Vietnam War, and I know of at least one reason for this which can now be mentioned.

All Australian Army unit commanders in Vietnam knew well that there were not enough awards to go around. I held the view that awards should be going first to the combat soldiers who were facing death regularly. We members of the Survey Troop were mainly fighting a six-day-a-week-war and facing little physical risk. The Survey Troop's soldiers were also earning high-skill pay, far higher than that of the infantry. Fellow commanders of similar technical units felt similarly. Accordingly, I submitted no recommendations for any awards for anyone in the Survey Troop.

In 1998 an End of War list of awards was promulgated by the Australian Government. This was intended to ease an unhappy situation which had lingered on after the Vietnam War. Sadly, it exacerbated the situation and did nothing to restore the existing imbalance of awards in favour of officers. Indeed, it made that imbalance even worse.

Those whose recommendations in Vietnam for awards had later been rejected back in Australia were now given what was deemed to be the modern equivalent of those awards. This was most unfair to those who had also been recommended for awards in Vietnam, but whose recommendations had been rejected differently. It was also unfair to those who had never been recommended at all due to the unit commander's policy, as in the case of the Survey Troop.

I made a detailed submission on this to the relevant committee in the Department of Defence, but received no reply. My subsequent phone queries led to assurances that my submission had been received and that I would receive a formal response in due course. But none came.

If only I could have known what was to follow in 1998, I would have recommended 30 years earlier two members of the Survey Troop for a Mention in Despatches. Sergeant Grant Small and Corporal Lindsay Rotherham performed their duties in Vietnam so outstandingly that they deserved recognition by an appropriate award.

Lindsay Rotherham was a resourceful and highly skilled national serviceman who was sent urgently to Vietnam in 1966 to tackle desperate problems encountered with screen printing in tropical conditions. He resolved those difficulties skilfully and effectively. After two months he was then brought back to Australia to attend a Battle Efficiency course and returned to Vietnam to complete his year there, before finally returning home in March 1968. He thus spent two Christmases in Vietnam, yet he continued cheerfully to give his all. His contribution to the Survey Troop's mapping achievements was immeasurable, and thoroughly deserving of an award.

Grant Small was a gifted man and an intuitive leader who was naturally good at everything he did. For a full year he was a tower of strength in the Survey Troop — calm, sensible, resourceful, skilful and ever dependable. It was the Army's loss that the deserved recommendation of Lieutenant Colonel Latchford (later Major General) that Grant Small be commissioned was rejected by the Director of Survey. It is also a shame that his sterling service in Vietnam has gone unrewarded.

Both these fine NCOs were excellent team men who contributed greatly to the high morale within the Survey Troop.

Although no member of the Survey Troop for the entire period from 1966 to 1971 received any Australian award for his Vietnam service, one member of the Survey Corps was rewarded. Corporal Dominic Yau was awarded the Commendation for Distinguished Service (the modern equivalent of a Mention in Despatches) in the End of War list in 1998. Fluent in English, Vietnamese and Chinese, he served in Vietnam for two and a half years as an interpreter.

wasn't quite as bad as usual. The Task Force Commander, absent at Fire Support Base Julia fighting the war, very kindly provided two bottles of Moselle with his compliments at lunch — a gesture that was much appreciated. After lunch we made a quick tour of the Task Force area, including a visit to the hilltop of Nui Dat itself. We then went down to Luscombe airfield where they caught the plane back to Bien Hoa — no super VIP twin turbo-prop Beechcraft this time, but a lowly Otter with a dashboard containing an on–off switch, a couple of knobs and a couple of gauges.

Noel Sproles, Eric Clutterbuck, Ted Morris all returned to Australia at dawn today. People who arrived here after me are now beginning to go home. Only three more depart before I go myself.

Wednesday 15 January

Quiet day with few interruptions. All work right up to date. But that won't last for long.

Thursday 16 January 1969

Off to Long Binh on orientation visit with Peter Constantine. Met most of the people at 66 Company by lunch time. We spent the afternoon hunting through the many PXs. Peter was searching for a tape recorder to send home, while I was hunting for a Yashica Lynx 1.4E camera for Corporal Oreste Biziak (a forlorn hope because I've seen none since I bought my own many months ago). Visited PXs at USARV, HQ USARV, Long Binh Post, 90th Replacement Battalion, II Field Force, 24th Evacuation Hospital and 93rd Evacuation Hospital. But no luck. The PXs have not re-stocked since the big Christmas rush.

Spent a most enjoyable (as usual) evening at 66 Company. Saw film *Dr Zhivago* (for second time in Vietnam) and enjoyed it again. Julie Christie certainly appealed greatly to most of the audience — pawing of the ground often heard, accompanied by speculative comments and deep growling.

Friday 17 January 1969

Peter received a VIP tour through 66 Company in great detail, while I attended to various tasks to be done at Long Binh — including paying our two men Colin Laybutt and Rod Offer, who have now been with 66 Company for a month or so.

Went to HQ USARV, met the other topographic officers there, had lunch, and then drove to Tan Son Nhut by jeep with Bill Harkins. Visited the huge Tan Son Nhut PX, possibly the biggest in Vietnam, but again no luck with camera or tape recorder. Went to HQ MACV and met the Mapping, Charting and Geodesy staff there, and then visited the tiny MACV PX, which is often full of surprises — and got Oreste's camera for him! Cost was $51.50, $7 cheaper than the same camera, if available, in an Australian PX. The Australian Canteens Service always makes a great show of being cheaper than the Americans, but of all their range of products, the only item for which I have found this claim to be true is toothpaste. For everything else, including all luxury goods and grog, the American PXs are usually 10 to 20% cheaper. Even *Playboy* magazine is 10% cheaper.

Walked from MACV to the RAAF office (a handy geographical coincidence in the mighty Tan Son Nhut complex — several kilometres across — surrounding the world's busiest airport) and caught the Caribou back to Nui Dat. Had a wild take-off but the landing was steadier.

Saturday 18 January 1969

Caught up on backlog of last two days. On duty as operations officer in the Task Force HQ Command Post from 16.00 until 24.30. A very busy session — missed dinner (which didn't bother me at all because it was a barbecue and the food's always terrible at barbecues) and was kept flat out for several hours. Many enemy contacts occurred, and there was a South Vietnamese Regional Force versus Viet Cong clash near Duc Thanh in which two civilians were badly wounded — a woman and a child were both shot several times in the stomach. I swung in the American casualty evacuation helicopter stationed with us, but the woman died before being evacuated. Indications were that the child would be OK. Not a good day today for the Australians — we had two killed and four wounded, while two enemy were killed and three wounded.

Meanwhile, just when things in the Command Post were at their most feverish, a phone call came from the Tank Squadron: 'The image on our TV set in the Boozer isn't good. Is this general throughout the Task Force?' I politely explained that in the Command Post we weren't watching TV, nor had we time to discuss such matters.

Sunday 19 January 1969

Quiet day. Slept in a bit, got washing and some letter writing done.

Monday 20 January 1969

Accepted invitation from a USAF friend to visit the USAF base at Vung Tau and stay overnight. Flew down to Vung Tau in RAAF Caribou and was met on arrival. Had lunch at USAF base in comfortable surroundings and then had a close look at the fascinating aircraft there, including the Mohawk, Skycrane and Huey Cobra. New helicopters for Vietnam are unloaded at Vung Tau and there were many brand-new helicopters there today.

In late afternoon, we drove into Vung Tau township to pick up another American officer from the Grand Hotel. I took advantage of being there to pass Susie a message from the Officers' Club at Long Binh, having been told there last week that they're prepared to raise her salary from $70 to $100 per month if she returns. She seemed very interested, although she's earning $700 to $900 per month as a bar girl at the Grand. I left her with the address of the officer to contact at Long Binh and returned to the air base with others. Spent a happy evening with the Americans, who were only too pleased to meet someone with an interest in their aircraft.

Tuesday 21 January 1969

Up very early to catch plane back to Nui Dat at 07.30. Learnt an hour or two later that only 25 minutes after my departure from Vung Tau, eight 122mm rockets (the nastiest and biggest of them all) had slammed into Vung Tau from Long Son Island to the north. Some landed in the USAF base, others in the US Navy area (damaging one vessel seriously), and others in the Vietnamese National Police Academy. Altogether two Americans were killed and 16 wounded, none of my friends being among them.

Into the Command Post from 16.00. Things were only moderately busy but warmed up at 22.00 when lights were seen moving along a known track in the Nui Dinh hills, some kilometres to our west. From experience, this was obviously a Viet Cong resupply mission, so with Captain John Grey, second-in-command of the Cavalry Squadron, observing and correcting the fire, I gave the necessary clearance to fire and directed 104 Field Battery (commanded by Major Mick Crawford) to open fire. The ranging rounds were well clear of the target and the resupply continued. The adjusted fire then landed fair smack among the lights. Half went out immediately, and the others went racing downhill. John Grey called another correction on the phone and I passed it to the guns, and the shells went quickly on their way again, landing right among the remaining lights, all of which now went out. End of shoot. Forty-two rounds were fired and almost certainly many were effective.

Remainder of evening was pretty quiet, save for an emergency casualty evacuation in 9th Battalion due to an accidental weapon discharge. The next operations officer, taking over at midnight from me, was on his first ever shift alone, so I stayed until 01.15, when we were both happy that he could handle anything likely to crop up during the night.

Wednesday 22 January 1969

Didn't get much done. Hoped to get a map fully checked prior to printing, but too many interruptions occurred — and a few personal problems cropped up as well. One of our men has collected VD from Vung Tau and a paternity lawsuit from Australia within only a fortnight. Got some pretty good help on the latter from Major Stan Miller, the new Legal Corps officer here, a practical and sensible man. Day slipped by very quickly.

Thursday 23 January 1969

Warrant Officers Glen Swarthout (Cartographic Platoon Commander) and George Caporale (Reproduction Platoon

Commander) came down from 66 Company at Long Binh to stay a few days and see this end of the country. This is Glen's second visit. Being excellent company they're doubly welcome here. They spent most of today with the Survey Troop and seeing around the Task Force.

Spike Jones's promotion to Warrant Officer First Class came through today, backdated to 1 October 1968, and he had even more trouble than I did in finding new badges of rank to wear. More understandable in his case — there are only five other WO1s in the whole Task Force of 5000 men — each of the three infantry battalions has a WO1 as Regimental Sergeant Major and so does the field artillery regiment. The only other WO1 in the Task Force besides Spike is a man in a similarly skilled technical posting in 547 Signals Troop.

Friday 24 January 1969

Glen and George went to Vung Tau for the day today and had a very interesting time. While there, they visited the Grand Hotel and saw Susie, much to her delight because she remembered them well from Long Binh. She told them she's returning to Long Binh at the end of the month, although it means a 90% drop in earnings. Still it's a better and easier job, and she will be home with her children all day every day, instead of seeing them about three times a month.

Farewell dinner for the Task Force Deputy Commander tonight. Colonel Dunstan's speech caused much mirth. He recounted many of the most amusing incidents during his year here, and almost all of them involved the Engineers in one way or the other. I felt good on realising that my blind, unreasonable, racial prejudice (developed over the past year) against our often ill-disciplined

Engineers is shared by someone else. I later discovered that just about everyone present (well, not entirely everyone, because there were three Engineer officers present) felt the same way about Colonel Dunstan's speech — during which, incidentally, there was considerable artillery firing.

We discovered later that one of the explosions was not artillery, but caused by a disgruntled Engineer who blew up a sergeant's tent with a heavy demolition charge. We also heard later that there had been two other attempts by Engineers to defy authority in the last few days. An upwards-directed claymore mine was found under a sergeant's bed with a pressure switch in the bed itself. Two hand grenades, less safety pins but with striker levers loosely taped with cellulose tape, were found under the pillow in another bed. Good, clean fun?

Saturday 25 January 1969

Quiet day. Caught up on outstanding tasks.

Sunday 26 January 1969

Due to an error, an important message warning of a major operational change didn't reach the units concerned, including the Survey Troop. Thus, we received no warning at all of an urgent and complicated task to be drawn and printed in an almost impossibly short time. Still, we did it. Spike Jones operated the printing press himself and many others helped with other tasks, such as making dyelines etc.

Monday 27 January 1969

Yesterday's job turned out to be no good, so we had to churn out another, starting from scratch. Fortunately, the fault wasn't ours. The Task Force HQ had given us an incorrect drawing to begin with.

Tuesday 28 January 1969

Quieter today, so finally got Sunday's washing done. Caught the new Task Force Deputy Commander, Colonel Ken McKenzie, at lunch today with the Hoa Long Dance trick. Innocently making conversation, I asked, 'Are you going to the Hoa Long Dance on Friday, sir?' Of course, he looked puzzled, so I explained, finishing with, 'Colonel Dunstan didn't go regularly and he never stayed late — it's not really all that much fun — but he attended now and then because it went over well with the locals when someone important took an interest in them.'

Colonel McKenzie fell for it completely. Beside us, Brigadier Pearson kept a perfectly straight face and said nothing. But then a couple of career-conscious majors at the same table got cold feet and blew the gaff. Nevertheless, it was obvious that both Commander and Deputy Commander enjoyed this frivolous interlude.

Went with Peter Constantine to Fire Support Base Julia in afternoon to discuss the urgent mapping problems of the past two days with the people there, to ensure against a recurrence. On the way back, small arms fire was directed from the ground against our helicopter but it missed us. That's the second occasion I've come under fire in Vietnam, this time enemy fire (presumably) for a change.

Wednesday 29 January
- Monday 3 February 1969

Fairly busy — many new tasks and got handover to Peter completed, and also January's operational report.

FEBRUARY

AUSTRALIAN MILITARY FORCES

AAB — 71A

Reprinted Dec, 1964

RECORD BOOK

CONTAINING 96 PAGES

RULED FEINT

In three years as a lieutenant and seven years as a captain, John Bullen had been engaged on technical duties in the Survey Corps, which, in its national mapping operations, was fairly isolated from the mainstream Australian Army. A year in Vietnam renewing associations with acquaintances, from Brigadier Sandy Pearson down to his own level, and establishing new friendships at the same time, had been a refreshing experience.

Naturally keen to get home after the best part of two years away, there were nonetheless some things he would miss, especially the camaraderie within the Task Force.

PAUL HAM

★

I'd done my best to brighten life for others, whether they wanted it brightened or not, and if at the same time I'd managed to produce a map or two, or do something useful, then I was more than happy.

★

Mauldin ® 1968....Chicago Sun-Times
"Dear Gen. Ky: I don't think much of the seating arrangements, either . . ."

Tuesday 4 February 1969

In Paris the Peace Talks delegates have finally decided on the shape of their conference table, after much palaver for the last few months, which has not impressed anyone at this end of the world where people are continuing to die in the war.

Captain Frank Thorogood, the new second-in-command of the Survey Troop, was due here today but didn't arrive, due to shortage of space in aircraft leaving Australia. I can't leave here until Frank arrives, but his non-arrival today doesn't affect me yet. I'm to go back on HMAS *Sydney* on 15 February, and there are two more flights here from Australia before then.

Peter Constantine is now in command of the Survey Troop, while I am doing various projects that have been shelved till now due to shortage of time.

Wednesday 5 February 1969

Received my confidential report today — for me to sight before it goes in. A very good report indeed, stressing my military value. I was surprised to see that it was prepared and signed by the Task Force Commander, Brigadier Sandy Pearson, himself. I was also pleased to note comments on my sense of humour, which indicate that my attempts to lighten the grim side of the war (including the 'Punch A Postie' episode) have been more appreciated than I'd realised. From this report and the previous one (also in Vietnam) it seems that I'm more readily accepted and more useful outside the Survey Corps than in it. This provides some food for thought.

Light rain today. This dry hasn't been at all like last year's — in fact, today we were almost threatened with the arrival of an early wet.

Thursday 6 February 1969

This letter came from the Task Force Commander today:

> *HQ 1 ATF*
> *Nui Dat*
> *2 Feb 69*
> *OC A Sect 1 Topo Svy Tp*
>
> *Dear John*
> *Two recent unsavoury incidents within the Task Force are causing me concern. They are:*
>   *The placing of an unfused Claymore near the bed of a sergeant by a private soldier. This act, presumably, was intended to warn the sergeant that his form of management was not appreciated.*
>   *The firing of a quantity of explosive in the unoccupied living quarters of a Staff Sergeant by a person unidentified at this time. I suspect the motive was the same as existed for the first incident.*

I have also seen a number of charge sheets involving soldiers who have used threatening language to NCOs.

I need hardly stress how serious these incidents could be to the morale of the Task Force, particularly if a trend developed. You will all be aware of the infamous Gnr Newman case.[1] A repetition of a tragedy of that kind would drag the reputation of the Task Force and the Army into the mud.

I want you to make it clear to the soldiers under your command that there is a proper way to gain redress of wrongs and that any attempt by soldiers to take intimidatory steps such as have already occurred is not only cowardly but totally against the spirit and letter of the law to say nothing of the comradeship which exists in the Australian Army.

I have written to all COs and OCs of units in the Task Force in similar vein.

Yours sincerely
(signed)
(C.M.I. PEARSON)
Brig
Comd

Brigadier 'Sandy' Pearson.

[1] Gunner Newman was a soldier in 4 Field Regiment who'd long had a reputation for his poor attitude. It was alleged that in December 1967 he threatened to kill Lieutenant Bob Birse (who had rebuked Newman over a drinking incident) and then to have carried out his threat by throwing a hand grenade into Birse's sleeping pit. Birse was mortally wounded and died in hospital at Vung Tau, after having lived long enough to state where the grenade had come from. Newman was court-martialled for murder, but found not guilty. He was, however, convicted of manslaughter, a sentence which was later overthrown on appeal back in Australia. The whole affair naturally received much publicity and made a big impact on the Australian Army at all levels. — PH

This letter is one of the neatest mixtures of seriousness and humour that I've seen for a long time. The mental impression of the 'development of a trend' along such unsportsmanlike lines is indeed amusing, despite the seriousness of the subject.

Caught the helicopter to Long Binh for a farewell visit to my many American friends there. Had a surprise on take-off — the aircraft, a Huey, slammed on full power and roared to 110 knots as it whizzed away from Nui Dat, heading not north-west towards Long Binh but south-east. Outside the Task Force area, the helicopter, still at top speed, dropped to about 4 metres off the ground and began weaving in and out amongst the scattered timber and scrub. Although this was fairly dangerous, the pilot was obviously enjoying himself a lot. He then began to bank the helicopter, first left then right, then left again, then right again, swinging the aircraft from side to side, dodging trees all the time. Then we flew over the flat rice fields around Dat Do and he dropped to 2 metres off the deck as, still banking and weaving left and right, we screamed across the rice fields at 105 knots, peasants hurling themselves flat, beasts plunging and galloping away in fright. This behaviour was utterly irresponsible, but nevertheless exhilarating to someone fascinated by helicopters to the extent that I am.

However, I got a bit of a fright when without warning we hurtled into a tearing turn to starboard, the aircraft banking at 70 or 80 degrees as it took this fearfully abrupt turn at full speed. My first thought was for the main rotor, but although the noise and shuddering were great, the rotor stayed with us. My next thought was of the ground. An aircraft must lose lift on banking, and we had virtually zero altitude to lose. Also, a helicopter almost on its side further loses lift due to loss of the cushioning effect gained from close proximity to the ground. This pilot had thrown the helicopter a few metres higher just as he began to bank, so there we were,

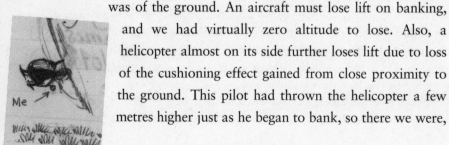

Me

about 5 metres above the ground, which was flashing by at 100 knots, the aircraft on its side in this crazy turn with me hanging out of the bottom side watching how close the tip of the main rotor was to the ground. It seemed we had about 3 metres to spare — as long as we didn't meet any high bunds in the rice paddy, and I hoped the pilot had thought of this before we began to turn.

Well, we made it, or these last pages wouldn't have been written, and immediately climbed straight up to 1000 feet and headed west from Dat Do, only to plunge down again as we reached Route 15. We then flew all the way to Long Binh, some 50 to 60 kilometres straight up the road and about 10 metres above it, travelling at 105 knots all the way. The pilot's enjoyment was obvious and he took pleasure in negotiating bends in the road designed for vehicles doing 20 to 30 miles per hour. We were well below tree level all the way, with extremely little clearance on either side along many stretches of road. It seemed impossible for there to be no overhead cables anywhere along so many kilometres of road, but this was indeed the case and we didn't hit a thing.

Had a diversion on the way when the pilot pounced on a herd of water buffalo, rounded them up with the helicopter, removed them from the control of the astonished herder and sent them charging straight into a vehicle convoy halted at a road block. The resulting confusion and chaos was tremendous, with excited beasts leaping everywhere. With no internal communication in the aircraft for passengers, I could do nothing except sit back and enjoy this wild and action-packed ride. We then resumed our race up the road, finally climbing to a safer altitude as we got to Long Binh.

This ride was quite a thrilling experience, but I think once is enough — in fact, more than enough, because as well as being dangerous it upset a lot of Vietnamese people and it is their country. The pilot was M.H. Drake, from Delaware, and I shan't forget his ride in a hurry.

Arrived at Long Binh. Visited HQ USARV in the afternoon to say goodbye to Colonel Maberry and Ed Wintz. Ed and I have only seen each other about once a month since he came in August, but we found we had a great deal in common. Did some shopping at the PX on the way back and bought a 2-gallon hot/cold drink container, complete with tap, for $2, and a 250 mL flask of Lanvin Arpège perfume for $6. Returned to 66 Company, where I was asked to attend a ceremony. They presented me with a certificate that acknowledged the assistance I've given them during the last year. The certificate was printed in four colours on plastic — in fact, it was a plastic proof, the same as proof copies of maps. Bill Harkins made a very kind speech and I responded similarly, my association with 66 Company (which amounts to almost 10% of my stay in Vietnam) having been very happy. The wording of the certificate is magnificent. It reads seriously, yet it makes reference to many matters that are not obvious but are hilarious to those who know their significance.

The officers of 66 Company took me out to dinner at the Officers' Club at II Field Force HQ — and we had a lovely dinner. There were seven of us altogether: Captain Bill Harkins, First Lieutenants Ken Steward and Roy McMichael, Chief Warrant Officers Glen Swarthout, George Caporale and David Huffine, and myself. First Lieutenant Jimmy Evers was on duty and couldn't come.

Returned to 66 Engineer Company and we entered the Officers' Club. There were only seven of us there when suddenly another officer entered with a projector and said that someone had got a blue movie. Within five minutes there were 30 officers in the club and someone had rung the Colonel (the Group Commander), who shouted, 'Don't start! Gimme five minutes.' A few minutes later the show (one 10-minute film) was to start, but it took over an hour to get the projector going.

'Waal,' said the Colonel, 'I'm gonna see this goddamn show

even if I have to view one frame at a time!' The experts tinkered feverishly with the machine while the Colonel, an unbelievable extrovert, kept everyone thoroughly entertained with his running commentary on the situation.

Finally, the show started. The title was *Full Treatment*, and it was too. The film featured two girls and a man who certainly did receive the 'full treatment'. I had seen the same film in Hong Kong, but it was far more entertaining here, thanks to the noisy and responsive audience. We saw it twice because the Colonel demanded a rerun.

'Wow!' said Roy McMichael at the end. 'That was rough!'

'Don't worry about it, son!' roared the Colonel, overhearing him. 'This is your first war!'

All told, what with Drake's plane (the first time I've ever travelled to Long Binh by road and in an aircraft), the presentation ceremony, the dinner, the *Full Treatment* and the Colonel, this was a memorable day.

Forgot to mention that the Colonel said to me, 'Say, we got your Engineer-in-Chief, Brigadier Charlie Flint, up here today on a visit from Australia. We gave him a thing or two to remember. We sent him out on a bulldozer on a land-clearing operation to show him how well our Rome Plow knocks down trees. We showed him all right. The tree went over and the meanest hornets' nest in this goddamn country landed on the 'dozer cabin. I ain't seen a brigadier move so fast for one helluva time.'

Friday 7 February 1969

Farewells all round then back to Nui Dat by helicopter, this time an extremely sedate flight. Arrived at Nui Dat to find things are livening up. 5th Battalion arrives on 15 February on HMAS *Sydney*. 1st Battalion leaves on *Sydney* the same day and I also go on the

Sydney. The Tet Festival is due to start on 17 February, and all intelligence sources indicate that fighting similar to last year's will blow up on 15 February. This makes the battalion changeover at this time both awkward and dangerous. Neither 1st Battalion nor I particularly want to be involved in a running battle from Nui Dat down to the ship, lying off Vung Tau. This could well occur, together with rocket attack against the ship itself. Minor actions are occurring along the Task Force perimeter, the first for a long time.

Met Steve Hart at lunch and heard him raving about an incredible helicopter ride he'd had. He wants to shoot the pilot and is very angry indeed, having obviously been considerably shaken, both physically and emotionally. It later transpired that this had occurred some 30 hours ago — he had got off (yes!) Pilot Drake's plane (from Long Binh) a few minutes before I got aboard. Steve obviously didn't enjoy the thrill to the same extent as I did. I agree that Drake is an idiot, but he really could handle that aircraft well — he had to!

Quiet afternoon getting a few things packed for home. Sorted out a year's collection of colour slides during the evening.

Saturday 8 February 1969

Got a few more things packed and organised for my return to Australia. During afternoon, Frank Thorogood arrived unexpectedly on an extra RAAF flight from Australia. I am now free to go home next Saturday.

Received letter from home with marvellous news: Grant Small, now in Queensland, has been promoted to warrant officer and posted to the same unit as myself, and called in at my home at Wodonga with his wife on their way down to the Survey Regiment at Bendigo. I'm very lucky to have Grant with me again.

Barbecue this evening — farewell party for Rocky Camps, who's now been here for a year and one week. Next will be myself, after having seen 27 others go from the Survey Troop, of strength 22.

Sunday 9 February 1969

The bugle stolen two months ago has been found! The Department of Customs in Australia intercepted it in the mail. Two or three members of 12 Field Regiment are being grilled (or should it be fried?) at the moment. The crime has apparently been at corporal level, or rather bombardier.

Quite busy today. Frank Thorogood went on orientation tours inside the Task Force (by Land Rover) and outside (by Sioux helicopter). The defence of the Task Force is being re-appraised, resulting in an additional weapon pit to be dug by the Survey Troop — and it has proved a killer. Basalt was encountered half a metre below the surface, so progress has been slow and arduous.

Monday 10 February 1969

Travelled with Frank to Vung Tau by RAAF Huey this morning. Couldn't get aboard the Caribou, so I hitched a lift on a Huey flown by a friend, Squadron Leader Tom Ward, which was far more satisfactory. Landed at 1 Australian Field Hospital helipad after a fast and easy flight, causing tremendous panic when we landed. A hospital helipad is for medical casualties, and the hospital must know of any incoming aircraft and whether or not it bears casualties. In this case Tom informed the RAAF base at Vung Tau but the message was not passed to the hospital. The Adjutant General, Major General Charles Long, on a short visit to Vietnam was expected to arrive at the hospital for an inspection, and they thought that this RAAF helicopter was bringing him — half an hour early! The Commanding Officer plus Wardmaster and entourage came racing out to the pad, while everyone else slammed full speed on to prepare the hospital for inspection. Anyway things soon calmed down again.

Visited the PX before lunch but bought nothing. After lunch Frank and I went on a trip through Vung Tau. Drove around the coast road and into the town in a hospital Land Rover. Stopped in town near a gathering of people and hauled aboard a drunken and unconscious Australian soldier from the gutter. Raced back to the hospital with him, threw him in and went back to Vung Tau. Visited the Grand Hotel — my friend the shoeshine boy has gone to Nha Trang (halfway up the country), Susie has gone home to Bien Hoa, and Snow also home to Bien Hoa. The reason for the departure of the latter two is to be home for Tet — whether or not they return afterwards depends on what happens during Tet.

Quiet evening. Visited this afternoon's casualty and found him fully recovered and just about ready for discharge.

While touring around the Vung Tau coast, we saw the USNS *Corpus Christi Bay*, the aircraft maintenance ship permanently anchored off Vung Tau. This ship is a most advanced floating workshop, ready to go anywhere in the world where most needed, but has been semi-permanently off the Vietnamese coast since 1966 — at first off Cam Ranh Bay and now off Vung Tau. The ship's crew of 130 is civilian, but they are heavily outnumbered by the battalion of 360 military technicians who perform the maintenance and laboratory work. As we watched, a Chinook took off from the aft helipad and returned to Vung Tau.

Unsettling night — Mohawks buzzing low overhead (lovely sound), wind blowing doors back and forth, Cap St Jacques lighthouse flashing through window, and third man in room (a doctor visiting from Australia) vomiting in bed while drunk. Slept soundly, however, having been up late.

Tuesday 11 February 1969

Up at 06.00 to catch ride back to Nui Dat on casualty evacuation helicopter at dawn. Fascinating ride. The Huey did a practice auto-rotation from 2000 feet to 100 feet, dropping at the rate of 3000 feet per minute. We did this above Van Kiep camp and then went from there to Nui Dat about 50 feet above the road. This was fun at 100 knots and without any nonsense or aerobatics. Frank was unhappy about it, so it was just as well he missed the wild flight of 6 February. Arrived at Nui Dat in time for breakfast. Drove to Ba Ria with Frank for farewell dinner given by Madame Minh Ha for me. Very nice meal and we enjoyed her company a lot — she is a kind soul. Said goodbye and then visited the orphanage to say goodbye to Sister Augustine.

Returned to Nui Dat and attended Tet party given by the ARVN liaison officer. Met the Task Force Commander there — temporarily back from Fire Support Base Julia — and said goodbye. He made some very kind remarks — he is obviously appreciative of my attempts to brighten up life in a war zone.

Earlier night tonight for a change.

Wednesday 12 February 1969

Attended brief farewell function held in the Officers' Mess in my honour and received a very nice engraved pewter mug from the Mess, presented by Colonel McKenzie, the Deputy Commander. Colonel McKenzie made a complimentary speech and expressed regret at the Task Force losing one of its more entertaining characters — so it seems I achieved one of my aims here. Then he dropped a bombshell by mentioning that the Commander had been going to appoint me as president of the Task Force Headquarters Officers' Mess a couple of weeks ago, but didn't do so on realising that I was about to return home. 'So,' said the Deputy Commander, 'that let you off the hook!'

'No,' I said. 'It let *you* off the hook!'

I must hand it to the Commander. He's a brave man if he was contemplating appointing me as president of the Mess. But, braver still, he appointed Major Alec Weaver instead, a renowned extrovert and eccentric, so it seems that his policy is to appoint someone who will probably introduce the unexpected into an otherwise very staid Mess.[2] Just as well it's not me though, as it is desirable that the Mess president be more senior than I am, and Alec Weaver qualifies well in this regard.

In referring to anecdotes of my stay in Vietnam, the Deputy Commander made it very plain that I have been more than acceptable here. I replied by saying that I'd like to be able to make as entertaining a farewell speech as did Colonel Dunstan but unfortunately I didn't outrank the Engineers present and this cramped my style. I said I hadn't wanted to come to Vietnam, but having come anyway I'd tried to make the best of it. I'd done my best to brighten life for others, whether they wanted it brightened or not, and if at the same time I'd managed to produce a map or two, or do something useful, then I was more than happy.

Returned to the Survey Troop and attended a small farewell party there too, and received another engraved pewter mug. Didn't stay late because I had to finish packing.

[2] The Mess president is responsible for conduct of the Mess and must exercise delicate judgement of when to be formal and when to relax. — PH

Thursday 13 February 1969

Up early, got everything together, said goodbye all round, and headed off to the Kangaroo pad, where I managed to hitch a lift by RAAF Huey to Vung Tau. As always, an interesting trip. Have now flown some 50 to 60 hours in Hueys in Vietnam and have enjoyed every minute of it in these wonderful aircraft. Powerful, reliable, fast, and with a good view, they are fun to ride in. I have now left Nui Dat for good and have only one more Huey ride to go — from Vung Tau to the ship on Saturday.

Landed at 1 Australian Field Hospital at 10.00. Spent a relaxing and pleasant day there, mostly in the company of John Lambie, Bruce Daniel and Lieutenants Jan McCarthy and Barbara Black.

Set up theodolite outside the Officers' Mess this evening. John and Bruce, both ex-Survey Corps men and due to leave Vietnam shortly, want to leave their mark on the Mess, so I've provided a brass survey ground plaque (marked AAS JBJ — Australian Army Survey, John Bruce John), and a theodolite for some angular observations. We had a practice run this evening and checked out the theodolite, it being many years (about 25 in Bruce's case) since they'd last used one. Made some observations on the Cap St Jacques lighthouse. From this close distance of about 5 kilometres, both sets of prisms could be seen swinging around the central light and this was most interesting. Sighted onto Sirius and Venus also before packing up.

Quiet night — just the occasional deep-pitched buzz of Mohawks flitting by.

Friday 14 February 1969

Very quiet day at 1 Australian Field Hospital. Wrote a few letters, tidied up a few things, changed my money to Australian currency

RETURN HOME

My decisions not to go to Australia for R&R leave and also to return to Australia by sea — headquarters staff in Saigon told me I was mad! — especially after being separated from my family for the best part of two years, might well puzzle readers. Maybe I should explain it.

Before I went to Vietnam and already aware of some pitfalls associated with leave, Yvonne and I had discussed the question of whether or not I should return home for my R&R leave and decided I would not.

As the year in Vietnam wore on, I began to hear many sad tales from those returning to Vietnam from leave in Australia. Having looked forward so much to their leave, many returned to Vietnam disappointed, the keenly anticipated rest having turned out to be loaded with stress and not at all relaxing.

Some had found it frustratingly impossible to fit the conflicting demands of extended family and friends into the bare five days allowed at home. Others sensed a clock ticking off the minutes from the moment they arrived home until they had to leave their families and get back on the aircraft. It seemed that five days were just not long enough for such a break to be effective.

For various reasons a few men chose not to return to their family on leave. I never met one who regretted having made that choice.

Due to my prior posting at Randwick in Sydney, I had been separated from my family for over a year by the time my R&R leave came up. By then, despite the pangs of separation, my family and I had all slipped into a routine that seemed to be working reasonably well. We felt confident that it would be better not to disturb the routine, and that we should carry on as we were until I could return home for good. After so long away already, the remaining months looked almost bearable.

So I went to Hong Kong, where the shopping appeared to be best, Yvonne and the boys both benefiting from my purchases. Unofficially, I also quietly visited the Portuguese colony of Macau.

At the end of 1968, my return home was at last coming into sight. It seemed that everyone automatically went home by air, except for the infantry battalions, each of which automatically returned in HMAS Sydney as a near complete battalion. But the pro forma that had to be filled out by all due to return to Australia actually did offer a choice. So, one could volunteer to return by sea, though apparently no one exercised that choice.

More discussion by mail with Yvonne resulted. I had not had a tough war, but towards the end I often felt tired and I had certainly been going short of sleep for months on end. Arriving home dead tired did not seem like a good idea, and Yvonne agreed. I had already done that in 1961 and 1962 after long field survey trips in remote regions of Western Australia. It had taken me weeks to recover and it wasn't fair to the family. Now, after the best part of two years away from home, an extra couple of weeks didn't really make all that much difference. And so we decided that I should elect to return in HMAS Sydney, which would be bringing our 1st Battalion back at just the right time for me.

When the date approached, I duly submitted my Return To Australia administrative pro forma to HQ AFV in Saigon. They phoned me immediately. 'Hey! Do you know you put a tick in the "return by sea" box?'

'Yes.'

'You mean you want to go home by sea?'

'Yes.'

'But have you any idea what it's like in HMAS Sydney?'

'Yes. I came up in her.'

'And you want to go in her again?'

'Yes. Her next trip home's at just the right time for me.'

By now HQ AFV was convinced I was mad, so they gave up and decided to humour me.

Thus I returned home by ship, arriving rested and refreshed. Over the years, Yvonne and I have felt our decisions for me not to come home for R&R leave and finally to return home by sea were sound. We believe we all benefited as a result.

and got everything organised for tomorrow. Just as well I've come early to Vung Tau and am only one short ride by Huey from the ship — transport for 1st Battalion is snarling up. Starting at dawn tomorrow they must travel in trucks, then by Chinook, then more trucks and finally the ship's landing craft. Well, that's the plan at the moment. An awful lot could go wrong.

After dinner Jan McCarthy, Barbara Black,[3] John Lambie and I went to the HQ 1ALSG Officers' Mess for a short while to say goodbye to Graham Pratt (Education Corps and formerly Survey Corps), who leaves for Australia by air next Tuesday. Returned early to the hospital.

Nurses leaving for Vietnam, May 1968. Lieutenant Barbara Black on right.

Ground shaken many times during night by the heaviest B-52 bomber strikes I've heard. The bombs must have been falling within 30 kilometres of Vung Tau and about 10 to 20 kilometres of Nui Dat. A truly colossal number of bombs were dropped. Mohawks were also whizzing over more frequently than usual. Obviously considerable enemy activity is suspected. Went to sleep amidst the friendly buzz of the Mohawks.

[3] In 1971 Captain Barbara Black died from leukaemia which developed in Vietnam and became Australia's only female casualty of the Vietnam War. Just 22 on arrival in Vietnam in 1968, she was also the youngest Nursing Corps officer to serve in the Vietnam War. Her name is on the bronze Roll of Honour in the Australian War Memorial, Canberra. Jan McCarthy, a highly regarded operating theatre nurse at 1 Australian Field Hospital, later became Colonel J.C.A. McCarthy, ARRC, Matron-in-Chief and Director of Nursing of the Australian Army. Jan, Barbara's daughter Emma and I still keep in touch. — JB

Saturday 15 February 1969

Up before dawn for an early breakfast and to catch the helicopter to ship. As usual I got an outside seat and a lovely view. Flew close to the Cap St Jacques lighthouse and low over the town of Vung Tau and then out to HMAS *Sydney* anchored close to USNS *Corpus Christi Bay*. Recognised many good Navy friends aboard *Sydney*. Atmosphere relaxing and enjoyable. Food wonderful. Ship got under way at 12.30 after a bare four and a half hours at anchor, during which time the 5th Battalion disembarked and 1st Battalion came aboard, and all stores and vehicles were loaded and unloaded. Cap St Jacques and 1 Australian Field Hospital slipped away over the horizon very quickly. With HMAS *Derwent* as an anti-submarine escort, we are heading for Singapore (to refuel from a Royal Navy tanker at sea), Darwin, Torres Strait and inside the Barrier Reef to Sydney.

Relaxed during evening, reading and listening to a Judith Durham tape. Looks like a delightful and restful trip. Today's Huey ride to the ship, my last in Vietnam, was a beauty — a very interesting one to finish on.

Now away from Vietnam, there are many things I shall miss:
1. My many Army friends.
2. The many fascinating aircraft — especially the Huey and the Mohawk.
3. The Cap St Jacques lighthouse, which always shone into my bed at Nui Dat, no matter how savage the fighting in between.
4. The children of Ap Suoi Nghe and at the orphanage at Ba Ria, and my shoeshine friend in Vung Tau.

Sunday 16 — Friday 28 February 1969

A wonderful and relaxing trip aboard HMAS *Sydney*. Unlike the voyage a year ago, when I was the senior officer among reinforcements on their way to Vietnam, this time I'm surrounded by officers and soldiers of the 1st Battalion and I have no responsibilities at all.[4]

Doing nothing and able to relax completely, suddenly I feel very tired. So I have just slept, read a bit, slept, written a few letters and slept. Still under the command of the redoubtable Captain D.A.H. 'Nobby' Clarke, HMAS *Sydney* has steamed at what feels like top speed, the ship often shuddering all over from its engines.

Inside the Great Barrier Reef, and a full day ahead of schedule, *Sydney* anchored at the Captain's favourite fishing spot. The Captain and his fellow fishing enthusiasts then set out in the ship's boats for a day's fishing. We all dined well in the Wardroom that evening.

Stopped again at Townsville where Australian Customs staff came aboard. They had everyone aboard checked for contraband before we reached Sydney, so that we could then disembark and disperse quickly.

Saturday 1 March 1969 and afterwards

Arrived at Sydney, refreshed and home again after thirteen and a half months in Vietnam. Welcomed back by my mother, Yvonne's mother and David.

Yvonne had sent David yesterday by plane to Sydney, where both his grandmothers picked him up and brought him to meet the ship. David was very keen to see over HMAS *Sydney*, and this time I was able to take him on a guided tour of the ship.

[4] Among the 1st Battalion troops on their voyage home was the future deputy prime minister Second Lieutenant T.A. Fischer.

Spent that night with family in Sydney and flew home with David the following morning — not without incident. We travelled by East-West Airlines in an F27 Fokker Friendship to Albury via Canberra. David, fascinated by all technology, was keen to see as much of the aircraft as possible, so I asked if we could visit the cockpit. Yes, of course. The pilot explained his instruments and controls to David and was surprised at the depth of David's questioning.

Warming to his enthusiastic audience, the pilot said that you couldn't really see how many of the instruments worked while we were in level flight and on course. He then hauled back on the controls, banked the aircraft, gave it plenty of rudder and headed upwards, thus demonstrating his instrument panel at work, with indicators and gauges now swinging rapidly. And then, to get the aircraft back on course, he did everything in reverse — nose down, steep bank the other way, reverse rudder and finally levelling out again. We thanked him gratefully for this excellent demonstration and headed back from the cockpit.

Big shock. White-knuckled, grim-faced passengers were glaring at us and muttering. One excited lady was vowing to report this to the authorities. Only then did I realise that the passengers had assumed that a six-year-old boy had been flying the plane and that an Army major had had a lot to do with it. No good trying to explain. We sat quietly in our seats, keeping a low profile for the rest of our trip.

At Albury airport, Yvonne and Peter, now aged two, were waiting to meet us. Home at last.

★ ACKNOWLEDGEMENTS ★

The relentless and indefatigable efforts of Ho Chi Minh and Mao Tse Tung must be acknowledged because, without them, this book would never have been written.

Too numerous to mention for their knowing contributions to this book are my many Army colleagues who, over a 40-year period, strongly encouraged me to publish my personal Vietnam diary. But one World War II veteran who rose above the military pack was the late author Kit Denton, who some 25 years ago wearily said to me, 'You bastard! I didn't get to bed until four o'clock this morning because I just couldn't put your bloody diary down till I'd finished it!'

Twenty years later Paul Ham, engaged in research for his own Vietnam book, sought to borrow a few quotes from my diary and the road to publication began. My special thanks go in chronological sequence to Paul, who kicked the ball off and edited the diaries; to agent Deborah Callaghan, who passed them so neatly to HarperCollins; and to the staff at HarperCollins.

Thanks also to my long-time friend Major General Steve Gower for the support generously given by the Australian War Memorial to a former staff member and donor of some of the items reproduced in this book.

Finally, I thank my dear wife, Yvonne, for her patience and support while I strove (sometimes successfully) to meet deadlines in a tight production schedule. I thank her too for her wonderful and uncomplaining efforts 40 years earlier in bringing up two lively boys on her own in Wodonga for the best part of two years.

Picture, illustration and text acknowledgements

Pictures and artwork pp. 4, 14, 22, 23, 40, 41, 55, 151, 202, 295, 320, 391, 431, 444 courtesy of the Australian War Memorial (AWM P05339.001 p. 295 copyright holder unknown); cartoon p. 370 by permission Geoff Hook; letter pp. 430-41 Department of Defence. Efforts have been made to contact identifiable copyright holders of material in these diaries; the publisher welcomes inquiries by copyright holders who have not been contacted.

★ INDEX ★

★ ABOUT THE AUTHORS ★

Captain John Bullen commanded 1 Topographical Survey Troop of the Australian Task Force at Nui Dat. He had previously served in national service, in the Citizen Military Forces, and with the Australian Regular Army as a soldier before being commissioned as a lieutenant in 1958. He retired from the Army in 1983 and joined the staff of the Australian War Memorial.

Paul Ham is the award-winning author of *Vietnam: the Australian War* and *Kokoda*.